Unearthly Powers

Why was religion so important for rulers in the pre-modern world? And how did the world come to be dominated by just a handful of religious traditions, especially Christianity, Islam, and Buddhism? Drawing on sociology and anthropology, as well as a huge range of historical literature from all regions and periods of world history, Alan Strathern sets out a new way of thinking about transformations in the fundamental nature of religion and its interaction with political authority. His analysis distinguishes between two quite different forms of religiosity – immanentism, which focused on worldly assistance, and transcendentalism, which centred on salvation from the human condition – and shows how their interaction shaped the course of history. Taking examples drawn from Ancient Rome to the Incas or nineteenth-century Tahiti, a host of phenomena, including sacred kingship, millenarianism, state–church struggles, reformations, iconoclasm, and, above all, conversions are revealed in a new light.

ALAN STRATHERN is an associate professor of history at the University of Oxford, and tutor and fellow in history at Brasenose College, Oxford. He is the author of *Kingship and Conversion in Sixteenth Century Sri Lanka: Portuguese Imperialism in a Buddhist Land*, and coeditor with Zoltán Biedermann of *Sri Lanka at the Crossroads of History*. He was awarded a Philip Leverhulme Prize in History in 2010.

Unearthly Powers

Religious and Political Change
in World History

ALAN STRATHERN
University of Oxford

CAMBRIDGE
UNIVERSITY PRESS

CAMBRIDGE
UNIVERSITY PRESS

University Printing House, Cambridge CB2 8BS, United Kingdom

One Liberty Plaza, 20th Floor, New York, NY 10006, USA

477 Williamstown Road, Port Melbourne, VIC 3207, Australia

314-321, 3rd Floor, Plot 3, Splendor Forum, Jasola District Centre, New Delhi - 110025, India

103 Penang Road, #05-06/07, Visioncrest Commercial, Singapore 238467

Cambridge University Press is part of the University of Cambridge.

It furthers the University's mission by disseminating knowledge in the pursuit of education, learning and research at the highest international levels of excellence.

www.cambridge.org
Information on this title: www.cambridge.org/9781108701952
DOI: 10.1017/9781108753371

First published 2019

A catalogue record for this publication is available from the British Library

ISBN 978-1-108-47714-7 Hardback
ISBN 978-1-108-70195-2 Paperback

For S.D

Contents

Figures

Preface and Acknowledgements

There is not much of Sri Lanka in the pages of this book, but it bulks large in the much longer, slower formation of thought that culminates here. Yielding to the narrative temptations of hindsight, let us put it like this: my experiences there as part of the extended family of my wife (as she became) from the mid-nineties onwards taught me much more about how religion works than my research as a doctoral student of its sixteenth-century past. In my encounter with the reality of Theravada Buddhism, I sensed a strikingly radical version of what I would later think of as transcendentalism: at once radiant and unforgiving. And yet at the same time, the majority of day-to-day religious life and conversation was of an entirely different order: deity supplications, astrologer consultations, healing rituals, buried charms, baleful curses, theatrical exorcisms, the evil eye – an omnivorous, eclectic, untheorised, and deeply practical approach to getting on in life. This was the true surprise (if this was what life was like in Weber's 'enchanted garden', I had evidently been living hitherto far beyond its walls). Here, the dead reappeared in dreams, or at the driveway gate at dusk, or hid in the top of a tree; fortunes were told in the flames of a fire; numerologists predicted the recovery of a stolen bag of A-level revision notes with complete accuracy; gods appeared unbidden at bedroom windows in the night to demand that oaths be fulfilled by sacrifice. Christian churches were vehicles for this appetite too, as in St. Anthony's in Colombo, where a crowd of people from all religious backgrounds were let in after the formal service was over to propitiate the figures of the miracle-generating saints, streaking their glass cases with their beseeching touch. (A sign admonished devotees that it was not appropriate to offer *puja* to the Virgin Mary.) Even Buddhist monks: while my father-in-law was growing up in a small village near Anuradhapura, an occasional visitor to the house was the Kondadeniya Hamuduruwo, famous nationwide for his awesome powers of magical protection and attack, courted and feared by the most senior politicians.[1]

Still, on another level, Buddhism remained a tradition of sublime disregard for such matters, and it was and is unquestionably hege-monic in several important ways. It has certainly been fundamental to any understanding of politics: in the sixteenth century, the Portuguese presence placed serious inducements to baptism before Sinhalese princes, to which some responded, but yet the foundational place of Buddhism ensured that conversion would come at the cost of a serious loss of legitimacy. This was one of the findings of my first book. Partly as a result, Sri Lanka did not succumb to Christianity any more than it did to Islam. But I knew that in other times and places, rulers had been able to *enhance* their authority, over the longer term, through their conversions to monotheism. Why? Indeed, why more generally have certain regions proved astonishingly vulnerable to the march of the world religions? I was born in Papua New Guinea, to anthropologists who worked in the highlands; this was a world in which no transcendentalist traditions had entered until the missionaries arrived and spread their creeds like wildfire in the twentieth century. The island became one of the most Christian countries on the planet – in world historical terms, within a mere blink of the eye.

Therefore, what emerged after my DPhil work was a concern, first expressed in a journal article in 2007, to understand why it was that ruler conversion should be a critical means by which the world religions expanded in many parts of the world, but was simply anath-ema in others.[2] This question is now properly answered in a compan-ion volume, *Converting Kings*, which compares specific cases where rulers sought to adopt or reject Christianity: Kongo 1480–1550; Japan 1560–1600; Ayutthaya (Thailand) 1680–1690; and Hawaii 1800–1830. All my work on these cases was written up before I worked on this volume, and has greatly shaped its content. This book has a much wider remit than its companion and a quite different methodology, but readers will find that they exist in constant dialogue with each other.

The project had thus yielded two books, but I am most conscious of what has been left out. A proper examination of how best to deploy the concept of the Axial Age could not be included. In particular, nowhere

---

[1] On the latter, also see Gunaratne 2017; Stirrat 1992: 93.   [2] Strathern 2007b.

in the present volume do I properly explain how Confucianism, Hinduism, and Judaism might or might not fit into the paradigm of transcendentalism. Apart from constraints of space, their absence reflects an early decision to leave China and India out of my four major case studies, and a very late decision to cut an appendix. I can only say that my thoughts have often returned to the complexities and opportunities involved in this exercise. While Chapters 1–3 compare Buddhism and Christianity as transcendentalisms, the remaining chapters largely use the latter to think about how transcendentalism spreads. It is a deferred ambition to show how the expansion of Buddhism could be analysed similarly. Thematically, I had to exclude consideration of the role of 'cultural glamour' in shaping the context for ruler conversions, and defer the issue of intellectual debate.[3] I have not explored here the role of resistance, popular scepticism, or the hidden transcript in any substantial manner. Equally, the contribution of apparently more 'secular' qualities of legitimacy – vaguely universal principles of good governance, justice, or dynastic breeding, for example – and their relationship with the religious sphere, has only been alluded to occasionally. In no sense do I preclude their significance: this book is concerned with the relationship between religion and power, rather than assuming that power is always about religion.

As for what does remain, readers will perceive that the range of literature drawn upon here goes far beyond what is attempted by any sensible historical monograph. Although I have sought to compensate for my lack of specialist expertise in all these areas by circulating chapters to the readers listed below, and as much as I have striven to the contrary, surely errors and infelicities will remain; at the very least I will be dependent on interpretations that split opinion at the level of specialist research. To make the avoidance of such sins the overriding task of intellectual enquiry, however, would be never to attempt a project of this scale.

* * *

Institutionally, I have to record my greatest gratitude to the Leverhulme Trust: the award of a Philip Leverhulme Prize in 2010 allowed me complete freedom to decide how I would spend two years.

---

[3] To CK.

In 2011–2013 I therefore completed most of the work for Africa, Oceania, and Japan, much of it destined for the companion volume. With this and subsequent work on Thailand behind me, I was now in a position to apply to the British Academy, which awarded a one year Mid-Career Fellowship, 2016–2017, in which the whole of this volume was written. I am most grateful, therefore, to the support of both bodies. I spent that year in Singapore, and part of that time as a visiting senior research fellow at the Asia Research Institute. This provided an excellent setting in which to engage scholars of Asia and was rather formative in coming to terms with certain conceptual issues. I particularly note my encounters with Ken Dean, Peter A. Jackson, and others noted below, and remain grateful to Prasenjit Duara for his support and conversations over the years.

But most important for their support and toleration have been my colleagues at Brasenose and St. John's Colleges in Oxford: Abigail Green, Rowena Archer, Lesley Abrams, William Whyte, Hannah Skoda, Leif Dixon, George Southcombe, Manjusha Kuruppath, Tom Marsden, Kevin Fogg, Helen Gittos, and Simon Smith. I have been lucky to have these people around me. This book, in fact, has its very first origins in Cambridge, and while I cannot list all my colleagues there, I'd like to record how vital the late and greatly lamented Chris Bayly was in encouraging my ambitions to think broadly and in supporting this book in its first formulation. Incidentally, the sheer range of topics both Cambridge and Oxford expect its lecturers to teach have surely enabled this book in quite different way. I am grateful too, to the History faculty at Oxford for their facilitation of research leave. Of the many congenial colleagues there I will single out Aileen Mooney for her wonderfully valuable assistance with all matters related to funding. This included support from the John Fell Fund for the means to employ Lucy Hennings for her excellent assistance with the bibliography and index. Cambridge University Press saw the merit of this project at a very early stage, and I am especially grateful to Lucy Rhymer for taking care of it during a long period of surface dormancy and shepherding it smoothly into its two-book format.

My debt to Marilyn Strathern is, of course, incalculable. To mention only the most elementary levels, she has read an entire draft, and acted as an unparalleled conversational route into what I consider as 'immanentism'. It is difficult to express the significance of Vic

Lieberman in my development: a model of fearless global comparative scholarship, a tireless reader and critic of my work, and an extremely valuable and generous source of wisdom. Joan-Pau Rubiés has been a touchstone and mentor in my career for even longer, and also provided incisive comments that have helped shaped the form of this book. Azfar Moin read the bulk of the manuscript, but more importantly has become an ideal source of inventive, theoretically alive, and broad-minded discussion.

Apart from the above, many others read and commented on drafts of particular chapters. Although they appear in a list, I feel a very personal sense of gratitude to and intellectual engagement with each of these readers – who, of course, cannot at all be associated with the inadequacies that remain. The Introduction and Chapter 1 were read by James Davidson, Will Sweetman, Edoardo Siani, Giuseppe Bolotta, Ben Schonthal, William Whyte, Roger Albin, Yoni Brack, Joel Robbins. Tomas Larrson and Alastair Gornall read these together with Chapter 2. John Watts read Chapter 3, Charles Stewart and Joel Robbins read Chapter 4, and Jonathan Shepard read Chapters 5 and 6.

The following provided more particular help with various points: Jonathan Bardill, Nicole Brisch, Nicholas Thomas, Robin Whelan, James Raeside, Richard Gombrich, Lesley Abrams, Lynette G. Mitchell, Stefano Zacchetti, and Peter B. R. Carey. Another army of regional specialists helped with the cases in the companion volume and will be acknowledged there. I must only record here particularly unstinting help from John K Thornton, the late J. D. Y. Peel, Chris Baker, and Kanda Chisato.

I'd like to record a special debt to Marshall Sahlins, whose influence on this book should be obvious, and who regularly sent me copies or oral papers and works in progress. Many of these were recently published, in collaboration with David Graeber, in *On Kings*. This came out after the first complete draft of *Unearthly Powers* was written, and in Graeber's contributions I found much that chimed with my understanding of how 'immanentist' or divinised kingship worked.

Nilmini Dissanayake has been an abiding source of fascinating conversation about Buddhism and much more general support. My wife, Samanthi Dissanayake, once pointed out to me the resemblance between Sahlins's model of the stranger-king and the origin myth of Sri Lanka, which set several balls of intellectual enquiry rolling. Without her, in sickness and in health, this book could never have appeared:

this book is dedicated to her with love. My two children, Leela and Aril Strathern, have never known me not to be working on this project, but they have brought joy and purpose of a more transcendent kind.

* * * *

Biblical quotations are from the New International Version. Unless otherwise stated, Pali quotations are from suttacentral.net, where I have privileged the translations of Bhikkhu Bodhi. Diacritics have not been used for Pali words that have a reasonable independent life in English.

Introduction

In Madakada Āranya, a forest monastery some two hours' drive from Colombo, a skeleton hangs from a hook in a small hut. This is the focus of a particular form of Buddhist meditation. The monk walks through sunlight towards a black square of a window, and as he approaches he will begin to see the skull emerge from the gloom and then the entire skeleton, suspended in the heat. What is the monk being invited to perceive? Reality. Not the horror of death but the horror of life that it should be so fleeting. Held in that window is a vision of the inherent suffering of the mundane world in which we all required to dwell; as such it also represents a denial of the ultimate significance of politics. Yet, such visions came to colonise the world, not despite politics, but through it.

A handful of religious systems now dominates our planet: Christianity, Islam, Hinduism, and Buddhism account for the vast majority of the religiously affiliated, while Judaism, Sikhism, and Jainism mop up a far smaller number.[1] Survey takers must then find a name for a forlorn category of the residuum: adherents of 'folk religions', which as of 2015 made up only 5.7 per cent of the world's population. Thus the countless, nameless traditions of ritual performance and mythic elaboration that lay outside the world religions, and that provided the distinct habitats of meaning in which humanity lived for most of its history, have been subject to a merciless winnowing. Profound religious diversity has given way to a weaker form of variegation playing out under the carapace of a few overarching traditions.

How did it happen? Perhaps, our first instinct would be to consider it a side effect of the movements of hard power. Christianity happened to hitch a ride on the Roman Empire before its demise, and after a long

---

[1] Pew Research Center 2017. Sikhism and Jainism are counted as 'other religions', 0.8 per cent, with Jews at 0.2 per cent. All the religions mentioned thus far could be classed as 'transcendentalist'.

incubation in Europe began to force its way into the outside world from 1492, flowing into the space carved out by Iberian steel in the Americas and subsequently into a world organised by the hegemony of the West. Islam, meanwhile, spread from Morocco to Afghanistan within a few generations of the revelations of its prophet through extremely rapid feats of conquest.

This takes us some way towards understanding the religious map of the world today – but not as far as one might think.[2] The Roman emperor Constantine was not forced by military pressure to become Christian, and barbarian Europe was subsequently converted through the essentially voluntary actions of its kings; across the other side of the world a thousand years later the peoples of much of Oceania also entered into Christianity in this way. Nothing suggests that the warring tribes of the Arabian Peninsula were set on world-transforming empire before the teachings of Muhammad himself transformed them. And in the second millennium, Islam tamed the superior military power of the Mongols and their warrior elite successors, and also spread into sub-Saharan Africa and Southeast Asia, largely through the conversion of princes, who received it from travelling scholars, holy men, and traders. Moreover, focusing on the two monotheisms ignores the earlier expansions of the Indic religions over Asia. Buddhism, for example, was carried by merchants and monks from South Asia along the silk roads into East Asia and across the Indian Ocean into Southeast Asia, finding patronage in the courts of kings and then, in many cases, coming to shape how those kings understood what kingship itself was for. Most of these transformations happened long before modern communications and transport technology shrank the globe.

Before receiving these new traditions, rulers and their subjects were already deeply invested in religious forms that shaped every aspect of their existence. From the start of history any substantial form of social cooperation – and therefore any concentration of political power – sought to draw upon religion to some extent. Wherever chiefs and kings emerged they did so with ritual responsibilities and claims. In some cases, they became quasi-divine beings, credited with powers to intercede with the highest supernatural forces ruling over human

---

[2] I will consider the issue of the relationship between military–political developments and religious change much more extensively in *Converting Kings*, referred to here as *CK*.

affairs, and personally exalted by the most elaborate forms of protocol. Still, they were prepared to give up these traditions for entirely new religious systems, which most of their subjects did not yet understand, and which in some ways transferred moral and religious authority to a formidable class of monastics, priests, or scholars.

How do we explain the victory of the named religions – which I refer to as 'transcendentalisms' – in the political sphere? Perhaps there were once ready answers to this question, relying on some assumption of inherent superiority for example, but in recent decades the premises they were built upon have been eroded or abandoned in much scholarship.[3] The recent rise of 'global history', however, has thrown down a gauntlet. If we are now invited to see the big picture in terms of shifts in economic capacity or the balance of power, or the global impact of disease or climate change – why not return also to the field of religion? To do so as a historian means learning from historical sociology, which has never abandoned the macro perspective, and also engaging with the findings of anthropology. This book exists at some intersection where these three disciplines meet.

It is not a global history in the sense of an attempt to tell a comprehensive story. It rather sets out to provide a means of understanding certain important features of religious change and the dynamics of its relationship with the political sphere on a global scale and over the very long term – but before the rise of modern nation states and secular political thought. It adopts a wide-ranging comparative perspective in order to help provide clarity to conceptual problems otherwise locked up in regional specialisms, and to identify particular patterns that might otherwise go unrecognised.

A Language of Religion

'Religion' is notoriously difficult to define.[4] Although this book must avoid the deconstructionist effervescence of the last generation of scholarship insofar as it impedes global comparative analysis, there is at least one very good reason why 'religion' tends to defeat attempts at encapsulation: it strains to cover two distinct phenomena, which

---

[3] For an older approach, see Latourette 1939: 240.
[4] And has been much historicised of late, see Asad 1993; Stroumsa 2010; Josephson 2012: 16, 23; Nongbri 2013; Lambek 2013a: 1–6.

Chapter 1 is devoted to describing at length.[5] The first is the tendency to imagine that the world plays host to supernatural forces and beings with whom we must interact in order to flourish. These beings are 'supernatural' because scientific knowledge finds no place for them in its account of the natural world: they include ghosts, spirits, demons, ancestors, gods, and the indwelling inhabitants of totems, masks, fetishes, and features of the landscape. The anthropologist Marshall Sahlins describes these beings as 'metapersons' because they have agency and motivation just as people have, but they are not present to the senses in the way that ordinary people are, and they usually possess a greater range of powers to effect their will.[6] Yet no society has lived without feeling these strange denizens moving amongst them; modernity has provided unusually congenial conditions for their eradication but has not yet succeeded. The fact that their presence has been so universally granted suggests that it has been driven by evolved features of human cognition – and indeed, when cognitive scientists refer to 'religion' this is normally what they mean.[7] To the extent that this disposition is concerned with such forces and beings as potentially present – or 'immanent' – in the world and influencing it for the good or ill of human society, it is referred to here as 'immanentism'.

This may, however, seem unappealingly reductive as a general definition of 'religion'. Is it not also to do with arriving at an understanding of ultimate truths about the nature and purpose of existence, truths that only became known to humankind at specific moments in history through the insight of extraordinary teachers, truths that some take to their hearts and others stubbornly reject? Isn't religion precisely to do with what is *not* present in this plane of reality, with that escape from

---

[5] It follows from the discussion here that no one simple definition of 'religion' is likely to work comprehensively and 'religion' is used in this book as an umbrella term for both immanentist and transcendentalist forms. However, if it *must* be reduced to a single definition, perhaps the most satisfactory one is very old indeed: that dimension of life which pertains to interactions with supernatural forces and metapersons. Definitions that focus on its role in the production of meaning make religion difficult to distinguish from culture, and those that focus on the production of society make it difficult to distinguish from other central and special features of social life. Still, this definition (close to Spiro 1994: 197; Sharot 2001: 23) has problems too, and is not put to analytical work here. On definitional complexities: Saler 2000.

[6] The term was introduced in his Hocart lecture (2016) and in Graeber and Sahlins 2017.

[7] See Laidlaw and Whitehouse 2007: 8.

the world that we know as salvation? And does it not involve the scrutiny and refashioning of one's inner self, the exercise of compassion, the cultivation of ethical discipline, and the attainment of theological understanding? Does it not have to do with belief and belonging? In fact, all these properly belong to a second phenomenon: 'transcendentalism'.[8] From a certain oblique perspective, all the traditions which exhibit these traits may seem to have a vast absence at their heart: they push their conception of the sacred towards visions that are literally ineffable, transcending any capacity of the human mind to represent it. Their followers yearn to attain that state nonetheless: this is salvation.[9]

It is important to grasp that none of this is implied by the first and most basic definition of religion above; these traits are quite extraneous to immanentism, the default mode of human religiosity. It is no coincidence that the term 'religion' should have arisen in Western intellectual culture. For one reason why it requires mental labour to separate out the phenomenon of transcendentalism and immanentism is the particular way that monotheism has fused them together by connecting salvation to the worship of a metaperson. It is easier to see their distinctiveness from the viewpoint of Buddhism, the other great transcendentalist tradition this book dwells upon: 'Gods are nothing to do with religion,' a Sri Lankan monk once remarked to Richard Gombrich.[10] Particularly in the Theravada tradition, metapersons are scarcely relevant to the pursuit of enlightenment. Gods may be unusually powerful but they are strapped to the wheel of rebirth nonetheless: their lives will end and begin again in this vale of tears just as any other unenlightened being. This is why Buddhism is so often the gate-crasher at any premature celebration of religious taxonomy, and particularly difficult for cognitive scientists to come to terms with.[11]

---

[8] The term 'transcendentalism' has naturally been used in many different ways, e.g., Mandelbaum 1966; Lambek 2013a.

[9] In practice, however, salvation is normally conceived in terms of perfection and bliss.

[10] Gombrich 1971: 46.

[11] See Laidlaw 2007: 221–222. On closer inspection, Buddhism may be less anomalous than it may seem, because (1) in practice all Buddhist cosmologies and much Buddhist practice involve relations with metapersons; (2) even in Theravada Buddhism, these metapersons may be linked to the soteriological project in many ways (Holt 1991); and (3) there is a tendency for the Buddha

Before proceeding any further, a few of the terminological issues that have beset the field of religion must be addressed. All the core concepts used here are profoundly etic categories, as the definition of the term 'supernatural' above should have made plain.[12] The notion of the 'supernatural' has been problematised since at least Durkheim because it finds so little emic resonance in many societies: it only makes sense in a worldview structured by the revolutionary eruption of 'naturalism'.[13] But, however uncomfortable it may be to acknowledge, this essentially secular and disenchanted vision remains the vantage point of nearly all scholarly enquiry.[14] The *emic* irrelevance of 'supernatural'– no less than that of 'religion' – to many societies is not only conceded here, but it is underlined as a ubiquitous feature of immanentism. However, this tells us little about the *etic* utility of these terms in undertaking cross-cultural comparison. Alternative concepts such as 'supramundane' or 'suprahuman' may sound a little less 'folk', but they are no more or less dualistic than 'supernatural'.[15]

In recent years, the notion of the 'world religions' has also fallen under a cloud. Nor is it preferred as a term here. 'Transcendentalism' is more precise in identifying a core feature – the ontological breach between a transcendentalist and mundane form of being – out of which many other features emerge. It does not take sheer size and expansiveness as fundamental criteria.[16] Religious traditions with

---

himself to be treated as a godlike being in popular worship (Pyysiäinen 2004: chapter 4).

[12] 'Etic' concepts are deployed for the purpose of analysis; they need not correspond to any 'emic' concepts, which are those deployed by the subjects of analysis themselves.

[13] Descola 2013a: 172–200, on naturalism. However, it may have a longer backstory ultimately reflecting the transcendentalist dimension of Christianity: consider Thomas Aquinas's distinctions between the supernatural, preternatural, and natural in Daston 1991: 97; compare Taylor 2007: 542.

[14] Anthropology sometimes flirts with the demotion of disenchanted secularism, as with the more radical voices in the ontological turn (Holbraad and Pedersen 2017) exploring an emic disruption of the etic. But very rarely does scholarship in history or anthropology explain religious phenomena in terms of the agency of the supernatural beings and forces that religion itself postulates. This would not count as 'explanation' as these disciplines currently construe it. This may change: Clossey et al. 2016.

[15] 'Super/suprahuman': Tweed 2006: 73; Riesebrodt 2010: xii.

[16] Bayly 2004: 332, distinguishes 'world religions' from nonexpansionary traditions such as Sikhism, Judaism, and Orthodox Christianity; Stroumsa 2011: 153, on Judaism.

a transcendentalist element include Buddhism, Hinduism, Jainism, Daoism, Judaism, Christianity, Manichaeism, Islam, and Sikhism, and there is considerable diversity here in how much each of these traditions has promoted proselytism at different points in their histories.

At the same time, the content of the conceptual dichotomy corresponds in important ways with categories developed by many generations of thinkers about religion using terms such as 'textual', 'historic', 'salvific', 'world' or 'universal' religions. Because the robust deployment of these related concepts has now fallen out of favour in certain areas of scholarship – particularly in history and anthropology, if not in sociology – it is important to distinguish, clarify, and nuance the transcendentalist/immanentist distinction in detail, which is what Chapter 1 sets out to do.

For example, it must be underlined that immanentism is a universal feature of religion, found in every society under the sun. Transcendentalism is not: it is rather the consequence of a series of intellectual revolutions that took place in particular parts of Eurasia in what has been called the 'Axial Age' of human history – the middle centuries of the first millennium BCE, which is introduced below. But transcendentalism cannot exist by itself; it always exists in a push-me–pull-you relationship with immanentism.[17] Note: the reverse is not true. Immanentism has existed untroubled by transcendentalism for most of human history, and many generations of anthropological work in particular have given us a fine sense of what these religious systems looked like. It follows that the terms *transcendentalism* and *immanentism* are used in this book in two ways: as labels for a *whole tradition* (such as Buddhism) or to describe an *element* of a tradition. Using it in the latter sense works to disrupt categorisations of whole traditions, and provides an opportunity for properly historical analysis, given that we can watch the dialogue between transcendentalism and immanentism shift about and buffet the sphere of politics.[18] Nevertheless, the taxonomy of whole traditions remains useful because it allows us to see that this dialogue only takes place within one kind of religious system.

In other related dichotomies, the systems that remain once world religions have been subtracted have been referred to as 'pagan', 'primitive', 'primal', 'local', 'communal', or 'traditional'. These are all

---

[17] Compare Gauchet 1999: 46.   [18] See 'An Unstable Synthesis' in Chapter 1.

problematic terms for various reasons. They frequently imply a range of characteristics that are *not* part of the construct of 'immanentism', including relatively simple and undeveloped cosmologies, an absence of literacy, unorganised and indistinct priesthoods, the nonexistence of an intellectual class or prophetic voices, and a confinement to locality and landscape.

An Overview of the Book

After Chapter 1 has established the fundamental framework for conceptualising religion, Chapter 2 undertakes to explain why religion was so prevalent as an integral dimension of state construction, absorbing the energies of warriors, chiefs, kings, and emperors. Much of the discussion in this chapter is in a universalist vein, as rulers everywhere looked to religion to secure both supernatural assistance and the social power that it generated so readily. The latter enabled rulers to establish their unique status, legitimise their position, and shape the feelings and behaviour of their subjects. The more ambitious they were in this regard, the more they sought to control or consolidate the religious field under their authority. However, the nature of the opportunities open to such rulers was shaped by whether the field was dominated by immanentist or transcendentalist traditions. The chapter also describes a political logic to the development of overarching 'higher' deities as a concomitant of expansive state building. This occurs frequently in immanentist settings and is therefore quite distinct from transcendentalism; however, there is an important affinity between the two dynamics. Where transcendentalist traditions arose and arrived they provided a compelling means of stepping outside and relativising the existing religious field in order to contain it within a higher narrative – with which the exercise of political authority may be equated. Over the longer term, however, transcendentalism bequeathed the potential for the religious field to seep away from central control by setting up a dialogue with a powerful class of clerisy (scholars, monks, priests) who were themselves prone to internal fragmentation.

Chapter 3 develops a set of concepts for understanding the phenomenon of sacred kingship, a major concern of early thinkers in anthropology, and the default form of political authority in the pre-modern world. After explaining why it should be such a confusing institution to analyse, the chapter takes on a similar structure to the first chapter, first setting out what the immanentist mode of sacralising the king looked like ('divinised kingship') and then the transcendentalist mode ('righteous kingship') before looking at how and why the latter eagerly sought to appropriate and combine with the former. For some purposes, divinised kingship may in turn be broken down into 'heroic' and 'cosmic' forms. However, the chapter is concerned with dynamics as well as types. For example, there seems to be a tendency for the charismatic display of warrior kings in the heroic mode to give way to the ritualised expression of cosmic kingship, and this in turn may ossify into ceremonial isolation (the 'ritualisation trap'). Meanwhile, it becomes clear that emphatic claims to royal divinisation often accompany attempts to consolidate the religious sphere.

Chapter 4 begins by considering the mechanics of religious change under the conditions of immanentism, dwelling on its innovatory, open, and experimental qualities, which ensure that it operates to some extent according to an 'economy of ritual efficacy'. Focusing on moments in which ritual systems are abandoned and new ones adopted allows us to intervene in scholarly debates as to what ritual is for. But the question arises: how do transcendentalist traditions – here represented by Christianity – manage to gain any kind of advantage in this economy? Amongst several answers, I shall draw attention to the capacity of missionaries to wage spiritual warfare through iconoclasm. Still, at the point of its reception transcendentalism has often been received as a species of supercharged immanentism, giving rise to prophetic, millenarian, and cargo movements in every corner of the planet.

Described in this condensed manner, these theoretical chapters may sound like abstract exercises indeed. Yet, at every point, the ideas and models suggested here have been constructed as means of thinking through the complex realities described by the specialist literature in history and anthropology. The discussion is grounded in a broad range of empirical material, including the empires of Ancient Mesopotamia, Qin China, Rome, and Angkor; the conquering warrior leaders Aśoka, Alexander, Chinggis Khan, and Queen Njinga; prophets of nineteenth-century Central Africa and the modern Philippines; royal cults of human sacrifice in Dahomey, Mexico, and Tahiti; and encounters involving the arrival of the Spanish conquistadors in the sixteenth-century Americas or fieldworkers amongst the highlands of Papua New Guinea in the 1960s.

The last two chapters of the book examine one of the most important ways in which transcendentalism actually spread: the conversion of
rulers. This involves descending from more long-term, objective, and
abstract assessments of the relationship between religion and politics
to what rulers facing the decision of whether to convert might actually
see on the ground or in the horizon of their imaginations. Here, the
investigation is confined to the arrival of Christianity into immanentist
societies. Much of the case study material is deliberately taken from the
two ends of the temporal spectrum, where the nature of the evidence is
most different: late antique and early medieval Europe from the conversion of Constantine (310s) to that of Vladimir of Rus (c. 988), and
the conversion of the chiefs of Oceania from Pomare of Tahiti (1812)
to Cakobau of Fiji (1854). There is no attempt here, then, to address
the issue of what happened when Christianity encountered a society
where a rival transcendentalism had already achieved hegemony – that
is explored in the companion volume (*Converting Kings*) written
alongside this one, where missionary encounters with royal courts in
Japan and Thailand are considered. Only then does it become possible
to arrive at an argument regarding the global patterns of ruler conversion to monotheism.[19] Nor does either volume consider what might be
called 'interschismatic' ruler conversions, as between the Sunni and
Shia branches of Islam or Catholic and Protestant forms of Christianity. These are fascinating in their own right but would appear to obey a
quite different logic.[20]

After describing a threefold model of ruler conversions, and reflecting on the meaning of 'conversion' as an analytical tool, Chapter 5
argues for the recurrent importance of the empirical demonstration of
immanent power in stimulating rulers to publicly commit to the new
faith; with surprising regularity, this took the form of military victories
and dramas of healing. Certain characteristics of immanentism also
shaped how Christianity was able to undermine the authority of the

---

[19] *Converting Kings*, referred to here as *CK*.
[20] It would take much more analytical work to consider how and whether the
   princely conversions of Reformation Europe, for example, might be brought
   into the paradigms assembled here – a task for future work perhaps. One of the
   reasons why interschismatic conversions appear to obey a different logic is that
   they are contained within certain shared understandings of the touchstones of
   legitimacy: they concern movements towards supposedly superior versions of
   existing religious commitments.

old religious order over the longer term. Chapter 6 analyses how rulers attempted to deploy the social power of Christianity to strengthen their authority, control the religious field, and pacify and unify their subjects – although such efforts might have ironic consequences. It finishes by considering this question: to what extent did divinised kingship form a bulwark against conversion, and what might Christianity offer in compensation?

The latter two chapters make much more use of primary sources than the preceding ones, particularly when drawing on early modern African and nineteenth-century Pacific material.[21] However, even in the latter case, there are simply very few contemporary indigenous sources to draw upon, and we are driven to texts written by outsiders or converted insiders. Meanwhile, all secondary scholarship on early medieval Europe must rely almost entirely on Christian sources, often written substantially later than the events they describe. All this raises significant questions of source criticism. The most acute concerns the role of supernatural interventions in accounts of ruler conversion, which is addressed at length in Chapter 5. Naturally, some will have alternative judgements about how to approach any given source: this is an occupational hazard of working with such partial and deficient material. But it was a working method to be conscious of these questions at all times and to develop a comparative sensitivity as to the ways in which missionary sources in particular are liable to be treacherous.

Some Matters of Methodology

A great range of other concepts, beyond those of transcendentalism and immanentism, are used in specific ways in this book. Defined whenever they arise, they are also gathered together in a glossary of theoretical terms as an appendix. This may be consulted if it becomes important to consider what is meant by terms such as 'state' or 'legitimation', for example. The much-discussed problems around the term 'conversion' are considered close to the start of Chapter 5.

What may be in order, however, are some brief comments on methodology. This can be skipped by those readers who discern in it an extended bout of scholarly throat-clearing. For others, however, it

---

[21] The case studies of *CK* are also based on primary material.

may help to allay misunderstandings about the approach adopted here. If this approach is somewhat unusual today, that is partly because of several tendencies in the humanities of the past generation: (1) an aversion to essentialism; (2) an esteem for genealogical deconstruction; (3) the prioritisation of the emic over the etic; (4) the avoidance of teleology. These tendencies have been assisted by broader intellectual moods of post-structuralism and post-modernism, by the consequences of the specialisation and professionalisation of academic disciplines, and also by political upheavals as the academy undergoes an entirely necessary process of globalisation. It must be underscored from the outset that that each of these now-dominant tendencies has served and will continue to serve important functions in the intellectual division of labour; this book has sought to incorporate their critiques and insights wherever it can. However, as ever, scholarship is prone to embalming once-radical movements into their own form of intellectual orthodoxy, in which subtleties are lost and taboos observed.

Anti-essentialism has its place as a reminder not to let our categories take more weight than they can bear in any given analytical endeavour. But it can lead to an overzealous category-crumbling – what Joel Robbins refers to as 'object-dissolving critique' – in which intellectual probity is demonstrated by breaking down any received concept into ever smaller particles.[22] The risk here, however, is in assuming that smaller-scale concepts necessarily attain a superior level of epistemo-logical purity – a point to which we shall return. It may be better in some contexts to refer to Sri Lankan Buddhism rather than Buddhism, but one has not hit upon something 'more real' by doing so, merely something 'more helpful' for a given purpose. While specialists may generate scholarly capital by performing the vanishing object act, comparativists can only look on with dismay. To work their magic, they need an array of distinct objects (cases, events, or processes) before them to shift around and manipulate. This is one reason why, in some corners of the humanities, comparison itself has become a suspect exercise.[23]

The deconstructive appetite has also been primed by genealogical analysis. This procedure is not only a significant historical exercise in its own right; it also prompts a healthy scrutiny of our received

[22] Robbins et al. 2014: 562; Peel 2016: 105–124, for some sensible comments.
[23] Dempsey 2011.

conceptual apparatus, and an awareness of the political implications they may once have had and may still be invoked to advance.[24] But it too carries a risk, of slipping into the genetic or genealogical fallacy. This is the tendency to assume that unveiling the origins of a concept is tantamount to demonstrating its analytical uselessness. Any concept inherited from previous generations is likely to be located in an intellectual context containing assumptions and endeavours that will be seen as morally deficient by modern standards. The concepts themselves are then seen as bearing this taint in their bones. But their malign influence must be demonstrated in the resulting distortions of the analysis itself rather than assumed from the mere fact of deployment. And since some concepts must, in the end, be used, will this involve their de facto acknowledgement as 'safe'?[25] It is as if, once the all-too-human genesis of a concept has been revealed, its capacity to convey insight is somehow tarnished – with genealogists themselves uniquely liberated from the chains of conceptual bondage. In reality, the scholarship in any one field tends to be rather selective in its problematisation of its basic concepts, all of which – including, for example, 'society', a term that started to gain something like its modern meaning in English from the seventeenth century – are historically contingent and 'impure'.[26]

Sometimes, there is even the suggestion that identifying the origin point of a concept is equivalent to identifying when the process or thing it describes came into being. That may sound absurd – we frequently refer to the existence of 'societies' existing long before the modern period – but this slippage is facilitated by the third tendency, a failure to acknowledge the integrity of the distinct domains of the emic and the etic.[27] To properly delineate the profundities and subtleties of the 'emic' – that is, the understanding of the society one studies – is

---

[24] Masuzawa 2005.
[25] See also Riesebrodt 2010: 6. Asad 1993: 29, argues that religion cannot be defined, partly because its definition 'is itself the historical product of discursive processes'. But which concepts are not?
[26] Though still not quite the modern meaning: Bossy 1982; Withington 2010: 102–133.
[27] See Bossy 1982 for purist emic objections to 'society'. For emic/etic wrangles in history: Yarrow 2014; in anthropology: Ortner 2016: 35. In one sense, emic and etic are always collapsing into one another, and the ontological turn (Holbraad and Pedersen 2017) attempts to push the emic into the etic in interesting ways (while deploying the most etic language imaginable).

the crowning purpose and achievement of anthropology and is almost as important to many areas of historiography and religious studies. It is a vital undertaking, both intellectually and politically. But it too holds no rights to exclusive explanatory power. Somehow, one may slip between noticing, for example, that a given society has no concept or term for 'religion' and arguing that the term must not be applied as an analytical term for it. This is a logical error of a kind. Even the most fine-grained and localised of scholarly interpretative acts involves the deployment of etic concepts, necessarily alien to the mental context they describe. And when it comes to comparative analysis in particular, the whole point is to develop concepts that do not correspond to the emic repertoire of any one society but which cut against the grain of the local in brutal but productive ways.

Lastly, there is the opprobrium in which 'teleology' now resides, especially in the field of history. This too reflects noble instincts: to protect the writing of history from the peddling of just-so stories, to ward off the terrors of anachronism and hindsight, to let the past live on its own terms rather than ours, and to maintain a due regard for the play of chaos and contingency in shaping the course of events. Yet antiteleology may become a no-less overbearing presence in turn, hampering reasonable questions about how we got where we are today, refusing to countenance the more patterned and structured dimensions of the past, and confusing explanatory projects for judgmental ones.

Every scale of analysis has been subject to these deconstructive tendencies: 'religion' is begging for disassembly (and I have not been able to resist either); the term 'world religions' is frequently regarded askance; 'Christianity' is reduced to multiple Christianities, and so on. At least let us recognise that there is no natural end to this. For example, in distancing themselves from earlier scholarly narratives, anthropologists and religious studies scholars have quite often urged us to beware viewing our material through a 'Protestant' lens, which may seem transparent but in fact colours and distorts our vision of religion in other times and climes.[28] Implicitly or explicitly, the Reformation is therefore invoked as a great watershed cutting off modern observers from other religious sensibilities. But meanwhile historians have been busy on their own deconstructionalist exercises,

---

[28] Meyer 2013: 322.

often aimed precisely at periodisations such as the Reformation or, indeed, the Enlightenment. There is a tendency now in some historical writing to downplay the coherence and distinctiveness of Protestantism, to rub away its revolutionary qualities as the residue of another grand narrative, or to at most acknowledge 'reformations' in the plural.[29] That's all very well, the anthropologist may insist, but over the longer term can we not agree that Protestantism did bring a profoundly different and profoundly influential sensibility into being (just as did the Enlightenment)? Quite. There are times when Calvin's Geneva of the 1550s may be the most respectable frame of analysis; other times in which the lumpen category of Protestantism is essential.

Just as deconstructing periodisation may hinder us from seeing profound forms of transformation over the very long term, so the cumulative effect of the unchecked deconstruction of cultural units is to move cultural diversity itself out of view, until we are left with a vista of monotonous granularity. Pressed up against a mountain with a magnifying glass, all we will see is the same banal variation in texture that may be found in the soil of the plains below. The point is: there is no law of epistemology which accords inherent propriety to any one scale of generalisation: neither the village, the nation, the macroregion, nor the planet; neither the year, decade, epoch, nor millennium. There are only more or less inappropriate deployments of these generalisations in any given context.[30]

This book and the companion volume therefore deploy the full range of scales of analysis in considering religion. An important level is that of rough universalism, in which global ubiquity is acknowledged. This derives, for example, from an appreciation of immanentism, which everywhere produces similar features of behaviour and perception and is nowhere entirely suppressed. It may be considered an alternative to regional or civilisational generalisations – such as 'African religion'

---

[29] Historians' concern to disembed Protestantism from modernisation and disenchantment narratives 'now represents something approaching the current historical consensus' (Walsham 2008: 500). Walsham 2014, however, combines teleology fear with an understanding of its costs in terms of a weakened grasp of long-term transformations. Contrast Eire 2016: 744–754, and see Cameron 2010: 12–14, 142–143.

[30] Much reasonable criticism will take place in exactly these terms; the problem comes when certain terms and levels of analysis acquire an inherently taboo quality.

or 'Southeast Asian religion' – which often lack a truly comparative rationale. More unusual is the deployment in this book of a level residing just underneath the universalism of religion, a dualist model, in which immanentist and transcendentalist modes of religiosity are differentiated, and which cuts across many received categorisations of religion and area studies.[31] Yet, transcendentalism is then broken down into its monotheistic and Indic variants, which were, in several respects, very different projects (See Chapter 1). Still, the Indic strand must also be teased apart so that we can recognise the coherence of Buddhism in particular as an important structure of the *longue durée*. At several places, the analysis will then crack the latter apart into Mahayana and Theravada Buddhism, which also developed distinctive tendencies.[32] Then again, in the Ayutthaya case study in the companion volume, the construct of the 'Theravada' tradition may be set aside in order to explore the distinctiveness of certain features of Thai Buddhism; and this in turn gives way to an exploration of the nuances of philosophical and religious thought in the cosmopolitan atmosphere of the court of the late seventeenth century, before finally pondering what can be discerned of the mental processes of an individual, King Narai, in the mid-1680s, as he performed his round of ceremonial and diplomatic duties and pondered how to keep the goodwill of Louis XIV, who was hell-bent on his conversion, while not angering the nobility and sangha he still depended on. In the heat of intradisciplinary debate, scholars are often drawn into arguing that one of these levels should be privileged while those above that level are 'reifications'. They are, in fact, all merely angles of vision that allow us to see some of what lies before us while occluding much else.

An openness to experimentation with scale is one of the central achievements of global history.[33] One solution to abiding by the scholarly tendencies above while working on a larger scale has been to pursue the 'connected history' method of tracing unexpected flows and circulations across macroregional or global space. This, indeed, is currently the most popular means of doing global history. It can be revelatory and exciting and is, in certain ways, indispensable.[34] But it

---

[31] The level of 'Axial' traditions could also be inserted, one level up from transcendentalism, but this fits awkwardly in a cascading taxonomy of 'religion' per se.

[32] On the controversy around 'Theravada', see Chapter 1.   [33] McKeown 2012.

[34] The case studies in *CK* are all moments of 'connectedness'.

can also be superficial in its approach to causation.[35] While it speaks clearly of the contemporary condition of globalisation, it may be less helpful in answering some of the big questions which those conditions have prompted and which in turn propelled the rise of global history. That is why the most influential debate to date in global history – 'the great divergence' question of when and why the West first rose to industry-fuelled economic dominance and not the East – has been framed in terms of a different method – that of comparative history. As soon as historians are forced – often by movements outside the academy – to return to questions of large-scale causation, to 'why' questions and not just 'how', the comparative method is likely to be invoked.

The major thinkers of the nineteenth century such as Marx and Weber did not avoid the religious dimension, but global comparative history in the early twenty-first century has largely confined its attention to economic, political, and military matters.[36] With comparativist instincts reemerging in anthropology too, and the lingering role of religion in the public sphere all too evident, it may now be time for historians to venture into these realms again.[37] To do so we will have to learn from historical sociology, which has never abandoned these ambitions, and which produced the literature of the 'Axial Age' – see the next section. In the arguments of this book, readers will no doubt be able to see similarities with ideas that go back to the nineteenth century and indeed much further, and which have naturally been subject to the misgivings of subsequent generations. But such ideas have not simply been 'inherited,' rather they have been discovered in dialogue with an array of empirical information, particularly in relation to the case studies of the companion volume – and also altered, tested, reformulated, or rejected, in the light of the now-hegemonic critiques that formed my real intellectual inheritance.[38] The comparative method employed in these volumes is not used primarily for the purposes of synchronic classification, but in order to explain patterns

---

[35] Risking collapse into diffusionism: Robbins 2004: 5–7, 319; Eaton 1997: 244.

[36] Clossey 2007. Lieberman 2009 is an exception in extending its purview to culture.

[37] In anthropology: Robbins 2014; Graeber and Sahlins 2017.

[38] That is to say, I came of age in an era dominated by such deconstructionalist misgivings – only slowly to find them strikingly unhelpful in meeting the challenges of global history.

of change. Chapters 5 and 6 (and all of the companion volume) take as their object of comparison societies facing the dilemmas and perplexities of cultural encounter and potentially on the verge of transformation.[39]

One feature of early historical, anthropological, and sociological theories obviously disavowed here is the arrangement of cultural difference along a line of primitive to advanced. For the avoidance of doubt, I do not set out here a line of progress, or stages of the evolution of consciousness.[40] Immanentism is the result of *universal* features of the human mind; it is only to lend some sense to that fact rather than in proposing a developmental model that I draw, very occasionally, and rudimentarily on cognitive science. The purpose of this book is to allow us to see transcendentalism as something wondrous in its peculiarity and contingency not as either some 'higher' stage of cognitive achievement or an inevitable and natural feature of human maturation. Indeed, the norms and values of the secularised stretches of the modern world are in many ways closer to immanentism than they are to those of transcendentalism. The truly teleological position would be to take the appearance and rise of transcendentalism for granted; once we refuse to do that it becomes important to explain how and why it could ever have become so dominant.[41] At the same time, the image of dominance itself is frequently qualified as this book traces circular movements which reinvoke the immanent at every stage.

Of the various grand narratives emergent in the nineteenth and twentieth centuries, secularisation theory has come under particular strain in the twenty-first.[42] This is not a primary concern of these volumes, but the material presented here does have one implication for this debate. Religion and politics are so obviously entwined around each other today that their current union may seem to be an eternal one. In that case: where have all the sacred kings gone? Across the

---

[39] In doing so, it follows what Peel 1987 (and see 2016: 105–124) advocated as the comparison of 'societies-in-change'; close to Puett's (2002): 233, argument for comparing the playing out of historical tensions rather than synchronic structures.

[40] Hefner 1993b: 6 discusses nineteenth-century views.

[41] Hefner 1993b:17: 'Impressive as it was ... anthropology's antievolutionist critique left unresolved whether global patterns are evident in religious conversion or broad commonalities exist among the civilization-based faiths we call world religions.'

[42] Katznelson and Stedman Jones 2010.

world our understanding of where political authority comes from and what it is for has undergone a great shift. If the primary means of generating legitimacy once came from the performance of divinised or righteous kingship, in which authority was a function of innate being or salvific justification, it now must find its origin in popular sovereignty as expressed in either democratic or authoritarian politics. This is surely one aspect of a larger phenomenon of secularisation – which some thinkers consider a legacy, in part, of transcendentalism itself.[43] Wherever one wants to locate the principal motor of this movement into the partially secular politics of modernity – the Enlightenment still seems an obvious reference point – its force cannot be denied. That is why the material relating to the relationship between religion and state in this book is largely confined to those times and places that had not yet been reshaped by it.[44] This is broadly referred to here as the 'pre-modern world', but only by making sure to bend chronology around geography. The chiefly conversions in the Pacific 1800–1850 may well have been taking place in a process of rapid interaction with the forces of the 'modern world' but – contrary to the synchronic implications of connected history perhaps – the key logics involved are comparable to those that took place a thousand years earlier with the conversion of Khan Boris of the Bulgars (c. 860s) or even, 500 years further back, Constantine himself.

The Axial Age

The explicit concept of the Axial Age was introduced by Karl Jaspers in 1949, though the origins of the key idea stretch back to the 1870s, and it received a decisive crystallisation with Shmuel Eisenstadt's 1986 volume, *The Origins and Diversity of Axial Civilizations*.[45] It has since become a major organising principle of the historical sociology of

---

[43] Casanova 2012: 192; Katznelson and Stedman Jones 2010: 8–9; Charles Taylor 2007. Transcendentalism helped prepare the ground for secularisation by suppressing the significance of immanent power.

[44] But note: material relating to religion or conversion in general, however, is drawn from all periods.

[45] Jaspers 1953; Eisenstadt 1986a; Halton 2014 identifies the founding figure as John Stuart Stuart-Glennie, in 1873. The general, though not specific influence of Max and Alfred Weber is often noted. Hefner 1993b has had an important influence on my reading of this literature and remains one of the best introductions to understanding religious diversity and change.

religion, notably extended by Robert Bellah.[46] Thinkers working in
the genre of philosophical history have naturally been drawn to it,
including Eric Voegelin, Ernest Gellner, Marcel Gauchet, and Charles
Taylor.[47] Within history, the concept has been picked up by some
historians in certain fields, such as Jan Assmann in Ancient Egypt;
Arnaldo Momigliano and S. C. Humphreys on Ancient Greece and
Rome; Jan Heesterman on India; Benjamin I. Schwarz, Heiner Roetz,
and Prasenjit Duara on China; Marshall Hodgson and Patricia Crone
on Islam; Steven Collins on Buddhism.[48] There have been a few signs
of some influence on anthropology in recent years, in the work of
Gananath Obeyesekere, David Graeber, and, in particular, Joel
Robbins.[49] It is no coincidence that Robbins is also a prominent figure
in the recent emergence of the anthropology of Christianity, and in
the promotion of a more explicitly comparative approach within the
discipline.[50]

Naturally, there is much debate among such scholars as to how best
to define the Axial Age, whether it works best as a periodisation or a
typology ('axiality'), whether the vague sense of synchronicity is worth
attending to, what its principal causes were and so on. There is not the
space here to make a proper intervention in these debates; what follows
is rather a greatly condensed, generalised, provisional, and speculative
summary.[51]

There was never any 'Axial Age' in the sense of an epoch that people
at the time – living in the dispersed clusters of Ancient Greece, Israel,
northern India, and China, in the first millennium BCE – understood
as such. It is a profoundly etic and abstract heuristic, then, which seeks
to capture the common ground shared by the visionary attempts

---

[46] See Bellah and Joas 2012 for a full list, but note especially Bellah 1964, 2005,
2011, Arnason, Eisenstadt, and Wittrock 2005; Wittrock 2015; Salvatore 2016.
Other sociologists to have engaged the concept include Jack Goldstone, Michael
Mann, Stephen Sharot, Ilana Friedrich Silber, and José Casanova. Political
scientists: Katzenstein 2010, Zarakol 2016. A popular take: Armstrong 2006.

[47] Gellner 1988, Voegelin 2000–1, Gauchet 1999; Taylor 2007, 2012.

[48] Momigliano 1990: 8–10; Humphreys 1975, 1986; Schwarz 1975; Roetz
2012; Duara 2015; Hodgson 1974; Crone 2003; Collins 1998. Also note Moore
2004.

[49] Obeyesekere 2002, 2012; Robbins 2012; Graeber 2011a; Tambiah 1986, Parry
1998.

[50] Robbins, Schieffelin, and Vilaça 2014.

[51] This is an inadequate account but readers deserve perhaps a statement of
what I see as the core of the 'Axial Age' revolution.

of thinkers in these regions to overcome a disturbing destabilisation of traditional thought patterns, including the immanentist form of religiosity.[52] The solutions it threw up were so successful in the long run that they came to establish the foundations for the civilisational structures that persist to this day, and perhaps not until the Enlightenment was any radical or lasting disavowal of them possible: Confucianism and Daoism, amongst other schools of thought, in China; Buddhism, Jainism, and forms of Hinduism in India; monotheism in West Asia, and the origins of European philosophy in Greece. It is impossible to imagine world history without these enormous Eurasian pivots of mental life.

There are two slightly more precise features which seem important to the overall vision of the Axial Age even if they cannot quite be applied to all four cases. First, in all but the case of the emergence of monotheism among the Jews, the Axial Age emerged within a context of philosophical ferment. In Greece, India, and China, the stage was set by the eruption of reflexivity, second-order thinking and competitive debate.[53] Everything was thrown open to question: species of scepticism, materialism, monism, and nihilism all found their champions and demanded to be addressed. Second, in the Judaic and Indic cases, there opened up an ontological breach between a 'transcendental' and 'mundane' sphere, only bridged eventually by salvific or eschatological hopes.[54] This was much less straightforwardly a feature of the Chinese case, while in Greece it perhaps only made a decisive

---

[52] Wittrock 2005: 68: 'Axiality is a form of reaction to a new type of human condition where neither the structures of kinship and physical proximity nor those of self-legitimizing empire, suffice any longer to embed the individual in a context of meaning and familiarity.'

[53] On second-order thinking: Elkana 1986. See the *Brahmajāla Sutta* I, 18, in Bodhi 1978: 57–58 for the Buddha's cautions about 'wrangling argumentation'. For Momigliano 1990: 9, the Axial Age was the 'age of criticism.'

[54] 'Salvation' or 'liberation' is a key element of Indic transcendentalism. But 'eventually' is crucial for the Judaic tradition, in which ideas about the afterlife were generally much more marginal and diverse, often taking the form of an immanentist bodily resurrection (Gilman 1997 argues for its growing importance from the second century BCE). Second Temple Judaism saw messianic or eschatological hopes emerge, in which God would descend to remake earth, while Christianity placed salvation centre stage. For further reflections on Judaism as transcendentalism, see Bellah 2011: 289–323; Uffenheimer 1986: 144; Eisenstadt 1992.

appearance in the later thought of Plato.[55] In Ancient Greece, then, the religious sphere per se was largely bypassed, and what the West came to know as 'philosophy' became the arena for asking ultimate questions.[56]

To some extent such intellectual revolutions are always underdetermined by the social, political, and economic context in which they occur. Nevertheless, given the focus of this book on the relation between politics and religion, we may note Karl Jaspers's observation that the main cases first emerged in contexts where empire was absent.[57] In China, this was the 'warring states' period before the unification under the Qin; the Indic sects emerged in a milieu of competing republics and kingdoms before the rise of the Mauryan Empire[58]; while in Greece, the context was the fiercely independent city-states before the conquests of Alexander the Great. In all cases, a distinct class of peripatetic intellectuals – teachers, debaters, advisors, but neither priests nor bureaucrats – roamed this polycentric landscape.[59] They helped promote a steep rise in the status of 'theoretic culture' as opposed to the 'mythic culture' which has always characterised humankind's account of reality.[60] Again, the case of the Jews is a little different, for some of the principal stages in the development of transcendent monotheism took place not in the absence of empire but as a victim of it in the shape of Egyptian and Neo-Babylonian

---

[55] But see Chapter 1 for qualifications. On the face of it, several of the movements of Qin and Han China described by Puett 2015, especially the Celestial Masters, could be drawn into a reconfigured transcendentalist paradigm.

[56] Indeed, the work of philosophers generated some important parallels with transcendentalism (see Chapters 1 and 3). Nevertheless, I agree with Wittrock 2004: 47, that 'Axiality' itself cannot be defined by transcendentalism, which is rather a major property of a major subset of it.

[57] Jaspers 1953: 51. This point would be qualified by the inclusion of Zoroastrian Persia in the paradigm.

[58] The rise of Magadha could look threateningly imperial in Buddha's milieu: see Obeyesekere 2012: 139.

[59] Humphreys 1975: 99–103. These are landscapes united by common language and culture but diverse enough to elicit sensations of nascent cultural relativism. Note that the Indian and Greek cases in particular saw experimentation in different political forms, including oligarchic republics as well as monarchies.

[60] 'Theoretic culture' is the ability, greatly assisted by literacy, 'to think analytically rather than narratively, to construct theories that can be criticized logically and empirically', according to Bellah 2011: 118, 273–274, following Donald 1991. I am not suggesting here that only Axial societies generate theoretic thought.

domination and enforced exile.[61] As a result, some of the key Jewish prophets were no less dis-embedded or alienated from the status quo than Greek sophists or Indian renouncers. In these cases, then, the promise of secular salvation implicit in imperialism was absent, resisted, or belied.[62] In the 'transcendentalist breakthroughs' of the Indic and monotheistic cases in particular, kinship, politics, and ritual – the normal means of attaining human flourishing – were inherently and shockingly devalued.

If one word sums up the nature of the threat that received world-views faced in the Axial Age, it would have to be relativism: it was the givenness of the status quo, its taken-for-granted meaningfulness, which gave way.[63] There is in many cases a distinct anxiety about impermanence, perhaps because certain forms of change really were moving these societies in more observably disruptive ways, and perhaps in some cases because the cumulative effects of literacy had created disturbing forms of historical consciousness.[64] The First Noble Truth of Buddhism is 'life is *dukkha*', and *dukkha* tends to elide suffering with transience.[65]

From this new historicised viewpoint, the lineaments of society could be rendered uncomfortably contingent, even artificial. As Marcel Gauchet suggested, the assumption of traditional forms as simply eternal, or as created in a time which was not-time by men who were

---

[61] Weber 1978, I: 450: they saw in 'the continuous peril from the pitiless bellicosity of terrible nations the anger and grace of a heavenly king'.

[62] The case of China is different given the relative idealisation of politics.

[63] By relativism I mean the understanding that truth and value are culturally constructed and therefore variable across time and space.

[64] See Carrithers 1983: 8–17; Obeyesekere 2012: 139–141; Thapar 1975: 124, and Graeber 2011: 21, the latter referring to the development of literacy, markets, cash transactions, and the development of materialism, to which the Axial Age was a paradoxical reaction. Bellah 2011: 270, also notes coincidence with coinage. Assmann 2012 examines certain uses of literacy as producing a 'cultural memory' which involves reflexivity.

[65] The *Maitrāyaṇīya Upaniṣad* (ed. van Buitenen 1962: 124–125) has a great king drawn towards a renouncer after reflecting that empires rise and fall, the great oceans dry up, the stars are cut from their moorings, the gods tumble out of their seats and 'I am trapped in this world like a frog in a sealed well.' Compare Roetz 2012: 262, on the breakdown of the old order in mid first-millennium BCE China: 'There is a very clear notion in Zhou texts that something unprecedented has commenced. They speak of a "chaotic" and "drowning" world that has lost its foundations and is falling apart ... The main directions of classical Chinese thought are answers to this crisis ...'

not-men, has done much to deflect the possibility of any more searching critiques of the status quo.[66] Contrast this with the following
quotation from the *Zhuangzi*: "Morals and regulations change
according to the times ... The old is as different from the new as a
monkey is different from the Duke of Zhou.'[67] Because previously
taken-for-granted local forms had been undermined, only universal
solutions would do.[68] For example, now that customary and locally
specific morality was no longer sufficient, all the major Axial Age
traditions arrived at the same solution in some form of the 'golden
rule', to treat others as one would be treated oneself: a stripped-down
maxim that could find widespread assent.

As Weber discerned, the problem of suffering was now experienced
as an acute burden.[69] How to account for apparently purposeless acts
of destruction or for the intrinsic rather than contingent pain of sheer
existence? It no longer seemed sufficient to simply conduct ritual affairs
appropriately, nor were the boons these promised held to be ultimately
satisfactory. For the Jews the result was a deity as strange and unknowable as their twisting fortunes.[70] For Buddhists, the result was something much more complete and radical: nirvana as the eradication of
any illusions of selfhood or desire whatsoever. It was precisely because
such visions of transcendence floated so freely above mundane reality
that they became such firm anchor points for epistemology and morality. Since the sacred was no longer entirely immanent in the world, the
world would no longer need to suffice as the locus of one's hopes and
aspirations. The new values that were imposed on the human being in
relation to this great unthinkable were unearthly, as we shall see.

The subsequent post-Axial Age transformations of monotheism –
Christianity and Islam – also first emerged among peoples who either
lay beyond empire or were uncomfortably subordinated to it. (These
are sometimes described as 'secondary breakthroughs' although the
term 'breakthrough' is unnecessarily celebratory). Christianity represents at once a deepening of the transcendentalist imperative, by transforming the Judaic inheritance into a universalist and more profoundly
salvific creed, and also an attempt to bridge the gap with immanentism
through its realisation of a quasi-human messiah.

---

[66] Gauchet 1999: chapter 1.   [67] Roetz 2012: 262–264.
[68] Charles Taylor 2012: 30.   [69] Weber 1961: 275.
[70] Berger 1967: 74, 115.

During their first emergence in the 'Axial Age,' the political implications of these movements had been rather slight.[71] It is one of the most
resonant ironies in human history that these traditions were subsequently exalted by the large imperial formations that began to seep
over the ancient world. Buddhism was established as an aspect of
imperial ideology under Aśoka (268 to 232 BCE), who ruled the first
vast empire in South Asia's history, and it is from this point that it
exhibits real missionary energy.[72] Confucianism attained its status as a
vital part of state ideology under the Han. And Rome finally held aloft
the image of its crucified victim as its master symbol following the
conversion of Constantine. In some ways this great accommodation
with political might negated dimensions of the Axial or transcendentalist vision, which now lay suppressed until specific conditions allowed
their release once again. At the same time, it allowed transcendentalism
to blossom as a social formation, as clerisies were afforded the wealth
and space to become strong institutional presences, and empowered to
draw boundaries and orthodoxies more starkly. As Guy Stroumsa and
others have argued, the monotheisms as we know them today were as
much a product of the milieu of late antiquity as of any earlier epoch.[73]

Little of substance has been said thus far about Confucianism and
the traditions that came to be known as Hinduism. They really deserve

---

[71] Casanova 2012: 210.

[72] Although Buddhism subsequently dwindled as a South Asian political ideology
according to Pollock 2005, and the exact place of Buddhism in Aśokan ideology
is contested. Certainly, later Buddhist kings took Aśoka as paradigmatic (Goh
2015).

[73] Assmann 2012: 399: 'If we insist on a first period of axialization, we could point
to the years about 200 BCE to 200 CE when the great canons were established:
the Confucian, the Daoist, and the Buddhist canons in the East, and the Avesta,
the Hebrew Bible and the canon of Greek "classics" in the West.' Stroumsa 2009
refers to the period from Jesus to Muhammad as another Axial period,
emphasising a new consciousness of the self and a boost to the text as a vehicle
for cultural memory following the invention of the codex. These shaped
Judaism, Manichaeism, and other cults, as well as Christianity. Indeed, to take a
broader Eurasian perspective, the emergence of Synagogue Judaism,
Christianity, Islam, Bhakti devotionalism, and Mahayana Buddhism all
popularised transcendentalist forms such as personal morality, ethics,
universalism, salvation – but also, and not coincidentally, generated forms of
immanentisation. They showed a new capacity to expand, to mobilise, and to
engage the political sphere. My thanks to Vic Lieberman for discussion. All this
points to the value in using 'axiality' as a concept rather than as a periodisation –
or indeed replacing it with transcendentalism in some contexts.

a full analysis of how they may or may not fit into various versions of the Axial Age thesis and the typology of transcendentalism. Such a discussion would have drawn out the profoundly different ways in which the relationship between transcendence and immanence was played out in each region. No one of these can be held up as an ideal type, in other words, against which the other Axial Age instantiations may be measured up.[74]

---

[74] As will become clear, the differences between the various forms of transcendentalism are easily as important as their commonalities for the purposes of global comparative analysis.

1 | *The Two Forms of Religion: Being and Nothingness*

Most of this chapter is devoted to distinguishing the characteristics of first immanentism and then transcendentalism. But while the former has often defined religious traditions in their entirety, the latter never has. The final section explains how and why *all* transcendentalist traditions have existed as an unstable synthesis with immanentism.[1]

The Characteristics of Immanentism

Again and again, historians and anthropologists articulate what is distinctive about religion as it functions in the particular society they study – in terms that could in fact apply to most societies that have ever existed. Eduardo Viveiros de Castro may be describing the Tupinambá of Brazil but in certain ways he is also describing any religious life untouched by transcendentalism.[2] These may be summarised by the following ten characteristics, all of which run into each another:

(1) The promiscuous attribution of personhood

As an element of human behaviour found in every society known to scholarship, it should be possible to understand immanentism in terms of the inherent characteristics of the evolved mind.[3] I will not attempt to proceed very far into the field of cognitive science, which has its own internal debates about how mental processing

---

[1] Note again that the reverse is not true.

[2] In other ways (such as perspectivism), of course, he is describing something more particular: Viveiros de Castro 2011.

[3] This does not mean that we *must* think as immanentists (or indeed as transcendentalists), contra the fears of Whitmarsh 2016: 5, about evolutionary psychology.

may or may not be organised and its own epistemological problems to overcome. Nevertheless, it has established some foundational points that all serious thinkers about religion must address. We are obliged, for example, to consider the implications of the fact that the human mind is not some force of pure intelligence that simply perceives the world as it is.[4] It is extremely good at some things and rather poor at others; it is inconsistently attentive. Some lines of thought are followed more readily and intuitively than others. One of the best examples of this also turns out to be the most significant for a comprehension of religion. Not for the first time, David Hume arrived at the point without the benefit of subsequent theories of evolution:

There is an universal tendency among mankind to conceive all beings like themselves, and to transfer to every object, those qualities, with which they are familiarly acquainted, and of which they are intimately conscious. We find human faces in the moon, ascribe malice or good-will to every thing, that hurts or pleases us.[5]

The profound tendency towards anthropomorphism is impossible to deny for anyone who has cursed a car that has broken down – exhibiting what Alfred Gell called 'vehicular animism'.[6] What informs such behaviour is the persistent assumption that significant effects are caused by somehow personlike agents rather than by the brute operations of nonconscious and nonintentional matter.

Some scholars working within an evolutionary perspective have argued that this was the product of various cognitive traits which promoted survival, such as predator detection: if a twig falls and snaps behind you, it pays to start as if it were a wolf rather than the wind.[7] Most promising, however, is the current interest in the supercharged development of social intelligence: the human mind appears to be distinguished by its capacity for complex feats of mind reading, speculating about the feelings, strategies, and intentions of

---

[4] Many cognitive scientists argue that this is because the brain is an intricately related set of tools for carrying out specific tasks (summarised in Larson 2016). For an alternative approach: Heyes 2012, 2018.
[5] Hume 2007 [1734–1737]: 40.   [6] Gell 1998: 18.
[7] Boyer 2001: 165; Atran 2002; Whitehouse and Laidlaw 2007: 13. Barrett 2007: 183. But see Willard 2017 on how 'predictive coding' may allow cultural expectations to shape perception.

other people.[8] Perhaps it became so important for survival and repro-
ductive success to understand the complexities of social relations that
it decisively altered the priorities of human cognition. However it
happened, it is as if this fixation upon the logic of the social was
inexorably transferred to other domains of cognition, such that it
structured the comprehension of powers, forces, qualities, or even
abstractions.[9] Of course, people in all societies discern 'natural' processes of cause and effect too. It is just that these are often held to
proceed alongside a deeper or more satisfying level of explanation
that revolves around the discernment of motivated agency.[10]

At a stroke, this perspective renders any social functionalist theory of
why religion exists unnecessary (although functionalism in the broad
sense is indispensable for understanding why it takes the forms it does,
as the following chapter suggests). Without some such appeal to
the evolved mind, moreover, it is difficult to comprehend why
certain features are independently invented time and again within
otherwise very diverse and disconnected cultures, including types comparable to witches, spirits of possession, ancestors, and so on.[11] Our
attention is also drawn to the way that de facto assumptions
(or 'nonreflective beliefs' in the terminology of Justin L. Barrett)
may diverge widely from ostensibly esteemed knowledge.[12] The cognitive tendency towards agency detection certainly helps explain the
promiscuous attribution of personhood in the historical and anthropological record.[13]

Two qualifications deserve brief acknowledgement: first that
'personhood' is used here to refer simply to motivated agency; emic
theories of what exactly personhood is and how exactly matter relates

---

[8] In neuroscience, the 'social brain' hypothesis makes such demands the driver of
the 'extraordinary size and complexity' of the human brain (Adolphs 2009).
Thanks to Roger Albin. Even the 'cultural evolutionary psychology' approach of
Heyes 2018, sees some genetically inherited predispositions towards pro-
sociality, while arguing that more specific features such as mind reading and
imitation are culturally transmitted – but still essentially universally present –
cognitive mechanisms. According to this approach, immanentism might be seen
as a 'grist' of these 'mills'. Where this book refers to the 'evolved mind' it could
potentially refer to such mechanisms insofar as they are universally established.
[9] Note also Esther Goody 1995.   [10] Evans-Pritchard 1976; Tambiah 1990: 58.
[11] Laidlaw and Whitehouse 2007: 24; Hutton 2004.
[12] Justin Barrett 2007: 181–189.
[13] Promiscuous by the standards of modern science, that is, which is unusually
parsimonious.

to non-matter, may vary enormously and are often composite.[14]
Secondly, many immanentist societies convey a sense that the capacity
to organise the underlying realities of the universe in terms of personhood has distinct limits, as if any such identities might be merely
shifting and plural masks allowing a dim apprehension of interacting
powers or processes.[15]

There is naturally some variety in how and where these metapersons
were located. To the extent that such metapersons are conceived to be
present in the animals, objects, and landscape of the observable world
around us, this disposition has been described as animism.[16] 'Animism'
sank into disrepute as a scholarly term for many decades due to its
association with old civilisational hierarchies, but in recent years
anthropology has cleared its head of this particular genealogical
fallacy.[17] 'Animism' has therefore been revived for its capacity to
convey an ontology radically different from that of modern Western
common sense, one in which the world is held to be full of subjects
rather than objects: 'The attribution by humans to non-humans of an
interiority identical to their own.'[18] One particularly striking subset of
animism has become known as perspectivism, which is found in a
number of societies in Amazonia and Siberia.[19] If, in the animist view,
non-humans such as animals are held to be essentially human, perp-
sectivalist cultures complete this logic: the humans that appear
as animals to us also see us as animals. These beings are not then
fundamentally 'other', they are merely endowed with different
bodies and perceptual equipment and therefore have a different, role-
reversed view of the world, one in which, for example, people may be
identified as prey.

---

[14] Marilyn Strathern 1988; Carrithers, Collins, Lukes 1985; Descola 2013a: 207–226; Selz 2008: 23; Puett 2015: 233.
[15] Maffie 2014: 88–89; Vernant 1991: 273; Valeri 1985: 9–18.
[16] Since Tylor 1871: 385–366.
[17] Aided by the ontological turn, current emphasis on the agency of the object, and Actor–Network Theory. Much of this work deliberately blurs (or ignores) the boundaries between the emic and the etic.
[18] Descola 2013a: 129. See also Lambek 2013a: 16; Viveiros de Castro 2012: 40–41: 'The world of immanent humanity is also a world of immanent divinity, a world where divinity is distributed under the form of a potential infinity of non-human subjects. This is a world where hosts of miniscule gods wander the earth... This is the world that has been called animist...'
[19] There is some ambiguity as to whether perspectivism should be a defining feature of 'animism'. See Viveiros de Castro 1998; Descola 2013b: 38.

The great majority of societies in the historical record, however, have attributed features of personhood not only to the animals and things around them, but to all manner of beings that are not usually visible nor inextricably tied to a single material instantiation, namely to ancestors, spirits, and deities. It is not always helpful to make strong distinctions between these entities, which is one reason why the term 'metaperson' may be preferable.[20] But a very large number of societies have arranged their metapersons in a hierarchy, in which moving up the scale entails both greater distance from and greater powers over normal persons.[21] In Bellah's view, a more acute sense of distance between man and metaperson, and thus stronger sensations of reverence – the emergence of 'gods' – was a hallmark of the 'archaic religion' that accompanied the rise of kings and states: religious and political differentiation proceeded hand in hand.[22] This must be qualified, for Sahlins has shown that societies without forms of political hierarchy have also imagined layers of godlike metapersons towering above them. They formed indeed a kind of invisible state before the state.[23]

(2) Cosmology is relatively monistic

The literature is emphatic that visions of reality existing before and outside those produced by the Axial Age tend to the monistic.[24] In the words of Bellah, 'Both tribal and archaic religions are "cosmological", in that supernature, nature, and society were all fused in a single cosmos.'[25] Monism is a concept of which it is easy to lose control, however. If it is pushed too far it might imply that the inhabitants of immanentist societies imagine metapersons as inhabiting the world in exactly the manner that normal persons do. There would be no sense in having special, set-apart ('sacred') modes of representing or interacting

---

[20] See Lambek 2013a: 14; Landau 1999: 16, for problems with 'gods'.

[21] In a recent schema by Descola 2013a: 41, 'Although they are in no way transcendent to human existence, deities are less immanent than spirits.' Sahlins 2016: 'Socially and categorically, divinity is a higher-order form of animism.'

[22] Bellah 2011: 141, 189. The emergence of statehood is not a precondition of Descola's 'analogical ontology', but it would seem that all state societies have been analogical (or more recently), naturalist.

[23] Graeber and Sahlins 2017: 23–64.

[24] Compare Oakley 2006: 15; Frankfort et al. 1946: 71.

[25] Bellah 2011: 266; Charles Taylor 2012: 34; Casanova 2012: 206.

with them. Evidently, the behaviour of ancestors, spirits, and gods is obstreperously obscured and mysterious.[26] The whole panoply of rite and sacrifice is an attempt to throw a rope bridge across the frustrating divide that separates person and metaperson. Moreover, it is precisely because there are normally some such emic distinctions between, say, cosmos and society, or gods and men, that so much energy is put into setting up relations between them (a truly monistic entity would allow for no inter-relationality).[27] Hence Jan Assmann refers not to monism but to

Conceptual compactness [which] results not so much from an inability to differentiate, a mere absence of later achievements, but from a will to connect and to integrate, to establish alliances, equations, and identities.[28]

Certainly, for some purposes, it may make sense to describe the spirits and gods of immanentist societies as existing 'beyond' or 'transcending' domestic human society in some form – indeed, it is this which allows them to underpin, represent, or legitimate it.[29] However, they do not 'transcend' the mundane world in a 'transcendentalist' manner! Assmann comments:

Transcendence in the sense of otherworldliness is common to all forms of religion and concepts of the sacred. These gods and spirits are, however, not extramundane. Their otherworldliness does not prevent them from being immanent in nature.[30]

The point is not then to deny that many immanentist cultures created special locations (otherworlds, underworlds, spirit worlds) for metapersons to inhabit, but rather that these locations were somehow

---

[26] Distinctions between men, spirits, and gods in Tahiti: Oliver 1974: 56; Hawaii: Valeri 1985: 32. Graeber 2015: 11, on the unknowability of *vazimba* spirits in Madagascar. Note Morris 2005: 313.

[27] Hence Descola 2013a: 201: analogical ontologies employ 'a mode of identification that divides up the whole collection of living beings into a multiplicity of essences, forms and substances'.

[28] Assmann 2012: 371–372, which also advances 'cosmotheism' to capture the 'cosmic immanence of the divine'.

[29] Bloch 1987.

[30] 'Otherworldliness' and 'extramundane' are almost synonyms, but twisted here in different directions, the latter implying a categorical break (Assmann 2012: 403, footnote 16).

circumscribed by or homologous to mundane reality in profound ways.[31] This is why, whenever anthropologists or historians are obliged to explain the nature of religion in any given immanentist society – to a readership universally assumed to have been reared within naturalism and/or transcendentalism – they have nearly always understood that their main exegetical duty is the explosion of dualisms. Repeatedly, we are told that distinctions between society and cosmos, man and god, god and thing, man and thing, thing and god, were consistently overcome by the intensity of analogical reasoning to which they are subject, the chains of cause and effect strung between them, and the routine nature of their mutual participation.[32] Above all, the nature/supernature distinction is often presented as an obstacle to grasping the emic sensibility.[33] Marshall Sahlins has recently referred to a raft of ethnographic literature in order to demonstrate the extent to which people of many societies have felt themselves to be living among metapersons, as empirical realities, as forces continuously dictating their fortunes, as *sharing their world* rather than inhabiting some distant other sphere.[34] Alfredo López Austin describes something like this as the experience of the sixteenth-century Nahua:

For the Nahuatl man, some of the supernatural beings had a reality as present, as immediate, as daily as he could capture through his senses. The supernatural was judged to be material, potentially visible, tangible, and audible. It was remote from man because of man's limitations, but man was immersed in the supernatural.[35]

In Ancient Greece, the gods may be described as being 'entirely of this world. They may have dwelled on the most remote, elevated mountain in Greece... they may have been capable of flight, but they nevertheless inhabited the same ecosystem as we do'.[36] Indeed, gods had once lived with men; their reign was contingent, their immortality only

---

[31] Eisenstadt 1986: 2; Obeyesekere 2002: 74.

[32] For example, Viveiros de Castro 2011: 30; Poirier 2013: 51.

[33] This is very widely remarked but recognised as long ago as Frazer's *The Golden Bough* [1890–1936] 1994: 24. See, however, Viveiros de Castro 1998: 483 for a defence of 'supernature'.

[34] Graeber and Sahlins 2017: 38, refers to Frederik Barth among the Baktaman of Papua New Guinea, on 'how *empirical* the spirits are'.

[35] Cited in Read 1994: 48.

[36] Whitmarsh 2016: 23, distinguishing from the transcendent Christian God.

maintained through nectar and ambrosia.[37] Scholars of contemporary Central Africa report widespread apprehensions of a 'spirit world'. In one sense this is distinct from mundane reality; in another sense it is not distinct all, insofar as it is a simulacrum of this world.[38] According to one account today, it has its universities, airports, government.[39] Among the Chukchi of Kamchatka, the spirit world is a kind of reversed, upside-down version of this one, where day is night.[40]

The submergence of the distinction between thing and spirit is no less important. This is again most fundamentally explicable in terms of the cognitive tendency towards agency or personhood attribution. Many behaviours, taking place within very divergent cultural systems, bear witness to this propensity to make objects into subjects, from the making of masks and fetishes in West Africa to the looting of temple icons in medieval India.[41] To take an example from early nineteenth-century Oceania, the English missionary John Williams reported a conversation among the recently converted Samoans debating how to destroy their god of war, apparently resident within a piece of matting. When burning was proposed it was deemed too cruel a death for the god, and so drowning was opted for.[42] In some of these cases, at the level of explicitly held knowledge there may well be important distinctions to be drawn between the object and the meta-person it represents or hosts. But at the level of non-explicit assumption, this distinction is often obliterated. Alfred Gell, in perhaps the most audacious act of liberation from the genealogical fallacy, has sought to resurrect the concept of the 'idol' in order to highlight such commonalities.[43]

For all traditions outside of the monotheisms, and especially for immanentist ones, their academic exegetes have also been concerned to highlight the liquidity of movement across the man/god frontier.[44] For J. D. Y. Peel,

In Yoruba ontology humans and *orisa* [deities] though early distinguished from each other in concept, were still seen as occupying different points on a

---

[37] Davidson 2007: 213.   [38] For Dahomey, see Bay 1998: 250.
[39] Ellis and ter Haar 2004: 51 (and 15, 40); 2007: 385–386.
[40] Willerslev 2013: 149.
[41] Mitchell 2006; Moin 2015: 495–496, drawing on Davis 1997.
[42] Williams 1837: 438–439.   [43] Gell 1998; Sissons 2014: 103–105.
[44] Examples from Ancient Greece: Whitmarsh 2016: 45; China: Puett 2002; and the Americas: Harris 1995: 14.

single scale of power or life/spirit, and there were various ways in which they could instantiate, partake of or be transformed into the divine.[45]

This has obvious significance for the matter of sacred kingship, as considered in Chapter 3.

(3) The afterlife is relatively undifferentiated and insignificant

In nearly all religious cultures, both immanentist and transcendentalist, however, there is one sense in which all persons must become somewhat 'meta': when they die. But to what extent is a form of ontological dualism entailed by the afterlife? In many societies, the dead are considered to remain within the community in an important sense and as the condition of the possibility of its existence. In some Central African societies the land of the dead has been seen as coterminous with the living, reachable through bodies of water, for example. Such substantial continuity is maintained across this boundary that 'death' itself may be a misnomer.[46] In the highlands of Papua New Guinea, recently dead ancestors could be imagined to take the form of Australian explorers making first contact.[47] In Hawaii, the dead Captain Cook could be identified with a volcano.[48] Wherever we find societies burying the dead surrounded by the paraphernalia of life such as chariots, money, or slaves, we surely also find afterlives that are simulacra of this life. Indeed such gravesites often indicate that social status – being a king, say – was something that could pass to the next life. The Jesuit Baltasar Barreira described his frustrations with West African interlocutors in the early seventeenth century: 'They evaluate all points about the next world in terms of things of this world, believing that the former are also material, and hence that they will employ in the other life what they used in this one.'[49] Hence, wherever in the world the archaeological record of gravesites suddenly plunges into mute emptiness it may be taken as an indication of the arrival of transcendentalism. Paradisical afterlives may be found in some forms

---

[45] Peel 2003: 83.   [46] MacGaffey 1994: 258.

[47] Schieffelin and Crittenden 1991.

[48] See *CK*. Julius Caesar's ascension to heaven was identified with a comet: Barton 1996: 152; Gradel 2002: 321.

[49] Brooks 1996: 307.

of immanentism but they tend to be concretely magnified versions of worldly good fortune.[50]

Frequently, if not quite invariably, the scholarship is at pains to observe the relative insignificance of the afterlife.[51] The definitive feature of the immanentist afterlife is simply that it is not the *raison d'être* of religious activity. As such, it may well be essentially untheorised. The missionary William Ellis recounted a conversation in Hawaii in the 1820s:

> We afterwards endeavoured to learn from them something respecting their opinions of a state of existence after death. But ... it could not be discovered whether they had any definite idea of the nature or even the existence, of such a state. Some said, that all the souls of the departed went to the Po, (place of night) and were annihilated, or eaten by the gods there. Others said, that some went to the regions of Akea and Miru ... But to most of the questions, they could give no answer, as they knew nothing about it; none had ever returned in open day-light, to tell them any thing respecting it; and all they knew was from visions or dreams of the priests.[52]

In these circumstances, it may be difficult to make people care about a new concept of the hereafter. The Welsh missionary John Davies in Tahiti found that even when working among people terribly afflicted by the new diseases brought by the English ships, they were irritated by talk of the next world and 'would say we want no other salvation but to live in this world'.[53] 'They cannot be persuaded that as to them, there is anything to be feared, or hoped for beyond the present life. Salvation from sin and its consequences is utterly despised. It is what they look upon as a useless and foolish tale.'[54]

(4) The purpose of religion is to access supernatural power for the flourishing of existence in the here and now

If the afterlife is usually a vague and minor detail of the immanentist canvas, what is the central motif? It is simply the pursuit of power – but power conceived in the broadest sense possible. The basic immanentist assumption is that the capacity to achieve any worthwhile objective is dependent on the approval or intervention of supernatural forces and

---

[50] Paredes 2006: 528.   [51] Firth 1996: 73; Gray 1990: 67–68.
[52] Ellis 1827: 368–369.   [53] Davies 1961: 62; cf Sahlins 2004: 201.
[54] Davies 1961: 101. Compare the Kingdom of Ndongo, Heywood 2017: 90.

metapersons. These constitute the fundamental origin of the ability to produce food, survive ill health, become wealthy, give birth, and wage war. Supernatural power may at times be imagined as a unified impersonal force – like electricity – that can be accessed both with and without the intervention of metapersons. The Polynesian concept of *mana* could stand as a label for the whole category.[55] But it is always also in the gift of ancestors, spirits, and gods with whom it is therefore vital to maintain good relations. This may seem like a very obvious point. But the more seriously we take the emic conception that all power is ultimately supernatural in origin – what Sahlins calls determination by religious basis – the more radical the implications for understanding how immanentist societies and politics works.[56]

(5) Morality is communal, local, and unsystematised

It follows that there is no sphere of religious values that may be differentiated from the values of society per se. What the stories and symbols and rites of immanentist religion embody are the normal appetites and desiderata of this world: heroism, consumption, fertility, sexuality, honour, order, peace, victory – in short, 'life', as A. M. Hocart put it.[57] (These are also the values of modern secular society.) This is not at all to suggest that immanentist religious activity is unrelated to morality, just that 'morality' here signifies the maintenance of successful communal living.[58] In seventeenth-century Central Africa, initiation cults aimed at the moral regeneration of society, punishing falsehood with sickness and death.[59] Everywhere, metapersons are ready to chastise oath breakers.[60] If Sahlins sees the precursor to the state in the heavenly hierarchies of metapersons,

---

[55] Valeri 1985: 98: *mana* is potency, efficacy, success. Among comparable terms and suffixes are perhaps *teotl* or *-teo* (Nahuatl: Maffie 2014: 31–32); *camac* (Quechua: Harrison 2014: 97); *evu* (among the Maka, see Geschiere 1997: 62–63 on its amorality); *ling* (Chinese); *-kis* (Bakongo), *baraka* (Arabic), *śakti*, (Hinduism), *saksit* (Thai).

[56] Graeber and Sahlins 2017: 53.

[57] Hooper 2006: 30–33; Charles Taylor 2012 refers to 'human flourishing'.

[58] Immanentist systems vary quite widely, however, in the extent to which metapersons concern themselves with human morality; see McKay and Whitehouse 2015: 46; Obeyesekere 2002: 98.

[59] Thornton 2001: 76–77. Compare the morality of cargo cults in Mount Hagen (Papua New Guinea): Andrew Strathern 1980: 162.

[60] See Chapter 2.

then evidently the invocation of their displeasure provided the police, judiciary, and penal systems (see Chapter 2). This may be held to be aroused by ritual infelicities – by neglecting sacrifice, for example – but also by the flouting of taboos, conventions, or moral rules of thumb.[61] More generally, ritual participation helps create communally oriented human subjects. However, immanentist systems have not developed systematic sets of ethical principles applicable to the whole of human-ity and which deserve to be followed regardless of their impact on community. They have not made the internalisation of such abstract ethical codes a central function of religious life. And they are not formed around a worship of or search for 'the good'. Ancestors in mid-twentieth-century Mount Hagen may have punished behaviour that was too egocentric, but they did so as social agents who have effectively thereby been ignored, who may themselves suffer from *popkl* (deep-seated anger and frustration), and may be partial or ambiguous in how they deal out sickness to those who have been wronged or done wrong.[62]

(6) Metapersons (and their relations with persons) are defined by power rather than ethics

That is to say: ancestors and spirits and deities are not defined by their role in a good–evil dualism. They are no more or less given to moral behaviour than visible human persons. The field of the sacred is set apart rather by its veiled and abnormal power, a power which is in itself ethically ambiguous.[63] It was understood, as many would under-stand today, that the origins of evil lay not in the very being of any agent but in their contingent motivations and strategies – and these may be opaque. From the Andes to Madagascar, from Nigeria to Fiji, metapersons have been as capricious as fate or the weather or any other cosmic force that may bear humanity on or grind it down.[64]

---

[61] Peel 2003: 99.

[62] Marilyn Strathern 1968: 559: 'Thieving, quarrelling, and sexual intercourse are not bad in themselves: they become offences when they occur between related persons who thereby show the have "forgotten" the ghost who links them.'

[63] Gray 1990: 5; Ellis and ter Haar 2004: 8.

[64] Ancient Greece: Whitmarsh 2016: 31: 'Gods strikingly uninterested in human morality', 'Their own behaviour can be disturbingly immoral'; Clendinnen 1991a: 76–80 on the Aztecs; Americas: Harris 1995: 14; Japan: Lin 2003: 67–68, and Hiroo 2003: 97; on the Chinese gods recognised by the Boxers:

They bring plague with one hand and cure it with the other. They may be terrifying, merciless, wrathful, violent. They may be petty, jealous, irritable, deceitful. They were, in that sense, no different from mortal lords and kings, who required constant appeasement and genuflection but could never quite be trusted.

Indeed, the tenor of relations with these entities is in many ways akin to that of normal social relations, and often takes on a decidedly transactional logic. Sacrifice is not quite a universal practice, for Philippe Descola has highlighted the importance of its absence in certain animist societies.[65] But in all other immanentist traditions, where some sort of distance has opened up between person and meta-person, sacrifice is the quintessential form of communication between them. One of the oldest (and therefore oft-critiqued) explanations of sacrifice is that it is a form of gift exchange with or debt payment to metapersons conducted to elicit the reciprocal bestowal of supernatural productivity and power.[66] This still remains the most compelling way of accounting for sacrifice as a global phenomenon, even if any given tradition of it may be loaded with all manner of other complex operations and significations.[67] The act of sacrifice therefore encodes something fundamental to the spirit of immanentism, which is the mutual dependency of life and death.[68] Like other immanent beings, the ancestors and gods require feeding – sacrifice can also be seen as the induction of metapersons into commensality – and that means they require violence, just as human must commit violence in order to eat.[69] But if this is gift exchange, it is with superior, unpredictable parties, who are by no means compelled to respond: like powerful humans, they may even simply require signs of submission.[70]

Cohen 1997: 112; on the 'thoroughly Olympian *orisa* of the Yoruba': Peel 2003: 94; on Ancient Egypt, Frankfort et al. 1949: 72; Madagascar: Astuti and Bloch 2013: 205; on Oceania, Hooper 2006: 31; Charles Taylor 2012; Bellah 2011: 143, 158, 166 on the Kalapolo, Australian Aborigines, and Navajo; and especially 219–221.

[65] Descola 2013b: 36.   [66] As Socrates argued: Lannstrom 2010.

[67] For example, the complex transferences of identity between victim, sacrifice, and deity. See Valeri 1985: 62–71; Sissons 2014: 56–58; Puett 2002: 40–41, 52–53; Collins 2014.

[68] For example, Maffie 2014: 158.

[69] As a result, ancestors may begrudge pork given to other spirits, see Andrew Strathern 1970: 577.

[70] Clendinnen 1991a: 74–75.

If sacrifice is the exchange mechanism for the economy of life force – the giving of life in order to obtain life – then it follows that the more precious the gift the more powerful the return. This is one reason why human sacrifice should be independently invented in entirely unconnected regions of the world; the other reason is its utility in the construction of divinised kingship (Chapter 3).

If it needed underlining that the 'transcendentalist revolution' is not some generic feature of societal development – a congeries of features that any society must produce once it attains a certain level of political complexity, urbanisation, and literacy – but rather a contingent and distinctive if extremely powerful cultural pattern, then we need only consider what happened when the Spanish reached the New World. When they arrived into the Aztec empire in 1519, the Spanish found at its centre the great city of Tenochtitlan, which – at more than 200,000 people – was larger than Madrid. It was radiantly attractive, clean, and orderly, and the setting for social behaviour that spoke to their preconceived notions of civility.[71] And yet at the heart of this city and the whole business of politics, was the Templo Mayor, dedicated to a god of war and a god of fertility, which churned through the slaughter of perhaps thousands of human victims every year, carried out by priests whose uncut hair was matted with their blood.[72] This is a scene that was unthinkable in any other major Eurasian polity by this time. And yet when Europeans reached Benin, one of the most important states in sub-Saharan Africa, around the same time, they also found human sacrifice at the heart of politics – and when finally they reached the isolated societies of the islands of Hawaii, Tahiti, and Fiji in the eighteenth century, they found it once more.[73]

The point here is not at all that such societies produced less ethical behaviours. All societies destroy human life in the name of some such ideal, whether justice or order or salvation, and once one accepts the basic immanentist proposition that all mortal flourishing lies in the hands of metapersons and the secondary proposition that these metapersons demand tribute or sustenance, then some

---

[71] Díaz 2008: 146; Dodds Pennock 2012: 283, 294.
[72] Dodds Pennock 2008: 21; Díaz 2008: 81 on Cempoala; the numbers are disputed, of course.
[73] Kirch 2010: 74.

kind of moral foundation for ritual homicide may readily be imagined.[74] Rather, these cases indicate what may happen to political theology in communities untouched by the transcendentalist devaluation of these immanentist propositions in favour of their universalised ethical codes – to which any reader vaguely shocked by such phenomena is indubitably the heir. Neither gods nor rulers are embodiments of the good here but are more or less successful participants in an economy of mutual fructification and destruction. One consequence is that the aesthetics of immanentist religiosity can sometimes embrace the themes of violence and darkness in a way that wreaks havoc among notions of the 'holy' or 'sacred' fashioned by the transcendentalisms.

Insofar as the purpose of ritual activity is the harnessing of power, then there is no reason why it must be conducted in a public and open context; indeed to the extent that this power is to be deployed for the benefit of an individual or select group rather than for the good of the community, it may well make sense to restrict access to it, and surround it with great secrecy.[75] In many parts of sub-Saharan Africa, indeed, the very hiddenness, scarcity, and exclusivity of rites have been taken as an index of their power.[76]

Nor is a reverential attitude mandated by the immanentist mentality. The German navigator Otto von Kotzebue, generally rather relativist and celebratory about Hawaiian culture, commented on the rites of *kapu pule*, set about by strict taboos:

We expected a certain seriousness during these sacrifices and prayers; and were astonished at the profane disposition which manifested itself; the indecorous sport that was made with the idols; and the tricks which they delighted to play us during the sacred ceremony. Children show more sedateness in playing with their dolls.[77]

The transactional quality to human–deity relations in immanentist traditions is nowhere clearer than when it breaks out into agonistic and antagonistic forms.[78] In Hawaii there was a procedure for 'casting

---

[74] For voluntary human sacrifice among the Chuchki of northern Kamchatka, see Willerslev 2013: 148.

[75] For Papua New Guinea, Andrew Strathern, 1980: 171.

[76] Ferme 2001: 3, Peel 2003: 224; Ellis and ter Haar 2004: 84.

[77] Kotzebue 1821: 249.

[78] Whitmarsh 2016: 43; Evans-Pritchard 1976: 284, on the 'huckstering' between man and spirit.

off the gods' who had become tiresome, terrifying, or ineffective – who no longer reciprocated.[79] Michael Puett has drawn on the scholarship of Hawaii to elucidate how the spirits of Ancient China were not just 'powers with which one harmonised; they were often powers one fought, cheated, appropriated and tried to become or transcend'.[80] In the seventeenth century, European writers were wont to observe, as did Louis Le Compte (1655–1728):

The Chinese are, however, sometimes weary of saying useless addresses to their idols, which are very numerous; for it often happens, that if after worshipping them a great while, the people do not obtain the blessing they desire, they use them in the most reproachful manner; some load them with hard names, and others with hard blows.[81]

In the early twentieth century, the inhabitants of one village in the New Territories of Hong Kong decided to abandon their 'useless' ancestors who had not helped them out of poverty over the past 200 years, by dragging them out of the hall to set fire to them.[82] In Ancient Rome the gods could be punished for national disasters – 'breach of contract' – by the closing of their temples.[83] Spanish missionaries found that the Mexica would weep to snag the attention of the gods but heap abuse on them if they were unresponsive.[84] As for the Incas, a story about their conquests of the fifteenth century had Topa Inca Yupanqui questioning why the *huacas* (the idols and metapersons they instantiated) had not rewarded him with victory after all the precious items and food he had given them. When they did not reply he threatened to burn all their possessions until they relented.[85] The *huacas* of subject people who rebelled would be whipped. When the Spanish arrived among the Incas and into a raging war of succession, both the main rivals angrily destroyed shrines and threatened *huacas* when prophecies went unfulfilled or battles were lost.[86]

---

[79] Sissons 2014: 40 ('I am wearied of thee – I am terrified of thee! I am expelling thee.')
[80] Puett 2002: 323, and 40–43, 230, 289.
[81] Cited in Reinders 2012: 94 (also 183); Gernet 1985: 82–84.
[82] Watson and Watson 2004.   [83] Gradel 2002: 370.
[84] Clendinnen 1991a: 71.   [85] Stern 1982: 15.
[86] Gose 1996a: 23; Lamana 2005: 11; Law 1991: 71.

(7) Religiosity tends to the empirical, pragmatic, and experimental

These examples indicate the *empirical* quality of immanentist religiosity. Relations with metapersons were expected to produce tangible results and, under certain circumstances, could be set aside if they failed to deliver.[87] This point raises some significant theoretical questions that will be addressed Chapter 4. For the moment, it is enough to simply note the diversity of societies for which scholarship has observed such utilitarianism or 'ruthless pragmatism' at work, in which particular metapersons, rituals, or ritual specialists may be dropped if they fail to work in favour of alternatives.[88] In this particular sense, immanentism is not characterised by an absence of scepticism but a particular form of it.[89] Among the Tupinambá of Brazil, for example, a sixteenth-century missionary reports that 'concerning some of those who make themselves into holy ones among them, they trust sometimes and sometimes not because most of the time they catch the holy ones in lies'.[90] As Eduardo Viveiros de Castro points out, missionaries who started out with an image of the universal credulity of the heathen realised that things were far more complicated. In Mount Hagen in the highlands of Papua New Guinea, a Big Man, Ru, recounted his leadership of a cult after a female spirit visited him in 1976. Since many people were dying he was able to convince people to join in the new form of cult activity, but then some children died and 'our pigs did not grow well, so I decided to forget about Kindip [a ritual specialist] and go get another set of experts'.[91] Ru had been involved

---

[87] I borrow the language of 'empirical religiosity' from Fletcher 1998: 6. See also Ando 2008: xiv–xvii, emphasising the importance of 'empirical verification' of ritual in Ancient Rome. Compare Peel 2003: 90–93.

[88] Eaton 1993: 274, referring to Melford Spiro. Widely invoked by Africanists, e.g., Iliffe 1995; 87. On Mongol eclecticism, see Jackson 2009: 115; Amitai 2013: 23.

[89] On scepticism as a general phenomenon, see Goody 1997.

[90] Viveiros de Castro 2011: 38–39. Graeber 2015:10, on hail charms in Madagascar: 'Arguments about the efficacy of one or another sort of *fanafody*, or of *fanafody* in general, were, in fact, so common I would even call them a popular form of entertainment.'

[91] *Ru*, translated Andrew Strathern 1993: 41.

in an earlier cult, the 'Red Box Money cult', about which a neigh-bouring Big Man, Ongka, had been sceptical all along.[92] The great majority of the time such scepticism does not extend to the overarch-ing system in which any given ritual effort takes place, but some-times quite significant shifts in religious practice may indeed be related to empirical adversity. Before the arrival of missionaries on the remote Pacific island of Niue, the institution of chieftainship itself had been badly undermined by failures in harvest, which had led to a resurgence of shamans who claimed they were better able to control the harvests and weather.[93]

(8) Dynamism, mutability, orality, and continuous revelation

This is one reason why immanentist religions display a particularly dynamic and mutable disposition. The most important reasons, how-ever, are that these religious systems are not defined and authorised by canonical texts, and they do not pivot around a single decisive moment of revelation. For John K. Thornton, Central African religion was characterised by 'continuous revelation and precarious priest-hood' in which a perpetual stream of knowledge arrived into this world through anybody who claimed to experience it.[94] There were few ways of arbitrating between valid and invalid revelations. Indeed, it may be tempting to attribute the key attributes of immanentism simply to a lack of literacy.[95] But note that immanentism has flourished in societies with large literate classes and magnificent feats of second-order thinking. It is not so much the absence of literacy that is crucial as the fact that no set of teachings have been enshrined as uniquely authoritative.

---

[92] Andrew Strathern 1980: 166–170.
[93] Nicholas Thomas 1991: 93; Tomlinson 2009: 71. The Tikopia ritual cycle 'the work of the gods' had no practitioners after the disastrous epidemic of 1955: Swain and Trompf, 1995: 211. The Romans adopted the cult of Cybele during a period of failed harvest, famine, and portents of defeat during the second Punic War: Beard 1996. Cf Friedel 2008: 199–200 on Maya divine kingship.
[94] Thornton 2001: 73–4; 1992: 246–248; Ellis and ter Haar 2004: 146.
[95] Iliffe 1995: 87.

(9) The concepts of 'religion', 'belief', and 'belonging' have little emic resonance

Scholars of immanentist societies are typically at pains to underline that the concept of 'religion' itself is alien to their subjects' self-understanding.[96] There are nearly always, as noted above, a web of concepts and behaviours surrounding relations with metapersons that mark them out as special in some way. But such relations tend to permeate all aspects of life, and the ideas, stories, habits, and rituals that pertain to them are not abstracted out into a conceptual unit of 'religion'.[97] The idea then that society is made up of individuals who may choose to 'belong' to a 'religion', as if it were one among several options, is also likely to be alien. Religion is therefore not an entity that can determine social identity in and of itself; it is simply part of one's cultural inheritance. Anthropologists in particular are likely to repudiate the emic relevance of the concept of 'belief' for many societies too.[98] The meaning of 'belief' is notoriously hard to pin down, but tends to be used for propositions that are affirmed in the light of the possibility that others may doubt their validity. Some of the societies that anthropologists have studied have simply been essentially unaware that profoundly different ways of understanding the world are possible. But even where such awareness is developed, it has usually not led to the habitual use of a concept for a type of knowledge that has such self-reflexivity built in. Instead 'all people act and react in the landscape of the real' as the Africanist Paul Landau put it.[99] For the Wari in Amazonia, the typical verb would simply be 'to see'.[100]

(10) Localism and translatable universalism

The absence of notions of either 'religion or 'a religion' lies at the heart of the question of the portability of immanentism, which is much more

---

[96] Africa: Ellis and ter Haar 2007, Greene 1996: 135, Baum 1999: 35, Peel 2003: 89; Pre-Islamic Central Asia: DeWeese 1994: 27; Pacific: Swain and Trompf 1995: 15; Amazonia: Viveiros de Castro 2011. Jonathan Smith 1998 on religion as an etic term more generally.

[97] Hooper 2006: 31.

[98] Needham 1972; Lambek, 2013b: 141; Boyer 2001: 10–11. For a dissenter see Morris 2005: 153.

[99] Landau 1999: 21.

[100] Vilaça 1997: 97. Handelman 2008 relates 'belief' to the fracture of monism by monotheism.

vexed than it may initially appear. 'Pagan', 'traditional', or 'tribal' religions are often contrasted with the 'world' or 'universal' religions by virtue of the way they were embedded in local milieux. There is a certain truth to this. The metapersons of the immanentist imagination are often grounded in important ways, rooted to particular temples or features of the landscape, and held to be the guardians of particular peoples, cities, or states.[101] When considered in terms of whole systems, the great majority of immanentist religious forms have remained tied to a particular society. In another sense, however, it would be entirely misleading to attribute an image of staticity and closure to immanentism. In fact, both individual metapersons, and particular ways of relating to them ('cults') have travelled large distances across immanentist societies: they can travel with conquerors (Hellenistic religion to West Asia) with the enslaved (Central African religion to the Caribbean), or be invited in from glamorous neighbours.[102] Indeed, in Chapter 4 we shall have cause to underline the particular appeal of rites from afar. Relatively recently before the missionaries arrived in Tahiti, the cult of the war god 'Oro had been imported into there from the Leeward island group, and was changing the social status of different political and ritual specialists in specific ways.[103] Partly in reaction to Robin Horton's arguments, some scholars of African religion emphasise the capacity of cults to traverse and express macrocosms.[104] Possession cults, for example, could claim initiates from across hundreds or thousands of square miles, facilitating the work of traders moving amongst many different peoples.[105]

It is not quite right to describe immanetism as 'tolerant' because that would assume a pre-existing notion of isolable and competing religious systems. Instead the religious field was rather borderless and elastic.[106] Assmann refers to the 'translatability' of religious forms across the diverse societies of ancient Mesopotamia or the Roman world.[107]

---

[101] See Scheer 2011 for concrete examples of how ritual embeddedness in landscape could and could not be overcome among Bunong converts in Cambodia.

[102] For the spread of a cult among different clans and tribes in Mount Hagen, Papua New Guinea, see Andrew Strathern 1970: 572; 1979: 99.

[103] Thomas 2010: 103.   [104] Hefner 1993b: 20–22; Fisher 1994: 71.

[105] Ranger 1993; Fisher 1973.   [106] Whitmarsh 2016: 26, 238; Peel 1968: 123

[107] Assmann 2010: 18–19; Momigliano 1986: 286; Ando 2008: 45.

This was not an automatic process, and the Durkheimian qualities of religion naturally allowed distinctions to be drawn between our cults and 'theirs'.[108] Yet equivalences could be found between particular metapersons, such that a sun god here was equivalent to a sun god there: the names and associations of metapersons could proliferate, combining and recombining with various others, taking in more local or more universal guises in different contexts. It was the shared, universal forms of immanentism that allowed such translatability to occur. There is an important sense in which immanentism is a more truly universalist – as well as universal – form of religiosity than the divisive transcendentalisms. It may seem as if appealing to a certain unity among extremely diverse worldviews steers us uncomfortably close to the Christian concept of 'paganism'. In fact it helps undermine a more insidious feature of the Christian worldview, which is that of a world of competing 'religions'.[109]

The Characteristics of Transcendentalism

The following discussion has two aims. The principal aim is to identify what makes transcendentalism distinctive in terms of fifteen attributes, which are exemplified by reference to Buddhism and Christianity. The set of transcendentalisms is of course wider than this, including forms of Islam, Judaism, Jainism, Hinduism, Sikhism, and perhaps Neo-Confucianism, but the discussion would need to be substantially adjusted as well as greatly expanded in order to incorporate them properly. The second objective is to show the rather different ways that Buddhism and Christianity have formulated the transcendentalist project. So often do the following attributes entail each other that readers will find points recapitulated under many headings.

(1) An ontological breach opens up between a transcendent realm and a mundane one

Transcendentalist traditions embody the frightening apprehension of meaninglessness and relativism that they have been constructed

---

[108] See Rüpke 2010 for evolving notions of religious pluralism in the Roman Empire – including that of 'foreign superstitions'.

[109] In its full and recent sense, the concept of religion itself is a product of post-sixteenth-century interactions, however; see Stroumsa 2010.

against. Indeed, they weaponise that apprehension and fiercely insist on it, but as the defining feature of only one plane of existence: our own. Mundane existence is therefore not just afflicted by transience, corruption, unsatisfactoriness, and negligibility, it is defined by it. It is cast into the shadows by the pure light of the transcendent. This dimension of reality is now considered as inherently superior to that of normal life, but it is so distant from us that it is radically unknowable and ineffable. This is what the literature of the Axial Age means by the ontological breach that cuts previously monistic worldviews in two.[110]

The transcendent dimension may be defined as that which is attained by liberation or salvation. In Buddhism this is nirvana – *nibbāna* in the language of the Pali canon.[111] In many Buddhist traditions, that which lies 'beyond this world' by pertaining to the realm of nirvana may be termed *lokottara*; it is defined against *laukika* to form a dichotomy that corresponds quite well to 'transcendent' versus 'mundane'.[112] One of the reasons why the nature of *parinibbāna* (attained on death) is still a matter of disagreement is because the Buddha is said to have refused to offer an account of it – even whether it was existence, nonexistence, both of these things or neither of them.[113] It could only

---

[110] Hefner 1993b: 9 on 'dualization' of cosmology.

[111] The Pali canon (or *Tipiṭaka*) is the basis of the Theravada tradition. However, current scholarship, as in the work of Gregory Schopen, tends to resist seeing these texts as a uniquely superior guide to early Buddhism, noting, for example, the evidence of other early corpuses such as the Sanskrit *Mūlasarvāstivāda vinaya*. The Pali texts are read here for their ideological vision rather than as documents of the reality of early Buddhism as a social movement. See also Collins 1990. My thanks to Benjamin Schonthal and Stefano Zacchetti for discussion.

[112] These are Sanskrit terms (in Pali; *lokkuttara* vs. *lokiya*). Holt 1991: 21–22. *Laukika* (worldly) is a common term in Sinhala; see also Southwold 1983: 77–79. See below for the *lokottaravāda* school.

[113] I therefore follow Collins 1998: 22–23, in seeing Buddhism as a soteriological system, but for a rather anti-transcendentalist and anti-metaphysical reading of *nibbāna*, see Kalupahana 1992: 90–100. Collins 1998: 164–165, sees *parinibbāna* as a form of real if ineffable existence, analysing the *sutta*-s in Udāna 80–81: 'That sphere (*āyatana*) exists, monks, where there is no earth, no water, no heat and no wind, where the sphere of infinite space does not exist, nor that of infinite consciousness, nor that of neither-perception-nor-non-perception; there is neither this world nor the other world, neither moon nor sun; there, I say, there is no coming and going, no duration (of life, to be followed by) death and rebirth; it is not stationed, it is without occurrence(s), and has no object. This, indeed, is the end of suffering.'

be talked about by describing what it was not: it was what happened when one escaped the cycle of rebirth, when desire was extinguished, when illusions fell away; it was permanence rather than transience. It was not a 'realm' in that sense but a status that stood completely outside of the normal laws of reality, including cause and effect, and the purchase of language or concepts.

The Christian heaven may often be granted more content than this, but it is still radically different from this worldly existence.[114] Moreover, heaven is really simply an attribute of, or way of talking about, God. God is therefore the principal transcendent dimension of reality in Christian ontology, surpassing the laws of existence as something unconditioned, uncaused, infinite, and sometimes ineffable. As with any theistic system, the basic anthropomorphic drive remains apparent in the attribution of conscious agency to cosmic forces, but the process of transcendentalisation attempts to tug the nature of the metaperson as far away from our normal concept of a person as it is possible to get. In one sense, of course, that is not very far at all: for God remains loving, judgemental, fatherly, and so on. In another sense, however, God is forbiddingly unknowable, inscrutable, and completely beyond the normal limitations of personhood.[115]

A resonant symbol of the new nothingness exalted by the transcendentalist traditions is the reluctance or hostility towards representing the divine or liberated state that has emerged from among these traditions from time to time. This is very far from a defining feature of transcendentalism, for it cuts too hard against the grain of human cognition (to be denied images to work with is to be forced into strenuous mental labour). Nevertheless it is striking that aniconism emerged among forms of Judaism, Islam, early Christianity, Protestantism, and the Byzantine orthodox church.[116] Tacitus noted of the Jews: 'They regard as impious those who make from perishable materials representations of gods in man's image; that supreme and eternal being is to them incapable of representation and without end.'[117]

---

[114] However, see the section 'An Unstable Synthesis' for the weak hold of apophatic visions of heaven.

[115] See Holbraad and Pedersen 2017: 268–269, for an assertion of the transcendentalist dimension to Christianity contra Bruno Latour 2010.

[116] For Byzantium's phase of iconoclasm: see Michael Humphreys 2015.

[117] 'Therefore they set up no statues in their cities, still less in their temples; this flattery is not paid their kings, nor this honour given to their Caesars': Tacitus 1931: 183 (*The Histories*, V, v).

An important aniconic movement developed among Jainism (Śvetām-
bara Jaina) in the fifteenth century. The first few centuries of Buddhist
material culture are characterised by a dearth of representations
of the Buddha – or, more interestingly, representations of his
absence.[118] Even in artistic scenes otherwise full of concretely realised
persons and metapersons, it was felt most appropriate to represent the
Buddha by an empty throne or a footprint: an evocation of the unrepresentable Buddha through his representable effects. As one climbs
the temple of Borobudur in Java (c. 800 CE) and reaches the upper-
most level representing enlightenment, the Buddha statues are hidden
by perforated stupas through which he may only be glimpsed
obliquely, and his enlightenment is fully expressed only by the pure
symbol of the complete stupa at the centre.[119] (See Figures 1.1 and 1.2)
The monotheistic strand is most given to aniconism due to its jealous
monopoly of metapersonhood. But wherever we find these movements
we find precisely an anxiety over some characteristic features of
immanentism: the human disposition to attribute personhood to
things; to convey ideas through images and to make images into ideas,
to fuse representation and substance, to speak the ineffable.

(2) Escape from mundane existence – or salvation – becomes the definitive goal

'For our Saints and Sages, to be blessed with life is a true joy. They
therefore have nothing in common with what these cunning Barbarians
say about the intelligent soul, which according to them is shackled at birth
and liberated at death as if it were emerging from a dark prison. They teach
people to regard life as a torment and death as a joy.'

Huang Zhen offering a Confucian critique of Christianity, 1639[120]

---

[118] It is unnecessary to imagine explicit prohibitions against iconic representation,
and the shift from aniconism to iconism was part of a larger shift in Indic
religious culture: DeCaroli 2015. Nevertheless, as Wenzel 2011, argues 'the
early "aniconic" phase of Indian Buddhism seems to share with Christianity the
notion that the highest truth—Buddhahood or enlightenment and the godhead
respectively —was ultimately invisible. Indeed, the invisibility of the Buddha
secured the truthfulness of the depiction.' Aniconic tendencies have sometimes
emerged outside transcendentalist traditions: Doak 2015.
[119] Seckel 2004: 63. See p. 9 for the editors' comparisons with other aniconic
dynamics.
[120] Gernet 1985: 171.

Figure 1.1 The upper level of Borobudur, a Buddhist temple in Java, constructed c. 800 CE.

Figure 1.2. A Buddha glimpsed through a stupa at Borobudur.

Transcendentalism launches an all-out assault on the immanentist project of securing a flourishing existence in the 'here and now' by insisting that any such 'flourishing' is relatively worthless. Ultimate purpose is drained out of mundane existence in order to concentrate it in the attainment of the transcendentalist objective. This is salvation, liberation, or enlightenment.[121] Again, it is Theravada Buddhism which shows how far removed this is from an 'afterlife' per se.[122] For most Buddhist cosmologies contain many layers of heavens and hell, which the good may enjoy and the wicked endure, but these are categorically distinct from nirvana: even the most glorious heaven populated by the most evolved divine being is still at bottom a form of suffering – at least for the hegemonic *nibbānnic* orientation pursued by the sangha (monastic community).[123] In Christianity, the newly distant form of afterlife is indicated by how deeply it problematises relationships with the ancestors that many immanentist societies have felt living amongst them: those who never converted are sucked away into an unreachable hell; while those who now convert are lifted up into a far distant heaven.[124] Not only is the soteriological objective incomprehensible by the standards of worldly existence, but it cannot be obtained by the normal forms of human success. One certainly does not enter it, like an Aztec warrior accompanying the passage of the sun or a Viking cast into Valhalla, by fighting courageously in battle.[125]

Instead, temporal *adversity* may indicate or stimulate soteriological prowess; indeed, transcendentalism may be considered a colossal effort to draw the sting of mundane misfortune: for the Anglican cleric Jeremy Taylor (1613–1667): 'Christ ... hath taken away the unhappiness of Sickness, and the sting of Death ... of decay and change,

---

[121] Apart from various Weberian thinkers, see also Okuyama 2000, discussing Shimazono Susumu. There are, naturally, diverse understandings of the afterlife that crosscut the immanentism/transcendentalism divide: see Tweed 2006: 150–156.

[122] See Pande 1995: 289, on the Upaniṣadic and particularly Buddhist shift towards 'the understanding that the fundamental need of man is not a utopian rearrangement of this world, nor a heaven, however fine – but a transcendence of it'.

[123] Which Spiro 1982 contrasted with the kammatic Buddhism of most layfolk, in which a better rebirth is sought. Moreover, where *nibbāna* is consciously desired, it is often interpreted in terms of superior saṃsāric flourishing – precisely akin to the attainment of heaven – see the section 'The Immanentisation of Buddhism'.

[124] For qualifications to this, see 'The Immanentisation of Christianity'. Nevertheless, the problem of the abandonment of the ancestors was a genuine one for many converting peoples. On heaven as radical alterity for Papuan converts, see Robbins 2009: 58.

[125] Dodds Pennock 2008: 36–37, 171–177; Clendinnen 1991a: 195–196.

and hath turned them into acts of favour.'[126] Christianity takes the tortured, destroyed human body as its symbol, as a visceral image of something higher, and many of the missionaries mentioned in the companion volume were inspired by dreams of martyrdom. The history of Christianity, as we shall see, is characterised by a particular ability to both stimulate and defy persecution. On one level, the Buddhist vision may work to deprecate worldly success: even a prince – as the Buddha once was – is no worthwhile object of jealousy, for he is still sunk into the cycle of craving and suffering. Transcendentalisms are therefore much less beholden to promises to secure a better existence in the here and now.

Both traditions do also find a way of connecting mundane fortune and soteriological status. But note the way that Christians may slip effortlessly between attributing any bounties they receive to the mercy of God (in the manner of an immanentist metaperson) while any setbacks they experience are attributed to the final mystery of his being (in the manner of a truly transcendent force): 'God moves in mysterious ways his wonders to perform' may seem a banal saying, but it encodes an important truth about Christian means of handling the empirical.[127] Buddhism attaches soteriology to worldly fortune more profoundly insofar as the effects of *kamma* also improve one's lot in this life: it may therefore act as an important buttress of social hierarchy.[128] But note how this potentially undercuts the basic immanentist proposition: by removing the gods out of the most fundamental understanding of cause and effect. Via the doctrine of *kamma*, fortune or misfortune become simply the product of one's past actions and thoughts.[129]

(3) Religious activity is profoundly restructured according to a process of ethicisation

The relativistic challenge to morality as a given quality of communal life resulted, in all variants of the Axial Age, in the attempt to produce much more comprehensive, abstract, and explicit understandings of ethics, founded upon on the golden rule and aiming for universal

---

[126] Davis 1974: 335.   [127] This is a form of 'conceptual control': see Chapter 4.
[128] For how this works in contemporary Thailand, see Bolotta 2018.
[129] On one level; on another level, metapersons remain at large and influential: several causalites coexist.

applicability. If these were expressed in the Greek and Chinese cases principally through the vehicle of what could be termed, with some reservations, 'philosophy', the transcendentalist systems made what is now usually identified as 'religion' the vehicle. Five further features distinguish transcendentalist morality from its immanentist counterpart: ethical norms are codified, arranged into lists of prohibitions and injunctions as in the Ten Commandments of Christianity or the Five Precepts of Buddhism[130]; adherence to ethical norms is connected to the attainment of liberation or salvation; that adherence is considered to be a matter of interiority more than mere obedience; the overall ethical vision is highly idealised to the point of utopianism; this vision represents an inversion of worldly norms in certain ways.

As Charles Taylor has realised, the transcendent dimension of existence is characterised by a moral absolutism: ethical ambiguity has been expunged from cosmic reality, and this pure vision of 'the good' is placed at the heart of religious life.[131] In fact this absolutist dualism – good versus evil or merit versus sin – was translated into real properties or forces in themselves that individuals may share in. As Hocart put it, most bluntly, about India: it is now 'better to be good than to be healthy and wealthy.'[132] Moreover, morality has been refitted for the macrocosm: transcendentalism creates moral communities which are potentially distinct from – and may far outstrip in scale – the communities to which one otherwise de facto belongs. These new communities are committed to a moral vision not only for its ability to preserve order among any one society, but for its essential role in facilitating individual salvation. If ritual is the characteristic mode of religious activity in the immanentist mode (and sacrifice the most typical form), then ethics is the characteristic mode of religious activity in the transcendentalist mode (and self-sacrifice the most typical form).[133]

Indeed, the radicalism of this ethical revolution is signified by a most shocking innovation: the repudiation of blood sacrifice.[134] In many ways, Buddhism presented itself as an inversion of the concepts and norms of prevailing Vedic culture, for which animal sacrifice was

---

[130] Assmann 2010: 44, 52, on the revolutionary arrival of God as lawgiver.
[131] Charles Taylor 2012: 33–39; 2007: 152.   [132] Hocart 1970: 72.
[133] Weber 1948: 273–274; Sharot 2001: 8.
[134] Muslim Eids are an exception. La Loubère 1987 [1691]: 376, on Siam. See Parry 1986: 467, for the way in which soteriological systems may affect gift exchange in general.

one of its greatest mysteries.[135] Indeed, as if intent on demonstrating the truth of its insight into the purely contingent nature of language, the Pali texts took the Vedic term for sacrifice or ritual foundations – *dhárman* – and twisted it to mean 'teachings'.[136] And one of those teachings was the utter worthlessness of sacrifice. The deliberate causation of suffering that it necessitated could now only be considered as grave karmic damage. A deprecation of bloody sacrifice is not therefore a peculiarity of Western or Christian rhetoric.[137] Instead, in parts of the world, such as Central and Inner Asia, where several transcendentalisms encountered and engaged each other, we find that they resorted to such accusations in order to disparage their rivals. Thus the Muslim ritual of halal could be attacked as animal sacrifice by Buddhists, while Muslims could assert that human sacrifice took place in Hindu temples.[138]

The extent to which memories of human sacrifice may linger on in the folk memory while also being castigated by transcendentalist morality is disclosed in Obeyesekere's analysis of events in the Sri Lankan chronicle, the *Mahāvamsa*.[139] There is a trace too of lingering sacrificial logic in the *jātaka* tales and paintings that dwell on bodhisattvas as giving up their body for the good of humankind –leaving their body parts behind as merit-filled lifeboats for the soteriologically adrift.[140] This idea is conveyed too by the story of Christ. Part of the power of Christianity is that it concedes the logic of sacrifice – indeed human sacrifice – in order then to banish it, just as it concedes the presence of a single metaperson in order to banish other metapersons.[141] 'It is finished,' says Christ from the cross: he is the sacrifice to end all

[135] Pollock 2005: 403–404. The Vedic tradition developed its own 'Axial' problematisation of sacrifice: see Collins 2014.

[136] Brereton 2004 for latter translation of *dhárman*. Meanwhile karma (Pali: *kamma)* was translated from 'action' to 'intention': Gombrich 1996: 51, who describes this 'ethicisation of the world' as a 'turning point in the history of civilisation.'

[137] Compare the Buddhist caricature of non-Buddhist societies through cannibalism: Monius 2002: 103. Note the disapproval of blood sacrifice by state officials and Buddhist monks in China: Dean 2017.

[138] Elverskog 2010, 62–64, 99. When the Mongols converted to Buddhism they tried to end animal sacrifices: Golden 2011: 111.

[139] Obeyesekere 1997.   [140] Ruppert 2000: 16–23.

[141] Parallels between Christian and pagan visions of human sacrifice go back to Frazer, *The Golden Bough*, 1994.

sacrifices.[142] The rationalisation of this is surprisingly weak: why the pain and bloodshed of the son of God should assist the salvific quests of others is most difficult to elucidate.[143] But because it meets the immanentist mentality part way, it became a powerful theme of evangelism. A chronicle account of the conversion of Vladimir of Rus in the late tenth century CE:

> No longer do we slay one another as offerings for demons, for now Christ is ever slain and segmented for us as an offering to God and the father. No longer do we drink the blood of the offering and perish for now we drink the pure blood of Christ.[144]

In medieval Christian culture, the importance of Christ's blood, his continual sacrifice, was replayed in the form of his ritual dismemberment and consumption in the mass.[145] Among the Tupi-Guarani in sixteenth- to eighteenth-century Brazil, the fact that the blood sacrifice was ingested by the flock spoke profoundly to local ideas of exocannibalism as a powerful ritual device.[146] In nineteenth-century Oceania, and among the Bunong in twentieth-century northern Cambodia, and no doubt in many other areas, missionaries recognised the powerful appeal of referring to Christ as the ultimate sacrifice, obviating the need for all further ones.[147]

For all the importance of this line of continuity, it would not do to obscure the profound implications of the transcendentalisation of sacrifice in Christianity. The single god did not need to be fed; he was not really going to benefit from burnt meat. If he demanded sacrifice from his followers, it was of their worldly self-seeking and pride.

(4) The inversion of worldly values and the soteriological virtuoso

How impressively did divine wisdom show the vanity of the mirth and wine, the pomp and pride, the distinction and power, of which these departed ones, for a brief period, could once boast; and how strikingly did the hand of God stamp transitoriness on things earthly, even the most

---

[142] Martin 2005: 303–304.
[143] Bossy 1985: 3–6, on the attempt at rationalisation by Anselm of Canterbury.
[144] Ilarion cited in Shephard 2009: 212.   [145] Bynum 2007.   [146] Lee 2017
[147] Scheer 2011; Marilyn Strathern field notes, Mount Hagen 1965: 'And Jesus told the whiteman to take his blood everywhere, all over the world, and everyone could eat communion' (I. 2016–8. 65).

coveted and valued, in order to call the attention of the thoughtless sons and daughters of Hawaii more strongly to the things that are heavenly!

> Hiram Bingham, on the death of high chiefs in Hawaii.[148]

How peaceful it is to live by dying each day.

> Francis Xavier, 1542, welcoming the hardships of missionary work in Goa.[149]

Christianity presupposes that man does not know, *cannot* know, what is good for him and what evil: he believes in God, who alone knows. Christian morality is a command; its origin is transcendent…

> Friedrich Nietzsche, *Twilight of the Idols.*[150]

As transcendentalism weaponised relativism so the values it came to exalt scrambled the usual signals of human success – as Nietzsche famously realised. Ethics took on an otherworldly quality, as if they were at war with human nature. The unattainability that Edward Westermarck noted for Christian ethics could apply no less well to Buddhism.[151] Normal human appetites were ruthlessly problematised. Is it any wonder that transcendentalism bucks against certain evolved tendencies of human cognition, given that it also bucks against the evolutionary imperatives of sexual gratification and kin preference? Consider Siddhartha waking up on the night of his renunciation after an evening of revelry and walking among the women of the palace now asleep and disgustingly contorted, the whole scene appearing 'like a cremation ground before the eyes'.[152] He walks outwards into the night, leaving his young wife and child behind. The real truth of the human body was simply foul decay. This is the insight revealed by the meditative practice of *aṭṭhika-saññā* or contemplation of thirty-eight parts of a skeleton, in the forest monasteries of Sri Lanka.

Immanentist traditions sometimes produced superficially similar forms of ascetic behaviour. Fasting or sexual abstinence or self-mutilation may be seen as means of corralling supernatural power, or as a form of auto-sacrifice.[153] Such forms of asceticism may have been

---

[148] Bingham 1849: 267.   [149] Francis Xavier, 20 September 1542: Xavier: 258.
[150] Nietzsche 1968: 70.
[151] See discussion in Robbins 2012: 7–9; cf Charles Taylor 2007: 614.
[152] Gornall and Henry 2017: 86.
[153] Clendinnen 1987: 230; Weber 1948: 271–274.

'ethicised' or 'axiologised' to use the language of Obeyesekere, by creeds such as Buddhism.[154] Transcendentalist asceticism may be understood as an attempt to deny the concrete, animal, and embodied qualities of the human person in order to somehow close the gap with the ethereal nothingness of the transcendentalist realm. It is an attempt to turn a human being into an idea. If this was unachievable within the normal structures of life, then the structures of life would have to change – at least for a few. These monastics, mendicants, and hermits are soteriological virtuosos, taking on the burden of the utopian strangeness of transcendentalist morality so that the rest of society does not need to.[155] But then the rest of society remains correspondingly further from liberation. And so many were attracted to the living out of self-denial: joining orders of monks such as the *paṃsukūlika* in medieval Sri Lanka who only wore rags from dust heaps and the crematorium, or religious orders in medieval England who worked with lepers, and identified with them, and only imitated Christ all the more successfully if they caught the disease themselves.[156]

How clearly this speaks to the redefinition of the sacred. In the immanentist mode one may become sacred by approximating the qualities of metapersons: amassing power, success, brilliance. In the transcendentalist mode one does it by denying the quest for power, success, brilliance. Therefore, when ascetic aesthetics arrived in immanentist societies they could be received with bemusement, as the Jesuit Francisco de Gouveia reported with some dismay from Angola in 1564.[157] He found that there was no intrinsic merit in the signals of poverty and hunger that he so diligently emitted.

What is monasticism but an institution that tears across kinship, which snubs marriage and lifts children away from their parents? Simon de La Loubère observed in Siam in the 1680s that a monk 'sins when he grieves his parents lost to death'.[158] In one of the most popular accounts of the Buddha's life, the *Vessantara Jātaka*, Siddhartha returns to his kingdom after having achieved enlightenment only to find that his elders refuse to accord him respect. He rises into

---

[154] Obeyesekere 2002: 75–76, 117, 122; Collins 1982: 36.
[155] Bellah 2011: 451, on the importance of renouncer types in all variants
[156] Coningham et al. 2017; Rawcliffe 2006: 141–142.
[157] Francisco de Gouveia, 1 January 1564, MMA, XV: 230. Compare Bartlett 2007: 68–69.
[158] La Loubère 1987 [1691]: 440.

the air and tells them a story of one of his past lives as the king Vessantara, in which he had given away not only his treasures and his kingdom but his children too. Caste was undermined no less than family or seniority: the brahmans, his rivals, were stripped of their pretensions to inherent superiority and left only with status as a matter of mere convention.[159] Thus the acid of relativism ate through all social conventions in order to make way for absolutist morality. Just as people left behind their old ascriptions as they began to 'take refuge with the Buddha' in parts of northern India, so the Christ of the New Testament welcomed the despised and impure.[160] All such traditional statuses were cast into irrelevance, along with the primacy of kinship again:[161]

Large crowds were travelling with Jesus, and turning to them he said: 'If anyone comes to me and does not hate father and mother, wife and children, brothers and sisters—yes, even their own life—such a person cannot be my disciple.'[162]

(5) Individual interiority rather than ritual action becomes the privileged arena of religious life

From a boy I had been led to consider that my Maker and I, His creature, were the two beings, luminously such, *in rerum naturâ*

John Henry Newman[163]

Your own self is your master; who else could be? With yourself well controlled, you gain a master very hard to find.

The Dhammapada, chapter 12, verse 160.[164]

This anti-communal quality to transcendentalism is extremely important. It reflects the fact that the fields of ethics and salvation arrived in a form that was not only universalised but individualised. It is

---

[159] Caste was soteriologically relativised but not rejected per se, according to Samuels 2006.
[160] Pollock 2005: 406.
[161] Pollock 2005: 407; Obeyesekere 2002: 182–189, on Buddha's social nominalism.
[162] Luke 14:26; see Kee 1993: 3, and Martin 2005:186: 'All basic social institutions and arrangements ... [had] a question mark put against them.'
[163] Newman 1890: 195 (thanks to William Whyte).   [164] Easwaran 2017: 157.

the self – not the social group – which becomes the most fundamental focus of religious life.[165] Each human being takes on alone the burden of responsibility for her liberation. This is important insofar as certain histories of the self have considered it to have been in some sense a creation of Western thought, the Renaissance, the Reformation, or even modernity. Yet evidently the self became the subject of intense focus in all the Axial Age bursts of creativity in first millennium BCE Eurasia, in keeping with the general context of reflexivity and second-order thinking.[166]

As will be considered in more detail in the section 'An Unstable Synthesis', in practice of course, religion never lost its Durkheimian dimension as a phenomenon of communal participation, ritual action, and external observance. But transcendentalism frames these activities within a powerful relativisation of them. They become merely secondary refractions of interior states, as the person within is made the locus of endeavour. In the Pali Buddhist canon, clinging to rules and rituals (*sīlabbata-parāmāsa*) is explicitly identified as an obstacle to progress towards nirvana.[167] In immanentist contexts such a critique of ritual as 'merely mechanical' would simply make no sense. But this is what Paul does when he twists the meaning of the term 'circumcision' such that it is no longer either a bodily fact or an illocutionary event:

For he is not a Jew who is one outwardly, nor is circumcision that which is outward in the flesh. But he is a Jew who is one inwardly; and circumcision is that which is of the heart, by the Spirit, not by the letter; and his praise is not from men, but from God (2:28–29).[168]

No doubt the principal reason why the focus on the self should have been so searching in the Indic traditions was because of the way they developed hand in hand with the ancient practices of yoga and meditation. These functioned as telescopes for the soul, magnifying the inner landscape to an exceptional degree. In Buddhism this resulted

---

[165] Compare Gauchet 1999: 45, on inwardness; Charles Taylor 2007: 154.
[166] See Assmann 2010: 36–37, on the arrival of 'a kind of inner transcendence', and Charles Taylor 2009: 32, for the social embeddedness against which it may be contrasted.
[167] Kalupahana 1992: 151.
[168] Compare the Buddha redefining 'brahman' from an ascriptive to an achieved inward status in the *Dhammapada* (e.g., verse 396, Easwaran 2017: 249). Thanks to Alastair Gornall.

in a paradox: the doctrine of *anattā* or 'no-self'.[169] Superficially, this may seem like a contradiction of the transcendentalist infatuation with the self; in fact it is a function of it. The focus on the self was so acute that, on a theoretical plane, it dissolved from sight, much as it may in the hands of modern philosophers. The result was a most extraordinary achievement of anti-anthropomorphic, anti-agential mental labour. It amounts to a kind of denial of personhood not only to all other forces in the world but the human subject itself. The Buddha's assault on the brahmans' reification of the self (*ātman*) was also an assault on their ascription of agency to the cosmos (*brahman*) and on sacrifice as the mediating term between the two: thus was the analogical exuberance of elaborated immanentism rubbished.[170] On another level, of course, the self – or the interior zone in which the illusion of the self was generated – remained the most significant realm of soteriological action. It was, as everywhere in the Axial Age vision, the contents of one's thoughts and feelings that ultimately determined one's progress. In Christianity, meanwhile, the self was also identified only to be chastened and disciplined. Joel Robbins's work on Christianisation of the Urapmin of the highlands of Papua New Guinea, has indicated how profoundly new and unsettling this sudden revelation of the self as the principal site of religious endeavour could be.[171] And, as in other Axial traditions, the revelation of the self also implied the imperative of its transcendence, in the sense that one was now obliged to value other selves just as one might value one's own.[172] This may be why explicit selfhood and explicit ethics arrive together.

(6) Truth, belief, and offensiveness

Gods word is flat contrarie to the nature and disposition of man.

William Perkins, 1608.[173]

---

[169] Collins 1982; Wynne 2010 for an argument as to its evolution.

[170] Tambiah 1976: 34.

[171] Robbins 2004; compare Holbraad and Pedersen 2017: 258–259, on Mongolia.

[172] There are some intriguing parallels with stoicism here, which arguably had much in common with transcendentalisms and Buddhism in particular. Notice that this conception of a multitude of selves – extensive to either humanity or all living beings – has no need for the *immediate* community.

[173] Dixon 2011: 799, citing Perkins 1608: 481.

On truth's path, wise is mad, insane is wise.

Jalâl al-Din Rumi (1207–1273)

May I gain access to the truth of the dhamma through my thought and my respect.

Yuan Phai, (Thai, late fifteenth century)[174]

Similarly to the history of the 'self', or 'religion', the cluster of concepts around 'truth' and 'belief' is sometimes held to be distinctively European or monotheistic or Reformation or Enlightenment in origin.[175] Once again this disguises the origins of a broadly equivalent mentality implicit in all the Axial Age revolutions. Here we may proceed from what Ernest Gellner made the definitive quality of 'ideological' systems: their offensiveness.[176] The transcendentalist teachings are offensive in that they are predicated on the assumption that alternative visions of reality exist and indeed typically predominate. Offensive systems are set up to be jarring, to challenge these alternative accounts masquerading as common sense. They generate hope and fear by virtue of the distance opened up between 'how things seem to be' and 'how things actually are'. The *Vessantara Jātaka* is an excellent example of the way that such counterintuitive accounts snag the emotions.[177] As it happens, this evocation of offensiveness comes close to Weber's portrayal of the prophet as the voice of anti-traditionalism, conveying an alarming message pitched at a higher level of meaning than ordinary discourse allows.[178]

There is no doubt much worthwhile scholarly discussion to be had with regard to how easily exact equivalents to the English terms 'truth' and 'belief' may be found in the various languages employed in the texts of the various transcendentalisms. But the essential conclusion

---

[174] Baker and Phongpaichit (trans.) 2017: 15.

[175] Anthropologists' historicisation of 'religion' tends to emphasise the Reformation and/or Enlightenment as fundamental cognitive watersheds. Asad 1993: 27–54, is sometimes interpreted as showing the irrelevance of 'belief' in Christianity before the seventeenth century. In fact, these comments pertain to something much more particular, and Asad himself acknowledges the importance of (power-authorised) truth (36–39). I shall affirm that Reformation/Catholic reform significantly intensified the significance of interiority and orthodoxy as doctrinal assent in the section 'A few notes on reform'. See also Tomlinson and Engelke 2006.

[176] Gellner 1979.   [177] Collins 2016: Introduction.   [178] Hefner 1993b:12.

would surely be that all such traditions peddle in the 'truth' rather than simply 'knowledge', and all aspire to ideological hegemony.[179] This may take its most aggressive form in the monotheistic traditions following what Assmann calls 'the Mosaic distinction', by which all other religions were rendered inherently false or evil.[180] But it is a recurrent theme of this book that Buddhism mounts a no less assertive claim to be the vehicle for profound truths that otherwise lie veiled. It had its origins, after all, in a milieu that valued formal and public debates in which all premises were laid open to question.[181] The Pali texts have the Buddha explicitly denounce tradition or any appeal to authority as invalid epistemology. They routinely frame their teachings within a description of the Buddha arriving in a public park where many other intellectuals and renunciants had set up their stall and then proceeding to win them all round.[182]

(7) The closure and textualisation of the canon and the historical singularity of primary revelation

If the transcendentalist traditions remained of 'axial' importance it was partly because of the astonishing durability of scripture as an authority structure.[183] In one sense, the flow of revelation suddenly became 'discontinuous', or at the very least impeded and hierarchicalised, simply because of the historical singularity of their founding teachers.[184] All subsequent claims could now only be evaluated in the light of their original insights. In fact, as Weber indicated, 'the closing of the canon' was a more drawn out and contingent process that was still evolving

---

[179] Duara 2015: 119; Bellah 2011: 276.

[180] Assmann 2010: 2–3. Therefore traditions based on textual doctrine, a founding figure and revelatory moments are 'counter religions'.

[181] Jayatilleke 1963: 233–242; Obeyesekere 2002: 110–112, 124.

[182] Schonthal 2017: 182. Gombrich 1988: 87, even suggests that *pasāda* in the Pali canon is reasonably equivalent to 'faith'. Some esoteric traditions of knowledge in immanentist societies (initiation cults, mystery cults) may seem approximate in their esteem for counterintuitive assertions, but the power of such knowledge is typically a function of its very secrecy and exclusivity. The transcendentalist traditions, on the other hand, are distinctive by their desire to broadcast their teachings as widely as possible (their power lies elsewhere).

[183] See d'Avray 2010: 102, on the fixity of literacy.

[184] Pollock 2005: 409, notes how Buddhism shifts 'scripture' from the anonymous and timeless voice of the Vedas to the arrival and preaching of the Buddha as concrete historical event.

centuries after the initial revelations.[185] This process of canonisation is greatly enhanced by the use of texts but it is not exactly dependent on it. The main body of Pali Buddhist works (*Tipiṭaka*) was apparently first established as an orally transmitted canon and only set down in texts many generations afterwards.[186] In other words, certain recitational devices and strategies employed within specialist institutions (such as the sangha) are apparently able to replicate some of the stability of cultural memory afforded by the text. This implies, too, that canonisation is not simply a function of the appearance of the technology of writing.

Immanentist traditions have shown the capacity to challenge and reformulate societal norms.[187] In this book we shall encounter developments – prophetic movements, witch hunts, bonfires of the idols – that sought to restructure religious life in quite general terms as a response to profound upheaval. But in the normal course of events they tended to dissipate as swiftly as they arose. It is possible that it is primarily the absence of a textual foundation that ensures that such movements do not turn into anything more lasting or far-reaching in their implications.[188]

The formation of a textual canon both reflects and drives the development of a clerisy who must act as its exegetes and who establish their authority upon it. It both reflects and drives the quest to fix upon 'the truth' and a codified set of ethical principles. And it both reflects and drives the creation of self-conscious moral communities defined by their relationship to the text.[189]

(8) Intellectualisation and conceptual control

One of the most problematic – but still somehow essential – features of the Weberian tradition is the theme of 'rationalisation'. It is perhaps in

---

[185] See Hefner 1993b: 11, for a good summary of Weber's sociology of knowledge as applied to the closing of the canon. Assmann 2012: 390–395, puts a great deal of emphasis on the 'secondary canonization' of the Axial Age. Stroumsa 2009.

[186] Wynne 2004.   [187] Hefner 1993b: 13–16.

[188] As suggested by Fisher 1973: 28–35; Iliffe 1995: 87; also see Ranger 1993: 85–86, on the impact of literacy on the exportability of renewed traditional forms of African religion. However, literacy is obviously not remotely a sufficient cause for the development of transcendentalism.

[189] Assmann 2012: 394, notes 'a strong alliance among revelation, transcendence, and secondary canonization'.

relation to this issue that genealogical critiques of nineteenth- and early twentieth-century developmental schemas deserve most consideration, lest we slip into a teleology of progressive mental liberation. It is therefore important to distinguish specific developments that have been discussed under the heading of 'rationalisation' from more sweeping evaluations of whole systems of thought as more or less 'rational' or superior at making sense of reality.[190] On this point, then, there is merit in not drawing too sharp a distinction between transcendentalist and immanentist religions.[191] Apart from their diversity, many of the latter have shown considerable intellectual dynamism, fecundity, and flexibility, and continued to produce compelling explanations of the world in the face of societal upheavals.[192] Many immanentist societies developed professional priesthoods that functioned as an intellectual class given to producing impressively systematised and elaborate cosmologies. Reading Valeri Valerio on Hawaii, Jan Assmann on Ancient Egypt, or James Maffie on the Aztecs is an antidote to any immediate assumptions of relative incoherence or simplicity of thought.[193] Lastly, it is also important to distinguish strongly between different versions of transcendentalism. The fact that monotheism did not emerge in the same milieu of philosophical ferment as found in other Axial Age cases means that the role of formal rationality was less central in both its initial formulation in Judaism and its reformulation as Christianity. Very early on its formulation, however, Christianity was already drawing upon the Greek intellectual tradition under the

---

[190] I follow here Hefner 1993b (e.g., 15); see also Obeyesekere 2002: 120–125. My discussion here does not represent a profound engagement with Weber's work and in particular his distinction between value rationality and instrumental rationality, on which see d'Avray 2010.

[191] As recognised by Geertz 1973: 174. Note Ghosh 2014: 251, 255, on Weber's approach to ideal types.

[192] Ellis and ter Haar 2004: 20; Ranger Intro 1975, and Hefner 1993b.

[193] Valeri 1985. However, Valeri may have oversystematised Hawaiian thought and smuggled in some Dumontian dualism: see Charlot 1987. Maffie 2014 is the most radically immanentist reading of any worldview I have come across, in which dualisms are repeatedly denied and the functioning of power (*teotl*) reigns supreme, 'without transcendent deities, purpose, truth, norms or commandments' (523). However, it does not demonstrate that the Aztecs produced a field of competing schools that deployed systematic second-order and reflexive thinking spurred by radical epistemological scepticism in the manner of Ancient Greek, Indian, and Chinese cases.

influence of Platonism, and its subsequent elaboration of monotheism exhibited intense rationalisation.

Indeed, let us consider the case of ancient Greece.[194] What happens to a religious field that is not itself wholly restructured according to transcendentalism but yet sits within a society in which intellectuals have laid everything open to searching criticism, exhibiting some of the most impressive feats of second-order thinking and explicit debate? The result is an unmistakable distance that starts to open up between these elites and their religious inheritance – and it is surely worth pausing on the fact that it was often the *immanentist* qualities to the gods, their anthropomorphic features, or their amorality, for instance, that troubled various Greek thinkers. If gods fight battles, can they be wounded?[195] Were cult statues instantiations of gods or representations of them?[196] Did sacrifice as some sort of commercial exchange make any sense?[197] Secular models of reality that simply left the gods out of the picture could be constructed; outright materialism asserted; idolatry mocked; tragic and comic poets could underline the perversity and unfathomableness of divine behaviour; and little bubbles of proto-transcendentalism could emerge, destined eventually to slip into the Christian tradition itself.[198]

It is very intriguing that a small but noticeable distance also opened up between some literati and their religious inheritance in the Chinese version of the Axial Age – where again much of the religious field was relatively unreconstructed by the intellectual ferment around it. The result is that from the age of Confucius onwards we find indications of a relativisation of popular religion, an awareness that ritual behaviour was more socially useful than grounded in unarguable truths, and a long-lingering suspicion of superstitious excess – all famously inspirational for much later European Enlightenment thinkers.[199]

This is suggestive that immanentist systems may strain to cope with exceptionally highly charged, combative, sophisticated, and open intellectual fields. And yet, Greek and Roman immanentism *did* survive into late antiquity; Chinese immanentism has persisted in some form

---

[194] Or ancient Rome: Rüpke 2010: 23, refers to 'rational argumentation' as 'resource of de-traditionalization'.
[195] Humphreys 1986: 95–98; Whitmarsh 2016: 37, 133.
[196] Ando 2008: 32–33.   [197] Lannstrom 2010 on Socrates' critique of sacrifice.
[198] See the section 'An Unstable Synthesis'.
[199] Paramore 2017: 21–22; Puett 2002; 2013; Sharot 2001: 88.

(albeit alongside Buddhism and Daoism) and was largely accepted by the literati into the twentieth century. Moreover, the freedom of intellectual enquiry in the case of Greece may contrast strikingly with long stretches of monotheistic history, for example, in which the closing of the canon entailed distinct limitations on the scope of rational enquiry.[200] And there is now much scholarship on the enchantment of the world under the conditions of modernity, in which, particularly in areas outside the West, the forces of modern capitalism, individualist competition, and digitalisation have driven recourse to novel, experimental, empirical, results-focused forms of ritual practice – have made immanentism particularly compelling, in other words.[201] All this speaks, again to the importance of distinguishing aspects of 'rationalisation' in a narrow sense from rationality in general.[202]

What remains of value, then, from the theme of rationalisation, for our purposes? It follows from the discussion thus far that if all religious traditions are means of understanding and ordering existence, transcendentalist traditions are ones that have been battle hardened against philosophical onslaught. It may be more helpful to refer to this process as 'intellectualisation' and to conceive this in four aspects:

First, the process of canonisation and textualisation necessitates the development of a class of literate intellectuals – a 'clerisy' – to act as its guardians and exegetes. Everywhere, this amounted to the establishment of a tradition of scholarship, insistently concerned with ordering, systematising, arguing, and providing intellectual justifications for their core commitments.[203] As a result, whatever their genesis, all the transcendentalisms create sophisticated traditions of philosophical thought. They subject the 'intuitive' understandings of religious life to unusually intense forms of scrutiny.[204] They pour energy into

---

[200] Hefner 1993b: 16. Rüpke 2013: 23, on an 'anti-intellectual current' among fourth-century Christian thinkers.

[201] Thanks to Peter A. Jackson (see 2016) and Giuseppe Bolotta for relevant conversation. Note, however, that these ritual forms seem quite weakly rationalised: they are not logically gathered together in a doctrinal mode and are subject to critique from secular or more transcendentally oriented elements.

[202] Hefner 1993b: 16. Wittrock 2004: 54.

[203] See Hefner 1993b: 14–18; Geertz 1973: 175; Peel 1968: 140; Tambiah 1976: 207–208.

[204] Larson 2016: 11–13, on intuitive and reflective cognition. If elaborate immanentist mythologies are the product of 'reflective' thought, transcendentalisms are hyperreflective.

elaborating and disseminating 'doctrine' – understood as a select but integrated bundle of truths as opposed to a general cultural inheritance of stories and practices. In Harvey Whitehouse's theoretical schema such doctrinalism involves a quite distinct cognitive mode to the 'imagistic' form that dominates much religious activity.[205]

Second, the 'offensive' quality of transcendentalist traditions means that they are engineered to engage in and provoke intellectual competition and debate.[206] They set out to prove their assertions and demand proof of the assertions of others.[207] Where other transcendentalisms are encountered they are likely to be engaged in both agonistic and mimetic relations.[208] And when the milk of pure immanentism is encountered, the acid of transcendentalism will proceed to curdle it, creating distinction and competition where there were none. Third, transcendentalisms appear to thrive amidst sensations of epistemological crisis, social upheaval, and multicultural challenge. This is what Robert Hefner means when he argues that the world religions 'often enjoy a competitive advantage over their rivals in that they are pre-adapted to the macrocosm. Catalysts of moral crisis, they stand ready to provide, or impose, prefigured ideals for a posttraditional world'.[209]

Fourth, transcendentalism provides generalised explanations of worldly vicissitudes which are impervious to empirical examination. For Weber, the most important features of rationalisation were the disenchantment or demagification of the world and a more holistic approach to the problem of evil and misfortune.[210] This involves the replacement of a plural, piecemeal, and *ad hoc* approach to the question of suffering – by engaging diverse metapersons through diverse ritual forms on the occasion of each setback – with a single story or account. As Clifford Geertz put it:

The problems of meaning, which in traditional systems are expressed only implicitly and fragmentarily, here get inclusive formulations and evoke

---

[205] Whitehouse 2000. Peel's analysis (2016: 76–78) of Yoruba *orişa* cults indicates how far towards more stable, expansive, doctrinal forms an oral immanentist system might go – while not matching that of Christianity and Islam.

[206] On the Buddhist tradition: Garrett 1997.

[207] For example, Elverskog 2010: 57. Of course, transcendentalism may rhetorically deplore reason: on Luther, Roper 2016: 106.

[208] Mimetic relations (stealing forms, arguments, properties from each other) have been particularly visible among Asian transcendentalisms: Duara 2015: 6.

[209] Hefner 1993b: 26.   [210] Ghosh 2014: 256–264; Sharot 2001.

comprehensive attitudes. They become conceptualized as universal and inherent qualities of human existence as such.[211]

In Buddhism the concept of *kamma* supplied a single principle as the explanation of all the vicissitudes of life. Indeed the process of converting villagers in far northwestern Thailand to Buddhism, as observed by Charles F. Keyes, was a matter of inducting them into seeing suffering 'not as the consequence of the malevolence of spirits, though these may still be the immediate agents, but as the result of a general 'law', namely that of *kamma*.'[212]

Again, it must be emphasised that whether the results of this were any more 'rational' in absolute terms is a moot point.[213] Christianity may be taken as an intensification of the problem of suffering as much as a solution to it. There is, however, one intriguing implication of the transcendentalist approach to explaining and dealing with misfortune: a certain enhancement of 'conceptual control' in the sense that the term has been used by certain cognitive scientists.[214] This derives from transcendentalism's devaluation of the mundane world: whatever happens in this plane of existence is ultimately irrelevant. The ostensible objective of religious activity is therefore withdrawn from empirical jeopardy. From one angle, at least, the moral underpinning provided by Christianity is little different from that provided in less absolute terms in some forms of immanentism: here we also have a metaperson who acts as a 'big brother' providing supernatural punishment of mundane wrongdoing. The key difference is that these sanctions are provided in an afterlife that lies beyond the discernment of mortals in the 'here and now'.[215] In this context, mundane disaster may entail transcendent rewards.[216] As for Buddhism, the operation of *kamma* could always be used to shift attention away from the business of metapersons and towards forms of ethical attainment. When the gods of Sri Lanka failed to protect the island from an invasion from southern India in the thirteenth century, the main Pali chronicle was

---

[211] Geertz 1973: 172; Hefner 1993b: 7, 21.   [212] Keyes, 1993: 268.

[213] In modern Bangkok and Colombo, for example, people from all social groups evidently find the immediacy of 'piecemeal' diagnoses and prescriptions relating to particular forces and deities to be intellectually and emotionally compelling: Jackson 2016, Gombrich and Obeyesekere 1988, Dean 2017 (for spirit mediumship in Singapore).

[214] See Chapter 4.   [215] Obeyesekere 2002: 74–75.

[216] Briggs 1996: 125–126.

able to explain it in terms of the sins of the Sinhala people.[217] It led to a redoubling of commitment to an authentic form of the Buddha's teaching.[218]

(9) Self-conscious identity and pugnacity – albeit construed differently by the Indic and monotheistic variants

We have already described the religious harmony of the ancient world, and the facility with which the most different and even hostile nations embraced, or at least respected, each other's superstitions. A single people refused to join in the common Intercourse of mankind

Edward Gibbon, *The History of the Decline and Fall of the Roman Empire*[219]

Implicit in the 'offensiveness' of the transcendentalisms is their potential mobilisation for identity construction: they create moral communities which are presented as compelling 'reference groups' for adherents, and these may be either coterminous with or in competition with their other social identities.[220] Yet this process worked quite differently in the Indic and monotheistic variants. Since the broad lines of the monotheistic understanding of identity are relatively widely understood, they will not be spelled out at length here. The case of Buddhism is more complex.

To avoid misunderstanding, it should first be noted that the dynamics of boundary construction are of course always historically contingent to some extent. The Ottoman emperor may cite an uncompromising verse from the Koran (71:26) when writing to his Safavid counterpart Ismail in 1514 – 'Do not leave a single unbeliever on the earth' – but the exigencies of Islamic empires had long meant that large numbers of unbelievers were peacefully incorporated in practice.[221] The characteristic intolerance of Christianity, meanwhile, only truly crystallised in the Papal revolution of the eleventh and

---

[217] Liyanagamage 2008: 78, implying a notion of 'sociokarma', briefly discussed later in this chapter.

[218] Gornall (forthcoming).

[219] Gibbon 1993, 1: 489; compare David Hume 2007 (1734–1737): 61.

[220] See Hefner 1993b: 25–29, on the theory of reference group formation, and 'the moral economy of self-identification'.

[221] www.fas.nus.edu.sg/hist/eia/documents_archive/selim.php.

twelfth centuries according to some historians.[222] Equally, Buddhism in China was subordinated to Confucianism in certain ways for much of Chinese history, while it was in a position to materialise its assertion of hegemony far more successfully in the Theravada world. And so on.

Nevertheless, from a global perspective, the divergence between the approaches to identity taken by the Indic and monotheistic forms are clear enough and no less clearly rooted in differences in their most fundamental orientation. Because monotheism is in a sense merely an inflation of immanentist anthropomorphism, it must deal with the sphere of the metaperson by monopolising it; because Buddhism side-steps the sphere of the metaperson it need only relativise it.[223] Monotheism is set up to destroy other religious forms; Buddhism to encompass and subordinate them.[224]

Since Buddhism does not depend on any anathemisation of other religions, it may share ground and combine with them in a way that monotheism tends to preclude. It leaves adherents free to engage in relations with metapersons of diverse origin in a rather pluralist or 'polytropic' fashion.[225] Buddhism was not founded upon a covenant with a jealous metaperson demanding 'faith', but rather invited adherents to become followers or receive instruction. In these respects it resembled many Hindu traditions and also Daoism. This enabled what Prasenjit Duara refers to as the 'dialogical transcendence' of the Asian traditions, which 'permits coexistence of different levels and expressions of truth'.[226] Of all the case studies explored in the companion volume, this was most characteristic of the 'combinatory field' of religion in Japan, as is evident in the letter by Toyotomi Hideyoshi to the Portuguese viceroy in 1591, lecturing him on the barbarity of exclusivism: 'The shin is spoken of India as the Buddhist dharma, in China it is regarded as the Confucian way, and in Japan it is called Shinto (Way of the Gods).'[227]

---

[222] Moore 2007; Iogna-Prat 2002.   [223] Keyes 1993: 266.

[224] Josephson 2012: 26, uses the phrase 'hierarchical inclusion'; cf Schonthal 2017: 189. Daoism, partly in reaction, could also be conceived in this way: Palumbo 2015: 100.

[225] By 'polytropism', or spiritual cosmopolitanism, Michael Carrithers 2000 meant the tendency to turn a disposition of reverence towards sacred entities of many different traditions in an *ad hoc* and pluralist fashion. Also see Chau 2011.

[226] Duara 2015: 6, and see 142.   [227] Takagi 2004: 62.

It is with good reason, then, that much scholarship of Buddhism is concerned to emphasise how different all this is from the field of exclusive identities set up by the monotheisms. Yet, if we push the distinction too far we end up failing to perceive something vital to the historical power of Buddhism, and which it indeed shared with all other transcendentalisms. In essence this is an assumed position of sublime ethical and soteriological superiority. Benjamin Schonthal has summarised the ways other views may be disparaged as 'misguided (*micchā*), counterproductive (*akusala*), wicked (*pāpaka*) or ignorant (*avidya*)' in the scriptures.[228] There was then certainly a potential concern with orthodoxy as well as the orthopraxy. It is true that Buddhist institutions rarely approached Christian churches in their desire or capacity to police these concerns among the lay population, principally because their focus was on maintaining the integrity of the monastic order rather than lay society, and this was most fundamentally a matter of adherence to a code of conduct rather than to a creed.[229] Yet, at certain historical moments, when Buddhism found its claim to hegemony under attack, it could indeed produce discourses of pugnacious ideological repudiation that spread well beyond the monastery.[230] We find this developing in seventeenth-century Japan and Siam and also in eighteenth-century Sri Lanka. In all these cases, such discourses arose as a reaction to Christianity itself, which became configured in both the official and popular imaginations as a kind of demonic sorcery.[231]

In contexts where several transcendentalisms compete for attention, the current scholarly emphasis on the artificiality of the concept of 'religion' can itself feel artificial. For here we find religious specialists (ulema, brahmans, mendicants, bhikkhus) making direct equivalences between themselves and their rivals, between their teachings and alternative ones.[232] Anyone who has seen the headless and defaced Buddha

---

[228] Schonthal 2017: 195; Collins 1982: 87. *Micchādiṭṭhi* is deployed in an Ayutthayan law of the 1660s: *CK*.

[229] I am grateful to Tomas Larsson for this point. Also Yao and Gombrich 2017: 220.

[230] Schonthal 2017: 183–184.

[231] *CK*; Josephson 2012; also see Young and Senanayaka 1998. But for earlier instances in Lankan history: Alan Strathern 2017b: 227.

[232] Elverskog 2010: 95–103, highlights the contingent, provisional nature of religious boundaries in the Silk Road region, but much of the material speaks to their sensed reality.

statues of Angkor, part of a systematic iconoclasm in the reassertion of Hinduism under Jayavarman VIII (r. 1243–1296), will appreciate that the Indic traditions do not always settle into dialogic accommodation.[233]

Genealogical and etymological approaches have enriched the scholarship of religion by highlighting the relative modernity of terms such as 'Buddhism' or 'Theravada'.[234] But such a focus on the late appearance of these concepts in emic usage may obscure their rough comparability with other emic terms or their etic utility in capturing important aspects of how agents in the past actually behaved. Buddhists did not need to wait for Western scholarship to produce an 'ism' for them to appreciate their kinship with other Buddhists. Chinese monks making journeys to Thailand or Sri Lanka or northern India knew they were operating in a shared ecumene.[235] Nor did they need to have any exact equivalent to the term 'religion' in order to represent to themselves the Buddha's dispensation as a distinct phenomenon: the term *sāsana* (the teachings and practices inaugurated by the Buddha) fulfilled a similar function, while *dhamma* (teachings, law) occupied a broadly equivalent semantic niche.[236] The *sāsana* was a contingent historical reality in a way that the *dhamma* was not; it required the active intervention and protection of human beings. The great reform of the Sangha in Sri Lanka by Parakramabāhu I (1153–1186) was described in a charter (*katikāvata*), which referred to monks 'who having succumbed themselves to the poisonous influences (arising from) the non-observance and ill-observance (of precepts) through ignorance and imperfect knowledge were destined to the sufferings of the *apāya* [a hellish plane of existence]'. He could not remain indifferent 'seeing such a blot on the immaculate Buddha-*sāsana*'.[237]

Similarly, it is quite proper to warn against assuming that 'taking refuge with the Buddha' may be understood in the same terms as a Pauline vision of 'conversion' or that the missionary mentality of Christianity was straightforwardly replicated in Buddhism. But from

---

[233] Coe 2003: 128.
[234] And also 'religion' or 'faith.' For example, Skilling 2007: 184.
[235] For a sense of participation in a shared Pali world, see Frasch 2017. In 1433, Ma Huan reported of Siam that 'the king is a firm believer in the Buddhist religion', according to the translation of Smithies and Bressan 2001:11.
[236] In Japan, the word *buppō* was used for 'Buddhist law': App 2012: 35.
[237] Tambiah 1976: 164.

a larger perspective it would be perverse not to recognise a common proselytising impetus.[238] The Vinaya enjoined monks to 'Wander forth, O monks, for the benefit of many... Do not two of you take the same road.'[239] The Lan Na chronicle of the early sixteenth century, *Jinakālamālīpakaraṇam*, reported that in 1523, the king of Lan Na offered sixty volumes of the Pali canon to a neighbouring ruler in order 'produce faith in him'.[240]

The conversion described here was to the new 'Theravada' form of Buddhism that had crystallised in the era of Parakramabāhu I, which established the Mahāvihāra vision at the centre of the reorganised Lankan monastic order. The Mahāvihāra worldview may also be seen as an explicit retrenchment of Buddhist soteriology against the movement towards theism that swept across first millennium CE Eurasia. While forms of Mahayana Buddhism elevated the soteriological significance of metapersons (Bodhisattvas), the Theravada school defined itself by its rejection of their ultimate significance. It reduces deities in a deliberate and conscious manner; it is Buddhism with its offensiveness towards the theistic, anthropomorphic urge hardened anew.[241]

(10) Universalist creeds fashioned for export as coherent packages

Transcendentalist traditions are not all equally concerned with expansion and conversion,[242] but their offensiveness engenders a strong potential for expansion. Christianity, Islam, and Buddhism in

---

[238] Brekke 2002: 45–55; Yao and Gombrich 2017: 231; Deeg 2015: 269–276, on Chinese terms for conversion centred on the concept of transformation, and Sanskrit and Pali terms 'to instruct'; Pollock 2005: 406; Elverskog 2010: 96; Keyes 1993, on late twentieth-century Thailand; Wyatt 2001: 28, on thirteenth-century Thailand; Palumbo 2015: 98–99, on sixth-century China; for seventeenth-century Chinese Chan Buddhist missions, see Wheeler 2007.

[239] Tambiah 1976: 65.

[240] As Grabowsky 2007: 125, gives the translation of '*pasāda jananat kaṃ pesei*'. (see above, footnote 182 on *pasāda*).

[241] The fifteenth-century Sinhalese monk Maitreya Vidāgama's *Buduguṇālaṅkāraya* attacks deity worship in a rationalist manner: 'Why call them gods ... if they hang about at the doors of people waiting to receive their gifts like beggars?' (Ilangasinha 1992: 214–215). Note Skilling 2013: 89–94.

[242] Sikhism has been relatively unconcerned with proselytism. Judaism has been a proselytising creed at points in its history but was also tied to ethnicity in an unusual way.

particular are distinguished by exceptional mobility. As noted in the previous sections, elements of immanentist traditions may move long distances too.[243] But what distinguishes the proselytising transcendentalisms is their capacity to move *as whole systems* that necessarily involve a radical reframing of other forms of knowledge. They may be seen as mechanisms for preserving the integrity of cultural transmission over space and time.[244] These transcendentalisms explode the de facto universalism of the immanentist world and replace it with a de jure universalism. The teachings of Christianity, Islam, and Buddhism are addressed to the whole of humanity – or even, in the latter case, all living beings. The touchstone of each tradition is not a particular temple or landscape but a portable, endlessly reproducible set of texts.

(11) The establishment of hegemony through the monopolisation (monotheism) or inferiorisation (Buddhism) of metapersons.

Transcendentalism recalibrates the meaning of relations with metapersons by redescribing them according to the language of soteriological–ethical endeavour.[245] In that sense, the Indic and monotheistic variants represent very different forms of the same project. In essence, the monotheistic approach looks relatively simple to comprehend: it is mass deicide, the exclusive monopolisation of metapersonhood. But such simplicity is deceptive. The Christian God is three beings as well as one being, much as a Hindu deity may be singular or plural at different levels of understanding. Moreover, Satan must be counted as a metaperson – indeed an extremely active one, and he has his minions, his devils, just as God has his angels. This is before we begin to consider the development of the cult of the saints. In this light, Christianity seems scarcely monotheistic: certainly, it has shown itself to be more promiscuous in the attribution of personhood than it may first appear.

The presumed existence of demons and fallen angels had many consequences for the mission field. Missionaries considered themselves

---

[243] See 'Localism and Translatable Universaism' under 'The Characteristics of Immanentism'.
[244] Hefner 1993b: 5. On Buddhism as universalism: Obeyesekere 2002: 120–121 and passim; Collins 1998: 28–29.
[245] Hefner 1993b: 14.

to be at war with these entities as agents of possession who could only be combatted through their rites of exorcism.[246] In practice, missionary discourse has often been ambivalent about the nature of the deities and spirits imagined by rival traditions. They may be deemed 'false' in the sense of being actually nonexistent, but they may also be 'false' in the sense of not deserving of worship – because they are in reality demons masquerading as gods.[247] Typically, converts have seen existing metapersons as overmastered rather than disproven.[248] Even doctrinally, Christianity does not so much as abolish all other metapersons as (a) wipe away other pantheons and replace them with a new simplified set, and (b) order that set according to ethical and soteriological principles.

In essence, Buddhism operated by sidelining the sphere of metapersons: neither their eradication nor their assistance was vital for enlightenment. This must be qualified with regard to traditions of Mahayana Buddhism, where Bodhisattvas may become godlike metapersons endowed with the power to release people into nirvana. Nevertheless, in all Buddhist cultures, the sphere of relations with metapersons is allowed to continue in a form that is recognisable from immanentism. Local pantheons endure or are bundled into an expanding Buddhist universe of gods.[249]

But the central point is that the gods themselves, in all forms of Buddhism, are subordinated to the Buddha.[250] This was conveyed by the image of the deities listening to the Buddha's first preaching of the dhamma, as described in the *Dhammacakkappavattana Sutta*. They cry out:

At Bārāṇasi, in the Deer Park at Isipatana, this unsurpassed Wheel of the Dhamma has been set in motion by the Blessed One, which cannot be stopped by any ascetic or brahmin or deva or Mārā or Brahmā or by anyone in the world.[251]

The gods were among the first converts to Buddhism, and as the Wheel of the *Dhamma* rolled into new lands, the new metapersons it encountered were converted and improved. They were not denied either

---

[246] In all the cases of *CK*, especially Japan.   [247] Paredes 2006.
[248] For example, Holbraad and Pedersen 2017: 255.   [249] Gombrich 1988: 25.
[250] See Obeyesekere 2002: 176–177, on the 'axialogisation' of Brahmanic deities in the canon.
[251] Bodhi 2000: 1846.

existence or power, but their power was configured as banal, wild, or ugly until it had been Buddhicised. Ancestors and spirits were therefore domesticated by the compassion of the Sangha.[252] This process is particularly clear in the scholarship on the taming of the gods of Japan, where monks founded shrine temples in locations associated with *kami* (gods, spirits).[253] It was not always a pacific process: the spirits and their ritual interlocutors could resist and strain against the leash.[254] But the result was a kind of permanent pacification of supernatural power: it was the quasi-human, nonethical, violent, and capricious qualities of the immanentist metapersons that were constrained and controlled. Buddhism converted both persons and metapersons and rendered them both more predictable, compassionate, harmonious. The gods were 'emptied of particularity' as Mark Teeuwen puts it, through their reclassification in Buddhist terms.[255] Thus were they encompassed.[256]

Notice that the field of metapersons is also ethicised in this vision, if less completely than in the Abrahamic traditions. The high gods are fashioned into beings who have amassed great quantities of merit and who now act in accordance with the Buddha's dispensation. In Sri Lanka the gods were conceived as recipients of a 'warrant' from the Buddha to protect the *sāsana*.[257] Contrariwise, the figure of Mara (mentioned in the quotation from the *Dhammacakkappavattana Sutta*) acts as the Buddha's negative, trying to tempt him away from the realisation of enlightenment just as Satan tempted Jesus in the wilderness. There are demonic beings too in this vision: evil metapersons who have failed to fashion themselves according to the *dhamma*.[258] In both Buddhism and Christianity, the evil beings are inferior to the Buddha/God in terms of both ethics and supernatural power. In both traditions, this assertion was stamped onto the landscape whenever a new church, monastery,

---

[252] DeCaroli 2004: 186–187.   [253] Rambelli and Teeuwen 2003a: 11.
[254] Grabowsky 2007: 123; Rambelli and Teeuwen 2003a: 30. For a wonderful example of the permanent placation of a thunder god, see Lin 2003.
[255] Teeuwen 2012: 74, and see 70.
[256] Schonthal 2017: 194, on 'a staccato tacking back and forth between' separation and encompassment in Buddhist boundary-making.
[257] Malalgoda 1976: 24.   [258] Josephson 2012: 32.

or Buddha footprint was planted on top of the site of an old shrine to a vanquished metaperson.[259]

(12) The ambivalent status of magic

Societies organised by immanentist religious traditions may identify forms of religious behaviour as negative from time to time, especially when they seem to have an *anti-social* or politically disruptive character. Indeed, Christianity acquired (and transformed) the language of superstition from pagan Roman discourse.[260] Magical activity aimed at delivering private personal advantage rather than more communal benefits has always needed to be policed.[261] But the strong discourses of vilification of magical practices that were deployed by Christianity and Islam were of a different order. These must wipe the slate of the supernatural clean so as to write on it anew.[262] The miracles of Jesus were then writ large. But the scriptures also represent Jesus' attitude towards the production of miracles with a degree of ambivalence.

In one sense, this is all quite different from Buddhism, which did not attempt to monopolise the manipulation of supernatural power. And yet, here too one may discern a certain relativisation of such practices. The scholarship of Buddhism is not currently always inclined to underline this point. Its task is to shake the field free from the legacy of orientalist scholarship, which preferred a super-rationalist figure of the Buddha, and sometimes viewed the mythical and miraculous elements of the stories and practices of real world Buddhists as embarrassing corruptions or trivial accretions. There is no doubt that from the Pali canonical texts onwards the Buddha is presented as acting within a world in which supernatural events and

---

[259] *Mahāvaṃsa* XVII: 28–31 (Guruge 1989: 40–42), on the foundation of Thūpārāma dagaba on the site of an important yakkha sacrificial rite; Grabowsky 2007: 129.

[260] Stephen Smith 2008. Both China and Rome inherited 'Axial Age' philosophical traditions; both developed something like a notion of superstition.

[261] I do not use 'magic' as a significant concept here – in a way, it is subsumed within the category of immanentism, a form of religiosity focused on mundane prosperity – but everyday use of the term gestures towards the more private, individual, amoral, technical, instrumental, and automatic of ritual acts.

[262] For example, 2 Kings 21:6.

powers are simply taken as a fact of life. However, from a global comparative perspective, it is more noteworthy that the Buddhist tradition preserves an unmistakeable ambivalence about the status of these affairs – which betrays the new values of transcendentalism.[263]

In the *Brahmajāla Sutta*, the Buddha presents a very comprehensive list of magical arts that renouncers might be tempted to practise, including all manner of prophesying, predicting the movements of enemy forces, harvests or astrological events, peddling demon-pacifying charms, reciting spells to bring on deafness, invoking the goddess of luck, and 'promising gifts to deities in return for favours': These are described as 'trifling and insignificant matters, those minor details of mere mortal virtue' – they are not 'evil' note, just *laukika* – worldly, and therefore ultimately distractions.[264,265] The Buddha granted that miraculous powers such as flying through the air or walking on water are quite accessible to the monk. But in the *Kevaṭṭa Sutta* he makes it clear that even though exhibiting these powers may win followers, they should be regarded as a source of humiliation and disgust.[266] In a typical manoeuvre of conceptual redefinition, the only 'miracle' worthy of the name is that of helping another being on the road to enlightenment – much as Muhammad's sole miracle was the Koran.[267] Here and there in the subsequent history of Buddhist monasticism, as in the eighth-century Taiho Code in Japan, meddling in magical arts was explicitly reproved.[268]

In an immanentist field, magical practices may be ambivalent insofar as they may be the source of harm as well as good for the wider community; in a transcendentalist field they are ambivalent insofar as they thwart or detract from the soteriological quest.

---

[263] Schonthal 2017: 191–192.

[264] *Brahmajāla Sutta* (the first sutta of the *Dīgha Nikāya*) III: 21–27, in Bodhi 1978: 58–61.

[265] Aśoka's rock edict IX refers to rites 'which may achieve their purpose or they may not. Moreover the purposes for which they are performed are limited to this world.' Tambiah 1976: 67.

[266] *Kevaṭṭa Sutta*.

[267] According to tradition: Buhl et al. 2017 (thanks to Azfar Moin).

[268] Piggott 1997: 217, 223; Conlan 2003: 186; compare Frasch 2017: 70.

(13) Clerisies form institutions with great organisational power, potential autonomy from state structures, and independent moral authority

The development of clerisies (learned guardians of transcendentalist scripture and interpretation) was noted previously in relation to the creation of traditions of scholarship. But on an institutional plane the consequences are no less significant. Sangha, church, and ulema have shown tremendous organisational power, maintaining their integrity, coherence, and techniques of discipline, their chains of command and common purpose even while states rose and fell around them. Indeed, states were driven to compete with, co-opt, or thwart such rival concentrations of hierarchy and organisation. Above all, the clerisy of transcendentalist tradition wields a moral authority that is quite distinct from that of the state.[269]

(14) Transcendentalist traditions emerge outside the development of state ideology

The transcendentalist traditions were neither in origin nor *in toto* an articulation of a political vision: they were only drawn upon for that purpose subsequently. Indeed, they preserve a certain strand – however fine or invisible for long stretches of time – of anti-political or at least extra-political normativity. Islam is an exception of sorts, given that it became the central feature of a rapidly expanding politico–legal entity within the lifetime of its founder. But Muhammad was not a prince when his revelations began. Instead the process of the translation to the political sphere merely happened unusually quickly, taking years rather than centuries.

---

[269] Eisenstadt 1986c: 4, the new elites 'were recruited and legitimized according to distinct, autonomous criteria, and were organised in autonomous settings, distinct from those of basic, ascriptive units. They acquired a country-wide status consciousness of their own. They also tended to become potentially independent of other categories of elites and subjects. They saw themselves not only as performing specific, technical, functional activities, but also as potentially autonomous carriers of a distinct cultural and social order related to the transcendental vision prevalent in their respective societies.' Also: Hefner 1993b: 19, 24.

(15) The dynamic of reform

All the foregoing characteristics are liable to erosion. But transcendentalism fights back: it generates movements of reform, which call on the authority of scripture, or the imagery surrounding their founders, or the soteriological imperative, in order to reassert its primacy. The following section considers why such impulses of reform were necessary.

An Unstable Synthesis

It is remarkable that the principles of religion have a kind of flux and reflux in the human mind, and that men have a natural tendency to rise from idolatry to theism, and to sink again from theism into idolatry.

David Hume[270]

The vision of transcendentalism set out in the previous section looks like no religious tradition that has ever been lived out in practice. That is because such traditions are always unstable syntheses of transcendentalist and immanentist forms. It is important to recognise that, in one sense, this is so *from their very inception*, as a matter of their core conceptual arrangements. It is no less important to grasp that it is also *a matter of history*, as the transcendentalist traditions are forced to gradually make peace with the structures of mundane reality in order to thrive and survive. Every single defining feature of transcendentalism was subject to reversal, contradiction, and subsumption. It would take a volume in itself to illustrate all the ways in which this took place.

Our task here is to acknowledge the historical significance of these lines of 'immanentisation' without losing sight of the overall distinctiveness of transcendentalism from a global comparative perspective. To take just one example, the individualist and anti-communal dimension of transcendentalism emphasised above only ever mattered in a very particular sense. Monasticism may trample across other forms of sociality such as kinship, but only to replace it with a new form of communal life.[271] And did Buddhist monks ever entirely detach

---

[270] Hume 2007 [1734–1737]: 58.
[271] It could even work to stabilise inheritance by dealing with the problem of second sons: Moore 1999: 145.

themselves from family ties? Unlikely.[272] As Christian villagers placed their salvation in the sacramental rituals that brought them together, or as townspeople joined confraternities of the devout, amongst many other developments, they effected the communalisation of soteriology. Indeed in both Buddhism and Christianity, collectivities such as kingdoms and nations could come to be seen as sharing a soteriological fate.[273] And yet, when we place Christianity alongside the immanentist traditions that have dominated the religiosity of humankind from the very beginning, the contrast is unmistakeable. For Christianity never lost that focus on the discipline and responsibility of the self, and if that focus weakened for stretches of time in its diverse local forms, myriad movements also emerged to clarify and intensify it.[274]

Transcendentalism is therefore treated here as a *historical* process as well as an ideal type. If this means considering its vicissitudes after the inception of its central vehicles, it may be no less worthwhile to seek intimations of it in earlier and other traditions.[275] There is no need to deny that interesting precursors and analogues may be found outside the core cases.[276] Movements towards the ethicisation of the afterlife may germinate outside the world religions.[277] Jan Assmann has delineated several ways in which Ancient Egyptian culture evolved some of the characteristics of transcendentalism while never reaching the fully fledged form it took in the Axial Age.[278] In particular the jealous monotheism and otherworldly aesthetics instituted by the fourteenth-century BCE Pharaoh Akhenaten are fascinating to consider in this light – although it is no less significant to register that subsequent pharaohs obliterated his top–down religious revolution almost entirely.

---

[272] Clarke 2014.   [273] On 'sociokarmic thinking': Walters 2003.

[274] See Robbins 2004: chapter 4, for the tension between individualist and 'relationalist' approaches to salvation among the Urapmin. See Bossy 1985: 94, on Martin Luther's reinterpretation of atonement as a 'rejection of the event from the field of social relations'.

[275] Indeed, the 'Axial Age' itself is merely a moderately convenient periodisation or typology with no more – and in some ways less – substance than terms such as 'Renaissance' or 'Enlightenment'. Apart from the fact that it has no emic basis, it is probably more useful as typology rather than periodisation.

[276] Just as with Renaissance and Enlightenment.

[277] Obeyesekere 2002: 174–176, argues that this is rare among 'small-scale societies' but notes a few examples of 'occasional ethicization'. Root 2013: 56.

[278] Assmann 2012: 396; 2010: 46–47. Also note Arnason: 2012: 341; Bellah 2011: 244.

The strongest parallels, intriguingly, are to be found in societies that participated in the 'Axial Age' without producing hegemonic transcendentalist world religions. Ancient Greek religious–philosophical culture shows several signs of what might be called 'proto-transcendentalism' here and there: developing notions of judgement of the soul upon death; the afterlife-focused sects inveighing against unbelievers revealed in the fourth-century BCE Derveni papyrus; Pythagorean reincarnation; Plato's creator god and the immortal souls trying to reach him.[279] Beyond the cult of Christ itself, some of the myriad forms of the late Roman Empire show some transcendentalist qualities.[280] The long history of Judaism has shown the evolution of some of the core characteristics of the 'transcendentalism' explored here while conspicuously not exhibiting others – most importantly in relation to the role of the afterlife. The visions of Jewish prophets and Christ may be placed in a continuum with the 'supernatural utopianism' exhibited by prophetic traditions in immanentist traditions too (Chapter 4). Zoroastrianism has invited much debate as to whether and to what extent it belongs in the paradigm.

These examples all derive from societies that participated in cultural currents swirling around Eurasia. In later periods, the influence of globally circulating cultural forms must also be acknowledged. The *babalawo* priests of the Ifa cult in nineteenth- and twentieth-century Yoruba land exhibited a few features that brought them closer to a transcendentalist clerisy, but they were, however, already in a social world that included the presence of Islam and Christianity.[281] Indeed, one particularly intriguing phenomenon is the way that immanentist systems may react to pressure from transcendentalist rivals by acquiring some of their characteristics – in particular that of hardened identity construction. The most striking example of this process is perhaps the formation of a self-conscious tradition of Shinto in Japan, discussed in the companion volume.[282]

---

[279] Emonds 2015: 559; Larson 2016: 250–276; Whitmarsh 2016: 115–116, 133; Ando 2008: 28–30 on platonic anti-idolatry and ineffability; Lannstrom 2010.

[280] Ando 2013; Rüpke 2010.

[281] Peel 1990 offers a limited comparison with Hindu Brahmans.

[282] *CK*; Compare Baum 1999, Mark 1999, on the Dioula of Senegambia and monotheistic influence.

Much more significant, however, is the way that fully realised transcendentalisms came to reproduce forms of immanentism. Most theorists of the Axial Age have sought to conceptualise this. Weber acknowledged the continuing appeal of magic, especially, but not only, among the peasantry, down to and beyond the Reformation.[283] Voegelin referred to the 'archaic mortgage'; Bellah has reiterated the principle that 'nothing is ever lost'; Eisenstadt was fascinated by the enduring power of 'pre-Axial' forms in Japan; Assmann refers to older forms relegated to the 'archive' of cultural memory, as in the encrypted cosmotheism that reemerged into the gnostic and magical forms of the Renaissance.[284]

There are four reasons why transcendentalist traditions always form amalgams with immanentism. The first is that the conceptual structure of transcendentalism entails endless paradox. The transcendent sphere can never float entirely free from the mundane world: it must materialise within the limitations of the human mind and human needs. As Michael Lambek puts it, 'Transcendence in this sense of unimaginable Otherness is not stable, it requires a completion through immanence.'[285] An inscription underneath an Amitābha statue from Tang China articulates it thus:

As a matter of general principle, while highest truth is devoid of any image, without images there would be nothing to make visible its [being the] truth; and while highest principle is devoid of all words, how, without words, would its [being the] principle be made known.[286]

The second reason is that the evolved structures of human cognition and need which produce the characteristic features of immanentism naturally remain in place. Most importantly, heaven and nirvana are always likely to register as paradisical versions of this world in the popular imagination.[287] This is crucial because it means that the actual

---

[283] Weber 1948: 277.
[284] Bellah 2011: 267; also Charles Taylor 2012: 37–38; Assmann 2012: 373; Moin (MS); Gauchet 1999: 46.
[285] Lambek 2013a:16; also Keane 2006.
[286] Wenzel 2011 notes this apologetic tone in many other votive inscriptions.
[287] For Buddhism see Spiro 1982: 69–70, but note villagers' incorporation of the hegemony of the *nibbānic* vision at a certain level of discourse (78). Spiro sees kammatic Buddhism as the result of both inherent elements of Buddhism and its *popularisation*: although it 'accompanied and developed in response to the sociological shift in Buddhism from an elitist to a mass religion', in fact it

soteriological objective for the great majority – even of Theravada Buddhist layfolk – will have been some enhanced or absolute conception of good fortune: it was a deferred form of being they were after rather than nothingness.[288] As Melford Spiro intuited, on some level, we all flinch from pain, reach out for pleasure, and fear nonexistence.[289] Meanwhile, the ceaseless desire to access supernatural power may shift the significance of the Koran from uniquely authorised logos to a receptacle for magical potency. The anthropomorphising tendency, the attribution of personhood or agency to chains of cause and effect, continues unabated. As Cicero understood, idol and deity will ever be conflated: 'The form resembling living creature has such powers over the affections of the miserable that it arouses prayers to itself.'[290] In modern European cities the capacity of holy images to produce 'spectacular miracles' continues.[291] Consider how hard it is to rid the mind of the notion that human beings contain immaterial persons and these persons stay around us in some form when they die. Even in societies subscribing to religious traditions that officially have no place for this notion – such as Christianity – ancestors find a way of making an appearance in the form of ghosts.[292] Indeed, if it is true that transcendentalism is less well supported by the mental tools cognitive scientists have hypothesised, then its rise to hegemony is all the more in need of explanation. Its susceptibility to immanentisation, on the other hand, is predicted by such theories.

Harvey Whitehouse has pointed out the vulnerability of doctrinal forms of religiosity to the tedium effect.[293] They may therefore give way to or require stimulus from religious forms that are conveyed through an 'imagistic' mode. Participation in a dramatic event such as an initiation ritual produces a 'flashbulb memory' that long endures thanks to the bombardment of the senses and the arousal of the emotions. For our purposes, we may note that imagistic events will tend to involve an immanentisation of the sacred, which is to say,

'merely transplanted seeds already sown by contradictions inherent in the very fabric of *nibbānic* Buddhism' (68). Compare Cannell 2005 on Mormon afterlife.
[288] While many Mahayana traditions will have explicitly heavenly visions of the afterlife.
[289] Spiro 1982. Thanks to Vic Lieberman for discussion.
[290] Cited in Ando 2008: 57; cf Versnel 2011: 479.
[291] Garnett and Rosser 2013.   [292] Cannell 2013.
[293] Whitehouse 2000:150ff; discussion in Peel 2016.

an evocation of its presence. Transcendentalism risks leaving the senses for dead, but rituals must bring them alive.[294] And as soon as transcendentalist traditions allow iconic representation, they open the possibility that these icons will be treated as if they are coterminous with what they represent. Furthermore, other universal propensities of cognition ensure that the attempt to halt the flow of revelation will always be in vain. Prophetesses, ecstatics, and visionaries continued to populate Christian and Buddhist history.[295] Above all, human beings continue to dream – in the literal sense. In all societies, dreams have been credited as an essential mode of communication with supernatural beings, and transcendentalism has only ever been able to frame rather than squash their interpretation, as Charles Stewart's work on Naxos shows so clearly.[296] Finally, a minority will continue to have 'religious experiences', profound, life-changing transformations of perspective and subjectivity, often characterised by a dissolution of the self–other barrier, which constantly demand the application of meaning.[297]

The third reason is the logic by which the transcendent takes on institutional forms that acquire social and political functions.[298] As Christianity, for example, worked its way from the margins into the centre ground of a society, it had to take on the Durkheimian roles that religion had always fulfilled: far from challenging the primacy of the family, the givenness of the cultural inheritance, or the justice of the political status quo, it had to become the most fundamental legitimator of each. The French ambassador to Ayutthaya in the 1680s, Simon de La Loubère, for example, noted that if the Gospel were placed in the hands of the Chinese they would surely be appalled at those passages where Jesus affects not to know his family or tells a disciple to follow him rather than bury his parents. Therefore,

---

[294] Note Gunson 1978: 233, on a spur for revivalist movements in Polynesia: 'We are all too formal here, too dead.'
[295] Christian 1981.
[296] Stewart 2012; Kinberg 1993. Julian 'the Apostate' dreaming of Asclepius, a proof of paganism: Momigliano 1986: 294.
[297] If religious experiences are not considered much in this book it is not because their emotional power is denied. For an atheist's account of an overwhelming 'religious experience', see Ehrenreich 2014.
[298] Martin 2005:12, refers to Christianity's encounter with the logic of social organisation.

missionaries must instead emphasise the capacity of Christianity to authorise obedience.[299]

Many processes may be placed under this heading, including the tendency for institutions such as cathedrals, temples, monasteries, mosques, and shrines to attract wealth: the more successful they were at convincing the surrounding population that they must look to their otherworldly status, the richer and more successful in worldly terms the institution itself tended to become. No less surely, locality and landscape were resacralised: the universal had to be brought down to the ground. In Japan, Buddha splintered into Bodhisattvas such as Hachiman who in turn splintered into different versions of himself to preside over different temples; in Christendom, saints emerged to sanctify villages and towns, and these too literally splintered into relics that cast them into geographical and bodily plurality; in Islam, the bodies of sufi saints splintered and seeded the ground no less spectacularly.

The fourth reason is that as the transcendentalisms expand – both into new sectors of any one society and into new societies tout court – so they must meet immanentism on its own terms in order to obtain victory. This is explored at length in Chapters 4–6.

Before considering some of the ways these processes worked in the *longue durée* histories of Buddhism and Christianity, it would be wise to relate this comparative procedure to historiographical tendencies within each field. In both, Weber is liable to be invoked as an old ghost who must be exorcised but is never quite laid fully to rest. In both, the notion of 'popular religion' has been identified as an obstacle to scholarly progress, especially insofar as it is conceived as some sort of vegetative immersion in the immanent.[300] In both, the tones of a domineering Protestant voice are discerned and reproved. Not just Hume, quoted previouslly, but a string of thinkers from Hobbes to Hocart may be charged with a Protestant disdain for the 'magical' proclivities of the masses.[301]

As always, such critiques have helped to develop fresh perspectives and reinvigorate their fields, while teetering on the edge of the genealogical fallacy in their more emphatic formulations. The fact that

---

[299] La Loubère 1987 [1691]: 418–419; Luke 9:59–60.
[300] On 'vegetative' mental life for Weber: Ghosh 2014: 263. Note Fletcher 1998: 239.
[301] Hobbes 2012, III: 1024 (*Leviathan* IV, 45); Hocart 1970: 78, on Buddhism.

a concept was developed in a context that modern sympathies find unpalatable – such as the deprecation of Catholicism – need have little bearing on its analytical utility. Why not consider instead that the particular historical predicament of Protestantism stimulated a certain kind of insight?[302] Or that resurgent transcendentalisms are likely to involve conceptualisations of an immanentism that otherwise had no need of a name?[303] The English Puritan William Perkins could come to see Catholicism as the natural religion of mankind after the fall, which always tends towards the man-centred, 'under new tearmes, maintaining the idolatrie of the heathen', once he realised how hard it was in practice to eliminate the immanentist urge.[304] It should go without saying that whatever value judgements were once hung from these concepts, they have long since fallen off in scholarly discourse.

There are several ways, however, in which the analysis presented here has been enriched by recent critiques. The teleological edge of past grand narratives is blunted by a recognition of the inevitable recurring power of immanentism, as a universal cognitive tendency that may be triggered in diverse ways.[305] For example, there is a certain common ground of empiricism that immanentism shares with the mentality of scientific endeavour, and which is observable in European history from at least the Renaissance, in the interest in astrology, alchemy, and natural magic.[306] Equally, there are features of modern capitalism, urbanisation, and globalisation which may propel a notably 'immanentist' and experimental approach to the manipulation of metapersons and supernatural powers – all in the expectation of enabling the individual to get ahead and gain mastery of the mysterious forces that propel some to fortune and others to inferiority.[307] The extraordinary proliferation of these forms in

---

[302] See Robbins 2012: 14. After all, we are all creatures of such predicaments.
[303] Protestant thinkers needed only to resurrect a language of idolatry deployed by Christians against paganism. See Cameron 2010: 208, on Heinrich Bullinger.
[304] Dixon 2011: 804; thanks to Leif Dixon for discussion.
[305] See 'A few notes on reform' for the immanentisation of Protestantism.
[306] Henry 2002: 54–67, on natural magic and the development of science; Moin MS.
[307] Comaroff and Comaroff 2000; Geschiere 1997. Thanks to Peter A. Jackson (and see 2016) for discussion. Note also the 'Prosperity Gospel' of some Pentecostalist and Charismatic preachers.

certain modern environments indicates how quickly they rise and fall according to an economy of perceived efficacy.[308]

The emphasis on the inherent rather than merely contingent union of transcendentalism and immanentism is also distinct. The 'split personality' or fundamental instability of Christianity in some recent anthropological writing ought rather to be seen as a property of all transcendentalisms.[309] Still, Jesus is a particularly vivid symbol of that tension: what is his story – the miracles of his life and death – but a provision of empirical proof for those who need it, a transformation of the distantly divine into vulnerable flesh and blood, and even a recapitulation of the awful logic of human sacrifice?[310] Thus was the 'hidden god' revealed in ungodlike suffering.[311] The implications of Christ's physical nature, the visceralities of childbirth and torture, could be rather repulsive to seventeenth-century East Asian Neo-Confucian and Buddhist scholars; it was, indeed, the confusion of the transcendent and the immanent in Christian doctrine that they found irrational.[312] Christ himself is just the first of many subsequent solutions to the impossible harshness of the transcendent vision. It has already been underlined that Christianity shares ground with immanentism insofar as it takes a metaperson as its essential focus, and that the journey from a violent and particular god of the Israelites to a transcendent, abstract entity can never truly be accomplished. This is a god who responds to entreaties just as immanentist deities do, and is therefore constantly interfering in the world in ways large and utterly small; who fills lowly priests and rural fonts with an overflowing grace. He remains a war god, as Chapter 5 will detail at length; he remains a god of the weather and can be as pitiless as the elements in his wrath.[313] This is the terrible god that the missionary William Ellis sensed as he climbed the slopes of the volcanoes of Kilauea in Hawaii in 1823, not so very different from the local

---

[308] Gombrich and Obeyesekere 1988.
[309] Cannell 2005, 2006; Robbins 2012; Mitchell and Mitchell 2008; Peel 2016: 105–124. On Christianity's combination of transcendence and immanence see: Lilla 2007: 31; Martin 2005: 183; Handelman 2008; Eisenstadt 1986b: 238–239; Kim 1987.
[310] But see Gauchet 1999: 119: his proximity was necessitated by 'unrepresentable remoteness'.
[311] Roper 2016: 106, on Luther's *deus absconditus*.
[312] Gernet 1985: 214–232.
[313] Boxer 1959; 309–310 (letter of 1564); Davis 1973: 59.

goddess deity Pele.[314] A truly apophatic vision of god has always struggled to gain purchase.[315]

Another paradox inherent in transcendentalism is worth our attention. The latter is defined by a particularly marked distinction between the clerisy and laity. But the more that distinction is conceived as corresponding to soteriological status (such that monastics or priests are closer to heaven or nirvana), the more that the layman's potential for salvation or liberation is problematised. It was partly in response to this that both Buddhism and Christianity developed, either in their canonical texts or their subsequent formulations, a concept of merit or grace.[316] This can be understood as an immanentisation of soteriological progress, such that what would otherwise be a matter of intrinsically individual moral–cognitive discipline becomes akin to a *mana* of the soul, a 'stuff' with real presence that may be stored, measured, transferred, or bestowed. It operates in that sense just like an immanentist supernatural force – except that instead of producing worldly benefit, it effects a salvific boost. The Catholic Church and the sangha thereby eased the soteriological burden they placed on the shoulders of the laity by setting up a new kind of gift exchange, receiving the tokens of immanentist endeavour (alms) or ritual (a mass, a *pirit* ceremony) in return for the priceless promise of liberation expressed in their sacraments or blessings. This also helped to soften too intense a focus on the self and rendered salvation more of a function of the proper conduct of social relations.

Ritual too was attacked but could never be defeated. It returned soon enough to the centre of religious life for the great majority.[317] Ritual action may be fashioned to express transcendentalist principles but it hardly does so reliably; indeed it is not a reliable vehicle of information in general. To the extent that symbolic action invokes ideas, they become meaningful in a more immediate and powerful but also diffuse, multivalent and unstable form.[318]

Considering how such paradoxes played out as Buddhism and Christianity evolved from fringe sects to become the presiding ideologies of large stretches of Eurasia again involves some delicacy in historiographical terms. Many historians have found the notion of

---

[314] Ellis 1827: 246, 252, 262.
[315] On debates around the apophatic god in Christian theology: Insole 2001.
[316] Samuels 2008 on Buddhist merit in scripture and practice.
[317] Hocart 1970: 174; McMullin 1989: 11, on Japan.   [318] Bell 1992: 182–186.

'popular religion' too crude a tool for the purposes of monographic research. It may be taken to assume class distinctions where none exist (princes are no less avid for relics than peasants), or to make the lower strata mere uncomprehending receptacles for religious energies issuing from above. 'Magic' is a vexed category, often in the eye of the beholder. When anthropology influenced cultural history in the 1960s and '70s, it helped historians see how all strata may participate in a common cultural life shaped by the same sacred landscape and subterranean structures of meaning.[319]

However, from a global comparative perspective we still need a conceptual language to help us grasp the apparently rather predictable ways in which the 'world religions' or 'great traditions' are shaped as they settle into society at large. 'Immanentisation' avoids some of the pitfalls of the language of popular religion without denying the force of the intuitions behind it. In fact, it is hardly implausible that monks and priests are likely to speak the voice of transcendentalism with greater consistency than peasants.[320] Nor is it implausible that sections of the population characterised by lack of education, low levels of literacy, relative immobility, distance from major urban centres, and closeness to the land, might show a loosely distinctive form of religiosity. It is just that such propositions are very rarely investigated in a systematic and globally comparative manner.[321] Stephen Sharot, at least, has examined the scholarship of China, the Indic world, and Europe, and concluded, amongst other things, that 'in the popular forms of all the world religions, soteriology has been overshadowed by thaumaturgy'.[322] Immanentist intuitions evidently recur regardless of the hostility of intellectual-hegemonic discourses of transcendence or secularisation. Still, 'immanentisation' does not in itself presuppose distinctions between classes/status groups nor any unidirectional flow of influence between them; we are free to acknowledge that bhikkhus and rajas may engage chthonic spirits just as intently as villagers.[323]

---

[319] Davis 1974.   [320] Johnson 2006 for a nuanced discussion of Europe.
[321] Moore 2003: 17, suggests the need for a comparative history of popular religion.
[322] Sharot 2001: 248. Sharot in fact distinguishes between elite/popular (referring to *religious* elite); great/little; and official/unofficial dichotomies, all of which are somewhat different but overlap. See also Riesebrodt 2010.
[323] See Schopen 1997 against the lay/monastic divide; and DeCaroli 2004: 17–18, who avoids terms such as 'rural', 'folk', 'village-based', or 'local' to

Indeed, the consistent and often overriding interest of lords and princes in immanent power is a principal argument of this book and its companion volume.

The Immanentisation of Buddhism

By contrast with the split personality of Christianity, Buddhism may appear much more uncompromisingly transcendentalist in terms of its core conceptualisation, and in one sense it is. In another sense, however, it makes a pact with immanentism that is even more whole-hearted: it simply leaves the sphere of relations with metapersons to proceed largely as it always did, albeit now subtly relativised and reframed.[324] But that process of reframing could take a very long time. The history of kami worship in Japan shows how for long stretches of time they could be considered as capricious amoral entities who must be implored, cajoled, and reprimanded into reciprocity.[325] While they were gradually tamed and endowed with Buddhist functions through the *honji suijaku* theory, still both layfolk and monks could interact with them in fundamentally immanentist ways.[326]

Moreover, the Buddha himself was no ordinary mortal. Just as with Christ, his soteriological perfection also endowed him with the ability to work miracles.[327] It is true that the Pali texts distinguish him from godhood per se (he is much more important than that), and that in the hegemonic doctrine of the Theravada tradition his attainment of nir-vana does not render him in a form ready to dispense boons. But what La Loubère reports of seventeenth-century Siam rings true: on the one hand the Buddha's enlightened status meant that he existed nowhere and with no ability to do good or evil to men, but 'nevertheless on the other hand they offer up prayers to him and demand of him whatever they want'.[328] In other words, whatever particular canonical texts say, there are in every tradition discernible urges to treat Buddha as a

---

describe the field of relations with spirits, but opts for '*laukika*', 'popular', and 'nonsoteriological'.

[324] Reynolds 2005: 214, 'Buddhism in almost all its manifold cultural settings is an amalgam, in which one of the elements bound with it is something called animism, shamanism, or the like.'

[325] Ohnuki-Tierney 1991.   [326] CK.

[327] As picked up by Gervaise 1688: 182–183. See Reynolds 2005: 217.

[328] La Loubère 1987 [1691]: 414.

conventional metaperson.[329] Indeed, from one angle, this is what the
Mahayana tradition formalised – albeit with great intellectual sophistication and complexity – through the reification of Bodhisattvas,
the various incarnations of the Buddha.[330]

From another angle, however, this development also derived from
an intellectual attempt to wrestle with an inherent transgression of the
transcendentalist/immanentist boundary equivalent to that embodied
in Christ: for Buddhists were likewise compelled to consider how a real
historical person could also surpass mundane existence in the most
complete form imaginable. Just as the first centuries of Christianity
were replete with arguments as to how to conceive the nature of Christ
qua God, so too Buddhists argued about whether the Buddha could
ever really have been a man. The *lokkottaravādins* – or 'transcendentalists' – denied this possibility, thereby producing a germ of
Mahayana Buddhology.[331]

Unless we grant the significance of the supernatural qualities of the
Buddha in all traditions, it is difficult to understand why a cult of his
relics should have become so important. Relics speak in a transcendentalist register, to be sure: they may be *memento mori*; they concretise
and immortalise the moral authority of their original persons. But they
also speak to the desire for embodied and tangible sacrality, and as
such they are always liable to be apprehended as condensations of
immanent power. The relics of the Buddha, then, were usually granted
a *mana*-like force, preserving his powers in this plane of existence long
after his *parinibbāna*. This is how they became central agents in the
establishment of capitals, the foundation of temples, the conduct of
diplomacy, and the waging of war.[332]

The underlying equation here is simply that soteriological virtuosity
equals immanentist power, and this is a paradoxical but irresistible
principle manifest in the historical development of all transcendentalist
traditions. Perhaps the self-discipline, liminality, and transgressive
otherworldliness conveyed by the ascetic practices of early Christian

---

[329] He is 'affectively divine': Collins 1982: 18. For an example from modern
ethnography see McKinley 2016: 1.
[330] Though the bodhisattva Avalokiteśvara merging *laukika* and *lokottara*
functions is popular in Theravada regions too, see Holt 1991.
[331] Kalupahana 1992: 141–143.
[332] Strong 2004; Scheible 2016: 98–99. Tambiah 1976: 87–88; Wyatt 2001:
34–35.

saints and mendicants, Islamic sufis, or Theravada forest monks intrinsically trigger sensations of supernatural mastery: these are people able to endure lives that others can only marvel at; their strange conquest of human nature signalling their power.[333] Tambiah, for example, analysed the manner in which Thai forest monks are liable to be attributed with magical powers that are of little use to themselves, having diminished their attachment to worldly benefits, but of great value to the laity.[334] In earlier periods of Thai history the accumulation of merit was expected to be visible in the demonstration of abnormal power.[335] In Japan, Zen monks pursuing the most abstruse and rationalised of philosophies could become the focus of popular hopes for their blessings.

The need to develop strategies of popularisation may be particularly clear in Buddhism given that its elite carriers are monastics rather than priests. This means that they are at once dependent on the laity and yet also not defined by an orientation to serve them. As DeCaroli has put it about both early Jains and Buddhists: 'How do those concentrating on a personal quest for enlightenment establish the religious authority and pertinence necessary to merit public support?'[336] Pattana Kitiarsa's fieldwork in the Thai temple of Wat Thepthanthong shows that recourse to the business of the immanent can be a quite conscious decision:

'The abbot once told me and other monks that "we need to find some tricks (*ubai*) to attract devotees to our temple. We cannot survive without patronage from laypeople. Magic is not encouraged in Buddhist teachings and ecclesiastical laws (*vinaya*) but sometimes it is quite necessary when we have to deal with popular expectation. I have built this temple with donations generated through magical and supernatural rites as much as by adhering to Buddhist teachings."'[337]

In more profound, holistic and intellectualised ways, a transcendentalist system may become repurposed for immanentist ends. This is one way of conceiving of the emergence of Tantric Buddhism from the seventh century CE. It is telling that tantrism constitutes an inversion

---

[333] Reynolds 2005: 225. Catholic saints must fulfil immanentist (miracles) and transcendentalist (virtue) criteria in order to qualify: Faubion 2006: 192.
[334] Tambiah 1984; Kitiarsa 2012: 36–37.
[335] See *CK;* cf Shugenja of Japan. Also see quotation in DeCaroli 2004: 31.
[336] DeCaroli 2004: 34.   [337] Kitiarsa 2012: xviii–xix, 1.

of transcendentalism across various dimensions simultaneously, and conveys a certain sense of the transgression and paradox that this entails. As a greater focus was placed on the capturing of supernatural forces, a highly intricate ritualism became the order of the day, and so a greater emphasis was placed on secrecy and esotericism to better preserve exclusive access to such powers; and so blood sacrifice reappeared; and so the aesthetic of the sacred returned to the earthy and the violent; and fierce warrior gods were exalted, and sexual activity celebrated.[338] Note, also, however, that all this was hung from a Buddhist framework, transcendentalist desiderata retained an ultimate hegemony, and some highly complex intellectual manoeuvres were carried out in order to rationalise the result.

Buddhist traditions, particularly the Mahayana, have often been explicit about the coexistence of different levels of truth corresponding to different capacities of comprehension.[339] Missionary observers, particularly as we shall see in Japan, noted that more difficult, radical, and abstract points of doctrine may be grasped by certain orders of monks or sections of the elite but were less digestible by the wider populace.[340] In particular, the radical qualities of the doctrine of no-self and *nibbāna* as complete annihilation were liable to be elided by popular conceptions of selves reincarnating and attaining heavenly planes.[341] In other words, it was precisely the attribution of continuing personhood (to themselves) and metapersonhood (to the Buddha) that was often difficult to deny outright. If David Hume saw theism as subject to an entropic fall towards idolatry, the history of Buddhism shows an entropic tendency towards theism. Indeed, more generally, from the early first millennium there was a shift towards theist devotionalism (*bhakti* in Hinduism, strands of Mahayana Buddhism) among the Indic traditions that had previously held up the way of the renouncer, ethical rigour and philosophical wisdom. It is tempting to speculate that the popularisation of soteriological fervour lay behind this.[342]

---

[338] Elverskog 2010: 79–86, 96. Tantrism has many strands (Gray 2016), and its actual origins are complex and debated. Note that some authors described the tantras as 'the *vidyādharasaṃvara*, the discipline of the sorcerer': Ronald M. Davidson 2015. Compare developments in Japanese Buddhism: Teeuwen 2012: 82.

[339] This is typical of 'dialogical transcendence': Duara 2015.

[340] Forest 1998, III: 222–224.   [341] Spiro 1982: 66–91.

[342] See Williams 2009: 24–27, for some more careful comments.

In the past, some Buddhist traditions have appealed to a grand cyclical conception of cosmic time, according to which the Buddha's current dispensation was undergoing a period of decline. This is one way in which the equation of *kami* (deity) and Bodhisattva was rationalised in Japan: because the people of such a degraded age would find deity worship easier to comprehend.[343] Teeuwen and Rambelli quote a fourteenth-century collection of shrine legends:

Sentient beings living in the corrupt world of the Final Age of the Dharma are not afraid of karmic retribution in their next life; their only concern is glory in this life, and for that purpose only do they visit Buddhist temples and perform rituals to the *kami*. They only believe what they see with their own eyes, and they are not concerned with the afterlife. For the benefit of such people [buddhas and bodhisattvas] dim the radiance of their original mind and transform into the dust [i.e. coarse material bodies of various different beings].[344]

One could not wish for a more conscious or explicit commentary on the way in which transcendentalist truths must become mingled with immanentist desires in order to maintain a foothold in the popular imagination.[345]

As transcendentalist traditions acquire cultural hegemony, they certainly do have the capacity to bring the masses into the soteriological vision, then – but as soon as this happens, ethically and ascetically severe modes of attainment simply become impractical: it is the arousal of (transcendentalist) hunger for salvation among the laity that drives the (immanentist) focus on ritual as the means of its satiation. This process reached a particularly striking form with the Pure Land Buddhist sects in Japan, in which the gravitational force of devotional theism pulled Buddhism as far as quasi-monotheism. These were genuinely popular movements that swept people from all social classes into worldviews with a strong ideological or 'offensive' implications. But this entailed the immanentisation of Buddhist soteriology in at least two senses: the ultimate end was conceived as a paradisical afterlife akin to popular views of Christian heaven; and the means of attaining it were radically simplified and ritualised. For elements of the *Jōdo*

---

[343] Teeuwen 2000: 206.   [344] Rambelli and Teeuwen 2003a: 20.
[345] Compare Valignano 1944: 160, where the equation of *kami* and Bodhisattva (*hotoke*) is presented as a deliberate way to boost the monks' authority over the people.

Shinshū school in Japan, the gates to heaven might now swing open to those merely willing to chant the name of Amida Buddha.[346]

The Immanentisation of Christianity

Having first explored a few of the ways in which Buddhism was subject to immanentisation, it may now be less controversial to extend that analysis to Christianity. At least the new anthropology of Christianity, unencumbered by the weight of generations of historiographical contention, has seen clearly that different varieties of Christianity found different ways of resolving the tensions between transcendentalism and immanentism.[347] In truth, at almost every level Christianity was immanentised over the course of its establishment. This was partly a function of the expansion of the faith, as it inevitably took on the functions of the paganism it displaced.[348] But it is in one sense unhelpful to think of this process as essentially a matter of pagan survival; instead it represents the universal salience of immanentist cognition and the inherent logic of its socialisation.[349] Doctrinalism was obscured by the breach between vernacular tongues and the Latin of church services. Ritualism took its place. A form of fetishism flourished in the cult of relics. The most worldly of tokens – money – could be exchanged for soteriological assistance. Kinship suffused the religious imagination. Jesus' mother and grandmother were sanctified; God acquired his own family of sorts in the saints; the Church came to grace life-cycle rituals.[350] If the cosmological dualism of Christianity had the distressing effect of sundering living humans from their ancestors, this was felt in medieval Europe too, where ways of bridging the divide with the dead were created so that the living could care for their ancestors who 'remained part of their kith and kin'.[351]

One of the most visible markers of the incessant immanentisation to which Catholicism was subject is the variety of forms that

---

[346] Alessandro Valignano therefore presented *Jōdo Shinshū* as a deliberate act of popularisation: Orii 2015: 202. Equally, sutra recitation in China might lead to miracles: ter Haar 1992: 20.

[347] Robbins 2012: 14. But see a clear statement in Eire 2016: 723.

[348] See Chapter 4, and Reff 2005: 24; Rapp 1998: 217.

[349] See Pina-Cabral 1992. Contemporary immanentism: Peter A. Jackson 2016: 838.

[350] Even if marriage rites were rather late to develop. Bossy 1985: 10–23.

[351] Davis 1974: 327–328; Geary 1994; Markus 1990: 21–26.

thaumaturgical ritual took and the variety of metapersons with whom people interacted in medieval Europe.[352] God even in his most unified and abstracted form is still a prayer-answering being: was this enough? It was not: saints materialised who answered to more specific concerns in more specific contexts.[353] Nor was this enough, for people continued to populate their environment with a multitude of sprites, ghosts, goblins, witches, demons, tree spirits, and so on.[354] Catholicism developed rites and objects that could be used to hold and channel supernatural power. The sacrament of the host could be attributed with miraculous efficacy, as could sacramentals such as holy water, which only clung on to transcendentalism though the proviso that they needed faith to work.[355] Was this enough? It was not: parasitic practices arose which aped, appropriated, and repurposed Church sacramentals, and beyond this a vast array of magical practices were deployed that stood entirely outside the teachings and often the toleration of the Church.[356] Robin Briggs describes healers in the Lorraine region of France:

These men and women operated without setting any clear boundaries between natural and supernatural, because they conceived their world as one permeated by hidden forces which they believed themselves able to mobilize or counteract, while they made no real distinction between knowledge and personal power...; for [their clients] an established reputation founded on previous cures was apparently what mattered.[357]

This could stand as an invocation of immanentism per se. In the witch hunts of sixteenth- and seventeenth-century Europe, people believed to have such powers became vulnerable to being identified as witches invovled in a diabolic pact – a transcendentalist reinterpretation of immanentist behaviour. Practices that always risked suspicion for their ability to cause harm as well as good to the local community now became subordinated to an absolutist morality by which they became an affront to the soteriological imperative, a sin with most grave and universal implications.

The tremendous profusion of practices and metapersons indicates that they were subject to empirical appraisal of their efficacy. If a single

---

[352] A vast literature, e.g., Thomas 1971.
[353] For example, St. Urban, the patron saint of vintners: Scribner 1987: 13.
[354] Cameron 2010.   [355] Cameron 1991: 15; Zika 1988; Scribner 2001a.
[356] Cameron 1991: 11; Gentilcore 1992.   [357] Briggs 2007: 181.

means of obtaining worldly fortune (such as a prayer to God or a dose of holy water) was regarded as reliably effective – as a matter of illocutionary effect rather than perlocutionary venture – then the constant generation of diverse other means makes little sense. It was at least partly because metapersons could visibly fail to reciprocate and rites fail to work that people were driven to seek new ones.

The most visible dimension of profusion in an official register was the cult of the saints. And for much of their careers across much of Europe the saints became vaguely amoral metapersons who were assumed to be actually present in their statues and figurines.[358] They were therefore subject to coercion in a manner that is immediately familiar from accounts of Inca lords whipping *huacas* or Chinese villagers burning their village deity for failing to protect them from the plague.[359] Healers in Lorraine had to devise rituals for working out which saint had afflicted a sufferer with illness and would respond to propitiation with pilgrimages and offerings.[360] Meanwhile 'in Pamiers, the Catholic vicar might drop his Black Virgin of Foix when she failed to bring good weather; but then he tenderly repaired her broken neck with an iron pin.'[361] What one Italian missionary observed of Portuguese Asia was not necessarily a reflection of the recent conversion of these areas so much as a manifestation of a mentality with deep European roots too: the laity had developed ceremonies for forcing the hand of a saint, giving its effigy

a thousand rough handlings and sacrilegious treatments ... for example they bite it indecently on the nose, the face, the ears, the hands etc and bind it with many chains, hang it outside a window in the sun and the rain, tie it with a rope and throw it into a well or a cistern, and similar things, and they say they do this to oblige the saint to intercede for them to gain that favour.[362]

Meanwhile, the capacity of saints for fractal subdivision allowed them to become local rather than universal protectors of worldly fortune – to become, for example, St. Tryphon of Kotor in the

---

[358] Geary 2004: 95–124; and see Delumeau 1977: 162.
[359] See the section 'Metapersons (and their relations with persons) are defined by power rather than ethics'.
[360] Briggs 2007: 215.
[361] Davis 1973: 77; see also Carroll 1992 for an immanentist religiosity of the Madonna in Italy.
[362] Alberts 2012: 29. Compare Thomas 1971: 29.

Adriatic – and therefore to enable the formation of local rather than universal allegiances.[363]

A Few Notes on Reform

However, the history of medieval Catholicism was no less punctuated by the impulses of reform, which could be as myriad and particular as the processes of immanentisation they fought against. Much of what scholars refer to when using the language of reform could happily be filed under the heading of 'retranscendentalisation'.[364] This is especially visible in – but by no means limited to – the cycles of encroaching worldliness and reestablished otherworldliness characterising the orders of monasticism and mendicancy. Their reform movements looked back to their founding figures such as St. Francis of Assisi, just as Christianity as a whole looked back to Christ: recapitulating within a microcosm the cyclical movements of the faith as a whole. Other kinds of reform might insist on the importance of access to scripture, or interiority, or salvation as a lay imperative, or self-sacrifice, or the inversion of worldly values, or the unity of God, and so on. Whenever these objectives were pursued in a way that pushed too vigorously against the established structure of compromise erected by the Church they were identified as heretical and persecuted.[365] Where it could, the Church also tried to appropriate and harness their energies.

The Reformation, of course, was driven by movements that generated enough power to sweep aside the Church's charges of heresy and develop their own structures of authority. It conveyed an urge to push apart the spiritual and temporal in certain ways, to reanimate an Augustinian vision of the relative worthlessness of man and the awesome majesty and otherness of God.[366] Whatever else the Reformation was, then, it was surely, at bottom, an attempt to reassert many of the defining features of transcendentalism – as were, indeed, in quite distinct and less radical ways, the contemporary waves of Catholic

---

[363] Grabačić 2010.

[364] See Brown 1975: 134, on a surge of transcendence, the 'disengagement of the sacred from the profane', in 1000–1200 CE.

[365] Cameron 2004.

[366] Roper 2016: 206; Scribner 2001b: 352–353; MacCulloch 2003: 109–123.

reform and Counter-Reformation.[367] This vision of it may be some-what blurred by recent historiography suspicious of Protestantism's role in modernisation narratives and concerned to restore the super-naturalism and strangeness of the Protestant worldview.[368] Much of this scholarship testifies to the inherent difficulties of inculcating cer-tain features of transcendentalism such as doctrinal knowledge.[369] Reformers working among rural parishes even close to major urban centres of Lutheranism in Germany could first report dismay at how little comprehension of Christianity was evinced by the peasantry and then how difficult it was to embed a reformed understanding of it amongst them.[370] We have also learned how incomplete the Protestant project of 'disenchantment' was in itself, how early moves were some-what blunted or reversed over time.[371] When Alexandra Walsham refers to the 'processes of adaptation that facilitated the rehabilitation of aspects of the medieval economy or system of the sacred in a distinctively Protestant guise', this may be taken as an expression of the fact that Protestantism was also of course moulded by the corruga-tions of the immanentist mind.[372] It too failed to shut the door of revelation.[373] Just as Christianity attempted to clear away the crowded field of pagan metapersonhood only to repopulate it with saints, angels, and demons, so forms of Protestantism tried to sweep it clean

---

[367] See Eire 2016: 744–754, for highly pertinent ideas of 'desacralization'; Cameron 2010: 207, on the transformed theology of miracles; Hendrix 2000 on this period as one of Christianisation or re-Christianisation; Nowakowska 2018: 222, on 'a paradigm shift in ... the very concept of orthodoxy'.

[368] Rublack 2005; Lotz-Heumann, 2017: 692–696. The work of Robert Scribner, who emphasised the immanentist qualities of life before and after the Reformation, was influential here. Scribner 1987: 13, referred to these qualities as 'crypto-materialism'.

[369] Yet at the same time, the current consensus is that much of late medieval society was profoundly Christianised – and therefore in one sense, transcendentalised, characterised by salvific hunger, for example – even in rural areas (Kümin 2016; Moeller 1972: 25; Van Engen 1986). This, of course, is partly why the message of reformist thinkers made sense in some areas.

[370] Parker 1992; Dixon 1996. Contrast with Scribner 1982: 4–5, on urban reception.

[371] Rublack 2005: 156.

[372] Walsham 2008: 526, for whom Christianity was subject to 'cycles of desacralization and resacralization, disenchantment and re-enchantment.' Compare Martin 2005: 3, on Christianisations and recoils.

[373] On Protestant prophets: Lotz-Heumann 2017: 694–695; popular stories of Luther as endowed with supernatural powers: Rublack, 2010: 151.

once more only to leave providence howling through the landscape and battling with the devil.

This story of reform and the immanentist digestion of reform could drop down a level to an analysis of certain sects of Protestantism. The most striking account here would concern Pentecostalism, now the fastest growing branch of Christianity in the world, in which the Holy Spirit takes the starring role in the drama of immanent power, making visible and real that which had been hidden, and the faith is once again returned to a mechanism for healing, exorcism, prophecy, and the bestowal of worldly fortune.[374] Or the story could move up a level to consider Islam as a seizure and reassertion of transcendent monotheism, and Sikhism likewise.[375] Contemporary Islamic reform may be seen as a reaction to the great compromises made with immanentism and other social realities during its journey of pre-modern expansion.[376]

In Buddhism, the impulse of reform is less visible before the modern period insofar as it less often took the form of politically explosive movements, and insofar as the whole area of immanentist relations was far less problematised to begin with.[377] Nevertheless, it is discernible in the ceaseless imperative to purify the monastic orders, to hold them to their adherence to the ascetic principles and their knowledge and understanding of the canon. It is evident in the steps taken to reintroduce higher ordination from other regions, and to ensure that correct versions of the canonical texts are reproduced and circulated. It is revealed whenever a particularly ascetic new order of forest monks is created or acquires authority.[378] And the elevation of the Mahāvihāra tradition in Sri Lanka and its establishment across the Theravada world may itself be seen as a project of reform reasserting the primacy of the Pali canon and a conservative text-oriented vision of truth.[379] Indeed, in the flowering of Pali literature in the twelfth and thirteenth centuries, Alastair Gornall sees a reformist attempt to return to the 'essential meanings' (*sārattha*) of the canonical texts that later

---

[374] Ellis and ter Haar 2007: 52–53; Peel 2016; Robbins 2004: 114.
[375] Wiesner-Hanks 2015.
[376] Kim 2007: chapter 6, on the ethicisation and problematisation of metapersons in a Yogyakarta village.
[377] For 'Protestant Buddhism' in the nineteenth century, see Gombrich and Obeyesekere 1988, but this was partially in response to Christian influence.
[378] Charney 2006.   [379] Collins 1990.

commentaries had obscured, a purified and systematised form of the *dhamma*.[380] In late eighteenth- and early nineteenth-century Siam following the fall of Ayutthaya, 'there was a radical shift in the interpretation of Buddhist thought, a process of reformation' involving canonical fundamentalism and stripping out traditional practices that obscured 'true Buddhism' as King Mongkut referred to it.[381] This impulse – which appears to predate the impact of obvious Western intellectual influences – also shaped Lankan Buddhism through the importation of the Siam Nikaya, while the Sudhamma monks played a similar role in Burma.[382]

In Japan, a newly intense focus on salvation had emerged in the Kamakura schools of Buddhism (Pure Land, Nichiren, Zen) originating in the late twelfth and thirteenth centuries but attaining their peak influence in the fifteenth and sixteenth. The first two sects empowered lay society to pursue salvation in a more direct and single-minded manner, and thereby posed a challenge to the established 'esoteric' system of compromise with immanentist tradition. The new sects might even be repudiated for their disregard for the *kami* (gods).[383] It was with some reason that the Jesuit Alessandro Valignano perceived the radical True Pure Land Buddhism (*Jōdo Shinshū*) as akin to Lutheranism.[384]

While engaged in the business of religious taxonomy, it may be in order to briefly reflect on the relationship between immanentism and discourses of philosophical monism that developed within certain transcendentalist religious fields. In the first place, the two must be seen as distinct, not least because the first is a form of religious behaviour and the second is the product of intellectual ratiocination. An Islamic example of the latter would be Ibn al-'Arabī's (d. 1240) pantheistic concept of *waḥdat al-wujūd*, the 'oneness of being' in the Islamic tradition, in which 'there was no sharp separation between scripture and cosmos or self and divinity'.[385] The Indic and East Asian

---

[380] Gornall (forthcoming).   [381] Hallisey 1995: 48.
[382] Blackburn 2001; Charney 2006: 13, 28, 48, passim, also linking these movements to various 'early modern' developments.
[383] A counter discourse of Japan as 'the Land of the Gods' developed partly in reaction: Kuroda 1996: 367–382.
[384] Orii 2015: 202.
[385] Moin [MS], noting Ibn Taymiyya's criticism of this as 'breaking from scriptural Islam in an attempt to conceive of the cosmos as the immanent divine'. Thanks to Azfar Moin and Francis Robinson for discussion.

traditions have a particular tendency to generate monistic concepts (such as Dao or Brahman). In Mahayana Buddhism, the notion of the supreme Buddha-body (*dharmakāya*) allowed the Buddha and his teachings to be conceived as a substratum of the cosmos.[386] These may be attributed to the inventiveness of the rationalising mind when faced with the paradox of the transcendentalist–immanentist boundary, or the very yearning to attain that transcendent realm on the part of mystics and philosophers.[387] A future project of comparative research might consider the extent to which the history of these intellectual developments proceeded essentially independent from de facto immanentism, or as post hoc rationalisations of it, or even helped to facilitate it.[388]

Supplementary Note: Christian Readings of Immanentism

How much of the distinction between transcendentalist and immanentist traditions was apparent to Christian missionaries? In their own faltering, often ignorant manner, missionaries did tend to register that there were some profound differences between the *kind* of thing that Christianity was and the relationships people had with supernatural beings and forces in parts of the world such as sub-Saharan Africa or Oceania. However, scholarship tends to consider the master concepts of the missionary, such as idolatry, superstition, and paganism, as obstacles to ethnological thought rather than as vehicles for genuine understanding. 'Idolatry', for example, may be taken to reduce cosmology to mere nullity, a spiritual void defined by what it lacks.[389] The pejorative function seems essential to these terms but even once it has been excised there is no doubt that they flatten and coarsen cultural variety profoundly.

---

[386] Rambelli and Reinders 2012: 8 (and note 16); Ooms 1985: 84–85, 94–104, on monistic dimensions to early modern Japanese thought.

[387] Religious experiences and meditation/yogic practices, help drive monistic apprehensions because so often the results are described as a dissolution of the boundaries between self/other, and matter/non-matter.

[388] Hence, for the latter, Ibn al-'Arabī as basis for Sufism.

[389] Miller 1985: 40, analysing European discourse on idolatry as 'nullity and an immanence in the religious realm, a violation of the transcendent nature of divinity', as also Baum 1999: 9, Ranger 1975: 4–5. However, also see Landau 1999: 24, on missionaries producing 'African religion(s)' intent on finding rivals.

Yet, from a rather distant comparative perspective, we may concede that missionaries in nineteenth-century Oceania were not wrong to conclude that the sincerity with which people related to their 'idols' did not entail a love of them in the Christian vision of worship, nor a counsel of morality in the Christian manner of rectitude.[390] And when earlier missionaries and travellers in West and Central Africa commented in confusion that they couldn't find 'religion'; that they weren't sure if the natives had religion as opposed to sorcery; that locals did not have notion of an afterlife or of sin; that their notions of deities seemed inextricable from actual objects or places; that people could be treated with the kind of awe which seemed fit only for a god; these observers were not only repeating prejudices but were also expressing an encounter with discomfiting realities.[391] None of this absolves the historian from the usual responsibility of source criticism.[392] Naturally, missionaries were influenced by a weighty discursive tradition about paganism that derived from the polemics of early Christian writers. But this was not necessarily inapposite: a core feature of 'paganism' is its orientation towards the elicitation of earthly benefits.[393]

Consider Sheldon Dibble's long discussion of the difficulties besetting the translation of the Christian message into the vernacular in Hawaii:

To these gods, of course, they attach the same attributes which pertain to them here on earth. If a missionary then wishes to speak of the high and holy God, what terms shall he use? There is no term in the language ... He wishes to say – self-existent and eternal: – the Sandwich Islanders ... had no such ideas and no such terms. He wishes to say holy: – the Sandwich Islanders had no notion of holiness and no word for it. He wishes to express God's justice, - they had some idea of justice but exceedingly inadequate, and their word for it was equally inexpressive.[394]

---

[390] See Davies 1961: 65, on Pomare.
[391] Ribeiro, 1 August 1548, Kongo, MMA XV: 163; de Marees (1987) [1602]: 72; d' Elbée (1671) II: 441–442. See Hastings 1994: 325–326 (also noting, however, another missionary tendency to perceive theism). Compare Chirino 2000 [1696]: 233, on the Philippines: 'And so they do not make sacrifices for devotion or religion, but rather for curiosity of knowing the outcome and as a way to see if they will have good health.' (Thanks to Natalie Cobo.)
[392] For example, on Dibble 1839: 113–130, see Weir 1998: 161–163.
[393] Bartlett 2007: 68; Gunson 1978: 210; Ryan 1981: 519–538. For attempts to retrieve the concept of paganism, see Fuglestad 2006; Auge 1982.
[394] Dibble 1839: 136, and 140–142.

Stripped of its judgementalism, this conveys an intimation of how unprecedented notions of eternity, ineffability, ethical assessment, salvation, and all the other hallmarks of transcendentalist religiosity were in the pre-existing cultural imagination. Indeed, as they reveal how much the old mentality persisted underneath the layering of Christian education (why did these converts feel so lightly the great burden of guilt?), such comments underline one of the central contentions of this book: that even the transcendentalist religions had first to obtain victory within the terms set by immanentist worldview.

In 1625, the Cape Verdean-Portuguese merchant, André Donelha described the Manes of the Sierra Leone region as having no religion or faith:

> They make idols for war, rain, sunshine, for famine or for whatever else they wish to undertake; and if things do not turn out as successfully as they hope, they throw the idols down and beat them and make new ones, or else they take up the original ones and implore them, caressing them and placing roasted and boiled meat, rice, wine and fruit before them in order to make them happy...'[395]

This was written close to the beginning of a long European tradition of discourse about the 'fetish', which tends now to be analysed for what it says about Europeans themselves (indeed it has been ascribed to a Protestant preoccupation, which the testimony of Donelha, as a Catholic certainly complicates).[396] But it clearly reflects something germane to parts of West and Central Africa in the importance given to the concrete effects produced by man-made items as repositories of immanent power. It also tells us something germane about immanentism per se – that is, if historians are willing to follow anthropologists in taking seriously Alfred Gell's resurrection of the concept of idolatry.

---

[395] Cited in Newitt 2010: 81. Compare d'Elbée 1671, II: 441; de Marees 1987 [1602]: 71.

[396] Pietz 1985, 1987; MacGaffey 1994: 264–266. It is reminiscent of the more famous report of Willelm Bosman 1705: 368 (see Sansi 2011: 31).

2 | *Religion as the Fabric of the State*

At first men had no kings but the gods.

Jean-Jacques Rousseau, *The Social Contract*[1]

There are kingly beings in heaven where there are no chiefs on earth. For Hobbes notwithstanding, the state of nature is already something of a political state. Indeed, it follows that, taken in its social totality and cultural reality, something like the state is the general condition of humankind. It is usually called 'religion'.

Marshall Sahlins, Inaugural Hocart Lecture[2]

This means: both before and after the advent of the state, there was the imaginary state.[3] Long before earthly governments emerged, heavenly governments had been called upon to order human affairs. According to Sahlins, even the most small-scale and egalitarian of societies in the historical and anthropological record, fiercely antagonistic to the emergence of lasting projects of human domination, have readily submitted to a hierarchy of superhuman beings encircling them. These metapersons demanded tribute, owned the land and its products, laid down laws, prescribed norms, and punished evildoers.[4] In this light it is not surprising that when people started to build their own edifices of domination they did so by referring to the supernatural structures already in place.

---

[1] Rousseau [1762] 1968: 176.   [2] Sahlins 2016.

[3] In some areas of scholarship statehood is seen as a necessarily modern phenomenon, but in a large swathe of global historical and sociological writing it has a much broader meaning. I follow Tilly 1990: 1 (and Lieberman 2009: 9, footnote 17): 'A coercion-wielding organization that is distinct from household and kinship groups and that exercises priority over all other organizations within a substantial territory.' This does not imply any emic reification of the state as an impersonal entity, but it does imply a set of institutions that allow rulers to intervene in the lives of their subjects by laying down laws and regulations and systematically extracting revenue.

[4] Graeber and Sahlins 2017.

The fabric of the earthly state is of course fashioned from many different materials – the arts of war and diplomacy, administration, and commerce – that may seem on the face of it to have little to do with religion, and this chapter does not advance some form of religious determinism. It may be worth speculating whether the ruler will be forced to rely more upon religion the more these other materials are in short supply. But it is quite difficult to argue for any general principle to that effect. Rather, the religious realm seems perennially unignorable for rulers or would-be rulers of the pre-modern world, for two reasons. First, the basic immanentist proposition that human flourishing lies in the hands of metapersons applies to politics and war no less than it does to agriculture. The more strongly this proposition grips the imagination the more that ritual activity will be seen as *creating* the power of the ruler – at the deep-lying level of supernatural agency – rather than merely reflecting, representing, or legitimating it. In Chinua Achebe's novel, *Arrow of God*, the origin story of the community of Umuaro tells of six villages coming together to ward off slave hunters by hiring 'a strong team of medicine-men to install a common deity for them'. From that day on they were never defeated.[5]

Men make the deity, to be sure, but it is the deity that makes them powerful. Of course, this is also a parable of the way that cooperation and emergent political hierarchy find their origins in common cult. The second reason, then, why religion was unignorable for rulers, then, is that it stretched out before them as a vast reservoir of *social power*. This was evident in the capacity of religion to (a) distinguish the rulers' status, (b) ground their moral authority, and (c) discipline, motivate, and cohere their subjects.[6]

The problem for any ruler, however, is that these forms of power might be controlled by ritual specialists or by rivals and rebels in the political arena. State construction is commonly understood as the struggle to monopolise violence or surplus produce, but in the pre-modern world it was no less serious a struggle to monopolise the supernatural and social powers of religion. In early nineteenth-century Tahiti, the missionary John Davies was caught up in the events surrounding the attempt of a dynasty to claw its way to pre-eminence,

---

[5] Achebe 2010: 15.

[6] The religious realm also often provided powerful forms of institutional and administrative power; this is discussed in this chapter, but is not a major theme of this volume (see Strathern 2016).

and his journal entries therefore stand as an unwitting record of what the attempt to fashion the basis for a state can look like: amidst all the violence and diplomacy, matters of ritual import – from chasing god images to arranging sacrifices – loom large.[7]

The Social Power of Religion

Status and Stratification

It is not hard to see why rulers may be drawn to sacralise and therefore exalt their status for its own sake: prestige, honour, and regard are inherently attractive. But whether they mean to or not, rulers are also thereby serving to legitimise their position through the assertion of sheer ontological superiority. This is chiefly explored in terms of the qualities of the monarchical role itself – as divinised or righteous – in Chapter 3. But this process may be placed in the context of a more general stratification of society that normally accompanies the emergence of states and empires. Kingship tends to emerge hand in hand with a wider ruling class which is able to control the deployment of violence and establish privileged access to the fruits of the land or trade. It is striking that in two nascent sites of primary state construction discussed in the companion volume, fifteenth-century Kongo and eighteenth-century Hawaii, an elite class had broken away from the mass of commoners relatively recently (and in both a lowest class of 'slaves' or outcasts had formed too).[8] In Kongo we know little about how this elite status was conceived before the advent of Christianity, which soon became a principal distinguishing feature of it. In the case of Hawaii, we can observe how far indigenous religion was deployed in this project before the arrival of Christianity: the commoners were denied genealogies while the *ali'i* set themselves apart by their genealogical closeness to the gods, which sent *mana* running through their veins.[9]

So religion may be implicated in two dimensions of state construction simultaneously, and these may well conflict: the *unification* of subjects such that people from diverse clans, lineages, or linguistic groups are gathered together into a single moral community, and the *division* of

---

[7] Davies 1961.   [8] *CK*. On the *kauwā* in Hawaii: Kirch 2010: 34.

[9] *CK*, compare Aztecs: Carrasco 2011: 49–50: Moctezuma I (r. 1441–1469) 'used this sacred prestige to divide his society internally so that the commoner class were forced into legal subservience to the noble class'.

subjects such that inequalities of political and economic advantage are rendered normative. The consequences of the importation of the 'Oro cult in Tahiti could stand as microcosm of the tensions that may result. The 'Oro cult helped drive the ascension of the warring aristocracy (*ari'i*) over that of the other ranks of society, but by the first decade of the nineteenth century this had given rise to discernible resentment.[10] Moreover, the corporate distinction of the *ari'i* was itself an obstacle to anyone intent on breaking through into unique paramountcy. A principal engine behind the development of ever more extravagant forms of royal sacralisation is the need for kings to distinguish themselves from the wider ruling class with whom they must both identify and transcend, and on whom they must depend and overmaster.

Moral Authority and Legitimation Theory

Nothing appears more surprizing to those, who consider human affairs with a philosophical eye, than the easiness with which the many are governed by the few; and the implicit submission, with which men resign their own sentiments and passions to those of their rulers. When we enquire by what means this wonder is effected, we shall find, that, as FORCE is always on the side of the governed, the governors have nothing to support them but opinion. It is, therefore, on opinion only that government is founded; and this maxim extends to the most despotic and most military governments, as well as to the most free and most popular.

David Hume, *Of the First Principles of Government*[11]

Numa [Pompilius] ... pretended to have private conferences with a nymph who advised him about the advice he should give to the people. This was because he wanted to introduce new institutions to which the city was unaccustomed, and doubted whether his own authority would suffice. Nor in fact was there ever a legislator who, in introducing extraordinary laws to a people, did not have recourse to God, for otherwise they would not have been accepted, since many benefits of which a prudent man is aware, are not so evident to reason that he can convince others of them.

Niccolò Machiavelli, *The Discourses*[12]

---

[10] Newbury 1967: 492.   [11] Hume 1987 (1777): 32.
[12] Machiavelli, *Discourses* I. 11 (1970: 140–141); see Stroumsa 2010: 140–141, for similar seventeenth-century views.

One of the reasons why the 'Oro cult exacerbated social tensions in the Society Islands is that it involved increasing recourse to human sacrifice.[13] This is an extreme example with which to make the point: that projects of status assertion must usually be articulated within a moral framework in order to be truly compelling. The moral framework which the exercise of power weaves around itself may be understood through the concept of legitimation. In the scholarship of the Indic world, this analytical language has been identified as problematic.[14] As should already be abundantly clear, legitimation is far from the only way of conceiving the relationship between rulership and religion; indeed, deployed by itself, it is an impoverished one. Nevertheless it remains an indispensable means of making sense of how kingship functions and the social consequences of how it is represented. The alternative is to imagine elite authority as simply a matter of brute coercion.

Four critiques of legitimation theory are worth addressing. First, does it assume that religion has to be manipulated in a conscious and cynical manner, as if rulers needed to step outside of their cultural inheritance in order to manipulate it?[15] The great bulk of sociological theory as to how the exercise of power is naturalised in society makes no such assumption. The way that the norms, values, and behavioural habits of hierarchy are suffused through the everyday lives of subjects is not reducible to individual strategising.[16] The urge to articulate rulership within the terms of a moral narrative does not need to arise from an attitude of insincerity.[17] For that matter, neither does legitimation theory require that subjects be endowed with an attitude of

---

[13] CK.

[14] Present in an extreme form in Pollock: 2006: 517–524. I have rarely found the concept so problematised in all other areas of scholarship.

[15] Pollock 2006: 517–518.

[16] See Bell 1992: 83–85, 190, on Antonio Gramsci. Note Pierre Bourdieu's (1977: 73) definition of habitus, which is apparently goal oriented in one sense, but which is 'collectively orchestrated without being the product of the organising action of a conductor'.

[17] Of West African rulers, Peel 1987: 108, notes, 'There had to be some independent strength in the religious ideas drawn upon. Religion had this power because it was already the shared idiom in which both chiefs and people confronted the pains and anxieties of the human situation.' 'If this was the bottom line of their reality, on what else could rulers better seek to build structures of higher obligation and control – but themselves remain constrained by its premises?'

blanket sincerity: what is really in play, as Ernest Gellner has argued, is their calculations about how others will behave.[18] In that sense, it is not so much whether one really believes that the king is a deity incarnate that matters, but how one expects others to act in relation to the king given that this vision is reliably acceded to in public.[19]

Second, does it assume that the principle of monarchy itself is ever in jeopardy unless sustained by regular doses of ideological fortification?[20] In some areas where *primary* state construction was underway, it is possible to see the cultural elaboration of kingship as involving an active disruption of the social values of egalitarianism and kinship. Moreover, the acceptance of any one form of kingship – or indeed any hierarchy – is not best seen as the product of an inevitable, natural, or timeless disposition, but rather one fashioned through generations of symbolic labour.[21] But it is true that the threat to kings of established dynasties rarely comes in the shape of a threat to kingship per se. If the nature of their authority remains a live concern, then, it is usually because they are in competition for the loyalties of their subjects with local lords, aristocracies, rival princes – and also religious specialists who might translate their social power into political opportunity. A Polynesian chief facing an upstart whose prowess indicates the *mana* coursing through him; a Japanese warlord facing the determined resistance of a fortified town held by the True Pure Land Buddhist sect; a Thai king facing a rebellion led by a monk wreathed in millenarian smoke: all would be compelled to wrestle with the force of religious ideas embedded deep within the fabric of political life.[22]

Third, is legitimation theory a species of structural functionalism, in which every act of cultural production is identified as a buttress of the status quo?[23] No: a discourse of legitimation is a sword that swipes both ways – it may be wielded to undercut the position of incumbents

---

[18] Gellner 1991: 94–99.

[19] Compare Scott 1990 on the 'public transcript'; Lukes 1979: 650–651.

[20] As implied in Pollock 2006: 522–523.

[21] Although, given the ubiquity of kingship as a form of state construction, it is probably facilitated by some basic human instincts and propensities.

[22] See *CK* for detailed examples of all of these.

[23] In relation to any given item of cultural production, legitimation theory may be an unnecessary and insufficient mode of interpretation, but in relation to understanding the relationship between cultural production and the construction of royal power per se it is necessary (but insufficient).

as well as to chop it into shape.[24] And, in practice theory fashion, it serves to constrain and shape the exercise of power as well as to naturalise it.[25] Religious traditions form part of the 'meta-institutional' framework, to use Armando Salvatore's phrase, which establish the norms governing how power and the purpose of power may be conceived; the 'master fictions' as Geertz describes them, by which the social order lives.[26]

Fourth, does the concept of legitimation invoke a legalist mentality, a world of constitutions and explicitly formulated criteria by which rulers are consciously assessed? The origins of the word might indeed point in that direction. However, most scholars mean by it something much more general than that – something closer to David Hume's 'opinion': the mental, cultural, and behavioural structures that allow power to be exercised with consent.[27] As Azfar Moin's examination of Safavid and Mughal kingship has shown so strongly, these cannot simply be equated with the texts and arguments of elite rationalisation.[28] Legitimacy is forged in the *mentalité*, habitus, and bricolage of the population at large, and evidence for it may be discerned in works of art, domestic rituals, or the behaviour of the crowd.[29]

The consistency and energy with which the most hard-headed rulers everywhere have attended to the elaboration of their role in religious terms is a strong clue as to its political significance.[30] Nevertheless, that significance cannot be assumed to be present in any uniform manner: it is to some extent culturally and historically variable. In any case study, the relevance of legitimacy will wink in and out of sight – sometimes seeming vital to the course of events, at other times swept aside by coercive force and material interest. And naturally, there is usually a range of less obviously religious discourses and norms of legitimacy in

---

[24] Bardwell L. Smith 1978: 76.

[25] Skinner 1998: 105, 'What it is possible to do in politics is generally limited by what it is possible to legitimise.' On practice theory see Ortner 1984.

[26] Salvatore 2016: 7; Geertz 1983: chapter 6.

[27] This may work by endowing power with inevitability as much as morality: Berger 1969: 33–36.

[28] Moin 2012, but note that Moin does not use the term.

[29] At times, then, it pays to distinguish 'theoretical legitimacy' from 'operational legitimacy'.

[30] Moin 2012: 69, on the role of such public acts where rulers 'had to establish their dominion without a centralizing bureaucratic order and an enumerating, naming, and documenting state'.

play too – ancestry, principles of succession, good governance, etc. – which also helps to determine the acceptability of rule; the relative weight of these must also be assessed. Furthermore: in whose eyes does legitimacy matter? Is it only the wider ruling elite whose judgements signify or might the feelings of more ordinary people become relevant? These are all matters of empirical enquiry rather than theoretical determination.

The Discipline, Motivation, and Cohesion of Subjects

Machiavelli saw the deployment of religion as a foundational element of successful governance, not only by legitimising the ruler but also by making their subjects more amenable to rule – or enhancing their 'governmentality' to borrow a term from Michel Foucault.[31] This is the third dimension of the social power of religion, and it concerns the capacity of the ruler to reach into the souls of his or her subjects: to make them more loyal, obedient, law-abiding, and self-restrained; to motivate them to collective action, as in times of war; and to induce feelings of participation in an imagined community much wider than that of their face-to-face relations. There is not the space here to sound out the theoretical dimensions of these issues.[32] Instead, we may simply note how consciously our historical agents might address themselves to such concerns. For example, missionaries could be induced to flirt with a de facto relativism by being drawn into arguments about the capacity of different religious systems to render subjects more amenable to rule.[33]

That utility was perhaps most blatantly apparent to all concerned in the area of law.[34] The threat of supernatural sanction, and therefore its

---

[31] Foucault 1991. Though Foucault's own genealogy of governmentality began with anti-Machiavellian writers: Korvela 2012: 201. See also on Mesopotamia, Bernbeck 2008: 158. Michael Mann (2013, I: 357) refers to 'normative pacification'.

[32] Except to quote Pierre Bourdieu 1987: 126, referring to competition over religious power, where 'what is at stake is the *monopoly of the legitimate exercise of the power to modify in a deep and lasting fashion, the practice and world-view of lay people* by imposing on and inculcating in them a particular religious *habitus*. By this I mean a lasting, generalized and transposable disposition to act and think in conformity with the principles of a (quasi-) systematic view of the world and human existence.'

[33] See the cases of Hawaii, Japan, and Siam in *CK*.

[34] A flourishing subfield of the cognitive science of religion focuses on the relationship between state construction and 'Big Moralising Gods' – as a means

capacity to serve the functions that the police and judiciary fulfil today, was very real.[35] This may be indicated by a very small and plain example. During one of his visits to Hawaii in 1815–1818, the sailor Peter Corney found that a shaving pot and a carving knife had been stolen from him. His remedy was to visit a Hawaiian priest; criers were sent out to convey that if the items were not returned to him the guilty parties would be 'prayed to death'; the following morning he found them duly returned. He commented that this was an excellent means of governance, 'As superstition prevails so strongly among them, as to be the only basis on which to build certain laws.'[36] The Capuchin friar Girolamo Merolla da Sorrento in late seventeenth-century Central Africa reported that ritual specialists dealt with cases of theft in a similar manner.[37] Or we might consider, in the coastal parts of this region, the use of fetishes to establish the trust on which commercial relations could be established with foreigners.[38] Compelling men to truthfulness was everywhere a function of metapersons, whether present in idols or not; divine vengeance was as vital an element of oath making in Siam and Japan as it was in Oceania and Africa.[39] It should not be underestimated how seriously and openly contemporaries could identify such oaths as the foundation of social order in making honest vassals of samurai and loyal officers out of the Siamese nobility.[40]

In 1612, the shogun of Japan, Tokugawa Ieyasu, wrote to the Spanish viceroy of Mexico to instruct him on these matters. Japanese society had always depended on the sanction of metapersons, he notes, and Christianity would only disrupt these arrangements:

We stand firm in the way of loyalty and duty between ruler and minster. Agreements between states we do not alter or change and in all things we swear by the kami, thereby making proof of our faith. Those who are able to

---

of allowing large communities of nonrelated people to escape the free-rider problem (e.g., Lovins 2015).

[35] Also see Sahlins 1981: 45. There is naturally much debate as to how the invocation of supernatural sanction works, on which see McKay and Whitehouse 2015.

[36] Corney 1896:104.

[37] Merolla 1814 [1692]: 272. These mechanisms occur outside the state too: Janzen 1982 on the Lemba initiation society.

[38] Graeber 2005; Sissons 2014: 102–105.   [39] CK.

[40] Japan: Ravina 1999: 35; Mayo 2015: 45. Ayutthaya: La Loubère 1987 [1691]: 304; Cushman 2000 passim; Wyatt 2001.

maintain uprightness will receive their reward; those who greedily do evil will receive their punishment.[41]

Or consider this inscription engraved on the pedestal of a bronze Buddha image from the kingdom of Lan Sang in mainland Southeast Asia: 'If someone is full of greed and comes to violate this royal edict, this person will be on fire in hell for four lifetimes. Don't be ambitious and insolent; don't be daring and violate the stipulations of the royal edict.'[42] Clearly, one did not need to be Machiavelli to recognise the utility of such invocations for improving the governability of one's subjects.

If religious cognition is not merely a by-product of the will to order social relations, in the pre-modern world it was nearly always used as the foundation stone of that project. And if it is not a by-product of the will to power, it is a found object that few who are hungry for dominion can resist picking up and brandishing. To recognise that religion may serve social and political functions is not to yield to a classic form of structural functionalism, however. The latter has long been criticised for its tendency to assume that any given cultural feature works its cohesive magic at the level of some organic whole community such as a tribe or a polity. The social power of religion is better seen as a kind of energy that state builders may try to harness and contain for their own ends but which rebels and local intermediaries, subgroups and splinter sects may also channel in order to break apart the larger order.[43]

The Dispersal and Agglomeration of the Social Power of Religion

To expand on this last point, the task of the ambitious ruler is to monopolise as far as possible all the resources that political power feeds upon, from pools of warrior elites to the flow of surplus produce. The more mobile, fluctuating, and dispersed these resources are the more difficult that task becomes. Many an empire has crumbled to dust because it has failed to adjust nimbly enough to the changing nature of economic growth, for example – as where a great edifice of agrarian

[41] Shimizu 1977: 282–283. I am very grateful to Richard Bowring for translating this extract.

[42] Grabowsky 2007:131. The edict sought to prevent the misappropriation of monastic endowments.

[43] That is, the social power of religion is not maintained reliably at any one level of social organisation.

revenue extraction fails to capture a gush of wealth from seaborne trade such that local princelings on the coast are left to fatten themselves upon it. So too the social power generated by a new religious form may be translated into political potency by upstart notables if the centre does not control it first.[44]

The purpose of this chapter is not to demonstrate the objective superiority of either immanentism or transcendentalism as vehicles of state formation. There are simply too many variables governing the success of any such project for the influence of religion itself to be isolated with conviction, and it is obvious that state builders will snatch at whatever kinds of cultural fabric are available in order to advance their cause: 'there is more than one way to skin a cat'. Not only is the historical record too messy in that sense, but it is also too consistent, in that many of the core patterns are essentially universal. The most basic pattern, for example, is simply the constant state of mutual jealousy which haunts the relationship between religious specialists and political specialists. Political agents naturally tend to be the more bullying, constantly reaching into the religious sphere for the riches of social power it may possess. But religious specialists often understand well enough that in the right circumstances they can exchange those riches for political influence themselves.

Nevertheless, I shall suggest that immanentism and transcendentalism present somewhat different kinds of problems and solutions to the state builder. In the eyes of rulers, the importation of transcendentalism could appear as a means of adopting a new approach to harnessing the social energies of religion. In reality, and from a much longer-term perspective, it also brought its own tensions and travails in train.

A small clarification before proceeding: from an emic perspective, contenders must compete for both the supernatural and social powers of religion; from an etic perspective, claims to access the former only signify as an element of the latter.

Centralisation under the Conditions of Immanentism

A priori, immanentism would seem to imply an extreme decentralisation of the religious sphere, in which supernatural power is precisely

---

[44] Most visible where great projects of state have disintegrated: see the section 'Clerisies and rulers steal each other's clothes and plunder each other's realms'.

'mobile, fluctuating, and dispersed', broadly diffused across the land-scape and coagulating in certain cult objects or shrines, or inherent in mountains, lakes, trees, at the command of fertility spirits and the ghosts of village communities. Revelations as to how such power may be accessed also poured into the world relatively unimpeded, and no one could be sure exactly when and where they might emerge.[45] Yet, this disaggregation of the religious field, and the fluidity of move-ment across the political–religious boundary, also presented state builders with opportunities for gathering the social power of religion in their hands.

Political and Religious Specialists Distinguished and Conflated

'Immanentist' societies have usually generated distinctions between figures who specialise in religious activity (priests, prophets, witches) and those who have assumed political power (kings, chiefs, warlords). Indeed, such distinctions may be implicated in the fashioning of polit-ical office itself, as priests are called upon to provide the essential mechanism by which chiefly or royal status is conferred and conse-crated.[46] In such scenarios, priests are not merely the 'legitimators' of 'thugs' as Gellner put it, but also the vehicle by which 'thugs' are turned into communally acceptable officeholders.[47] Through such relations wider society imposes the norms and taboos by which it expects rulers to abide.[48]

A number of immanentist societies generated a distinct class of reli-gious specialists who specialise in revelation as opposed to ritual offici-ation, which the literature often refers to as 'prophets'.[49] In fact, it is not easy to ascertain the extent to which prophetism is an unusual reaction to contact with the transcendentalism-wielding outsiders, given that so

---

[45] See Ellis and ter Haar 2004: 88, on parts of contemporary Africa: 'For while secular government and politics may be managed with appropriate doses of patronage and coercion, the spirit world is less easy to govern, particularly in a continent where access to spiritual power is believed to be within the reach of anyone... This poses a constant threat to the ideological order and thus to political stability.'
[46] Quigley 2005b: 19 (though possibly over-Indianised).   [47] Gellner 1991.
[48] Schoffeleers 1992: 11; Gray 1990: 3–4. On governors subjected to priests in seventeenth-century Kongo installation rituals: Hilton 1985: 46–48.
[49] Evans-Pritchard 1956: 308; Firth 1970: 32.

much evidence comes from precisely such contact scenarios.[50] For present purposes, however, if we assume that such prophetic traditions are indeed autonomous elements of immanentism, they then testify to its capacity to provide quite radical critiques of the status quo inspired by utopian visions of possibility – particularly in periods of great societal upheaval and strain. To briefly adopt a teleological perspective, these could be considered as the kernels from which mature transcendental-isms elsewhere had sprouted. In Tahiti and Hawaii such liminal figures (*taura/kaula*) seemed to rise in significance as contact with the West increased.[51] The Hawaiian scholar David Malo described the *kaula* as able to foretell the death of a king or the overthrow of a government; they were 'a singular class of men; they lived separately from other men, and in solitary places ... their great thought was about the gods.'[52] Across Polynesia, indeed, such figures were quite distinct from the *marae* priests who served the cultic needs of the chiefs; one can even see the stock of the two types as rising and falling in inverse relation to each other.[53] In sub-Saharan Africa, meanwhile, prophet figures could spearhead movements of religious-cum-political purification against unpopular chiefs or witchcraft, as in the Mbona cult of the Lundu kingdom, which was focused on a murdered rain priest.[54]

In these ways, then, immanentism may certainly generate distance and tension between political and religious specialists. But as a rule, the distinction between the two is likely to be less marked, more readily overcome than is typically the case in transcendentalist traditions. Wyatt MacGaffey presents a fourfold schema of roles in the region of the historic kingdom of Kongo. He begins by distinguishing the *nganga* (magician) from the *ngunza* (prophet) by the fact that the former works through charms and offers his services in return for money, whereas the latter acts as a personal mediator of divine force in the public interest.[55] More pertinent is the next pair:

---

[50] Hefner 1993b: 9–13. Evans-Pritchard 1956: 310, concedes the possibility of Islamic influence on Nuer prophets.

[51] *CK*; Valeri 1985: 138–139; Oliver 1974: 1334–1335.

[52] Lyon 2013: 48. Compare Evans-Pritchard 1956: 305–308.

[53] Thanks to Nicholas Thomas for discussion. See Thomas and Humphrey's 'Introduction' to 1996: 6–8; Oliver 1974: 1336, on 'Oro-inspired prophet Tino's translation into political power.

[54] Present-day Malawi: Schoffeleers 1992; Ranger 1993: 78.

[55] MacGaffey 1977: 179. The distinction is slightly compromised by the possibility of Christian influence on the figure of the prophet: the two main historic

These two figures, prophet and magician, belong to an exclusive set of four power-bearing roles. The "chief" (*mfumu*), like the prophet, represents a hierarchical, authoritarian order, but is otherwise identified by the power to kill rather than to heal. The "witch" (*ndoki*) is also a killer, but he exercises his power in his own interest... Further scrutiny of the content of these roles reveals, besides these contrasts, many similarities. All four are popularly supposed to possess "the wisdom of darkness" and to be capable of seeing and moving "at night," in "the land of the dead," and therefore to be capable of modifying the states of being of ordinary persons. The common environment of all the roles in this set is their relationship to *mbevo*, the afflicted individual, whose affliction is healed by prophet or magician but caused by chief or witch.[56]

In essence then, it is not the type of power (e.g., 'secular' versus 'spiritual') that determines office, for all are marked out by access to the same sort of supernatural force which issues from the land of the dead; it is rather whether that power is exercised for private or public ends, and whether to kill or to heal. These are of course matters of argument and perception, and therein lies the potential for chiefs to be deemed anti-social, or to themselves launch widespread anti-witchcraft drives in order to establish their authority.[57]

Two ancestral figures of anthropology, James Frazer and A. M. Hocart, spent their careers elaborating the thesis that kingship arose first as a ritual device which only subsequently acquired political functions.[58] This is not best interpreted as a general prediction of how any one tradition of kingship actually came into existence.[59] But in a few parts of the world – invariably immanentist – where state construction has been relatively recent or nascent, scholars have indeed identified or speculated about cases where something like this has happened. James Frazer himself referred to rainmaker kings in parts of Africa and suggested that they could be murdered if they failed to produce the life-giving rains.[60] The work of Simon Simonse has managed to substantiate Frazer's claim for the southern Sudan region at least, documenting cases of regicide. Indeed there are clues that the

phenomena of prophetic movements discussed, Kimbanguism and the Antonine movement, were both influenced by Christianity.
[56] MacGaffey 1977: 179; 1986: 171.   [57] MacGaffey 1986: 175.
[58] Frazer 1994. Late nineteenth-century social science tended to recognise that the 'early stages of social evolution, the secular and the sacred are but little distinguished': Spencer 1898: 602.
[59] Graeber 2011b: 6.   [60] De Heusch 2005.

accumulation of material coercive force by rainmakers – by acquiring firearms, for example – was spurred by the need to protect themselves from the precariousness of the ritual situation they occupied, forever in empirical jeopardy.[61]

Across Polynesia, the chiefly title of *ariki* (as in *ali'i*, etc.) seems to have been a sacerdotal one originally, indicating that the differentiation of the elite had first rested on ritual expertise.[62] Among those Amazonian societies exhibiting more complex, ranked formations, the more powerful few were often shamans who oversaw ancestor-oriented life-crisis rituals.[63] The Assyrian monarch was original referred to as 'priest' or 'vicar' and only later as 'king'.[64]

Equally, actors whose role seems chiefly defined by their stock of political capital may well identify ritual activity as an important means of enhancing it. Among the peoples of Mount Hagen in late twentieth-century Papua New Guinea, the more dominant individuals ('big men') managed to achieve influence, wealth, and wives without establishing any more effective or heritable dominion approaching chieftaincy or 'rulership'. Their position was secured by oratorical prowess and the clever working of gift exchange – but they also took the lead in initiating and organising cults.[65] The big man Ru, mentioned in the previous chapter, was himself the recipient of the revelation that set off the Female Spirit Cult in the 1970s, and he was in a position to carry out the spirit's injunctions and channel social energy towards it because of his wealth in pigs. (Here the economy of ritual exchange with metapersons interlocked with the economy of ritualised exchange with persons.)[66] Elsewhere in the highlands, among the Paiela, 'the Sun [deity] and big man complete each other as "head". The sun speaks through the big man, sees through the big man.'[67]

The central point here is not the genealogy of kingship: it is simply the translatability of power across the boundary between the roles of 'political' and 'religious' specialists in immanentist systems.[68]

---

[61] Simonse 1992, 2005; Graeber 2011b: 11–12; also see de Heusch 2005: 28.
[62] Kirch 2010: 19. African examples of statehood emerging from priestly authority: Greene 1996:131; Boahen 1992: 412–413, 426.
[63] Hugh-Jones 1996.   [64] Tadmor 1986: 207.
[65] Andrew Strathern 1970: 571.
[66] Andrew Strathern 1993: 39–41. On specialist warriors (ramo) becoming priests in later life in Malaita, Solomon Islands, see Keesing and Corris 1980: 17, 21.
[67] Biersack 1991: 260.   [68] Hocart 1941: chapter VI.

Expansion and the Struggle Over Supernatural Power

But even if a chief or a prince has succeeded in gaining control of the ritual affairs of his own people, what will happen when he manages to extend his control over new territories inhabited by diverse groups with their own traditions in the hands of their own specialists?[69] This scenario is particularly pertinent for parts of Africa, for which scholarship often now prefers a picture of migrations, empire formation, and long-distance trade over that of discrete homogenous society–polities.[70]

A glimpse of what could result is afforded by a stretch of narrative in the Kano chronicle about the reigns of kings leading up to the arrival of Islam in this part of West Africa. The struggle over esoteric knowledge – in this instance a snake cult – is assumed to be a vital element of political control. It tells us that the sixth Sarki (king), Naguji, who was the first ruler to collect a land tax of one-eighth of the crop, found the people of Kano in revolt, so he executed their leaders, and the people there said, 'We are willing to follow you, O Sarki, because we must.' The Sarki said to them, 'If you are willing to follow me show me the secrets of this god of yours.'[71] When they refused, he punished them. Similar tussles characterised the reigns of the seventh and eighth kings, with the people refusing to yield because 'if we show him the secrets of our god we shall lose all our power and we and our generation will be forgotten'. The ninth is finally successful after a battle with a fire-breathing man holding a red snake.

This is oral tradition rendered into written form no earlier than the nineteenth century, but it is interesting not for its historical facts but for the politico-theological mentality it discloses.[72] Note, for example, the equation between secrecy and power. Above all, the tradition seems to make no distinction between the people's political independence and their relationship with local metapersons or, conversely, between the king's control over the people and his mastery over their snake god.[73]

---

[69] For example, Ranger 1975: 6.

[70] Ranger 1993; Fisher 1994; Ellis and ter Haar 2007; Peel 1968: 123.

[71] Palmer 1928: 101–102.

[72] Last 1980: 161–178; Hunwick 1993 on mid-seventeenth-century or nineteenth-century origination.

[73] Palmer 1928: 104. It is no coincidence that the ruling dynasty then sought to establish Islam decisively in the reign of the eleventh Sarki, Yaji (r. 1349–1385),

Indeed, Clyde Mitchell argued for a quite general model by which the fact of conquest would 'set up an ambiguous relationship between the victors and the vanquished since the victors have no direct communication with the spirits of the ancestors of the autochthons'.[74] Hocart, meanwhile, pointed out that the worship of spirits housed in sticks or clubs in Fiji was seen as incompatible with rule by the colonial office. Therefore 'the struggle between idolaters and iconoclasts is at bottom a struggle between local autonomists and centralizers'.[75]

The supernatural power held by local shrines and cults might threaten overlords in a more menacingly personal way. If royal power was conceived as propelled by the conduct of rites, so it was vulnerable to them too: those who sought rebellion or revenge might turn to witchcraft, the deployment of magical objects, or sacrifices in the precincts of recalcitrant shrines.[76] And the link between secrecy and power could also produce a certain instability, as political ascension invited suspicions of deception and concealment.[77] In any society that takes seriously immanentist principles, the recourse to the more 'magical' arts – ritual acts most directly concerned with empirical outcomes for the benefit of individual clients – in particular is likely to become a matter of political concern. The result could be a kind of supernatural arms race.[78] The emergence of the emperorship in Rome is associated with the rise of astrologers, who could provide a cosmic narrative by which individual ascension was rendered an operation of fate. But how then to prevent others from using astrology in the same way? Consultation of astrologers by others could be construed as conspiracy; the Roman emperor Tiberius could be depicted as 'shut up in Capri with a sort of "occult cabinet", whose chief job was to

---

with the arrival of Wangara traders, which forces another showdown with the chief pagan. On the actual chronology of Islamisation: Haour 2007: 110–115.

[74] Cited in Schoffeleers 1992: 8.

[75] Hocart 1970: 248; Sissons 2014: 54, 115. In the northwestern Himalayas (nineteenth and twentieth centuries), where communities were ruled by gods as kings, such deities were the vehicle for resistance to princely or colonial centralisation: Moran 2007.

[76] Francisco de Gouveia, 1 January 1564, MMA XV: 231, on death as always a product of sorcery, especially for rulers. Also Olfert Dapper in Ogilby 1670: 513 on Loango; Peel 2003: 80–82.

[77] Ferme 2001: 161: 'Both the exercise of power and the subjection to that power are more unstable in the presence of pervasive strategies of concealment.'

[78] Compare Melvin-Koushki 2016: 360, on the post-Mongol Islamic world.

locate those marked out for great destinies by the stars so they could be destroyed'.[79] In seventeenth-century Siam, the king's name was strictly interdicted: this was not only a symbol of his unreachable status but an anxious recognition that he was after all reachable by magical attack.[80]

The Consolidation of the Religious Field

Immanentism undoubtedly presents certain problems to the state-builder, then, but no bar to finding solutions. There were many ways in which the social power of religion could be yoked to the interests of rulers. This is what is meant by the 'consolidation' of the religious field hereafter: the process by which religious activity is both centralised and instrumentalised under the auspices of political authority. J. D. Y. Peel meant something similar when describing certain African societies as more 'geared-up' than others.[81] The main vehicle for the consolidation of the religious field in immanentism is the creation of a state cult devoted to the patron deity of the state or to the ruler himself, or his ancestors, or some such conflation of these. This is likely to benefit from an equation between the obvious success of the elite and the power of the spirits and deities they invoke.

Where rulers amassed substantial economic and coercive power, they were able to stage great ritual dramas at their capital set against the backdrop of sacred architecture that brooked no argument; they could even insist upon the enactment of mandated rituals in outlying areas.[82] The priests of state-sponsored cults might fan out across the territory in a hierarchy capped by the king himself or a subordinated appointee. Local metapersons could be incorporated within a vision of the supernatural realm that mirrored the political hierarchy created by human beings.

Indeed, immanentist priesthoods did not tend to emerge as powerful and enduring institutional structures autonomously from the state.[83]

---

[79] Barton 1996: 155. Compare also the 'magical' arms race under the Kamakura Shogunate in Japan (1185–1333) as described by Conlan 2003: 170–172.

[80] La Loubère 1987 [1691]: 345.   [81] Peel 1987.

[82] For example, Paramore 2016: 707–709, on Tang regulations for Ancestral and Heavenly shrines.

[83] One – probably minor – aspect of this was their potential vulnerability to empirical disconfirmation: Thornton 1992: 247–248, also referring to the absence of landed property: 'Priests lived at the pleasure of their clients, whether

This was because their moral authority was less distinct and commanding than that of their transcendentalist counterparts and because they were not drawn together by a common purpose defined by an 'offensive' revelation. Therefore, when priesthoods did become more unified, organised, and doctrine focused, it was usually as a function of the growth of state power itself.[84]

Furthermore, to the extent that the attainment of rulership was associated with productive access to the supernatural sphere, the chief or king was already a kind of priest. It was not therefore strange for the ruler to present himself or herself as the pinnacle of priestly endeavour. Amidst the nascent state construction of Ndongo in Central Africa, there was a high priest who presided over the cult of the local deities, but a Portuguese report from 1575 also remarked that the *ngola,* or king 'says openly that he is the lord of the sun and rain, and he orders it to rain or not to rain as it seems fit to him'.[85] His predecessor had taken advantage of a failure by rainmaker 'sorcerers' to bring rain during a drought, which had in turn allowed him to order the execution of eleven of them.[86]

Chinggis Khan followed a similar course of action. He owed his title to the visions of the Mongol's paramount shaman, Kököchü, who had spoken with Tenggeri ('the universal victory-granting sky god') and reported that 'all the face of the earth' has been given to the khan', in 1206. But, as Joseph Fletcher points out, 'Chinggis Khan could never rest secure in his mandate while such a shaman-turned-priest lived: what Tenggeri had given through Kököchü, might also be revoked through the same intermediary. The conqueror's best course of action would be to do away with him altogether, communicate directly with Tenggeri himself directly, and thus, becoming priest and emperor, monopolize both religion and empire.'[87] This, indeed, is what he did.

Sheldon Dibble overgeneralises in this account of Hawaii as he experienced it in the 1820s, but his main point holds:

they were rulers or others.' Compare the rough empiricism with which the Kubaka of Buganda dealt with priests (Peel 1977: 119).

[84] MacGaffey 1977: 186; 1986: 196, on a hierarchy of priests (*kitomi*) and spirits linking the regions in Kongo.

[85] Garcia Simões, 20 October 1575, MMA III: 134; Heywood and Thornton 2007: 79.

[86] António Mendes, 9 May 1563, MMA II: 509–510. Compare Shaka Zulu's expulsion of rainmakers from his kingdom: Schoffeleers 1992: 8.

[87] Joseph Fletcher 1986: 34–35.

The King was head of their superstitions, as well as of the state; the temples were his temples, the idols were his idols, the priests were his priests, the prophets were his prophets and he used the whole machinery to further his designs. If human enemies were needed for the altars the King's enemies were the persons to be sacrificed. The idolatrous system threw immense power into the hands of the chiefs.[88]

This system owed much to the innovations of Kamehameha (d. 1819), who was engaged in a significant centralisation of power – to the extent of pushing Hawaii into true statehood according to one analysis.[89] He was using religion 'as an engine of government'.[90] As Lord Byron observed in 1825:

In the early part of his reign, finding that the great and separate power of the priests was dangerous to his authority, especially since he was often absent from his capital, then fixed in Hawaii near Karakakua [Kealakekua], he had taken upon himself the office of priest as well as king.[91]

In the Makahiki rites of the New Year in honour of the god Lono, the tribute to the gods brought by subordinate parties was the means by which surplus produce was gathered by the centre.[92]

If immanentist priests were vulnerable to elite domination in this way, so too were the instantiations of the metapersons they represented. The more that metapersons are held to be immanent within icons or idols the more open they are to coercion and theft by political agents. A number of imperial centres have demanded that vassals yield present the images of their chief deities to their overlord: the Incas took the main idol of a newly conquered province to be installed in Cuzco and held as a hostage in case the province should rebel; when the Aztecs conquered a city, they burned down the temple of the patron

---

[88] Dibble 1843: 94. Predictably, he is also thinking of Catholicism in this context. Compare Niumeitolu 2007: 66–67, on Tonga.

[89] Grinin 2011: 250.

[90] According to Hira Bingham: Mykkänen 2003: 77; Mathison 1825: 442.

[91] Byron 1826: 42. Sahlins 1995: 134 (and see 71, 256), interprets this as reference to the Lono priests in particular. However, it is possible that the writer/editor has been confused by the operation of divinised kingship and rationalised it thus (compare, for example, Panoplist, 1820 [July], 334–335).

[92] Sahlins, 1995: 208–219; Kirch 2010: 61–63, 208–210; see *CK*. Compare Bloch 1987: 284, on the New Year rites of the Merina of Madagascar, the occasion for a tax 'the price of life' paid to the sovereign as recognition of his part in the ritual of renewal of life.

deity and locked its main idol into a special building in the central temple district of Tenochtitlan.[93] Thus were the gods overmastered by a higher form of supernatural agency. In emic terms, these were far from being merely symbolic acts: the subordination and incorporation of persons and metapersons were simply two sides of the same coin, as the Kano chronicle already intimated.

Normally, imperial immanentism could incorporate deities – whether old, or new, domestic or foreign – into a hierarchy rather peacefully, thanks to its universalist qualities. The Huarochirí manuscript from c. 1608, gives a striking account of how quickly and instrumentally Inca overlords could move to co-opt any new shoots of cultic growth at a local level. When a young woman discovered the deity Llocllay Huancupa, who then became the subject of a shrine, an 'emissary of the Inca' turned up and swiftly intervened. This emissary was endowed with the power to force any *huaca* to speak, and so Llocllay Huancupa was made to declare that he was a 'child' of Pacha Kamaq, a great state-sponsored *huaca*. This father deity had initially sent him to the village, then withdrawn him when he was not being taken care of, and had now returned him once more.[94]

But sometimes more blatant and aggressive policies could be adopted. The fifteenth-century Aztec ruler (*tlatoani*), Itzcoatl, who did much to elaborate the state cult, also seized hold of the books of the commoners and burned them. As David Carrasco says, 'The royal religion celebrating Huitzilopochtli, Quetzalcoatl and Tezcatlipoca would face no competition from local shamans and commoner priests.'[95] The Aztec patron deity, Huitzilopochtli, the hummingbird god of war, the sun, and human sacrifice, was a young upstart. Each morning, the rising of the sun reenacted the myth of his victory over his

---

[93] Rowe 1982; Also Rostworowski and Morris 1999: 788–789; Read 1994: 60–61. Compare: the rulers of Vijayanagara in southern India incorporated the deities of new lands by bringing their images to the capital: Rubiés 2000: 237. Jayavarman VII (r. 1181–1281) requested that vassal kings bring deity images to Angkor for ritual lustration at New Year ceremonies: Wyatt 2001: 17–18. On the less coercive practice of *evocatio* in Rome: Ando 2008: 128–148.

[94] Salomon and Urioste 1991: 101–102; Rostworowski and Morris 1999: 796. MacCormack 1991: 59–62, for diverse strategies in dealing with rival *huaca*s.

[95] Carrasco 2011: 49.

enemies: he threw them off the top of a mountain, just as sacrificial victims tumbled down the steps of the Templo Mayor.[96]

Among the Incas, and in many other societies, high deities of the heavens and dead kings have provided a central focus of state cult. The patron deity of the Incas was Inti, god of the sun, who was closely linked to the welfare of the emperor, the *Sapa Inca*.[97] Of the Inca ruler, Huayna Cupac, it was said that when he took office the first thing he did was to take on the position of the high priest of the Sun himself, visiting all the shrines and oracles in person.[98] Each province had to have a Sun temple, and had to set aside one part their lands and herds to the cult.[99] The Incas also established a highly elaborate cult of 'living ancestors' in the form of mummified kings who retained their own devotees and huge landholdings.[100] The prevalence of royal ancestor worship reflects the fact that it is an inflation of widespread notions about the powers of ancestors in general. King Agaja of Dahomey in West Africa (r. 1718–1740) in a 1726 letter to King George I of England, referred to his 'deceased Relations' who had the 'Power of revenging any Wrongs done to them by violating the Laws and Customs of their Country and Ancestors; and that it is in their Power also to prosper us, or frustrate our Designs; nay, even to take away our Lives'.[101]

Dahomey has been interpreted as exhibiting a classic problem of early state formation in which the authority of lineage groups was held in tension with the ambitions of the state.[102] In response, rulers sought to consolidate the religious field in various ways and produce the state as a common endeavour. The success of this may be glimpsed in the image of the king as a pot perforated by holes into which each subject had to sink their finger for the pot to hold water.[103] The reign of Tegbesu (1740–1774), marked an important step. He ruled over a

---

[96] My thanks to Emily Umberger for discussion. Defeated enemies were compelled to worship Huitzilopotchli according to Durán 1994: 155.
[97] One of the founding siblings of Cuzco, Ayar Oche, turned into an idol in order to propitiate their father the sun 'to protect them, increase their number, give them children and send good weather': Juan de Betanzos, 1996: 15.
[98] Gose 1996b: 402.
[99] Rostworowski and Morris 1999: 800; D'Altroy 2003: 148.
[100] Rostworowski and Morris 1999: 782.
[101] Law 2002: 267, and Heywood and Thornton 2009: 105. Compare the Sango cult in Oyo: Iliffe 1995: 89.
[102] Diamond 1996.   [103] Peel 1987.

cosmopolitan mix of populations who had been left bruised by the way he had crushed opposition to his succession, and he also perceived the necessity of creating centralised structures for dealing effectively with the slave trade. His response was a 'religious revolution' that involved a new control over the ancestor cult.[104] He also introduced an official cult of a high god known as Mawu, redefined as 'the ultimate controller of the universe, parent of the other gods'.[105] Thus he sought to overcome 'the disaffection of the people who were being swayed by the priesthoods of the autochthonous gods to resist the monarch ... and under the aegis of the powerful gods of the Sky to cement his rule and gain the spiritual submission of his subjects'.[106] As with the Incas, Aztecs, and in Hawaii, human sacrifice was also a crucial aspect of public religion. European commentators reported that by the 1770s the result was not simply fear, but a certain reverence for the king of this upstart polity.[107]

There are good reasons, then, why political transformation so often proceeds hand in hand with religious innovation. Michael Puett's analysis of sacred kingship in early China brings out the restless need of the 'First Emperor' of Qin (r. 220–210 BCE), who ruled a unified China for the first time, to appropriate the reserves of supernatural power strewn across the landscape. Bearing the title of the 'august god' (*huangdi*), he deployed a distinctly immanentist discourse in which he claimed divine powers and the command of lesser spirits. This entailed undertaking several tours of his vast territories and visiting all the principal regional cultic cites, personally performing many of the most significant sacrifices.[108] The Emperor Wu (r. 140–147 BCE) revived this approach, constantly touring the regions to sequester their ritual powers.[109]

---

[104] Yai 1993: 256–257: Tegbesu sets up an official priest over 'all the other priests of the inter-ethnic deities...introducing an embryo of verticality into a hitherto horizontal and a hierarchal religious system'. Also Law 1991.

[105] Melville J. Herskovits cited in Greene 1996: 127. Bay 1998: 315, refers to a male–female pair of gods, Mawu and Lisa, introduced by a high priestess and 'reign-mate' of Tegbesu.

[106] Herskovits 1938, II: 104; Law 1991: 67.

[107] Heywood and Thornton 2009: 101–103.

[108] Puett, 2002: 240. This was also an attempt to achieve immortality.

[109] Puett 2002: 245: The goal of the Qin-Han sacrificial system was 'for the ruler to contact personally as many divine powers as possible in order to obtain their power'.

It is important to note, however, that the state cult typically only coexists with other strata of religious life rather than crowding them out altogether – and this is especially so in empires covering vast tracts of land and numerous societies.[110] According to Michal Tymowski, across much of Africa, higher forms of rule sat on top of local, ethnic, lineage-based units which retained their individual cultic systems without being dissolved into a higher unity.[111] Over much of East Asian history and to this day, spirit mediumship, a profoundly immanentist practice, has dispersed ritual power far outside established orders of priesthoods. Despite the provincial diffusion of a state cult and the constant attempt of the Chinese centre to slot local deities into a heavenly bureaucracy, Chinese religious culture has therefore remained stubbornly open to 'the spontaneous eruption of supernatural power or *ling*'.[112] These have in turn played an important role in many countermovements against the state, including most strikingly the Taiping Rebellion (1850–1864). By this time, the Chinese state had been determinedly trying to control the religious field for almost 2,000 years. When the Spanish attacked the Inca empire, by contrast, it was only a few generations old. As gloriously elaborated as its state cult of the emperor as sun god was, and as etched into the sacred landscape its cosmic vision, still the local communities and their leaders (*kurakas*) had kept their old traditions which proved much more enduring once the Incas themselves fell.

Nevertheless, what should have emerged from this discussion is the dynamism and flexibility of immanentism, which certainly included potential for consolidation in the interests of a political elite.[113] If all such acts of consolidation risk stimulating resistance, the incorporative capacity of immanentism meant that it did not need to risk antagonising subjects through the imposition of homogeneity.[114] There were many ways of acknowledging, translating, and subordinating the deities of conquered peoples.[115] The diffuse, unmediated, and

---

[110] Woolf 2008: 249: The worship of emperors in Rome was organised separately within the various 'notionally autonomous religious systems'.
[111] Until the arrival of Islam: Tymowski 2011: 113–115.
[112] Dean 2017, leaning towards the scholarship that emphasises the 'ritual autarky' in parts of Chinese rural life.
[113] Descola 2013b: 42, on the flexibility of 'analogist' pantheons.
[114] Although states could try to control the religion arena and ban subversive cults. Rome: Woolf 2008: 248.
[115] Hume 2007 (1734–1737): 60.

decentralised nature of supernatural power was both problem and opportunity. On the one hand, the local roots of such powers could be deep indeed, and only ever overlain rarely than completely effaced by projects of state cult. Innovations, too, might erupt at any time. And yet, ritual specialists not in the service of the state remained relatively atomised and heterogeneous, stubborn in their particularity rather than unity. Ambitious rulers might be able to establish state cults in which they became, in effect, the highest religious authority in the land, the apex of a priestly hierarchy which functioned as an arm of government.

Centralisation under the Conditions of Transcendentalism

If the Buddha represents the absence of power, then he leaves a very large black hole that exerts immense gravitational forces on those in its orbit.

Craig J. Reynolds[116]

None of the transcendentalist traditions emerged in the centres of great empires, and figures such as Christ or the Buddha repudiated the ultimate significance of violence and politics.[117] And yet their fate was often to become the ideological *raison d'être* of imperial machines. What might explain the 'gravitational force' their nullity produced? The answer lies deep in the logic of legitimation itself. To seek legitimacy for a mode of action is to refer to something definitively 'beyond' it: it is the unusually radical and stark vision of what lies 'beyond' produced by transcendentalism that compelled attention. In other words, it was precisely because they did *not* arise as state cults that Buddhism and Christianity became such good cults of state. This paradox is explored more fully in relation to 'righteous kingship' in the following chapter, where the implications of transcendentalism for the status and moral authority of the ruler him or herself are more extensively addressed.

This chapter is the place to consider in quite abstract terms what transcendentalism offered to the ruler wishing to consolidate the religious field more generally. It is difficult to avoid noticing a striking isomorphism between transcendentalism and the project of the state: the former effects an unusually comprehensive form of dominance on

---

[116] Reynolds 2005: 200.   [117] Bellah 2011: 269.

the religious plane to match what the ruler hopes to achieve on the political one.[118] Both Buddhism and Christianity set out to dominate and relegate the field of supernatural power, and both came endowed with massive reserves of social power. The latter was particularly evident in emphatic discourses of unimpeachable moral authority, techniques of pacification, and governability; the new orders of hegemonic religious specialists organised into strong, centralisable institutions.

The Sovereignty of the Sky and the Sovereignty of the Earth

There is, of course, no *necessary* connection between transcendentalism and state expansion, monotheism and empire, or even between high gods and macrocosms – but it is more difficult to deny that there are intriguing associations. As examined above, the universal qualities of immanentism and the translatability of its metapersons worked to knit together the different religious fields of an expansionary state in a loose manner, and this expanded pantheon could be fashioned into a hierarchy in order to serve power more directly. And yet the establishment of the principal deity or pantheon of the ruling people as supreme already points the way towards the urge to make political and metapersonal realities commensurate.[119] Here I shall argue that transcendentalism whether in the form of monotheism, East/Central Asian visions of 'Heaven', or Buddhist encompassment, offers a particularly satisfying means of establishing that commensurability. However, we must begin by noting that the dynamic which these principles resolve is already visible in empire formation in immanentist ecologies.

Most basically, warrior elites may simply project the primacy of a war god in ever more assertive terms.[120] But many peoples have had conceptions of a deity of the sky or sun who is seen as particularly all-encompassing or abstract in their remit. Although these could be rather otiose or distant from human affairs, they also made natural candidates for deities who were granted unlimited sovereignty in order to articulate royal and, especially, imperial pretensions – as in Tegbesu of Dahomey's importation of the sky god Mawu or the Inca patron deity

---

[118] Pollock 2005: 411, is critical of political–cultural homologies.
[119] Compare Weber 1978, I: 416.
[120] As perhaps with Odin in Anglo-Saxon England (Yorke 2016: 245) or 'Oro in Tahiti.

of the sun, Inti.[121] When the Assyrian ruler, Sennacherib (r. 705–681 BCE) smashed apart Babylon (and its gods) he did so in the name of Ashur, who may have been a solar deity, but was now rendered almost henotheistically as 'king of all the gods, creator of himself, father of the gods, whose form developed in the deep, king of heaven and earth, lord of all the gods'.[122]

It is surely an extension of this same urge that we see finally expressed in monotheism. The Abrahamic monotheism we know today was pre-empted by the brief flash of monotheism in the history of Ancient Egypt during the reign of Akhenaten. Like many other rulers of greatly expanded regimes, the pharaohs had long been identified with the sun, but Akhenaten was the first in history, as Hocart remarked, to mandate iconoclasm as form of centralisation: he came to insist that this sun-god Aten was the only god whose worship was sanctioned.[123]

The Chinese Emperor Wu, mentioned previously, introduced sacrifices to an overarching deity, 'the Great One'.[124] But throughout most of East Asian history, the encompassing principle was Heaven (*tianxia*), a rather opaque and abstract entity with which rulers claimed a unique relationship.[125] Such conceptions fed the Mongol notion of Sky or Heaven (Tenggeri), to which Güyüg Qa'an (d. 1248) referred in a letter to Pope Innocent IV: 'By the command of the Living God, Chinggis Khan, the dear and revered son of God, says that God, the Highest over all things, is God immortal, and Chinggis Khan is the sole ruler on earth.'[126] After the conversion of the Ilkhanid Mongols to

[121] There is a debate in African scholarship about how common and significant such deities were before contact with Christianity and Islam. It certainly seems plausible that attempts at religious consolidation within a local idiom could receive inspiration from monotheistic contact in this way. See Yai 1993: 259; Greene 1996; Horton 1971, 1975a, 1975b for Africa; compare Biersack 1991: 260–261, on the Paiela (Papua New Guinea).

[122] Tadmor 1986: 213–214; Levine 2005: 412.

[123] Hocart 1970: 245–246; Landes 2011: 50–70; Assmann 2008: 37–38. Compare Byzantium: 'Iconoclasm involved the general reassertion of central control over centrifugal tendencies': Michael Humphreys 2015: 266. Mughal ritual under Akbar became directed towards a personified sun: Moin [MS]. On recurrent association between kingship and sun/sky: Al-Azmeh 1997: 17; Oakley 2006: 97.

[124] Puett 2002: 304–305; 2015: 39–41.   [125] Duara 2015: 24.

[126] Peter Jackson 2006: 7; also Humphrey 1996. Fletcher 1986: 30–31: 'The idea of a universal supreme god – of which Semitic monotheism is only one form – contains within it the potentiality of a single universal realm on earth and

Islam in 1295, in one sense at least, their diplomatic rhetoric of political theology did not need to shift that far.[127]

This is the point: there seems to be a recurrent logic arising out of the process of state and empire construction itself that pushes ambitious rulers towards the exaltation of an overarching deity of the sun or skies or towards fully fledged monotheism, and yet which is quite distinct from – and emerges under different conditions from – that of Axial transcendentalism.

Rome following the conversion of Constantine may be seen as the site in which these two logics merged in west Eurasian history. Indeed, one way of understanding the possibility of Constantine's conversion in the years before and after the Battle of Milvian Bridge (312), is by recognising how the ground was prepared by pre-existing tendencies to conceive of the emperor as a sunlike saviour being intimately associated with abstract principles and overarchingly powerful metapersons.[128] Henotheistic images of a divine ruler mirroring the earthly ruler, such that piety for the former entailed obedience to the latter, had already emerged.[129] In particular there seems to have been a conflation of the 'Unconquered Sun' (Sol Invictus) with the Christian God.[130] A strong Christian tradition exemplified in the writings of the Eusebius (Bishop of Caesarea, d. c. 340), but drawing on earlier pagan philosophy, explicitly asserted that there was an inevitable association between the unicity of God and the unicity of the Roman Empire from Constantine onwards.[131] But was this logic merely a reflection of cognitive holism or did it bring more concrete political advantages?

the potentiality that the supreme god may destine a single ruler to establish his dominion over that entire universal realm.'
[127] Peter Jackson 2006: 7. But see Chapter 3 for the moralisation of the Mongol Heaven under transcendentalist influence.
[128] The ideology of virtuous sacral kingship fashioned by henotheistic pagan philosophers shows some striking common ground with transcendentalism: Bardill 2011: 80, 340.
[129] Ando 2013: 97–99; Rüpke 2010: 761.
[130] Bardill 2012: 281; Potter 2013: 156; Whitmarsh 2016: 235. Even the apostate emperor Julian 'never really ceased to be a monotheist', according to Momigliano 1986: 294–296. He saw the multitude of lesser gods residing beneath the authority of a nameless God of absolute Goodness, with Helios the sun god as an intermediary between the two dimensions.
[131] Bardill 2012: 353–354; Al-Azmeh 1997: 31–33 (comparing with Islam); Oakley 2006: 73; Momigliano 1986: 291–293. Geréby 2008, drawing on Erik Peterson, mentions the complications brought about by Trinitarian theology, but the practical consequences of this can be overplayed.

Supernatural Power Subdued

Hocart thought that the equation was obvious: 'Why does it matter whether there be one God or many? Because by abolishing minor gods you abolish minor sovereignties.'[132] Christianity offered the tempting opportunity to simply destroy the temples, cult objects, and priestly groups of one's subordinates and rivals. Many immanentist traditions already exhibited a certain 'auto-iconoclastic' potential (see Chapter 4) that centralisers could deploy: cult sites, objects, and officiants could be targeted as malign or antisocial. But this impetus was massively enhanced by the outright and permanent attack on rival forms endorsed by Christianity.

Buddhism could be seen as arriving at an analogous outcome, for the Buddha is also a being who lords over all other metapersons. But the distinct means by which the Indic and monotheistic traditions tackle the question of supernatural power must again be appreciated: monotheism seeks to eradicate all other forms of it; Buddhism to encompass and subordinate them. There is an intriguing homology here with the way that their respective traditions of statehood conceived the nature of political authority. In Christendom, sovereignty tended to be understood in more absolute terms such that the symbolism of kingship was confined to a single individual or dynasty at the top.[133] In the Buddhist and Hindu regions of South and Southeast Asia, sovereignty was 'nested': great rajas contained chains of lesser rajas – just as higher versions of Hindu gods encompass myriad lesser forms, and just as Buddhism frames and contains rather than dissolves regional metapersons.[134] This was partly, but not merely, a political strategy, for lording it over lesser kings also became the standard by which the greatness of kingship could be measured. As Tambiah

---

[132] Hocart 1970: 85.

[133] The 'King of Kings' motif could be used in Europe to describe unusual imperial situations (e.g., the Portuguese monarchy as liege to Asian vassals) but was not a fundamental constituent of how sovereignty per se was constructed.

[134] Pollock 2005: 420–421. Compare Alexis Sanderson 2006: 5: Śaivism 'mirrored and validated the incorporative structure of the state's power by elaborating an inclusivist model that ranked other religious systems as stages of an ascent to liberation in Śaivism... In this way, Śaivism became an integral and indispensable part of the early medieval polity, achieving as it progressed a

puts it, 'The *cakkavatti* in effect grants back their domains to subdued kings once they have submitted to the basic five morals of Buddhism.'[135] This homology may be simple coincidence but arguably it speaks to the way that religious and political unification were subject to the same cognitive template.

The way that Buddhism sought to incorporate existing spirits and deities within its cosmological vision is broadly comparable to immanentist strategies of translation. But the Buddhist version was more far-reaching, draining deities of some of their local uniqueness and local threat, and subordinating the whole dimension of metaper-sonhood to a higher vision organised by ethics rather than power.[136] According to Mark Teeuwen, the Nara court which established Buddhism in eighth-century Japan used the 'universalizing powers of Buddhism to convert clan shrines into court temples, at times provoking local protests that took the form of violence attributed to the kami'.[137] The identification of *kami* and *bodhisattva* in the 'trace-manifestation' theory (*honji-suijaku*) could 'function as a political model by which local communities, represented by local *kami*, were considered as manifestations of lofty central state institutions'.[138] Here is another homology then: the promise of liberation from the unpredictability and violence of the local gods was akin to the claims of imperial states to release local populations from the tyrannies of local lords into the peace and justice of the higher order. But the central point here is simply that Buddhism, just like Christianity, offered a means by which the supernatural power of diverse and localised cultic sites was both tamed and taken out of the hands of local actors.

transregional organization and a consequent standardization of its rituals and doctrines'. This incorporative sovereignty pattern does not hold for the Mahayana regions of East Asia, perhaps because Buddhism arrived in a form subordinate to an entrenched and authoritative Confucian vision of state authority.

[135] Tambiah 1976: 46. Conversion is therefore coextensive with processes of political expansion or unification. Baker and Phongpaichit 2014: 9, refer to the process of kings containing sub-kings (Thailand) as 'emboxment'.

[136] Chapter 1.

[137] Teeuwen 2012: 73, comparing with Buddhist kingship as the tamer of the *nat* spirits in Burma.

[138] Rambelli and Teeuwen 2003b; 44.

Moral Authority and Community

Consequently, you are no longer foreigners and strangers, but fellow citizens with God's people and also members of his household.

Ephesians 2:19

As they settled into established elements of society, Buddhism and Christianity rarely repudiated other kinds of identity, but they did offer a transcendence of them. Because they arose in milieux in which local and customary norms had come under great strain, they were 'preadapted to the macrocosm', as Hefner puts it.[139] The individualism–universalism at their core provided a means by which kinship, ethnicity, and even language could be overcome as forces of allegiance and self-understanding. Their texts, core symbols, and institutions were portable and replicable across all such boundaries. Christianity in particular created what Louis Dumont called a 'pseudo-holism', by which an imagined community defined by common possession of one especially important characteristic springs into being.[140] If the Tower of Babel had split men into squabbling nations, Christianity would reunite them.

In their recent comparative history of empire, Burbank and Cooper considered how imperial systems might 'harness monotheism to solve problems inherent in the structure of empire: how to capture the imaginations of people across a broad and differentiated space and how to keep intermediaries in line'.[141] Clifford Ando has presented Rome's acceptance of Christianity as a natural corollary of the 'disembedding' of religion under the conditions of empire, arriving 'when a homology was achieved between its social-theoretical postulates and the wider political culture of the day'.[142] In the decree issued by Theodosius (r. 379–395) in 380 that pronounced Christianity the official religion of the empire, 'the omnipotent Christian god and

---

[139] Hefner 1993b: 26, 34; Turchin 2011: 8; Eaton 1999: 174.

[140] I am drawing upon the discussion of Dumont 1986 in Robbins 2004: 309.

[141] Burbank and Cooper 2010: 62. Compare Kippenberg 1986: 279, on Christianity's embodiment of a 'depoliticization' ethic, abrogating primordial loyalties.

[142] Ando 2013: 101.

the emperor stand in a relationship of exact analogy.'[143] The most compelling illustration of the social power that might be unleashed by the unifying and motivating potential of monotheism would have to be the extraordinary explosion of Islam out of the Arabian Peninsula to cover a vast tract of territory within a few generations after Muhammad.[144]

In these cases, diverse groups were brought within the embrace of a single 'moral community'.[145] This means that they not only shared a common set of moral understandings, values and norms, but were conscious of doing so. Moral communities also have the unfortunate (albeit far from inevitable) tendency to value the lives of those outside the community rather less than of those within. They may also become soteriological communities, in which an individual's chances of achieving salvation or liberation are somehow seen as dependent on the collective fortunes and piety of the entire kingdom.[146] If rulers became interested in the unification of their subjects – or even a subset of them such as the ruling elite – Buddhism and Christianity provided a clear mechanism for achieving it.[147] They thereby disseminated and stabilised the norms by which their own legitimacy would be conceded.

In a very specific sense, the eruption of statehood entails a shift of focus from kinship to kingship.[148] Kinship hardly goes away, of course, but there is a sense in which it must be dislodged from the centre stage of the social order so that monarchy may find the spotlight: indeed this is one way of reading the transgressive symbolism of some forms of immanentist kingship explored in Chapter 3. Again there is an intriguing isomorphism with the way that

---

[143] Whitmarsh 2016: 6, presenting Christianity as a means of creating 'unity out of diversity without the armature of modern nationalism.' Compare Papaconstantinou 2015: xxviii; and Sanderson 2006: 5, and Thapar 2012: 182–184 on Aśoka.

[144] Hodgson 1974.

[145] See Obeyesekere 1995: 237–238, referring to the creation of a Sinhala Buddhist moral community out of diverse village communities through pilgrimage, etc.

[146] See Ruddick 2013: 273; Lieberman 2003 passim, for Buddhist parallels.

[147] Islam as unifying African imperial elites: Tymowski 2011: 114.

[148] Duindam 2016: 3–4, sensibly sees kingship as both a move away from and an extension of kinship; for an anthropological take see Da Col 2011: vi–xxxv.

transcendentalism also subtly devalues kinship in favour of infinitely expandable moral–soteriological ties.[149]

Pacification and Governability

All under Heaven is unified and yielding in will.

An inscription of the 'First Emperor' of China[150]

Hocart noted that war kings needed to become law kings. Georges Dumézil described kingship as an oppositional play between *celeritas* and *gravitas*: in the establishment of dominion the chaotic, magical, youthful violence of the former prevails, but over the longer term it must unite with the wisdom and justice of the latter.[151] This movement is precisely what is described by accounts of the archetypal Buddhist king, the Mauryan emperor Aśoka, who is said to have turned to the promulgation of Buddhism in revulsion at his bloody feats in conquering the state of Kalinga.[152]

But war and law are also different ends to which the social power of religion in general may be directed: sweeping people up into rebellions or crusades, assaulting the status quo on the one hand, or disarming subjects, quietening them, and drawing them together in the name of amity and order on the other. For the latter project, transcendentalism would appear, at least, exceptionally well suited. For there is one final homology to consider. If the transcendentalist rejection of violence seems to sit oddly with the imperatives of politics, that is because we associate the business of state with the state of war. But the business of the state is also the business of internal peace, and this is secured through the monopolisation of violence. God (even the Buddha in some of his guises) also reserves the use of dreadful force to himself while mandating nonviolence to man – or rather delegating the righteous deployment of violence to earthly representatives. How to create

---

[149] The way in which Buddhism and Christianity transformed communities' relationship with their ancestors – and therefore their local landscape – is just one dimension of this.

[150] Puett 2015: 240.

[151] See discussion of Dumézil in Sahlins 1985: 90–92. Hocart 1970: 161.

[152] Echoes, perhaps, with Pomare (Tahiti): see Chapter 6. The actual connection between Aśoka and Buddhism is much debated, but at issue here is his image in later Buddhist thought: Strong 2014: 13–14.

an ethic of peace, particularly for societies shaped by warrior honour codes and afflicted by cycles of retributive violence, may well be an immediately pressing concern. The inherent esteem for nonviolence in Christianity and Buddhism could present a solution. No less significant for many a ruler hoping for loyal vassals: how to implant truthfulness as an inherent value and not just a contingently useful social strategy. This is where transcendentalism's qualities as a technology of self-control became most pertinent. It offered a means by which subjects would be inducted into the surveillance not just of their own behaviour but their thoughts and feelings too. This is the *ne plus ultra* of governability.

Administrative and Institutional Power

All priesthoods are likely to become the bearers of the broader cultural inheritance of the societies they serve, but transcendentalist clerisies functioned as the autonomous repositories of skills that state builders tend to value particularly highly. Their profound orientation to the textual tradition meant that they became the primary carriers of literacy and scholarship, and this normally included all forms of knowledge from medicine to astrology. They were also thus the main providers of education, and an important resource for ruling elites who wished to take records, make accounts, write chronicles, receive advice, consult history, and draft laws. Because transcendentalist clerisies are connected to great transregional networks, and perhaps also because they are framed by the imagery of nonviolence, they were also valued as envoys and diplomatic agents. But their capacity to assemble networks within the domain of the state was more important. The more that transcendentalist clerisies were 'established' within a society – that is, dispersed vertically (across all levels of society) and horizontally (across the different regions of a kingdom) – the more that they formed an institutional fabric unrivalled by anything that the state itself could produce until perhaps the modern era. At times, they were able to keep that fabric in good repair even as dynasties and states rose and fell about them.[153] Monasteries, lodges, and temples often functioned at the frontier of the state, indeed often at the frontier of

---

[153] Particularly Christianity; Theravada Buddhist monasticism was more vulnerable to state vicissitudes.

population expansion and agricultural cultivation.[154] Just one of the reasons for the institutional power of monasticism is its capacity to chisel away the claims of kinship, allowing bureaucratic or even meritocratic principles to take the place of kin sentiment and preference.[155] The material fabric of that network – churches, temples, and monasteries – came to form the physical and social focal point of local communities. Their works of charity served by way of welfare.

The Instabilities of Transcendentalism

Because the priesthood of the gentiles and the whole worship of their gods existed merely for the acquisition of temporal goods (which were all ordained to the common good of the multitude, whose care devolved upon the king), the priests of the gentiles were very properly subject to the kings. But in the new law there is a higher priesthood by which men are guided to heavenly goods. Consequently, in the law of Christ, kings must be subject to priests.

Thomas Aquinas, *On Kingship*[156]

For our religion, having taught us the truth and the true way of life, leads us to ascribe less esteem to worldly honour. Hence the gentiles, who held it in high esteem and looked upon it as their highest good, displayed in their actions more ferocity than we do.

Niccolò Machiavelli, *The Discourses*[157]

For Machiavelli, as indeed for Edward Gibbon, Christianity presented serious drawbacks for the ambitious ruler.[158] In Machiavelli's eyes, the principle of pacification had worked too well, and sapped the other function of religion: to rouse men to coherent violent action. The ethic of Roman paganism, advertised in its bloody sacrifices and glorification of conquering generals, produced a more militaristic populace. What Machiavelli and Gibbon had in their sights was a core characteristic of transcendentalism, its otherworldliness. They may have conceived the impact of this in too literal and direct a manner. Nevertheless they

---

[154] Eaton 1993: 194–267.   [155] Gellner 1991: 95.
[156] Aquinas 1949: 62–63 (II, 3); compare Gelasius I (492–496) in Oakley 2006: 77.
[157] Machiavelli 1970: 277–278 (II, 2); Stroumsa 2010: 152.
[158] Gibbon 1993: 517–518.

were right in intuiting that transcendentalism was not merely something that was deployed by the state, but an entity that deployed the state for its own ends! This is frankly what Thomas Aquinas asserts. Transcendentalism was indeed a great source of social power, then, but not one that was so readily dominated after all.

Ethical Arbitration and Dissent

The attractions and the frustrations of the transcendentalist clerisy for the ruler both derived from its potential autonomy, which was in turn a function of its moral primacy. This autonomy was apparent from the very start of Buddhist, Christian, and Islamic history, but it burgeoned over the first millennium CE. In Christendom it achieved a decisive form during the Papal Revolution of the eleventh to twelfth centuries CE, in which the primacy of the Church over religious matters – and above all the question of the election of the Pope – was settled. The trajectory of Islam differed insofar as prophetic charisma was translated into political, legal, and social force almost immediately. Muhammad begat a race of sacred kings in the guise of the caliphs. It was only gradually that the ulema entrenched their institutional autonomy and corporate identity and came to assert 'the doctrine of priestly primacy in the public sphere'. This crystallised by about the mid-thirteenth century, coinciding with the waning of the caliphate.[159]

The moral authority of the clerisy was expressed in their explicit vocation to hold kings to account according to their ethics and piety. Ideally, of course, these should be internalised by the ruler. Hence a fifteenth-century court chronicle of Samudra-Pasai, the *Hikayat Raja-Raja Pasai,* has a dying king express these by now conventional sentiments to his successor:

Do not transgress the commandments of God, the Exalted, or the sayings of the Prophet Muhammad, the Apostle of God... So conduct yourself that you are always on your guard against the things which are not in accordance with Holy Law. Do not oppress or despoil the servants of God the Exalted by unjust treatment. Do not be backward in enjoining good and eschewing evil ... for this mortal world will pass away and only the world to come will last for ever.[160]

[159] Al-Azmeh 1997: 103–104; von Sivers 2000: 22–23.
[160] Hall 2001: 212, citing Hill 1960: 133–134.

The last phrase is where the sting lies: the pretensions of kingship are here punctured on the blade of the hereafter. Francis Xavier would express a very similar admonishment to the Portuguese king Dom João III (r. 1521–1557).[161] For Buddhist monks, 'the true ruler is the one who upholds the *dhamma*'.[162] While immanentist priests could also act as the vehicles for imposing communal norms and expectations on rulership, transcendentalist clerisies took on this task with much greater force and clarity.[163] It was, after all, not easy to rid oneself of turbulent priests. After the ruler of Male in the Maldives invited in a Syrian-born Sufi *sayyid*, Muhammad Shams al-Dīn, in the late seventeenth century, a chronicle describes him as enraged by the criticism he subsequently received. But although he attempted to ban anyone from attending the *sayyid*, his subjects forsook his injunctions for 'they loved [Shams al-Dīn] very much, and they continued to attend the *sayyid* every Friday and Monday'.[164] In the end, Shams al-Dīn himself would succeed to the throne in 1692. If transcendentalism could be used as a means of pacifying a populace, it was no less a means for pacifying the king.

Clerisies and Rulers Steal Each Other's Clothes and Plunder Each Other's Realms

The history of the world may, from one perspective, be seen as the recurrent capture and institutionalization of transcendent authority.

Prasenjit Duara, *The Crisis of Global Modernity*[165]

R. A. L. H. Gunawardana described the relationship between king and sangha in Sri Lanka as one of 'antagonistic symbiosis': this may be taken as an expression of the tension between ruler and clerisy in transcendentalist societies more generally. They are in an important sense now kept quite distinct, like neighbours divided by a common fence; but they are jealous neighbours, always casting covetous eyes over the boundary and stealing each other's clothes from the washing line. This is what Ernst Kantorowicz described for medieval Christianity:

---

[161] Francis Xavier, 26 January 1549, in Schurhammer and Voretzsch 1928: 534.
[162] Duara 2015: 137.   [163] Runciman 2012.
[164] Peacock 2018: 68; see Duindam 2016: 27.   [165] Duara 2015: 6.

Infinite cross-relations between church and state, active in every century of
the Middle Ages, produced hybrids in either camp. Mutual borrowings and
exchanges of insignia, political symbols, prerogatives, and rights of honour
had been carried on perpetually between the spiritual and secular leaders of
Christian society. The pope adorned his tiara with a golden crown, donned
the imperial purple, and was preceded by the imperial banners when riding in
solemn procession through the streets of Rome. The emperor wore under his
crown a mitre, donned the pontifical shoes and other clerical rainments, and
received, like a bishop, the ring at his coronation. These borrowings affected,
in the earlier Middle Ages, chiefly the ruling individuals, both spiritual and
secular, until finally the *sacerdotium* had an imperial appearance and the
regnum a clerical touch.'[166]

These sartorial interplays are but the surface signals of a much
deeper rhythm. The clerisy is always tempted to translate its moral
authority into wealth, privilege, and political influence, while ruling
elites seek to use their political power to plunder the religious realm
for its reserves of status enhancement, moral authority, and tech-
nologies of governmentality.[167] This tension creates such flux that it
is often easier to see common dynamics of ruler–clerisy relations
across all traditions (Christianity, Islam, Buddhism) than it is to
generalise about structural differences between them. Within
Christianity, for example, the relative monopolisation of the religious realm by the ruler – often called *caesaropapism* – would be
represented by the Byzantine tradition.[168] At the other end of this
spectrum might be found the papacy at the height of its power in
late medieval Europe, when it had become a state in its own right
(levying taxes and raising troops), as well as a statelike agent operating within the jurisdiction of other kingdoms (appointing ecclesiastical personnel, overseeing canon law). Here, the capacity
of transcendentalism to fashion institutional networks across huge
ecumenes could be a source of frustration to rulers: it might mean

---

[166] Kantorowicz 2016: 193.
[167] See the discussion in Eisenstadt 1962: 283–286: 'Thus the rulers would often
attempt to control entirely the activities of the religious elite and to claim for
themselves the sole right to represent the major religious and cultural symbols
of the society, while the religious elites would often attempt to usurp various
central political offices and to remove the religious organizations from the
political control and influence of the rulers.'
[168] Al-Azmeh 1997: 50–54.

conceding a degree of authority to an organisation such as the Catholic Church which existed above and beyond the reach of any temporal prince.[169]

The accumulation of land, tax privileges, and wealth was an obvious flashpoint. The notions of merit or grace encouraged laymen to become patrons, in which they exchanged the fruits of their mortal toil for the promise of immortal reward. Kings were such patrons writ large, and frequently exercised the power to grant the use of land or exemption from taxation to monasteries and temples. The cumulative result could be that more and more stretches of economic activity were removed from the reach of the state. Naturally, rulers might be sorely tempted to appropriate this wealth for themselves. This could be undertaken in a spirit of blatant aggression, in which rulers simply 'cocked a snook' at clerical anger.[170] But it could also take place through an appropriation of moral authority, by proceeding under the auspices of reform.

For the accumulation of worldly goods and powers on the part of the clerisy always carried the risk of diminishing their transcendentalist aura – and thus conceding moral authority to rulers who stepped in to purify them. In this sense, the boundary wall between the transcendent and mundane spheres was rather useful for rulers. It set up a peculiar paradox: the power of transcendentalist clerisies to intervene in the mundane world depended on them holding themselves above and apart from the mundane world![171] Just as clerisies reserved the right to moralise about the ruler's governance of temporal affairs, rulers could also reserve the right to moralise about the clerisy's governance of the spiritual realm. This was in particular a structural feature of the Theravada world, in which kings had the duty to purge the sangha and examine them for scriptural knowledge, but there are clear echoes in phases of Christian history too.

Something like this process can be seen in the role of princes and civic authorities in implementing the European Reformation and the

---

[169] This formed an obstacle Christianity in Japan (CK). This principle applies to the monotheistic traditions but was much less a feature of the Buddhist world. Reynolds 2005: 13.

[170] Sri Lankan chronicles castigate kings for this: Liyanagamage 2008: 57–58.

[171] Just one example: the growing political influence in late eighteenth- and nineteenth-century Burma of the reformist forest-dwelling Sudhamma monks: Charney 2006.

appropriation of monastic wealth and ecclesiastical administration that accompanied it. At the other end of Eurasia in the sixteenth century, anticlerical discourses could be deployed by unifier warlords in Japan intent on crushing recalcitrant temples and leagues – although they also revelled in sheer coercive might. When temples raised armies and siphoned off taxes, or when the Nichiren and True Pure Land (*Jōdo Shinshū*) sects clashed in Kyoto and burned down each other's temples (and much of the city) as they did in the 1530s, they forfeited legitimacy to strong men who would restore order – and therefore forfeited wealth and manpower too.[172] In Sri Lanka, the unification of the sangha under Parakramabāhu I (r. 1153–1186) crystallised a Theravada template of royal oversight.[173] Each of these were also in fact relatively decisive moments in which the state managed to fundamentally contain and subdue the worldly power of the clerisy in a lasting manner.[174]

The rulers of vast imperial complexes that incorporated elites of more than one transcendentalist clerisy had another option: to set these clerisies against each other, and to subordinate them to a still higher vision of order. This is one way of considering the approach of the Mughal emperor Akbar, who relativised the authority of his ulema by pitting them against other religious traditions in formal debate, and made himself the highest authority in certain religious matters.[175] He effected this project symbolically through his own divinisation as a sunlike millennial being: here we see, somewhat ironically, immanentist kingship as a means of creating a universal language across transcendentalist boundaries.[176]

Equally, however, rulers who flaunted their coercive power over the clerisy too nakedly – without pulling over suitable ideological

---

[172] CK.

[173] Walters 2000: 144. The three *nikayas* had been degraded due to Cōḷa invasions, but tellingly were also damaged by Vikramabāhu I's (r. 1111–1132) seizure of monastic wealth: Gunawardana 1979: 89–91, 328. However, following Parakramabāhu I, the sangha again gained some autonomy and presented itself as akin to an independent royal court: Gornall (forthcoming).

[174] In China, the state sought to contain Buddhism rather fundamentally from early on, in the Tang period, but its continuing social power was seen as a recurrent problem: note the draconian legislation passed by the founding emperor of the Ming dynasty, Zhu Yuanzhang (r. 1368–1398). Brook 2005: Chapter 7.

[175] Compare the policy of the Safavid Shah 'Abbas I in Matthee 2010.

[176] Moin 2012.

cover – risked damaging the 'opinion' on which government relies.[177] In the Theravada world, the sangha might be involved in generating rebellions against incumbents, but more often showed their hand during the liminal period of succession in which questions of legitimacy tended to become exceptionally acute.[178] Yet, it was in zones of relatively fragmented and fluid authority, especially following the collapse of imperial power, that religious specialists were most likely to translate the social power of religion into real political force. Japan during the protracted vicissitudes of central authority in the second millennium is the outstanding example. Buddhist institutions moved into this power vacuum left by the faltering emperorship and shogunate in several guises, including huge wealthy temple complexes with armies of warrior monks such as the Tendai monastery of Enryakuji on Mount Hiei. Even more strikingly, horizontal bandings (leagues, *ikki*) of urban and rural commoners emerged and were brought together in self-governance in the name of the new sects of Kamakura Buddhism. The communal discipline of these leagues, especially the True Pure Land *Ikko Ikki*, was a cause of great alarm and frustration to the warlords intent on reunifying the land under their authority.[179]

Or consider what happened once the Mongols had smashed apart the structures of the Islamic world in the thirteenth century: Sufi holy men often became key power brokers in the fluid conditions that followed.[180] The charisma of Sufis stemmed from their otherworldly attributes but also from the thaumaturgic powers they evidently accessed and the prophetic insight they achieved (revelation was, if you like, partially unblocked) – immanentist qualities that would stimulate the attention of later reformers. The Sufi order (*tariqa*) was a powerful means of creating new corporate identities. The most

---

[177] Reid 1993: 282, on the Toungoo king Nandabayin (r. 1581–1599), and Lieberman 2003: 156.

[178] Reid 1993: 194–197; Liyanagamage 2008: 116.

[179] Deal and Ruppert 2015: 174–179. Compare the rise of the theocratic 'kingdom' of Fang after fall of Ayutthaya, 1767 (Gesick 1983: 93); and the mini theocracy created by the Han monk Wang Foye among the eighteenth-century Lahu (Walker 2003: 508–511).

[180] See Moin 2012: 154–156, on the Naqshbandi Sufi saint in Central Asia, Khwaja Makhdumi Nura, which 'highlights how Sufis imbued with hereditary charisma would attempt to exchange their symbolic capital for more tangible forms of wealth and influence. Such Sufis pursued power and status as much as any king or warlord'.

striking example of the way that Sufis could parlay charisma and
social discipline into political force is the transformation of the Safavid
lineage into a royal-cum-saintly dynasty in Persia.[181] In parts of India,
meanwhile, Sufi lineages also sought to acquire royal powers
for themselves, and were closely associated with the origins of
dynasties.[182]

The Challenge of Millenarianism

Since transcendentalism always forms an amalgam, the 'conditions' of
immanentism never quite go away: the process of subduing and containing supernatural power, for example, is never-ending, and this in
itself is a kind of instability. One of the ways this was apparent is in
the phenomenon of millenarianism. This is in fact slightly misleading
as a general term for movements that I describe as supernatural
utopianism.[183] Such movements anticipate the permanent transformation of mundane reality into a perfect, heavenly order. They normally
revolve around a special agent of that transformation – a messiah,
Maitreya Buddha, or *mujaddid* (renewer) – who is either already
present or about to arrive. Millenarian movements also tend to reserve
the benefits of the new perfect dispensation for their own followers
who must abide by special strictures and taboos. The precise nature of
the anticipated transformation resides on a spectrum from substantial
immanence (in which it is already happening in the shape of a new
community on earth) to relative transcendence (in which it is located in
a dim and abstract future).

As Chapter 4 explains, supernatural utopianism may be found in
societies founded on both immanentist and transcendentalist traditions. Here, we need only note its role in generating political instability
and innovation in the latter. Many of the insurgent agents discussed in
the last section fashioned themselves by the light of such expectations.
Although, in transcendentalist traditions, the authentic prophetic
voice has already spoken, centuries ago, millenarianism allows it to
speak again in a more specific register by interpreting the attainment of

---

[181] Moin 2012.   [182] Moin 2012; Digby 1990; Bayly 1989: 164, 183–184.
[183] Misleading because it refers to Abrahamic notions of time, when the underlying
phenomenon is far broader. However, I retain the term here as a more familiar
term for discussing transcendentalist variants of supernatural utopianism,
which are based on chronologies underpinned by historic revelation.

the transcendent realm as both immanent and imminent. Indeed, monotheism itself may have started, in each of its three Abrahamic iterations, in essentially this form.[184] Millenarianism provides a mechanism for tapping the latent capacity for dissent within transcendentalism when it translates soteriological aspiration into social and political utopianism. In fact, it is the primary means by which the anti-status quo dimension to transcendentalism is actually materialised in premodernity; it was also the primary means by which radical social or political change could be conceived as the end point of political movements before the French Revolution.[185]

More simply, it was a way in which anyone apparently defeated by the status quo could present a convincing narrative of their own status and moral authority regardless. In this way Prince Dipanagara (1785–1855) in Java framed himself as the messianic 'just king', the *Ratu Adil*, who would first arrive poor and unknown, in order to rouse a widespread rebellion against Dutch rule (the eruption of Mount Merapi at the end of 1822 helped convince people that the 'time of madness' before the Ratu Adil's arrival was at hand).[186] Indeed millenarianism was a widespread reaction to the imposition of European imperial power across the world. All the transcendentalist traditions have generated such movements, and the political implications have rarely been trivial.

Millenarianism drags the transcendent down to earth so that it may be realised in the persons or projects of charismatic monks, peasants, rebels, and princes.[187] As a special kind of immanentisation, then, it sparked new possibilities in fusing political and religious leadership, but it also reintroduced a dispersal of access to supernatural power – because once hopes of a coming and final disruption of mundane reality were unleashed they were not easy to contain or monopolise.[188] And it also brought religious claims into a kind of radical – and typically immanentist – empirical jeopardy, which meant that such

---

[184] Landes 2011 argues that intellectual rationalisers then kicked the eschatological aspiration into the long grass – or transcendentalised it.

[185] For examples, such as the Free Spirit heresy, from medieval Europe, see Cohn 1970.

[186] Carey 2008: 513–516 and passim. See Elverskog 2010: 98.

[187] On rebels, see the origins of the first Ming emperor Zhu Yuanzhang (1328–1398) among Red Turban Daoist millenarianists taking advantage of the chaotic conditions in the last decades of Yuan rule: Dubois 2011: 38–39.

[188] See also Gilmartin 2017: 4.

movements, in their more urgent and apocalyptic guises, were prone to desperate measures and self-combustion.[189]

If the boundaries between political and religious roles were rendered unusually fluid, divinised kings were often the result. Thus Sufi saints could become Safavid kings; Hong Xiuquan – the leader of the quasi-Christian millenarian spirit-medium 'Heavenly Kingdom of Supreme Peace' movement behind the Taiping rebellion of 1850–1864 – could end by becoming a secluded emperor-like figure in his palace in Nanjing; the prophet Yali came to style himself the King of New Guinea and twice ran for a seat in parliament in the 1960s.[190] If, in normal terms, the millennial kingdom turned out to be just that – a state ruled by a prophet-turned-king – it could also unleash new social compacts based on idealised principles such as egalitarianism.[191] The quasi-monotheist *Ikko Ikki* in Japan helped bring into being quite radical visions of an alternative sociopolitical order, in which lords were unnecessary and ordained priests took prominent leadership roles.[192]

Why is the social energy deployed by millenarianism so formidable? Because the imminence of the great event utterly overwhelms normal cost-benefit calculations.[193] Are you ready to wager that the second coming is *not* coming? What will it matter if you lose your cattle today or if you abandon your village and snub your lord, if soon enough cows and neighbours and lords will be subject to a cosmic maelstrom? In transcendentalist millenarianism the result is a great ratcheting up of hopes and anxieties about salvation or liberation and therefore a new readiness to be subject to disciplined action in order to attain it.

Schism, Plurality, and Reform

It was in these circumstances that Jesus came to establish a spiritual kingdom on earth; this kingdom, by separating the theological system from the political, meant that the state ceased to be a unity, and it caused the intestine divisions which have never ceased to disturb Christian peoples.

Jean-Jacques Rousseau, *The Social Contract*[194]

---

[189] Landes 2011. This point applies much less to forms of millennialism deployed by rulers *in situ*.

[190] Landes 2011: 127.   [191] Reilly 2004: 140–142.

[192] Souyri 2001: 193–195.   [193] Landes 2011: 43–55.

[194] Rousseau [1762] 1968: 176.

Transcendentalism sought to shift attention from the realm of super-natural power to that of truth–ethics–salvation. However, over the longer term, the latter might also become the grounds for division rather than unity. Clerisies patrolled these grounds with vigilance and – at least in the case of many monotheistic traditions – with coercive instruments at the ready. But the intellectualisation they pro-pelled was a source of fragmentation as well as strength.[195] While it helped to smooth over rational difficulties and obscurities, and weave the core teachings into a logical frame, it could also throw light on such problems, invite speculative attempts to solve them, and thereby gener-ate doctrinal innovation and dissent. Moreover the historical singular-ity of transcendentalist revelation and its enshrinement in the text set up the unique possibility of 'reform', by which such innovations and organic evolutions – especially insofar as they served to accommodate immanentisation and its concessions to social realities – were made vulnerable to challenges.[196] Reform movements were also generated by a recurring irony: the more successful the clerisy was at establishing transcendentalist norms, the more vulnerable it became to being judged wanting in those terms. The severe or idealised standards of other-worldly self-abnegation they established were always liable to be com-promised in ways large and small, as popular traditions of anticlericalism mercilessly pointed out. The moral authority of the clerisy might therefore be cast into jeopardy. From this perspective, then, it was the very success of the late medieval Catholic Church in inducting parts of the European population into transcendentalist desiderata that paved the way for the Reformation movements which sought to attack the Church. And it was the success of Buddhism in Japan in making people care about salvation that stimulated the emer-gence of lay movements which sought to bypass the sangha altogether.

None of this would matter much to rulers if it were not for the fact that innovative and reformist movements threatened to fracture the insti-tutional carapace of the clerisy and thus in turn undermine the consoli-dation of the religious field under political authority. In short, such developments robbed the centre of its command of the social energy of religion, and conceded to new actors the ability to plunder its reserves of status enhancement, moral authority, and disciplinary technology.

---

[195] Burbank and Cooper 2010: 62 on monotheism as a two-edged sword.
[196] See Chapter 2.

Rulers might of course immediately try to appropriate those reserves for themselves. This is what princes and civic authorities did in Germany during the Reformation, particularly once the Peasants' War of 1524–1525 and urban iconoclastic fervour had shown how dangerous Reformation enthusiasm was if left unharnessed. But in many parts of Europe, princes now saw themselves ruling over subjects split into two or more warring moral-soteriological communities of Catholic and Reformed persuasions, each with their own conflicting norms of what a legitimate ruler looked like. This was the basis for the wars of religion that wracked much of the Continent over the later sixteenth and seventeenth centuries. In the Buddhist world, where plural and combinatory commitments were rather the norm, the generation of diverse sects in Mahayana regions was much less likely to cause such problems. But the plurality of schools of thought and monastic lineages did, in a more modest sense, make the religious field harder to control. Indeed, as was intimated earlier, by the sixteenth century in Japan, the religious scene was rather spectacularly unconsolidated, and the Kamakura schools had even acquired something like the hard edges of monotheistic commitment and the threat of schismatic violence. No wonder the Tokugawa regime quickly set about enmeshing Buddhist institutions into a single network firmly under state control. First millennium CE Buddhism in Sri Lanka had also been faction-ridden until the establishment of the Mahāvihāra vision, which appears to have been unusually successful in keeping doctrinal divisions under control.

The Gamble of Monotheistic Consolidation

Christian and Islamic rulers do not always seek to use their faith as a means of effecting comprehensive religious consolidation: Muslim empire builders have tended to see it as a means of uniting elites rather than homogenising the subjects beneath them, while kings in sub-Saharan Africa might keep it as a dimension of court ritual rather than a tool for shaping their subjects. However, where it is used for this purpose, it can be considered a high-risk, high-yield strategy. Successful imperial strategy in general is often a delicate and flexible balancing act between *laissez-faire* and *dirigiste* modes – as may be seen in the way that the British Empire tended to cycle between informal and formal forms. But the imposition of Christianity is an emphatically *dirigiste* policy of the cultural plane, which holds great potential for centralisation while also risking the generation of resistance. Indeed, the aggressive face it presents to opposing religious forms often stimulated them to become more belligerent in response.[197]

Conclusion

From one perspective, all the relationships described in this chapter fall into a simple and universal pattern: regardless of the cultural inheritance they draw upon, political and religious specialists simply cannot leave each other alone. To ambitious rulers, the social power of religion was obvious in its ability to confer status, establish legitimacy through moral narrative, and shape and discipline subjects. Indeed, it is striking how consistently rulers wishing to centralise political power have sought to subdue and manipulate the religious sphere. In rather generalised terms, immanentism facilitated this process by supporting an equation between ritual efficacy and worldly success, and by placing few obstacles in the way of rulers who wished to establish state cults associated with their authority. In the following chapter, I shall suggest that that radical attempts to 'consolidate' the religious sphere in this way can be linked with unusually strong claims to divinise the ruler. However state cults only ever slid over the top of other strata of religious life, which normally continued untroubled and disaggregated.

Transcendentalist traditions – considered here in the form of Buddhism or Christianity – generally arrived as far more thoroughgoing attempts to reconfigure the entire religious field. As a matter of profound irony, their very transcendence – even repudiation – of politics set up an affinity with a quite different dynamic in the political sphere itself. As rulers made more and more expansive claims for their dominions, they tended to articulate hegemony in terms of ever more 'ultimate' gods of the skies or conceptions of Heaven. Buddhism and Christianity could therefore function as a trump card which might be played to either destroy or encompass other cultic sources of supernatural and social power; they also carried a certain technology of interiority that promised new forms of governability.

Transcendentalist traditions, did this, however, in a manner that defined the ruler's role not primarily in terms of his sheer status but

---

[197] Alan Strathern 2007a: chapter 10.

in terms of a soteriological–ethical project that was far greater than the king or polity itself. The ability of the Christian church and Buddhist sangha to confer legitimacy was a function of their very moral and institutional autonomy from power and institutional terms. And in some contexts this could amount to a certain diminution of the king's control over the religious field: it set up a dialogue at the pinnacle of political-ritual affairs rather than the monologue of the immanentist state cult. Indeed, transcendentalist traditions contain the seeds of their own forms of instability, above all as a result of the cycles of immanentisation and reform discussed in Chapter 1. This might fragment the religious field through sectarian fissure and – particularly in the case of Christianity – even create rival moral communities instead of unified ones.

The purpose of this discussion was therefore to establish the somewhat *different* conditions and possibilities of centralisation presented by either immanentism or transcendentalism – rather than to conclude that either system was *better* suited for this purpose over the long term. Moreover, looking forward to the concern of ruler conversion in the last two chapters of this book, it should be noted that the dynamics sketched here in rather abstract and objective terms cannot be translated directly into the subjective motivations of individual lords deciding whether or not to adopt Christianity. These men and women were not afforded the bird's-eye perspective of global history: they had to cast their vision into the future from the ground and typically against a backdrop of imminent conflict and existential crisis.[198]

---

[198] See Chapter 5.

3 The Two Forms of Sacred Kingship: Divinisation and Righteousness

> Let him go, Gertrude; do not fear our person.
> There's such divinity doth hedge a king
> That treason can but peep to what it would.
> *Hamlet*, Act IV, Scene V

The irony of these words is not subtle. Claudius, who speaks them, has become king only by murdering the previous incumbent. He had poured poison into the ear of the sleeping old Hamlet, and no divinity had stooped to scoop it out. Instead treason had been victorious, as it so often is. Kings are divine; kings are mortal. Shakespeare famously withholds, but in this instance the ambiguities he conveys are inherent to sacred kingship itself.[1] In the first part of this chapter, the ambiguity of sacred kingship is explored as a matter of its plural origins and functions, as a creature of both dispositions and cognition, and as a mirage of both royal presentation and popular culture. Kingship is sacralised to serve the ends of kings; but also, it seems, to serve the ends of their subjects – and beyond all discussions of means and ends, it is the product of more mysterious and deep-rooted patterns of thought. In the second part of the chapter, the features of immanentist or 'divinised' kingship are laid out, and for some purposes, this may in turn be broken into its 'heroic' and 'cosmic' forms. Divinised kingship, it is suggested, is an attempt to ambiguate the ontological status of incumbents so that they are in-between things, straddling the worlds of men and metapersons. The moral status of divinised kings may be no less ambiguous too. The third part of the chapter shows how transcendentalism generates an altogether distinct means of sacralising kingship by rendering it 'righteous'. Yet, in a final ambiguity, the fourth

---

[1] Shakespeare belonged to a post-Machiavellian world in which the theatrical nature of both sacral and political authority was uneasily disclosed (Greenblatt 1985; Sharpe 2006: 110) within a censorious climate (Lake 2016: 49–58).

section sets out to explain why such discourses of righteousness so often developed hand-in-hand with some form of divinisation.

Some Notes on How to Think About Sacred Kingship

Sacralisation from Below and the Isomorphic Languages of Hierarchy

If sacred kingship is a play scripted at court, it is one that must pay acute attention to the tastes and expectations of its shifting audiences. It is no coincidence that when Alexander the Great transformed the possibilities of Ancient Greek political culture by showing that world-transforming might lay in the hands of an outstanding individual, his own divinisation followed.[2] This was in part a matter of his own self-understanding. But it was also a matter of deliberate policy, as he took on the styles of kingship of some of the peoples he conquered; thus was he welcomed as the son of Amun by the high priest at Siwa, shortly before adopting his pharaonic titles of rule in Egypt.[3] In a typical example of immanentist translatability, in the Greek world Amun had already been identified with Zeus, to whom the Macedonian royal house traced their ancestry through Heracles. Greek cities in Asia Minor liberated from Persian overlordship began to offer Alexander cult honours too.[4] His brief reign impressed itself so powerfully on the imagination that after his death his Ptolemaic and Seleucid successors developed their own cults of divinised kingship, and over the much longer term legendary tales of his miraculous exploits came to circulate across the expanse of Eurasia.[5]

All this follows readily from the immanentist proposition: what else could such extraordinary power be than a manifestation of a supernatural potency? Never mind the business of securing popular legitimacy, how does an Alexander *explain* his conquests to himself? How do his subjects explain it, as they find themselves part of an improbable new

---

[2] Mitchell 2013.
[3] This is a complex episode: Lane Fox 1973: 200–208; Hölbl 2000: 10–12. Collins 2014: 64, argues for personal motivation.
[4] Lane Fox 1973: 438–447; and Woolf 2008 for currents of sacred kingship in Mediterranean. Thanks to Lynette G. Mitchell for discussion and for sharing her manuscript in private correspondence.
[5] Stoneman 2010; Erickson 2013.

empire stretching from Macedonia to Pakistan? (Much later the extraordinary ascensions of Zhu Yuanzhang [1328–1398], the founder of
the Ming Dynasty, and Timur [r. 1370–1405], the founder of the
Timurids, would also stimulate rumours of their recourse to supernatural assistance.)[6] To be sure, the Greek cities of Asia Minor probably
offered divine cult to Alexander in anticipation of gaining leverage
with their new master. Later Greek communities offered Roman
magistrates divine honours, and repeatedly asked permission to bestow
them on emperors, which the latter either acceded to or declined.[7]
This dimension of divinisation from below may be considered an
example of what Arjun Appadurai referred to as 'ritualised coercive
deference', in which flattery is designed to trap the superior into
acceding to the inferior's supplications.[8]

But is this form of gift exchange not what relations with metapersons
are like more generally? Note, then, that such supplications may have
the elicitation of entirely supernatural boons in mind. Such a popular
capture of royal potency may be seen in the annual Dasara rites of the
kingdom of Bastar state (now in Madhya Pradesh), as analysed by
Gell: 'A massive ritual event which played a key role in preserving
Bastar as a large, unified, kingdom' by drawing in the scattered tribal
populations.[9] The Hindu raja was abducted in a palanquin and taken
to spend the night in the tribal encampment, feasting on wild meats
and alcohol, before being returned to the centre. Thus he was domesticated into a locally useful goddess through induction into commensality, just in the normal manner of sacrifice to metapersons.[10]

Quite apart from this, there is also the simple and ubiquitous tendency to use the same symbolic and behavioural codes for constructing
both earthly and supernatural hierarchies.[11] The homology that may

---

[6] Moin 2012: 33; Dubois 2011: 37. Compare Ellis and ter Haar 2004: 85.
[7] Woolf 2008: 244–245; Price 1987: 84. Compare the apparent role of popular
    acclamation in the first Mesopotamian ruler to attain a clearly divine status,
    Naram-sin (2254–2218 BCE): Michalowski 2008: 33–34.
[8] Gell 1997: 436. Ancient Rome: Gradel 2002: 59.   [9] Gell 1997: 436.
[10] Gell 1997: 442.
[11] Maurice Bloch 1974: 79, sees religion originating as a 'special strategy of
    leadership', making rulers by dehumanising them. Graeber and Sahlins 2017:
    67, argue that 'the state came from heaven to earth—rather than the gods from
    earth to heaven', given that egalitarian societies also have heavenly hierarchies.
    Ando 2013 argues the opposite for Roman cult – that the governance of heaven
    comes to conform to the governance of earth. Whichever: the point is that when
    mortal hierarchies did emerge it was often through a mutually constitutive

result is most famously expressed in the bureaucratic vision of Heaven in China. The celestial Jade Emperor ruled over a court of gods closely resembling that of his imperial counterpart below, in which deities functioned as officers and magistrates with their particular worldly remits, and appeared dressed as such in village temples.[12]

This is not at all strange: rulers, just like gods, are present in their subjects' lives as concentrations of power.[13] As King James I of England (and VI of Scotland) argued in 1610: 'Kings are justly called gods for that they exercise a manner or resemblance of Divine power upon earth.'[14] There is, in short, a recurring tendency to equate the two forms of hierarchy such that they are understood in terms of each other.[15] This is a behavioural as well as cognitive principle, for the same codes of embodied respect – *puja* in a South Asian context – are likely to be deployed for metapersons and kings alike.[16] I am suggesting that this has its own logic, which is to some degree distinct from the play of political interest. It is, at least, not only kings who think this way: in the *Mahāparinibbāna Sutta*, the Buddha is asked how his body should be treated after death and he replies – like that of a universal monarch (*cakkavatti*), who would be placed under a stupa at a crossroads, pointing to all four directions.[17] From at least the early second millennium, Sinhala kings in Sri Lanka could only rule in possession of the Buddha's Tooth Relic, which was housed in a building grander than the palace and sometimes known as the palace. The implication of this symbolism is that the Buddha is the real king, and the mortal ruler is king by association.[18]

---

dialogue with supernatural hierarchies. Indeed, see Graeber and Sahlins 2017: 411, for some pregnant reflections on a universal logic of deference in which encompassment is signified by disembodiment.

[12] Wolf 1974; Barrett 2000: 14; Puett 2013: 96–97; Dean 2017: 19, on modern Singapore.

[13] In Hawaii: Valeri 1985: 151; in the Andes: Stern 1982: 17.

[14] *Speech to the Lords and Commons of the Parliament at White-Hall*, cited in Asch 2014: 43.

[15] Al-Azmeh 1997: 4, refers to the 'metaphorisation of power in terms of the sacred'; see also Ronald M. Davidson 2002: 71–74.

[16] Carrithers 2000.

[17] *Mahāparinibbāna Sutta*, part V, verse 26. Bandaranayake 2012: 253. At Buddha's birth, a prophecy had it that he would be either a *cakkavatti* or a Buddha: Reynolds 2005: 220.

[18] Obeyesekere 2017: 28–29.

Pluralities of Disposition and Cognition

Representations of sacred kingship may be plural and even incoherent because of the different audiences they must address. Indeed, the primary audience may not be their subjects at all, but other royal centres. Insofar as the sacralisation of kingship is concerned with the assertion of status, it is nearly always driven in part by peer-to-peer consciousness and rivalry. The question is acute: Am I a king in the way that other kings will recognise? As a result, courts may even fashion one 'face' for the outside world, while another visage altogether turns to look inwards. This is perhaps most notable in the selective Islamisation of certain sub-Saharan African courts.[19] But this domestic face too may take on a chameleon quality: the more diverse and far-flung the subject groups are – which is to say, the more 'imperial' the polity – the more diverse the performances they may invite. Indeed, in such circumstances, the main target may be an imperial elite rather than the broad mass of subjects beneath them.

However, sacred kingship is also conveyed through various genres of performance and artistic contrivance and each of these may induct the same audience into subtly different sensations of what it signifies. These are heavily aestheticised and embodied experiences in which ideas are conveyed symbolically and vaguely.[20] Royal ritual, the bulk of which surely enhanced the 'governmentality' of the court or ruling elite rather than the wider populace more directly, works by creating social situations of high arousal and high tension, in which the potential failure to conduct oneself according to strict protocol is a source of anxiety.[21] If the king is exalted by drama, colour, sensation, thrill, nervousness, excitement, disorientation, spectacle, and the psychology of the crowd, such modes may not reflect explicitly articulated principles or consciously formulated doctrine in any straightforward way. In Christian settings, for example, where assertions of substantial and personal divinisation were often awkward to assert, ceremonial forms could nudge the emotions in that direction regardless.[22] From one perspective, then, theological discriminations may matter less than cultivated dispositions.[23]

---

[19] Fisher 1994. [20] See also Al-Azmeh 1997: 4–5. [21] Bernbeck 2008: 161.
[22] Al-Azmeh 1997: 29. [23] Oakley 2006: 106; Woolf 2008: 257.

Indeed, the question of whether or not an individual holds certain ideas or even proceeds according to a particular assumption, is not at all a straightforward matter. Cognitive scientists have alerted us to the prevalence of context-dependent thinking. Rita Astuti has drawn upon fieldwork in a Vezo village on the west coast of Madagascar to illustrate the point. She reports the elder of a family calling upon the ancestors to talk with them, and adopting a special seating position, tone, and demeanour to do so. But when this is over, he stretches his legs and announces, 'It's over and there is not going to be a reply,' which makes people laugh as they resume ordinary existence. It is a joke that 'shatters the representation of the ancestors as sentient and agentive beings'.[24] In the same way people understand that sacrificial meat is eaten by the gods during the ritual but also that it will in fact be eaten by priests or celebrants afterwards. There is a direct analogy to be made here with sacred kingship, given that members of the court must in some contexts bow to the awesome numinousness of the king while in others they may gossip about his sexual affairs or change his chamber pot. Sacred kingship is so obviously 'staged' and yet compels acquiescence nonetheless. Perhaps this is a feature of ritual in general.[25]

Appreciating the significance of sacred kingship is therefore not quite the same as identifying what people 'believe' about it. To some extent, those beliefs may even be secondary elaborations of a common grammar of kingship that seems to transcend cultural boundaries.[26] Certainly, the institution has a reality which cannot be reduced to the explicitly articulated, publicly sanctioned, and culturally specific ideas about it. And yet, no less evidently, ideas or assumptions – that is, both explicitly and implicitly adhered to – must also be of vital importance. As Simon de La Loubère noted while comparing forms of reverence for royalty in different Asian societies in in the late seventeenth century, 'there is nothing that may be taken in more diverse senses, nor which may receive more different interpretations than exterior worship.'[27]

---

[24] Astuti and Bloch 2013: 108. Also relevant here is the disconnect between 'locally accepted doctrine' and spontaneous and implicit reasoning; see Boyer 2010.

[25] Compare Geertz 1983: 124; Whitmarsh 2016: 43. Versnel 2011 provides a brilliant analysis of the ambiguities of ritualised context-dependent 'as-if' thinking – 'honest hypocrisy'.

[26] Al-Azmeh 1997: 67; pertinent reflections in Puett 2013.

[27] La Loubère 1987 [1691]: 417.

He appreciated, in other words, that although the bodily grammar of kingship was often remarkably repetitive, the 'interpretations' which it expressed may be quite different.

Mere Metaphor, Meaningful Metaphor, and Beyond Metaphor

The same point may be made with more force about the aesthetic sphere. There is a risk that artistic representations in particular may be *less* significant than they appear because they do not correspond to widely held ideas and norms; that is to say, they are not so much the tip of a submerged iceberg of meaning as a dash of glitter cast upon a mundane sea. This means that we are obliged to assess the cultural *weight* of claims made and symbols contrived, and this sets up problems for the comparative method in particular, especially where the nature of the evidence for different cases is incommensurate. Especially when we are left with decontextualised and fragmentary sources, it may well be difficult to be sure what a divine analogy signifies: a playful literary flourish or a sudden insight into an inner cultural mechanism. Perhaps we may distinguish between three different ways of understanding the role of metaphorical cognition: first, 'mere metaphor' is useful for situations in which the language and imagery of divinity is deployed as a matter of court artifice or rather conscious artistic expression without corresponding to significant patterns of thought and behaviour in wider culture.[28] 'Meaningful metaphor' invokes situations where such correspondences are indeed present.[29] 'Beyond metaphor' describes propositions that describe substantive identity rather than analogy.

In early modern Europe, for example, royal courts started experimenting with classical motifs, which involved themes and gods from Greek and Roman mythology. These framed the monarch within the prestigious high culture of renaissance humanism, dignified them with the borrowed glamour of the ancient world, and fashioned vivid symbols for their prowess.[30] Louis XIV (r. 1643–1715), at the apogee of his claims to absolute sovereignty, was depicted in art according to a heroic repertoire that included Apollo/Helios or Alexander the Great

---

[28] On not confusing 'poetic personification with conceptual animism': Gaster 1955: 422–426.

[29] See Moin 2012 for sacred kingship as 'social phenomenon'.

[30] Gunn 1999: 116.

as role models; he might even take part in *ballets de cour* where he took on the role of an ancient god.[31] His predecessor, Henry IV, had been received into papal Avignon in 1600 with imagery dominated by the figure of Hercules.[32] It is not that such pomp necessarily lacked resonance; and it is surely telling that pagan antiquity was plundered for quasi-divinising purposes.[33] But what, ultimately, did it signify in terms of popular apprehension of the supernatural dimension of existence? Surely, rather little.[34] In this period of reformed Christian commitment, there were distinct limits to the extent to which a monarch could assert the reality of the pagan gods and align him or herself with them.[35] In one sense, all was mere metaphor. Perhaps the strangely theatrical quality to the discourse of sacred kingship invoked by historians and some contemporaries in this period is one result.[36]

But if this is the case then how ought we to approach the royal praise poetry (*praśasti*) of South Asia? A rock inscription eulogised King Parākramabāhu I (r. 1153–1186) of Sri Lanka, as one 'who surpasses the Sun in his own glory, Maheśvara in prowess, Viṣṇu in pride, Indra in deportment, Kuvera in wealth … the Moon in gentleness, Kāmadeva in the excellence of his beauty, and the Bodhisattva in the fullness of his benevolence'.[37] In Indic courtly literature, as in many other courtly genres worldwide, kings are repeatedly *compared* with the gods in this way, then, but what did this mean exactly? It was probably a 'meaningful metaphor' – or, in this case, analogy – which disclosed broadly diffused patterns of thought about the equivalence of divine and earthly hierarchy, but this could only be confirmed by

---

[31] Asch 2014: 113, though an outcry against this in 1680s: Blanning 2002: 34–37.

[32] Asch 2014: 29–30, notes the opacity of 'sophisticated and often arcane pagan symbolism' to many; Rowe 2017: 75, for Habsburgs and Hercules.

[33] The implied continuity with ancient Rome, and the use of a language which escapes the domain of the Church is also significant: see Bergin 2014. My thanks to Sarah Mortimer for discussion.

[34] But even this was enough to spur accusations of idolatry and blasphemy: Asch 2014: 115. Still Burke 1992: 127, does suggest of Hercules that 'the aura of the demigod rubbed off on' French rulers as a result.

[35] Monod 1999: 46–47.

[36] That is, conveying an uneasy apprehension of its artificiality. Nevertheless, recall that context-dependent embodied and aesthetic experience (as in the theatre of the court) may work its magic somewhat independent of ideas and beliefs.

[37] Berkwitz 2016: 329, and for fifteenth- and sixteenth-entury praise poetry Berkwitz 2017. Also *Mahāvaṃsa* XVII: 31–32 (Devānampiyatissa as 'the god among men' or manussadeva, 'human god' – Guruge 1989: 587, 836).

analysing a range of evidence issuing from beyond the sphere of court aesthetics and formal flattery itself.[38] And this is different again from inferring that it went 'beyond metaphor' to signal actual assumptions about the nature of royal being. (At the same time, it is wise to recall that what the classicist Henk Versnel referred to as 'the ambiguity of the ludic in the deification of mortals' may entail a deliberate blurring of all such boundaries.[39])

It is as if there are some common track lines that guide the progress of thinking about monarchy, but in some contexts these lead to assumptions about cause and effect, while in other contexts – where those notions have become taboo or implausible, perhaps – they stay at the level of metaphorical modes of representation.[40] For example, there is a common tendency to envisage society as somehow summed up in the body of the king, which we can find from Hawaii to the famous front-cover image of Thomas Hobbes's *Leviathan*.[41] The king *is* society, this imagery says; he is the very condition of its possibility – this is surely a meaningful metaphor. But Hobbes's use of it did not go 'beyond metaphor' as did the understandings that sustained some forms of African kingship. Here the relationship was conceived as a matter of concrete causation such that if the king became ill he must abdicate or be killed, lest his bodily affliction bring misfortune upon the whole of society.[42]

Another pervasive association is between kingship and the weather. In Shakespeare's *Henry IV Part I*, for example, the weather is mystically connected with great affairs of state, such that rebellion is accompanied by unnatural portents – much as Chinese officials scanned the skies for the appearance of dragons and comets as an augury of upheaval.[43] Yet while Shakespeare was influenced by a genuine strain

---

[38] See Charlot 1987: 138, for a similar problem of interpretation in the case of Hawaii.

[39] Versnel 2011: 441.

[40] On the broad context for the disenchantment of monarchy in Europe: Burke 1992: 125–133.

[41] Hobbes: Malcolm 1998: 141; Hawaii: Valeri 1985: 146; France, Louis XIV: Asch 2014: 112; Akwapim of Ghana: Gilbert 2008: 172; Japan: Rambelli and Teeuwen 2003b: 3; Nepal: Burghart 1987: 247; Mughals: Juneja: 2011: 236–237.

[42] These include the Akuropon and Akwapin in Ghana among others: Gilbert 1987: 326; de Heusch 2005; Graeber 2011b.

[43] Marchant 2008; Brook 2010: Ch. 1.

of cosmic thinking in the chronicles on which he drew, an English king would not be held as directly accountable for unfavourable weather in the manner of a Chinese emperor. In 1832, after failing to obstruct drought after many sacrifices, the Daoguang emperor (r. 1820–1850) performed an exceptional prayer for rain in which he announced, 'I tremble as I consider the causes of the drought; the fault must be mine.'[44] Nor would rulers from either England or China actually be killed if they failed to provide the right weather, as some rainmaker kings were in Africa.[45] Any comparative analysis must find a way of appreciating the common ground of such phenomena and their crucial divergences.

The Divinised King

Among many peoples the task of government has been greatly facilitated by a superstition that the governors belong to a superior order of beings and possess certain supernatural or magical powers to which the governed can make no claim and can offer no resistance.

James Frazer, *The Devil's Advocate*[46]

Immanentist societies vary widely over time and space in how far they attempt to sacralise their kings. When they do, however, it will be in the mode of 'divinisation'. *Kings are divinised when they are regarded as godlike and treated as if they were metapersons.*

The sacrality of the king is therefore a matter of the nature of his being, which is conceived as somehow *close* to divinity or even sharing in it.[47] Making a king becomes like raising a cathedral spire, pushing him up and out as far as possible to the realm of the ancestors, spirits, or gods. While this category of 'divinised kingship' is used consistently in this book as a summation of the immanentist mode of sacralisation, on occasion it may be helpful to make a further distinction between two different subtypes: (1) *heroic divinisation* entails the assertion of individual or dynastic superiority that exceeds normal human capabilities; and (2) *cosmic divinisation* entails the presentation of the king as a ritual pivot, an intermediary between human society and the divine

---

[44] Duindam 2016: 50.
[45] Simonse 2005. Echoes in Buddhist *jātaka* stories: Gombrich 1988: 63–64.
[46] Frazer 1927: 6.
[47] Hocart 1941: Chapter I; Bellah 2011: 231; Al-Azmeh 1997: 18.

forces that govern its affairs. This is by way of allowing us to see, for example, that the divinisation of Alexander as an expression of his personal prowess has a different quality from that of the Tui Tonga in early nineteenth century, a ritual focal point as a living representative of deity but increasingly denuded of real political power. Alexander did not merely inherit an office or take on a ritual function, he unveiled his unparalleled being and sundry offices and titles followed.[48] Consider the table below:

Type:	Heroic	Cosmic
Achieved through:	Deeds	Ritual
Relation to society:	Exposed	Isolated
Achieves:	Status	Legitimacy
Stability:	Brief	Enduring
Archetypal Location	Battlefield	Palace
Normativity:	Transgressive	Ordered

These associations are rather loose: they barely amount even to the formation of ideal types; certainly no attempt is made here to force any one kingship system into either side of the dichotomy. In real life a dense of web of interconnections will stretch across both sides. For example, in some cases, it was by demonstrating their heroic qualities that kings most effectively proved their cosmic centrality.[49] Rather, this tablature is a way of summarising certain analytical suggestions. For example, it would seem that the heroic form carries more weight when it is accompanied by *deeds*, which display the extent of the individual's supernatural power, while the cosmic form is chiefly expressed through *ritual*, which effaces his humanity and mortality. The heroic assertion rings most true when the king has generated a charismatic aura through feats of conquest, feeding off popular fascination from below and egomania from above. The cosmic form often lends itself to expression through highly orchestrated action or stillness. In these cases, the objective is not to establish the unique personality of the ruler but to smother it in ceremonial propriety. The king's body may be withdrawn from sight or displayed in artificial and stylised form.

[48] Mitchell and Melville 2013b: 7.
[49] Further, the divinisation of rulers through genealogy, discussed in the section 'Intimacy with the Gods', spreads across both columns in important ways, while charismatic kings acquire legitimacy through their status.

Heroic Divinisation and the Instability of Charisma

A further hypothesis follows: that strongly divinised kings usually only adopt a relatively open, sociable, and free style when they can rely on heroic claims underpinned by charisma. But this possibility is usually limited in duration: as the reign proceeds or as setbacks are endured, or, more often, as reign follows reign, and as feats of military magic (or *celeritas*) give way to palace routine and administration (*gravitas*), then there is likely to be a greater reliance on the ritualised form, and this is likely to involve the elaboration of sociocosmic claims.[50]

This hypothesis no doubt carries Weberian overtones. The value of Weber's approach to charisma is that it identifies a source of authority deriving from the tangible achievements of the individual that allows him or her to both shape and attract popular visions of their supernatural qualities but which is subject to empirical jeopardy and therefore unstable.[51] All this fits very well with the 'immanentist' mentality explored in Chapter 1. Indeed, the concepts that so many societies have generated to indicate supernatural power as evident in prowess and fortune (variations on the theme of *mana*) can be understood as rather explicit emic examples of what the etic concept of charisma aims at: these are the mechanisms by which success in battle, for example, is immediately translated into authority and legitimacy.[52] Surely, also, the prevalent centrality of such concepts helps explain the common absence of fixed principles of succession such as primogeniture in monarchical systems – and therefore the prevalence of violent clashes and interregna – which otherwise may seem merely dysfunctional. They are presumably often informed by the recognition that contenders ought to be granted the opportunity not only to demonstrate their practical fitness to rule through competition but also to generate charisma through victory.[53]

---

[50] Hence the difference between accessible, charisma-based Greek kingship and the inaccessible ritualised form of their Achaemenid neighbours may be an effect as well as a cause of the relative instability of the former, rarely lasting more than a few generations. See Mitchell [MS].

[51] Weber 1978, I: 242–245. Exegesis: Keyes 2002; 247–249. In what follows, I do not, however, attempt here to deploy Weber's specific concept of charisma in any faithful manner.

[52] See Geertz 1983: 136; Lamana 2005: 29, on *camac* among Incas.

[53] As Schnepel 1995: 10, has it for the Shilluk.

Weber suggested that charisma could be rendered into a more stable form through its 'routinisation'. This is most apt in relation to the genealogical principle whereby rulers claimed descent from actual founder heroes or deities, and which is discussed further below.[54] It is a little less helpful as a description of the process by which heroic claims (focused on the intrinsic nature of the individual) subside in favour of a greater emphasis on cosmic kingship (focused on intercessory function).[55] Charisma is not a central concept of this book, but where it is used it is therefore reserved for the attribution of supernatural qualities and powers to individuals as revealed most particularly in heroic accomplishment. This also helps to preserve Weber's insight into the potentially transgressive nature of charismatic authority, the way that unprecedented achievement may smash through existing cultural norms, as in Akbar surpassing aspects of ulema Islam.[56] Equally, Julius Caesar's exploits in Republican Rome surely fuelled plans in his final dictatorial phase for a cult to him as a 'divus' – originally a synonym for god, but now defined as a god who had once been a man – with his own priest ('flamen') and cult statue, and so on. (Indeed, this is often given as one reason for his assassination.)[57] The unruly warlord unifier Oda Nobunaga (1534–1592) might stand as a Japanese example. A number of scholars are sceptical about the suggestion that he had himself deified towards the end of his life, pointing to the absence of precedent amongst other reasons, but a comparative perspective would prompt us to take such evidence seriously.[58] (Meanwhile, the emperors of Japan in this period represent a decayed and almost redundant version of cosmic kingship.)

Traditions that normally placed distinct limits on the monarch's identification with the divine might therefore be overwhelmed by demonstrations of heroic prowess. One of the suggestions emerging out of a recent forum on ancient sacred kingship is that more explicit claims to divinity were most forcefully asserted during periods of particular crisis or achievement, and especially when great empires

---

[54] Compare Weber 1978: 248. See the 'Intimacy with the Gods' section'.
[55] Less apt insofar as there is not some initial store of 'charisma' stuff that is somehow stabilised; rather authority is differently derived.
[56] Puett 2002: 234–235, on the principle of transgressive innovation.
[57] Woolf 2008: 246–250; Price 1987: 70–78. Gradel 2002: 68–72, for a slightly different reading.
[58] CK.

were created or rapidly expanded.[59] The first instance of explicit claims of divinity in Mesopotamia, by Naram-sin, (2254–2218 BCE) occurred during the 'first world empire' of Akkad.[60] The second king in Mesopotamia to be identified by scholars as 'actually' divine in status was King Shulgi (2094–2047 BCE) of the third dynasty of Ur, who is identified also with abnormal feats – this time holding the empire together after 'almost fatal state collapse' and then expanding into foreign lands.[61] But neither Shulgi nor his predecessor, Naram-Sin, passed on their particular kind of unqualified divine status to successors.[62] Such claims are therefore usually relatively ephemeral or punctuated, and under normal circumstances more muted claims were advanced.

This is to compare forms of sacred kingship as dynamic entities, ever 'on the move'. Applying this approach to Ancient China, Michael Puett shows how 'empire and deification happened together', when the First Emperor of China (of the Qin dynasty) sought the best ritual masters and drugs in order to acquire immortality by ascending to the state of godhood. This would have sociocosmic implications but was also a reflection of his will to power.[63] There is, then, a dimension of the elaboration of heroic divinisation that has little to do with popular legitimacy or communal expectations but is all about the pretensions and sensations that a rapid ascent to power – the heady assertion of status – will generate in the ruler himself.[64] Subsequently, however, particularly once the overreach of the state was exposed following Emperor Wu (r. 140–187 BCE), the form of divine kingship switched to a more passive cosmic mode in which the king was not himself a being stretching for divinity but an interlocutor with Heaven, a stationary ritual pivot.[65]

---

[59] Bernbeck 2008, Winter 2008, Michalowski 2008, and compare Duindam 2016: 302.

[60] Brisch 2008b: 7; Michalowski 2008.

[61] His year name first took on the cuneiform signifier for 'god' in the twenty-first year of his reign, which marks the start of extensive military campaigns.

[62] Michalowski 2008: 40.   [63] Puett 2002: 236–237.

[64] Compare Gose 1996a: 15, on Incas: 'The goal of the ruler was to aggrandize himself in a manner that knew of no distinction between the spiritual and the worldly … to constitute his own divinity through an irresistible display of imperialist might.'

[65] And an embodiment of virtue: Puett 2002: 307–310. Note that Wu's own form of self-deification had accompanied 'massive military expansion': Puett 2015: 241.

In Ayutthaya (Siam), there were multiple ways of asserting both heroic and cosmic understandings of kingship from the start, but there is an observable shift in style from the open approach of warrior kings such as Naresuan (r. 1590–1605) to the far more circumscribed and ritualised forms of Prasat Thong (r. 1629–1656) and Narai (r. 1656–1688), who had ceased to lead their troops into battle. But after this elaborate edifice of monarchy was pulled to the floor with the sacking of Ayutthaya by the Burmese in 1767, it was as if the cycle could start again. The subsequent disintegration of central authority presented a typical scene for the emergence of (unstable) charismatic authority. A minor provincial official, Taksin, engineered an ascent to become the leader of a resurgent Siam, retaking the conquered territories and expanding them. He lacked the inherited authority of royal blood but more than made up for it with the charisma generated by preternatural success in battle. At this point he began to experiment in practices that would concretise his godhood, claimed that he was able to fly, and announced in diplomatic letters that he had the twelve marks of the *cakkavatti*.[66] He had overreached in the spiritual realm, transgressed too violently, and was deposed.[67] Similarly, there are clues that the warrior king Rājasiṃha I (r. 1581–1593) of the upstart city of Sītāvaka, who almost drove the Portuguese from Sri Lanka, was drawn to self-deification and ended up suffering a loss of legitimacy (and a fearful popular postmortem deification).[68] Such cases again indicate that a complex psychology influencing both leader and followers lies behind newly forceful claims of heroic divinisation.

Cosmic Kingship

The project of cosmic kingship does not depend on the revelation of the superlative individual. It is rather sustained by the cognitive tendency to leave the biological, social, political, and cosmological realms relatively undifferentiated.[69] All are held to be subject to the operations of supernatural power. The figure of the king, which modern common sense would locate in just the political domain, can thus be established

---

[66] See *CK*; Gesick 1983c: 100; Reynolds 2006: 144–145.
[67] His parvenu status may have made him particularly vulnerable to such criticisms. (Thanks to Vic Lieberman.)
[68] Alan Strathern 2007a: 190–192.   [69] Oakley 2006: 7.

as the central pivot of all of them.[70] Indeed, metapersons and kings are comparable means to the same end. From one angle, at least, gods are ways of making the awesome and unfeeling powers of the universe approachable by endowing them with more or less human qualities such that they may become amenable to gift exchange and supplication. Cosmic kingship, on the other hand, may be seen as a way of dealing with such powers from the opposite direction, by pushing a man into their sphere in order to contend with them on the basis of greater parity.

The scholarship of certain forms of kingship in sub-Saharan Africa (among, for example, the Jukun, Bemba, and Nyakyusa) has sometimes presented the institution as less a mechanism of mediation with the gods than as a potent ritual object with more direct and immediate effects.[71] Among these societies we find the kings and queens who are held responsible for natural or social disasters, whose bodies must be healthy in order to ensure the health of the society.[72] Elsewhere, I have referred to this as 'magical kingship'.[73] More active warrior chiefs, such as the rulers of the Imbangala or Ndongo, credited with very direct control over the elements and apparently the main focus of religious reverence themselves, might also be placed in this category.[74] However, in a larger perspective these types still sit firmly within the category of the 'cosmic', for they are also attempts to place the king at the heart of a ritual attempt to access and regulate the forces and metapersons that surge around the human community.

---

[70] Many analysts of monarchy have noted its role in establishing harmony between supernatural and natural realms; see especially Oakley 2006: 7–22, and Duindam 2016: 22; Assmann 2012: 372, on 'mutual modelling', also discussing Voegelin on 'microcosmos' and 'macranthropos'; Tambiah 1976: 256; Berger 1970: 34; Frankfort et al. 1946: 241; Burghart 1987: 260–269.

[71] De Heusch 2005: 26–27.

[72] Beattie 1971: 197. It is this that allows kings also to be scapegoats, blamed when things go wrong: Friedman 1985: 269.

[73] Alan Strathern 2009: 17. See essays on Africa in Quigley 2005a; Hooper 2006: 38, on Oceania.

[74] Heywood 2017: 15, 22. The Dominican friar, João dos Santos, reported that the Imbangalas (Zimbas) 'do not adore idols or recognize any God, but instead they venerate and honour their king, whom they regard as a divinity ... [who says] that he alone is god of the earth, for which reason if it rains when he does not wish it to do so, or is too hot, he shoots arrows at the sky for not obeying him'. Schoffeleers 1992: 124.

The ritual activity of the ruler allowed the supernatural or cosmic realm to be brought into productive alignment with the mundane.[75] It was this idea, of course, that propelled the construction of vast architectural schemes establishing the microcosm–macrocosm equation in concrete form.[76] Ancient Egyptian kingship, for example, was understood as a vital mechanism for the maintenance of creation and the exercise of *maat*, the principle of world order.[77] Given the unchecked parallelism between different domains of reality, natural disorders (strange births, comets) were often understood as corollaries of political disorders (a rebellion).[78]

It is as if the regularities of nature could not be relied upon to be regular without the agency of a regulator in the form of a king. One recurrent means of calling the world to order was through the rites of New Year festivals. So the king becomes a champion of the liminal period in which the old year becomes the new among the Swazi; enacts the battle between Marduk and a female sea goddess in the New Year festival in Babylonia; carries out the climatic ceremony of the royal bath of the Merina in Madagascar; or reclaims the land for the use of chiefs from the fertility god Lono in the Makahiki rites in Hawaii.[79] Rulers were thereby fashioned as the means by which cycles of death and life, chaos and order, darkness and light were stabilised.

The more that we understand these symbolic themes as not 'merely metaphorical' elaborations but as corresponding to deeply lodged ontologies, the more it becomes possible to grasp the sense in which cosmic kingship functioned as a communal project. If, in the previous chapter, it was noted that rulers may use religion to discipline their subjects, here it can be noted that subjects use religion to discipline their kings – to make sure that their powers are harnessed for

---

[75] Duindam 2016: 48–51; Bellah 2011: 186–187.

[76] An inscription of Jayavarman VII has him 'marrying' his new city of Angkor Thom 'with the intention of procreating well-being in the Universe' (Groslier 2006: 90). Note Puett's criticisms (2002: 32–33, 42) of the Wheatley hypothesis of the general origin of the urban centre as Axis Mundi.

[77] Frandsen 2008: 47.   [78] Moin 2012.

[79] Valeri 1985: 226; Babylonia: Kuhrt 1987: 30–37, Al-Azmeh 1997: 36; Feeley-Harnik 1985: 281; Oakley 2006: 15–16; Maurice Bloch 1987: 276–277, 'By the ritual, the authority of the king was naturalised, in that it was merged with cycles beyond human action and therefore human challenge.'

the benefit of society as a whole.[80] As Evans-Pritchard noted, for the
Shilluk, the king is an instantiation of the ancestor-god, Nyikang,
in whom 'are centred all those interests which are common to all the
people: success in war against foreigners and the fertility and
health of men, cattle, crops, and of those wild beasts which are of
service to man'.[81] Visiting Loango to the north of Kongo, in the first
years of the seventeenth century, the Englishman Andrew Battell
remarked, 'The king is so honoured as though he were a god among
them, and is called Sanibe and Pongo [*Nzambi-ampungu*, 'the most
high God']. And they believe that he can give them rain when he
listeth. So once a year, when it is time to rain, that is in December,
the people come to beg rain and bring their gifts to the king, for
none come empty.'[82]

The more completely the basic immanentist proposition is adhered
to – that all forms of flourishing have a supernatural origin – the
more concretely divinised kings may be considered as its solution. It
is only in this light that Clifford Geertz's famous argument that in
Balinese kingship 'power served pomp, and not pomp power' begins
to make sense.[83] Geertz's theoretical focus on meaning creation
rather than reality manipulation perhaps obscured, however, the
fact that 'pomp' (ritual) was after all a means to power – but the
supernatural power to sustain the universe as a hospitable environment for human life.

Little wonder, then, that the death of kings could signal a communal
sensation of vertiginous destabilisation, in which social norms were
subverted and a genuinely distraught form of limited anarchy played
out.[84] In early nineteenth-century Hawaii, William Ellis reported that
when the high-ranking chief Keopulani died, the people of Maui
dreaded the disturbances that would ensue with the suspension of
tabus, and sought to transfer their properties to the missionary enclos-
ure for safety. For the custom was that

---

[80] On ruler–subject reciprocity in Africa: Ellis and ter Haar 2004: 146, Duindam
2016: 45.
[81] Evans-Pritchard 2011: 414; Schnepel 1995: 61.   [82] Ravenstein 1901: 46.
[83] Geertz 1980: 13.
[84] Bellah 2011: 206; Oakley 2006: 27. At the death of Tiberius's heir, Germanicus,
in 19 CE, 'the populace stoned temples and upset altars of the gods; people
threw their household deities into the streets and exposed their new born
children'. Price 1987: 62.

as soon as the chief had expired, the whole neighbourhood exhibited a scene of confusion, wickedness, and cruelty, seldom witnessed even in the most barbarous society. The people ran to and fro without their clothes, appearing and acting more like demons than human beings; every vice was practiced, and almost every species of crime perpetrated.[85]

The cosmic theme thus emerges out of a dialogue between ruling elites and their subjects, but there is no need to imagine that it was politically innocent. In the previous chapter, it was suggested that immanentism facilitates a certain fluidity of movement between political and ritual roles, and that rulers attempted to take advantage of this by dominating the priestly function in order to consolidate the religious field. Chinese state ritual was conducted by the emperor and the imperial clan or officials rather than by a distinct priesthood.[86] Roman emperors were '*pontifex maximus*'.[87] In Hawaii, kings were distinguished by their unique role in consecrating human sacrifice.

The Ambiguities of Divinity

It may have been noticed that this book avoids the phrase 'divine kingship' (opting for the rather less resonant 'divinised' instead). Surveying the mass of anthropological and historical literature on the subject, it becomes clear how few areas of scholarship have lent their unanimous assent to the term.[88] At times, emic concepts come to our rescue, where we can pick up on explicit contemporary debates on the propriety of rulers moving from more implicit or limited associations with divinity to more outright assertions – as with the Mesopotamian Shulgi, or Julius Caesar in his last days. But these do not get us far in setting up globally useful etic concepts. These scholarly disagreements reflect ambiguities inherent in the nature of cognition and representation (as noted above)[89] and also in what 'divinity' might be as a concept of cross-cultural comparison.

---

[85] Ellis 1832: 177. See also Valeri 1985: 220.   [86] McMullen 1987: 186.

[87] Woolf 2008: 252. Compare Tonga: Niumeitolu 2007: 66–67; Tahiti: Newbury 1961: xxxiv; Tikopia: Bellah 2011: 184; Egypt: Frandsen 2008: 47; Dahomey: Yai 1993: 257.

[88] For example, Brisch 2008b. Ancient Egyptian scholarship is unusual in its consensus on divine kingship, according to Frandsen 2008.

[89] See the section 'Pluralities of Disposition and Cognition'.

Yet they also reflect a real ambiguity at the heart of the project of divinised kingship itself.[90] Eminent scholars of 'divine kingship' such as Hocart and Evans-Pritchard have warned that kings are very rarely 'divine' in any unqualified sense.[91] But it may be added: rarely are they 'merely human' in an unqualified sense. They are in-between things, neither one thing nor the other. In the cosmic mode that is their purpose and their power, for they are meeting points between persons and metapersons: they are channels, conduits, pivots, cruxes. And, consistently, it has been understood that this may be achieved by making them *godlike*. Already human, they are pushed part way into the divine, treated as if they were divine, or equivalent to it substantial ways.[92] Their humanity is blurred and smudged until it shades into something higher.[93]

They may be pushed greater or lesser distances, of course. This spectrum of greater or lesser divinisation applies not only to different cultural traditions, but to different reigns of the same dynasty and even between different genres of representation issuing from any one point in a reign. In general terms, however, at one end may be placed rulers whose normal humanity is entirely taken for granted but are yet endowed with the responsibility of priestly supplication. At the other end might be placed rulers who have become the subjects of cult worship in their own lifetime.[94] Admittedly, it is a weakness of the term 'divinisation' that it resonates less well with the former end of the spectrum (the subtype term 'cosmic' kingship is more usefully vague on this point). Nevertheless, the term does have the advantage of signalling that kings are rarely simply priests, by virtue of the centrality of their intercessory role and the density of their symbolic functions.[95] The relationship between divinised kings and gods is often understood as more intimate, permanent, inherent, critical, and familial than that between the priests and gods.

---

[90] Morrison 2008: 270, refers to 'a kind of orgy of ambiguation'. The mediatory role of cosmic kingship seems equivalent to what Mesopotamian scholarship (Michalowski 2008: 34) describes as 'sacred kingship'.
[91] Piggott 1997: 211; Sahlins 2004: 161, drawing on Hocart. Graeber 2011b: 3–4.
[92] Graeber 2011b: 1; Versnel 2011.   [93] Root 2013: 50–61.
[94] Mesopotamia: Michalowski 2008: 38–40; Rome: Woolf 2008; Maya: Friedel 2008: 193; Tonga: Niumeitolu 2007: 127; Incas: D'Altroy 2003: 91.
[95] For example, Valeri 1985: 130–171.

The project of rendering a man godlike is always liable to be fraught and incomplete.[96] What makes it at all feasible are immanentist conceptions of the entities and forces for which the English words of 'gods' and 'divinity' stand as an inexact placeholders. Once again, exegetes of immanentist cultures – from the classical world to pre-Columbian Americas – habitually must begin by noting the absence of any great ontological breach between mundane and the divine, and the presence, therefore, of a single fluid domain housing both normal persons and metapersons.[97] Hence, as Woolf says about Rome, for 'many of the religious cultures of the empire it is preferable to imagine a continuum stretching from men to the greatest creator deities. Emperors were the lowest of the gods, and the greatest of men. They were the greatest of priests and the least of all those beings that were paid cult.'[98]

Recall how human-like deities of the immanentist imagination may be in their emotions and motives, as examined in Chapter 1.[99] Deities can be seen as more or less anthropomorphised ways of talking about the powers everywhere at work in mundane reality. As Steven Hooper says of Oceania, 'Gods in most cultural contexts were not remote omniscient beings but were persons or things with life to give.'[100] In Japan, according to Piggott, 'An ordinary human can assign divinity even to a toothpick.'[101] Visible human beings may be understood as sharing in the 'divine stuff' that nonvisible metapersons possessed. Lorraine Gesick, describing common properties of Southeast Asian polities, referred to the 'belief that all beings ranked hierarchically according to their relative proximity to the sacred. The higher one's status, the more sacral stuff – merit, *pon, barami, śakti*, white blood – one was believed to possess in one's person.'[102] This would express no less well the possession of *mana* by the Hawaiian elite (*ali'i*). The latter was partly a matter of genealogical inheritance, but it was also demonstrated by prowess, and it was this that rendered the

---

[96] Gilbert 2008: 186.
[97] Stern 1982: 53–56; Al-Azmeh 1997: 19; Burghart 1987: 237; Bellah 2011: 212; Howe 1996.
[98] Woolf 2008: 256. Therefore it is wrong to assume that the priestly function of the king rules out his divinity (consider the scholarship of Ancient Egyptian kingship, emphatic on both). Momigliano 1986: 99, on Roman emperors.
[99] Bernbeck 2008: 158.   [100] Hooper 2006: 36.
[101] Piggott 1997: 209–210.   [102] Gesick 1983b: 1, 4.

paramount chief or king in Hawaii suitable to intercede with the gods.[103] No wonder then that cosmic kings could be credited with godlike supernatural powers – over the rain, over disease, over enemies, over the rough seas.[104]

One way that scholarship has attempted to resolve the paradoxes of the divinised king is through the Kantorowiczian device of distinguishing between the person and office – in which 'it is the kingship, and not the king who is divine', as Evans-Pritchard put it.[105] This has the merit of gaining some purchase on the way in which the position of strongly divinised kings may be distinctly conditional – subject to election, dethronement, or assassination – who anyway must at some point confront the unavoidable fact of their mortality.[106] And it is certainly true that there is often a certain sense in which kings are man-made objects that may be unmade by men too.[107] But, it is also true that the linguistic and behavioural structures of divinised kingship strive to obscure that fact and represent the person of the king as *embodying* divine powers and qualities – particularly where a more heroic mode is in evidence. The differentiation of person and office is often de facto irrelevant. The result may seem logically incoherent at one level; but we may just need to rest content with paradox as an integral quality of king creation.

Intimacy with the Gods

In ontological terms, kings are divinised not so much by asserting their identity with godhead, as by their intimacy with and proximity to the gods. Monarchs are commonly credited with divine descent, which implies bodily continuity. The origin stories of the Inca rulers traced them back to Inti, the Sun.[108] By the end of the seventh century,

---

[103] Here the distinction between heroic and cosmic divinised kingship is a hindrance.

[104] These documented in *CK*. Also Friedel 2008: 191; Tomlinson 2009: 76, chiefs in Fiji 'were believed to speak with *mana*, that is, to utter words that carried automatic efficacy'.

[105] Graeber 2011b: 3; Evans-Pritchard 2011: 34–35.

[106] For example, Read 1994: 58, 'People supported and responded to the ruler as long as it looked like he was possessed by Huitzilopochtli.'

[107] Sahlins 2004: 161.

[108] Rostworowski and Morris 1999: 792. Lamana 2005: 11, has the Inca as a 'semi-divine, supernatural being.'

the Tennō ('heavenly sovereign' or 'emperor') of Japan was presented as descended from the sun deity Amaterasu, which allowed court edicts and poems to describe him 'as a very God' (*kamunagara*).[109] Thus an edict read out at Monmu's accession in 697 refers to him as a 'Sovereign that is a manifest God (*akitsu mi-kami*) ruling over the Great land of many Islands'.[110] Piggott presents this as a 'shamanic' role of 'conditional' divinity, which did not efface the humanity of the sovereign.[111] No doubt; cosmic kings are always 'twinned beings'.[112] The intercessory role of the sovereign is very clear in the early Japanese material, in particular with regard to ensuring fertility, but this surely drove rather than hindered claims of divine descent: it was because the emperor was in effect dealing with his own past family members that he was so plausible an interlocutor with them.[113] Indeed, the climax of the famous *daijōsai*, a greatly expanded harvest ceremony marking the ascension of a new emperor, was (and is) a private act of commensality and communion with the ancestral kami, in order to ensure the provision of their bounty.[114]

Kings may be conceived as kin to the gods: as their children, siblings, or marriage partners. The ritual cycle of Ayutthaya royalty at one point included a rite which climaxed with intercourse with female spirits.[115] This was probably influenced by elements of neighbouring Khmer kingship. At the end of the thirteenth century, the Chinese ambassador Zhou Daguan wrote an account of his stay in Angkor. He reported the story that every night the king alone ascended the steep steps of the mountainous royal temple ('celestial palace') of Phimeanakas, in order to couple with a *naga* (a nine-headed snake spirit) in the shape of a woman – for the prosperity of the country depended on it.[116] (See Figure 3.1.) A similar idea, of the sultan's

---

[109] Bowring 2005: 45–46. Kuroda 1996: 361, refers to the Ise notion that Amaterasu thereby became an 'earthly deity'.

[110] Thanks to Laurence Mann for checking the translation of the edict in K. Kitagawa 1987: 3.

[111] And refers to a line of succession of Sovereign August Children of the God of Heaven: Piggott 1997: 208–209.

[112] To borrow from Schnepel 1995.   [113] Naumann 2000: 63–65.

[114] Bowring 2005: 44–45; Breen and Teeuwen 2010: 168–199.

[115] Baker and Phongpaichit 2016: 72, 124–125 on the *Bophok* rite.

[116] Daguan 2016: 25. Coe 2003: 33, 112, describes this as 'probably legendary' but popular belief is perhaps more telling than actuality. Moreover, it reflects

Figure 3.1 Phimeanakas, a temple inside Angkor Thom, Cambodia.

marriage to the serpent queen of the Southern Ocean, animated stories and rites of kingship in Yogyakarta into the twentieth century.[117] The ruler's marriage to this metaperson of the water was directly credited with powers of protection and fructification.[118]

In a hymn to an aspect of the goddess Inanna (identified with the Venus star), the fourth king of the Isin dynasty, Iddin-Dagan, takes her as his lover: the hymn describes how a chapel was built for her and 'the king, as if he were a god, lives with her there ... She bathes (her) loins for the king.'[119] The first Mesopotamian ruler regarded as 'deified' by scholarship, Naram-Sin, may have been presented as the consort of this goddess in her Akkadian form, Ishtar. The next 'deified' Mesoptamian ruler, Shulgi, claimed to be the brother of Gilgamesh.[120] The Sapa Inca, meanwhile, had formidable parents to be hosted: 'As the son of the Sun he drank to Him and induced Him to send his life-giving rains;

the Khmer origin story of the union between a Brahman and a naga princess, and a more general understanding of the success of the Khmer polity/ society as a union of two symbolic poles, the first associated with water, and indigenous female local spirits, and the second conflating land, royal sovereignty, the phallus, Sanskritic culture, and Indic gods. See also Groslier 2006.

[117] Hughes-Freeland 1991: 149–150.   [118] Levenda 2011: 247–257.
[119] Michalowski 2008. Thanks to Nicole Brisch for discussion.
[120] Michalowski 2008. 34–36; cf Selz 2008: 20.

as the son of the Earth he prevented the Flood by way of his heavy drinking.'[121]

In other cases the dual nature of kings may be expressed through the notion that they are intermittently possessed by the gods, or instantiate them, or are copresent with them.[122] The following, taken from the first formal address to a new ruler of the Aztecs, is eloquent on the resulting paradox:

Although thou art human, as we are, although thou art our friend, although thou art our son, our younger brother, our older brother, no more art thou human, as we are; we do not look on thee as human ... Thou callest out to, thou speakest in a strange tongue to the god, the Lord of the Near, of the Nigh. And within thee he calleth out to thee; he is within thee; he speaketh from thy mouth. Thou art his lip, thou art his jaw, thou art his tongue.[123]

The word for ruler of a city-state among the Aztecs was 'the speaker' (*tlatoani*): he speaks to direct the life of his people, of course, but he also speaks for the gods.[124] He was the 'flute of Tezcatlipoca', and possessed by him in certain rituals, but he could also be associated with Quetzalcoatl, the deity of priestly wisdom, or proceed into battle in the garb of the war god Huitzilopochtli.[125] Hence some scholars speak of such rulers as 'man-gods'.[126]

In Hawaii, the king, as 'the most divine of men ... instantiates different major gods ... according to a precise ritual calendar', although the connection with the war god Ku was pre-eminent.[127] In Fiji, the sacred king 'had a human form by nature that embodied a divine form by consecration', as Sahlins put it.[128] If gods could also be embodied in certain animals or priests during temple rituals, what set apart the king was that his whole life, pervasively ritualised, 'testified to this duality', and made him permanently 'by way of a human god [*kalou tamata*]'.[129] Across the Pacific, chiefs 'were embodiments of

[121] Zuidema 1989. Compare Chinese emperors as 'Sons of Heaven' worshipping the Heaven and Earth as their parents.
[122] Compare the possession of the Shilluk king by Nyikang: Graeber 2011b: 38; elder/ancestor conflation among the Merina: Maurice Bloch 1974: 78.
[123] Clendinnen 1991a: 80.   [124] Carrasco 1998: 127–128.
[125] Clendinnen 1991a: 80. Carrasco 2008; Read 1994: 55, 63; Elliott 2009: 221–223.
[126] Carrasco 2011: 47; Gruzinski 1989: 21. Compare Oakley 2006: 26–27 on the Kuba king.
[127] Valeri 1985: 142; see debate with Charlot 1987.   [128] Sahlins 2004: 161.
[129] Sahlins 2004: 161, quoting Hocart 1952: 93.

ancestral gods, who spoke through them and for whom chiefs' bodies acted as a kind of shrine'.[130]

Sheldon Pollock has described kings as conceived in the Sanskrit imagination as 'consubstantial god-men'.[131] Samudragupta (r. 335–380) of the Gupta Empire could be described as 'a human being only insofar as he performs the rites and conventions of the world – he is [in fact] a god whose residence is in this world'.[132] Hindu kings could be divinised by means of the notion that they somehow embodied elements of presiding deities.[133] According to Kulke, this same idea lies behind the claims of the kings of Angkor that they possessed a 'subtle inner self' that was understood as being a 'portion' of the god Śiva, and which was in turn located in a transportable *linga*.[134] And in Ayutthaya, the consecration rites conveyed the Brahmanical idea that the king was a purposive creation of the principal deities of the Hindu pantheon who united to bring him about.[135] The Palace Law of Ayutthaya begins with the consecration of the king Boromma Trailokanat (r. 1448–1488) as a *thep manut* or 'divine human'.[136]

Such terms illustrate rather perfectly the inherent ambiguity of the being that results from the manufacture of a king. There was, however, a means of short-circuiting such paradoxes of divinisation: to place the focus on kings who were already dead. This followed naturally from immmanentist ontology, in which people are usually assumed to become metapersons with notable powers (ancestors) when they die. A deceased king is merely a magnified ancestor spirit; the problem of his mortality solved by acknowledgement of his ascension and the problems of fallibility and corporeality banished for good.[137]

---

[130] Hooper 2006: 36–37; Tcherkézoff 2008: 120, on Samoa: 'The chief is a temporary "body" of the founding ancestor,' and see 140–141.
[131] Pollock 2006: 278. A twelfth-century inscription from Sri Lanka described kings as 'human divinities' (*naradēvatā*): Alan Strathern 2017b: 255.
[132] Pollock 2006: 278.
[133] Although Hinduism generated a range of forms of divinisation, including the king as the god's intimate deputy on earth: Schnepel 1995 on early Orissa.
[134] Kulke 1993: 362–375.
[135] See CK. Compare a Mahayana sutra explaining why the king is known as the 'Son of the Gods' in Embree and Hay 1988: 182.
[136] Baker and Phongpaichit 2016: 77.
[137] Indeed, Friedman 1985: 267, notes that later in the Kongo region kings might be executed after coronation, as as a means of creating an ancestor-god.

But the point here is how the cult of a parent or special ancestor, often a founder figure or great conqueror, benefits the incumbent king. The charisma of the ancestor's heroic exploits is thereby enshrined in a form that descendants may benefit from. The reigning king may not only gain a divine genealogy in this way but could also be taken as a more direct instantiation of the ancestor – as in the classic case of the king of the Shilluk.[138] Intriguingly, it seems as if this logic could be foreseen by actual founder kings who arranged for their postmortem deification. Almost as soon as Japan was brought under central control at the end of the sixteenth century, the unifier warlords of Japan – Toyotomi Hideyoshi and Tokugawa Ieyasu – successively attempted to institute a cult to themselves as *kami* that would be inaugurated with their deaths.[139] Julius Caesar had followed a similar course, and the transition from republic to empire in Rome can be seen in the changing patterns of funerals for its dead rulers. The first emperor of Rome, Octavian/Augustus, first proceeded by declaring himself '*divi filius*', son of the deified Julius, and by promoting the cult to his adoptive father in the provinces.[140] One of the few pieces of evidence that we have about royal ritual in pre-Christian Kongo concerns the importance of the grove of royal graves as a cultic site.[141]

If kings are great concentrations of supernatural power in their lifetime, it may make sense to keep them intact for that purpose after death. The chronicler and translator Juan de Betanzos reported in one of the earliest European accounts of the Incas:

You must know that while these lords were alive they were held in awe and reverenced as sons of the Sun and once dead their mummies were held in awe and reverenced like gods and thus they made sacrifices in front of them just as was done for the image of the Sun.[142]

---

[138] See the section 'Cosmic Kingship' above, and Schnepel 1995: 19; Graeber 2011b. The partly human, partly god, hero figure of Gilgamesh could take on this role in Mesopotamia: Selz 2008: 21; Michalowski 2008: 36–37; Bernbeck 2008: 158.

[139] *CK*; and Ooms 1985: 45–62.

[140] Woolf 2008: 250, 'From this point on it became common for emperors in Rome to associate themselves with their deified predecessors, but not to seek worship in their own lifetimes.' See Price 1987 for changing funerals.

[141] *CK*, part of a much wider phenomenon of cults of royal tombs in Africa: Feeley-Harnik 1985: 297.

[142] Juan de Betanzos, *Suma y narración de los Incas* (1551), quoted in Gose 1996a: 19.

The Inca were so intent on maintaining the continuing presence of dead kings that they were skilfully embalmed and treated almost as if they were alive by their large descent group (*panaka*).[143] Deceased kings remained, in effect, considerable property and estate owners, to the extent that vast tracts of land were alienated from the living monarch. Indeed, the civil war into which the Spaniards arrived was partly driven by the frustration of one contender at the debilitating consequences for government. Peter Gose notes, however, that reverence for dead monarchs was partly conditional on accumulated charisma: 'Dead sovereigns were worshipped only to the extent that they had conquered in life', and were therefore able to remain a source of oracular wisdom, fertility, and prosperity.[144] The system also allowed living rulers to be divinised to the extent that they were treated in the same manner as the mummified ancestors.[145]

But, once again, this is not merely a top–down process; there may be a popular will to access the power of dead kings associated with great deeds. The fourth-century Sri Lankan King Mahasen, who was known to have overseen the creation of an extraordinary large reservoir in the dry zone of the island, is still the recipient of worship to this day. (See Figure 3.2.) The capacity of these processes to quite outstrip official intentions is illustrated by the fate of a statue of the Thai king Chulalongkorn (Rama V, r. 1868–1910) in Bangkok. 'Originally intended as a symbol of an independent Siam ruled by a modernist, rational and scientifically minded Buddhist monarch', by the 1980s it had become the focal point for a major prosperity cult devoted to his deified spirit.[146]

Remoteness from Humanity

As Hocart suggested, the similarities of enthronement rituals indicate their common interest in allowing the normal humanity of the would-be king to be cast off so that an altogether different being may be born.[147]

---

[143] Rostworowski and Morris 1999: 779–783.
[144] Gose 1996b: 407, 'Thus, there was not even an incipient sense in which the Inkas approached a Hindu-Christian distinction between secular politics and religious transcendence.'
[145] Gose 2008: 16.   [146] Peter A. Jackson 2016: 845.
[147] Hocart 1941: Chapter IV. Mitchell [MS] notes Herodotus's (book 1, chapters 96–101) representation of the first ruler of the Medes, who secluded

Figure 3.2 A recent statue to Mahasen at the temple of Sella Kataragama, in southeast Sri Lanka.

With the election of a prince to become the *reth* of the Shilluk, the elders will inform him: 'You are our Dinka slave, we want to kill you.'[148]

In behavioural terms, kings are divinised in the cosmic mode by their distance from the rest of humanity. It is true that there may be a consideration of bodily protection and a basic psychology of glamour behind royal isolation that operate independently of any such assumptions. Shakespeare's Henry IV explains as much to his prodigal son Prince Hal: during his bid for power he had withdrawn his presence 'like a robe pontifical/Ne'er seen but wonder'd at', while his rival, the consecrated king, Richard II, had 'mingled his royalty with capering fools', being thus regarded

> with such eyes
> As, sick and blunted with community,
> Afford no extraordinary gaze,
> Such as is bent on sun-like majesty
> When it shines seldom in admiring eyes.[149]

himself in his palace because if his peers 'could not see him he would seem to them to have become of a different kind'.
[148] Schnepel 1995: 103.   [149] *Henry IV Part One*, 3.2.76–80.

But in fact European kings, whose cosmic function was relatively suppressed and divinisation relatively forestalled, were also relatively free with their presence in comparative terms. Where cosmic kingship took on a more concrete form, it was often accompanied by a much more consistent urge to shield the king from normal human contact, stationing him deep within the protective recesses of a palace and a complex web of taboo and protocol.[150] The effect was to obscure his humanity and mortality. This emerges particularly clearly in the case of Ayutthaya in the companion book. In Hawaii, the two highest ranks of *ali'i* were subject to the *kapu moe*, the prostrating taboo, which meant that others had to take off their upper clothing and lie flat on the ground in their presence – they often travelled at night as a result.[151] Among the Aztecs, after a *tlatoani* was elevated, commoners could not look upon his face; his eating and visits to women were concealed; in public rites he was borne on his lords' shoulders.[152] Indeed, eating, given the obvious carnality of the alimentary canal, was a recurrent source of anxiety: kings – whether the *Sapa Inca* or the king of Benin – often dined alone.[153] Inca rulers, like many others, were not to touch the earth but were carried in a litter, and, again, like many others, were not to endure normal human discourse for speech was heavily restricted and heavily scripted.[154]

In short, to a greater or lesser extent, the cosmic king is dehumanised as he is fashioned into a kind of sacred object: he may therefore be understood as a man-idol as much as a man-god. The process is

---

[150] Feeley Harnik 1985: 296; on the kings of Ardah: Law 2002: 268.

[151] Kirch 2010: 40; Valeri 1985: 147. The *Ali'i Nui* (divine kings) meanwhile stood at the centre of the *kapu* (tabu) system because 'they were the *akua* (gods) on earth who mediated between ordinary humans and the destructive-reproductive forces of the unseen divinities of the cosmos': Kame'elehiwa 1992: 36. See debate between Charlot (1987: 110–111) and Valeri (1987: 155) on whether it was the highest etiquette for a high chief not to move. When Cook visited in Tahiti in the 1760s and 1770s, the aspirant paramount chief Pomare I did not meet him because he had assumed an untouchable status: Newbury 1967: 488.

[152] Clendinnen 1991a: 81.

[153] On Persia: Lane Fox 1986: 273; Mitchell [MS]; a 1540 Portuguese account of the Guinea to Kongo region: 'The kings are worshipped by their subjects, who believe they come from heaven ... Great ceremony surrounds them, and many of these kings never allow themselves to be seen eating, so as not to destroy the belief of their subjects that they can live without food'; Blake 1942: 145. On the Natchez Kingdom (now southern Louisiana), see Graeber and Sahlins 2017: 391.

[154] Betanzos 1996: 27–29.

comparable to the creation of a sacred statue such that mere clay or stone becomes the embodiment of a metaperson. But whereas ritual may be needed to effect the animation of an idol by the painting of an eye or the opening of a mouth, kings are already all too real and animated; indeed this is both an attraction and a problem for them as a cult object.[155] Instead, the task of ritual is to reduce and control the human-like agency of the king.[156] In both cases, the effect is stylised, inhibited, non-human agency. For Michelle Gilbert, among the Akwapim, a small Akan kingdom in Ghana:

The king does not occupy ordinary space: he neither steps barefoot on the ground, nor walks without an umbrella over his head, showing that he is neither of the earth nor the sky, the domains of people and deities. The king's freedom of movement is carefully controlled and when he walks, he is supported by attendants, as he must not fall. The king appears neither to eat nor drink since he does these things only in seclusion in the palace. He is prevented from talking or being addressed in the same way as are ordinary people. Because he speaks with the power of his ancestors, his words are dangerous.[157]

Moreover, given that he straddles the spheres of the living and the dead, he does not really die. 'If we say he is dead, it is almost like ... a curse, a sacrilege."[158]

There may be another dimension to the relative isolation of the king, which derives from a particularly concrete understanding of him as a conduit for supernatural power. This is most evident in the literature on the Pacific and parts of sub-Saharan Africa.[159] As this power is morally neutral it is potentially dangerous, like electricity. No wonder they must not be touched! In the eyes of some societies then, it is not so much that the king must be protected from the desacralising gaze of his subjects as that the subjects must be protected from the 'sacral' (that is, immanent) force of the king.

---

[155] As attraction, see Whitmarsh 2016: 151–152, on the divinisation of Demetrius the Besieger, who liberated Athens in 308 BCE. His obvious powers as a visible being are contrasted with the more uncertain ones of the Olympian gods.

[156] Selz 2008: 23; Hooper 2006: 36–37.

[157] Gilbert 2008: 174–175; compare Peel: 1977, 118, on the Awujale of the Ijebu; Vansina 2004: 194.

[158] Gilbert 2008: 174.   [159] Gilbert 1987: 328.

The Ritualisation Trap and the Diarchical Escape

There were, then, strong currents drawing the divinised monarch's existence towards ritualisation, objectification, and dehumanisation. The king's desire for status and society's desire for a cosmic access point united on it. But this process carried within it the seeds of political irrelevance: subordinates, ministers, and nobles could exploit the ceremonial rigmarole surrounding the cosmic king in order to detach him from the levers of rule.[160] In some cases it may be possible to see this in terms of a shift from the charismatic (heroic) authority of founder figures and kingdom expanders to a greater reliance on the claims of cosmic kingship by less fortunate or ambitious successors. Here ritualisation may also be either a compensation for or a facilitator of territorial retreat and sub-royal elite assertion.

Whatever the cause, the result was that in some cases, kings could become trapped within their subject's ritual needs or their nobles' political designs, or even denuded eventually of cosmic power to become symbolic touchstones.[161] In the eighteenth century, this happened to the much reduced Christian kings of Kongo, who were confined to their dwellings and could only leave them to attend Mass or go to war.[162] The *obas* of Benin further up the coast had also become secluded ritualised figures in the seventeenth century as their chiefs came to dominate the stuff of politics.[163] In 1651 a Spanish Capuchin reported that one of the court officials was

... a great magician, who consulted the devil on all matters, and enjoyed so much favour with the king that the latter was entirely under his influence, and nothing whatsoever was decided in the kingdom without his advice. In order that the king might not know what was happening among his subjects,

---

[160] This is equivalent to what Graeber and Sahlins 2017: 8, 403, refer to as 'adverse sacralization'. However, I would see a noble/chiefly assertion of power here rather than a more generic communal process.

[161] Narēndrasinha of Kandy (Obeyesekere 2017a: 175–176) may be an example; Bellah 2011: 196, on Mangai, a Southern Cook island; Duindam 2016: 4–5, 49–58. The Safavids at first combined genuine political power, an 'unusual level of royal visibility' compared to the Ottomans and relatively strong divinisation, at least for an Islamic context. Nevertheless, Matthee 2010: 247, also notes a decrease in royal accessibility over the seventeenth century. Friedman 1985.

[162] Hilton 1985: 219 and 224, on Mani Sonho. Compare Graeber and Sahlins 2017: 407–408, on the Jukun of Nigeria.

[163] Iliffe 1995: 78; Graeber and Sahlins 2017: 415.

he had been persuaded, on the pretext of enhancing his greatness, to leave his palace only once a year, and allow no-one to see him.[164]

It may be that the rupture of direct hereditary succession had damaged the claims of kings to be incarnated ancestors, necessitating a more emphatic ritualisation in response.[165] (Note also that the official is already generating his own, more active, form of charismatic appeal.) The thrust of this sort of interpretation is to turn Hocart on his head.[166]

The emperorship of Japan underwent a slow and uneven confinement to the world of the aesthetic, symbolic, and ritual over the second millennium, as actual political power was usurped, first by Fujiwara regents, then by abdicated emperors, then by shoguns – followed by warlords usurping the shogun during the *sengoku* period. According to Nelly Naumann, then, 'The divinity of the emperor, derived from his office, becomes the more conscious the more he is deprived of real power, and the more his role is restricted by the court ceremonies.'[167] Something similar happened to the caliphs of the Islamic world, who could not be simply overthrown so much as bundled into the ceremonial. As a Seljuq ruler explained: 'If the Caliph is the imam, then his constant occupation must be the performance of prayer, as prayer is the foundation of the faith ... the interference of the Caliph in the affairs of temporal rule is senseless; they must be entrusted to the sultans.'[168] Azfar Moin notes that in the seventh century, the caliph had been treated like an ordinary man; 'by the tenth century, the powerless figure was treated like a god'.[169] European colonialism sometimes worked in an equivalent fashion, allowing nominally independent princes in India, for example, to reign rather than rule, as they themselves sequestered the work of actual governance.[170] Hence, Herman Kulke argues that the kings of Orissa evolved from being the servant or deputy of the deity Jagannath to becoming an actual incarnation of him during the

---

[164] Ryder 1969: 17.
[165] Ben-Amos Girshick and Thornton 2001: 362–364; Ben-Amos 1999: 34–45; Ryder 1969: 16.
[166] See Friedman's (1985) criticisms of the ahistoricism of Pierre Clastres and others. The scapegoat, fetish, or slaughtered kings of Africa do not represent the origins of kingship but the ballooning of the cosmic, ritual function as the political function dwindles.
[167] Naumann 2000: 65. [168] Moin 2015: 482. [169] Moin 2015: 473.
[170] Dirks 1987.

period when they were slowly denuded of real power under Mughal, Maratha, and especially British overlordship.[171]

In Nepal, the kings' identification with Viṣṇu was particularly emphasised in the nineteenth century, when they began to cede political power to prime ministers.[172] This monarch–prime minister model, also in evidence in Thailand and in the United Kingdom today, for example, is just one variant of the tendency of kingship towards diarchy, by which the ceremonial and the executive functions of authority are disassociated. One figure in the diarchy is sprung from the ritualisation trap and freed to undertake work in a less hampered form. The prevalence of diarchy has been widely observed in scholarship.[173] It is not quite apposite to fold it within a secular–religious dichotomy, however.[174] The more politically active and militaristic role is also likely to carry sacred signification and responsibilities, if less onerous and restrictive than that of his counterpart.[175]

In these cases, then, it may be preferable to envisage diarchy as a split along the heroic and cosmic forms of divinised kingship, as listed previously. It is the relatively free and potentially charismatic display of prowess in battle and politics which falls to one king, while the responsibilities of cosmic integration rest on the shoulders of the other. This would describe the case in Tonga, where the senior chief was the 'Tui' and the junior chief bore the title 'God of War'. Naturally, Europeans might consider the former office vestigial – the Tui Tonga being once described as having 'as much utility to the Island as a large mole to a man's face' – but their superior status in emic terms was real.[176] A similar diarchic principle structured high chiefship in Hawaii and Tahiti. We meet *celeritas* and *gravitas* once again. Given that in Ayutthaya also there was a tradition of a lesser king residing in the more open 'front palace' while the reigning monarch occupied the more secluded rear palace, it means that we find distinct manifestations of the diarchic logic in all the case study regions of the companion volume.[177]

---

[171] Kulke, discussed in Schnepel 1995: 71.   [172] Graeber 2011b: 13.
[173] Sahlins 2014: 137; Oakley 2006: 11–14; Duindam 2016: 33, 42, 55; Hocart 1970: 162–179.
[174] As Hocart 1970: 163, realised; Sahlins 2011.
[175] Philips 2007: 198, on Tonga.
[176] Latukefu 1974: 84, citing Reverend S. Rabone in 1838.
[177] *CK*; Reid 1993: 264.

The foregoing discussion leaves us with a clue: that the status and authority brought by cosmic divinisation through ritualisation must be weighed in the balance against the risk of yielding the ability to wield power and interact with subordinates.

Non-Euphemised Kingship: Strangers, Transgressors, and Aggressors

Everything is happening as if the *reth*'s subjects were resisting both the institutionalization of power, and the euphemization of power that seems to inevitably accompany it. Power remained predatory.

David Graeber[178]

How else to strip humanity from a king and cast him into productive liminality? By making him a stranger, a transgressor and an aggressor, such that he becomes both the very heart of domestic order and yet – or therefore – also quite beyond it. A dense bundle of symbolic logic may be implicated in any such representations.[179] But here let us note how it may tally with two imperatives: (a) the project of turning him into a cosmic intercessor, and (b) the need to express the experience of subjection to kings, who may often in fact be foreigners, the breakers of local rules, or the source of terror.

This not to argue that the process of 'divinising' a monarch – that is, sacralising him or her in the immanentist mode – *necessarily* involves the exploration of a darker register of symbolism. The tendency may be more region specific than that, being particularly clear in some American, but particularly aspects of the African and Pacific material. The point is rather that immanentism *allows* this symbolism to flourish by virtue of its steady gaze upon power rather than ethics. It does not need to swaddle the figure of the king in moralising gauze, euphemising what the business of wielding power actually entails. This is surely a major reason why kingship symbolism in immanentist societies can simply feel so different from its counterparts in Eurasia after the advent of transcendentalist domination.[180]

---

[178] Graeber 2011: 30. I take the phrase 'euphemisation' from Graeber but use it rather differently.

[179] See, for example, Alan Strathern 2009.

[180] Graeber and Sahlins 2017 make the transgressive repertoire more central. Their distinction (7–9) between divine kingship (aiming at absolute and

Once again, this should not be confused with the question as to whether the actual conduct of kingship was any more ethical. In seventeenth-century Ayutthaya, for example, we find the representation of kingship subject to relentless Buddhist moralising, and a ritual repertoire in which animal, let alone human, sacrifice would be anathema. Yet the fundamental political reality of contested succession and structural insecurity meant that the monarchy resorted to the most horrifying punishments and torture to keep control over its officers.[181]

For kings everywhere are the ultimate wielders of violence, whose own ascent to the throne is often a bloody one. Non-euphemised kingship not only allows greater expression to resentment and fear of the king – even to the extent of depicting him as an enemy of his people in certain contexts – but integrates these sensations into an appreciation of his sacred status.[182] In some cases, its appearance may reflect the relatively recent emergence of kingship itself, such that the strains involved in wresting lineage-based societies into a newly authoritarian form of human organisation are still acknowledged in the collective imagination.[183] One function of the ritual or mythical repertoire of transgression that accompanies king creation may be to underscore the king's unique escape from the clutches of kinship: now he can arbitrate between diverse clans and families, imperiously transcending domestic morality.[184] An eighteenth-century story about Afonso I (r. 1509–1542), the Christian king of Kongo, relates that he had his mother buried alive because she would not remove a small idol from her neck. This no doubt expressed his austere Christian commitment, but it also revealed the unnatural cruelty that a disinterested approach to relatives entails.[185] Other stories of kingship from the wider region reveal the theme of kin-murder as revelatory of its solitary exceptionality. Such a king has 'denied the ancient order; he has acquired an autonomy which can only be explained by the possession of

transgressive power) and sacred kingship (in which the community douses the fire of tyranny with a blanket of ceremony and taboo) may be compared with my heroic kingship, (with an emphasis on its non-euphemised expression), and cosmic kingship (with an emphasis on the ritualisation trap).

[181] See *CK*.   [182] Gluckman 1963: 238–239; Simonse 1992: chapter 9.

[183] Graeber and Sahlins 2017: 154–156, drawing on Luc de Heusch, as noted previously. In another sense, kingship also involves the reification of kinship, as the royal kin-group and ancestry is exalted above all others.

[184] Quigley 2005b: 8; Graeber 2011b; de Heusch 2000, 2005.

[185] Balandier 1968: 50; Hilton 1985, 45, also 37; Fromont 2014: 38.

extraordinary powers', as Balandier put it, and may therefore construct society on the basis of new principles.[186] Drawing on fieldwork from the mid-twentieth century, Wyatt MacGaffey notes:

Ideally the chief is a benevolent despot whose authentic relation to the ancestors is assured by some ordeal or test, such as a successful hunt for a particular kind of animal, or some other demonstration of the power to kill. Modern informants said, 'If we choose someone to be chief, we would require him to kill one of his nephews. If he could not, we would have to find someone else to be chief.'[187]

This is a heroic act, generating charisma through sheer transgression. It signals a being to whom the normal rules do not apply.[188] Indeed, for some parts of the world, scholars have seen spontaneous and unpredictable violence as part of the repertoire of kingliness, advertising immunity from human constraints and norms.[189] This finds some resonance in the Pacific.[190] It is intriguing that Pomare II, who was attempting to raise himself into a more monarchical position in the Society Islands (Tahiti), began to display a tendency to mete out sudden and disproportionate punishments, and indeed his anger might take a cosmic form: one missionary report has it that a wind which prevented the passage of some thirty sailing canoes was attributed to the anger of the king. The thwarted travellers then decided to take a pig to Pomare as an atonement.[191] The would-be king has become an ill wind.

An underlying structure behind this tendency is therefore simply the amorality of supernatural beings or forces with which divinised kings are pushed into contiguity. In the immanentist imagination gods are lawmakers and boon providers but also whimsical tyrants and threatening monsters; they participate in conflict and violence as a condition of the generation of life on a cosmic level. Why then obscure these themes in the vision of kings?[192]

---

[186] Balandier 1968: 37.
[187] MacGaffey 1986: 176. Graeber and Sahlins 2017: 157. Njinga of Angola actually murdered her nephew in the 1620s: Heywood 2017: 120.
[188] Duindam 2016: 99; Feeley-Harnik 1985: 287.
[189] Graeber 2011b, 8; Graeber and Sahlins 2017: 394, 445.
[190] The Hawaiian proverb that a chief is 'a shark who travels on land' has been widely noted: Sahlins 1981: 10.
[191] Oliver 1974: 1328.   [192] Simonse 2005: 72.

The process of making a ruler, according to Inga Clendinnen, included a night spent standing naked before an image of Tezcatlipoca, the deity associated with fickleness and worldly power: 'It was this principle of subversion, of wanton, casual, antisocial power which was particularly implicated in Aztec notions of rule and was embodied (at least on occasion) in the Aztec ruler.'[193] One analysis of the Rwandan genocide of 1994 related it to ideas about the flow of supernatural power (*imaana*) that was held to irrigate the country with prosperity as it circulated. In an earlier age this was held to be channelled through the office of the king, who was thus both its source and potentially a blocking agent: 'It was through obstruction, impoverishment, strangulation, murder and sorcery that the Rwandan king manifested the coercive aspect of his power over subjects and adversaries.'[194] That which mediates between the sky and earth might equally serve to sever them. The Dutch compiler Olfert Dapper, using sources from 1660s, reported that the king of Loango was referred to by the people as a *nkisi* (spirit, or the fetish it inhabits), who could, with a word, kill a man or ruin the entire country, cause rain, or metamorphose into a beast 'which all serve to manifest his greatness, and strike awe into the Subjects of his Potency. Thus also it stands with the other Lords, whose might, honour and esteem grows from the same root'.[195]

Human Sacrifice

Kings are also like the gods of the immanentist imaginary because they feed off society, devouring the fruits of its labours in order to fructify it in turn. And when they demand victims for rituals of human sacrifice, gods and kings devour humanity in a most explicit way.[196] The practice of ritual homicide was usually set within an overall moral vision, in which the generation of life depended on the production of death.[197] One origin story for it from Tahiti nicely encapsulates both royal agency and communal benefit: it tells of a king 'moved to pity for his people' during a great drought, who directs his priests to offer a man

---

[193] Clendinnen 1991a: 79–80.   [194] Taylor 1999: 121, 126.
[195] Ogilby 1670, II: 514 (a translation of Olfert Dapper).
[196] Feeley-Harnik 1985: 273.
[197] This was a central argument of James Frazer [1890–1936] 1994; Feeley-Harnik 1985: 273.

as sacrifice; the rain falls and 'thus it was shown that the gods liked human flesh'.[198] Indeed, to evoke briefly the ghost of Frazer, in emic terms the symbolism sometimes suggest that kings, victims, and deities are curiously interchangeable, each standing in for each other. It may even be intimated that, on one level, it is the king or the deity who is symbolically killed for consumption.[199] To see ritual homicide as simply a means of terrifying subjects is therefore inadequate.[200] But equally, to see it simply as a necessary ethical intervention (once certain immanentist postulates are granted) would be to muffle its potency under a blanket of idealised political theology. It is surely doubtful whether it ever lost its fearful and awesome qualities, wherever it was practised.[201]

The regular appearance of ritual homicide in the historical record now looks simply undeniable.[202] It can certainly be found among stateless peoples, but it seems to be particularly associated with the rise of stratified societies.[203] The most common form it took, from Ancient Egypt onwards, was retainer sacrifice, in which slaves, wives, or officials were killed to accompany a deceased ruler into an afterlife – again underlining how concretely the immanentist vision conceived of that domain.[204] But it could also be used for the appeasement and delectation of metapersons. Portuguese sources, for example, relate the importance of funereal sacrifice for the kings of Bissau in the seventeenth century, but also note how it was his task to have a woman taken out to sea to be sacrificed in order to make the waters calm.[205] Indeed, human sacrifice as a form of metaperson propitiation was a most ubiquitous feature of pre-Columbian South and Central American history, and was central to Aztec, Inca, and Maya ritual life.

---

[198] Oliver 1974: 908; Henry 1928: 196.
[199] Graulich 2007; Valeri 1985; Olivier 2016: 279.
[200] But not ridiculous in itself: Iliffe 1995: 152.
[201] See Read 1994: 43, 49, 53, 66.
[202] Post-Saidian scholarship sometimes doubts the prevalence of ritual homicide, rather acknowledging its utility in discourses of otherness (Obeyesekere 2005). But see Davidson 1998 (on archaeology of Carthage); Bremmer 2007a; Kirch 2010: 55; Trigger 2003: 472, 484–485.
[203] Watts et al. 2016. Zhou China: Mair 2011: 100.
[204] Egypt: Iliffe 1995: 152; Ndongo: Heywood 2017: 76; Dahomey: Heywood and Thornton: 2009: 105; Ashanti: Ellis and ter Haar 2004: 90–91; Law 1991: 72; Brooks 1996: 307; Aztecs: Dodds Pennock 2008: 176; Bellah 2011: 213, 234.
[205] Hair 1982: 24–25.

It is amply attested in parts of West and Central Africa. It occurred in pagan Europe.[206] In the Philippines.[207] And it was found right across the far-flung islands of the Pacific, from Fiji to the Marquesas.[208] In many of these areas it seems to have been pushed to new heights by more predatory states routinely on a war footing, where the war gods who granted victory demanded human flesh.[209] In some cases, kings themselves carried out or consecrated the ritual.[210]

Outside of the funerary context, then, the fundamental logic of human sacrifice is simply that it represents the most powerful move one can make in the procedures of gift exchange with metapersons.[211] There was normally a tendency to draw victims from populations who were not too close to home – foreigners, war captives, slaves, and criminals – presumably in order to avoid undermining the morale of core groups of subjects.[212] And yet, the underlying logic also pulled against that tendency, drawing to the conclusion that the most precious humans would be the most precious gift of all. This is presumably what lies behind the rites involving the sacrifice to the god Tlaloc of children taken from families of Tenochtitlan at the heart of the Aztec empire.[213] The following words were spoken by an informant on the consecration of the king of the Akwapim through the fashioning of the 'Black Stool' on which he sat:

The Black Stool has power, but you must get that power from a relative who is important to you. You do not just take any man from anywhere to make a Black Stool. It must be a fellow lineage member. His head is cut off to make the stool ... You use an executioner's knife to pierce the neck and the blood comes out and is poured onto the stool. You put the head on the stool, and the heart and sex organs, you put them on the stool for a while. Then power [*tumi*] has come into the stool. The head will be taken later and buried; the power is already in the stool.[214]

---

[206] Scandinavians: Bartlett 2007: 59–61; England: Chaney 1970: 38–40.
[207] McCoy 1982: 152.
[208] Nicholas Thomas 1996: 22, on Marquesas; Bellah 2011: 196, on Mangaia.
[209] Aztecs: See Chapter 1, 'Metapersons (and their relations with persons) are defined by power rather than ethics'; Dahomey: Bay 1998: 65.
[210] Valeri 1985: 141.   [211] Valeri 1985: 49–50.
[212] Bremmer 2007b: 3. Excessive use could lead to rebellion; for seventeenth-century Benin, see Ben-Amos Girshick and Thornton 2001: 370; Ben-Amos 1999: 42. Compare Graeber and Sahlins 2017: 444.
[213] Clendinnen 1991a: 98.   [214] Gilbert 1987: 308.

Thus the king is connected to his ancestors through the death of a relative. Note also the deliberately transgressive register deployed to effect that transformation.[215] Yet another quintessentially immanentist theme brought out of this account is the way that human sacrifice might allow the capturing of raw supernatural power or *mana* by the sacrificer. In Hawaii, contenders for the throne who killed and sacrificed their rivals and relatives were in effect absorbing their *mana*.[216] Kings participated in the cycles of life and death that operated on every dimension of existence: immanentism allowed that reality to be looked at square in the face.

The Righteous King

> Protecting his realm according to the Dharma
> Teaching well the laws of the Dharma too,
> Those engaged in virtue should be encouraged
> And he himself must refrain from evil deeds.
> > *The Golden Light Sutra*, Chapter 12, 'The Inviolable
> > Commitments of Divine Kings'[217]

Thus, just as in the heavens, the sun, the moon and the stars exhibit to the world as if in a mirror a certain likeness of God, so on earth a far truer image of God is provided by those good rulers who love and reverence Him, and display to their people the resplendent light of His justice accompanied by a semblance of the divine reason and intellect ... Thus men have been trusted by God to the protection of their rulers ... So the Prince must not only be good but make others good.
> Baldesar Castiglione, *The Book of the Courtier*[218]

Kings may be radiant, heavenly beings in the transcendentalist vision too. The logic by which earthly and celestial hierarchies are equated continues unabated. But what is it now to be heavenly and to shine like the sun? It is to radiate goodness. It is the moral status of kings and their place in an overarching soteriological vision that matters now. Kings remain mediators of sorts then, but not primarily as the crux of a

---

[215] Gilbert 2008: 179.   [216] Valeri 1985: 161.
[217] Prazniak 2017: 668; Sango 2015. *The Golden Light Sutra* is a very influential Mahayana Buddhist text, first translated into Chinese in the fourth century CE and then into Japanese in the eighth.
[218] Castiglione 1967: 299–300, influenced too by classical ideals of virtue.

system of ritual intercession; rather they would establish the conditions within which their subjects might attain salvation.[219] They have become *righteous*.

Moreover, that mediatory role is circumscribed by the authority of the clerisy or virtuosi who stand as the ineradicable guardians of the transcendentalist project. In a rather abstract sense, the king must yield to the higher purpose the clerisy represents. As Jonathan Parry put it, 'In a world in which ultimate value is located in a transcendent realm, status is likely to be distinguished from power.'[220] Parry means here the kind of status which a renouncer may attain, profoundly antithetical and superior to all that kingship stands for.

An Emphatic Moralisation

The introduction of transcendentalism entails a shift of focus from the ontological status of the king and his ability to capture supernatural power to the question of his moral authority.[221] Recall the simple proposition that the act of legitimation depends on an appeal to an order of reality beyond the object of legitimation. This is one way of reading Durkheim's formulation that society 'worships itself' through the vehicle of religion. It is as if the clunky machinery of society construction cannot be operated in plain sight, but only once it has been transfigured by a veil of supernatural purpose. But if that is so, in the immanentist mode, the worldly order throws a barely altered version of itself into that dimension beyond the veil. With the eruption of transcendentalism, however, that other dimension is more profoundly transformed according to new values and norms.

In the previous chapter the similarities between the developing Mongol notion of Sky or Heaven (*Tenggeri*) and monotheistic or Buddhist forms were noted; but in truth a crucial rupture attended

---

[219] In Buddhist societies, this was often understood in a particularly direct way, not only because of the responsibilities of kings to purify and patronise the sangha but because kings could be seen as treasure houses of merit in themselves. (Thanks to Vic Lieberman.)

[220] Parry 1998: 167–168 (drawing on Dumont): 'I am suggesting that a radical opposition between this world and the other world is likely to encourage [the clear separation between status and power], and to make temporal rulers dependent for the legitimation of their power on those with transcendent authority.'

[221] Hocart 1924–28: 34. Duara 2015: 4, on transcendence as 'a source of non-worldly *moral authority* that can speak back to power'.

the shift from the former to the latter. As Brian Baumann puts it: 'This new form of government transcends the empirical reality of heaven with a heaven that exists beyond the lines of separation that apportion time and space,' for it is one given by 'everlasting moral order'.[222] How firmly kingship may be anchored to this sphere of higher values is conveyed in a praise poem to Parākramabāhu VI (r. 1411–1467), the king of Kōṭṭe in Sri Lanka: he is lauded as a 'Buddha-aspirant' (*budukuru*), who venerates the Buddha, has a profound knowledge of the *Tipiṭaka*, and promotes the flourishing of Buddhist teachings and practices.[223] He is defined, in other words, according to the transcendentalist trinity of truth, ethics, and salvation. It would therefore be an understatement to say that the king must adhere to the teachings of the tradition in question in order to be considered legitimate in the eyes of the clerisy. Normally this simply goes without saying, but where the tradition is explicitly placed under threat it may be explicitly articulated. According to the thirteenth-century Lankan text, *Pūjāvaliya*: 'If any non-believer becomes a king of Sri Lanka by force at any time, that dynasty will not last owing to the special influence of the Buddha. Because this Lanka is rightfully those of kings who have right views.'[224] When King Boris of the Bulgars was converted in the mid-860s, the Patriarch of Constantinople finished his long letter to him by exclaiming: 'May you be for me a model and an example of every virtue and piety not only to those under you but also a beautiful and great encouragement to the entire race of mankind to achieve noble ends.'[225]

Is this not a severe expectation?[226] When kings are divinised, it is their human mortality and weakness that must somehow be obscured; when kings are made righteous, it is their human immorality and violence that must be effaced. Naturally, that process may be pursued more or less insistently: Buddhist kings for example, are generally more comprehensively moralised than monotheistic ones. And it is the clerisy and virtuosi (priests, monks, renouncers, or holy men) who must take

---

[222] Baumann 2013: 274–275; and see also Jackson 2009: 113.

[223] Berkwitz 2016: 334. Compare Piggot 1997: 96, on Buddhist texts envisaging the 'king as a charismatic teacher and saviour of his people' in Japan; Duindam 2016: 34–35.

[224] Written following rule by Saivite Cōlas: Obeyesekere 1995: 234. See the first entries in a list of attributes of Ottoman sultans (1596): Woodhead 1987: 127.

[225] Photius 1982: 79.

[226] And yet when Machiavelli attempted to escape the discourse of righteousness to describe rulership, Christendom was appalled.

on the full burden of embodying the new transcendent values. Yet the more the king aspires to take centre stage in the drama of religion the more that he will also be represented as realising those values most perfectly in himself.

The non-euphemised vision of kingship explored above was not presented as a generic feature of immanentism,[227] but rather as a possibility permitted by it. The analytical significance of this is only apparent once we realise that this possibility is suffocated by the arrival of transcendentalism. An obvious consequence is the disappearance of human sacrifice as the pinnacle of royal ritual, only leaving behind traces here and there in mainland Eurasia.[228] But indeed a whole repertoire of monarchical symbolism now dwindles away. Can we imagine in Christian, Islamic, or Buddhist societies, a consecration ritual that involves incest or cannibalism? Violence is not erased from the sacralisation of kingship, but it is a violence with the moral horror drained from it: it has become exquisitely legitimate.[229]

And yet kings may fail at righteous kingship. It is important then to grasp hold of a certain point which may initially appear paradoxical. It is not that transcendentalist discourses *must* euphemise power. Quite the contrary: they hold within themselves the threat of a devastating critique of the exercise of temporal authority.[230] Indeed, this is why their potential for legitimisation is so great. It is rather that when transcendentalism *is* mobilised to sacralise royal authority, it will entail its moralisation by association with the salvific imperative.

This development should not be seen then simply in terms of the interests of kings. All societies must protect themselves against the obvious threat presented by individual aggrandisement. Across Eurasia, and no doubt far beyond, therefore, a range of literatures in the *Mirror for Princes* genre counselled broadly similar virtues: of reason, self-control, justice, masculine steadfastness, and charity.[231]

---

[227] See the section 'Non-Euphemised Kingship'.

[228] Naturally, many societies with non-transcendentalist traditions also repudiated human sacrifice. Pagan Greece, Rome, and China are obvious examples – although note that all three were influenced by other forms of Axial Age thought.

[229] Crouzet 2011; *Mahāvaṃsa* passim (Guruge 1989).

[230] Gauchet 1999: 50, 'There is now something permanently beyond the reach of power: what sustains power will soon be able to be used against it.'

[231] Van Leeuwen 2017: 74; also Photius 1982: 66. However, van Leeuwen's Eurasian cases are all influenced by Axial or transcendentalist traditions, which

The central weakness of kingship as an institution is the way it subjects the well-being of all to the passions of one human being. The more powerful in concrete political terms that kings became, the more urgent became the communal imperative to lodge an intrinsic mechanism of self-control in the person of the king. Transcendentalism did not invent this prince-taming imperative.[232] But by shifting the mode of royal sacralisation from divinisation to righteousness, it was rooted more firmly than ever before in the deepest elements of the worldview.[233] Spontaneous violence or vaulting transgression was no longer a sign of sacred power, but a sign of the all-too-human frailties of the king – brought under control by a concern for salvation that must afflict his conscience no less than that of his subjects. Henry V is made to articulate it well:

> We are no tyrant, but a Christian king
> Unto whose grace our passions is as subject
> As our wretches fettered in our prisons.[234]

If divinisation allows a community to build something godlike out of a man in order to save them from mortal terrors, righteousness specialises in saving them from the king himself.

A Subtle Disenchantment?

> Put not your trust in princes, nor in the son of man, in whom
> there is no help.
> His breath goeth forth, he returneth to his earth; in that very day
> his thoughts perish.
>
> Psalm 146:3–5

may be why ideal sovereignty there is always disciplined rather than transgressive and arbitrary in the manner emphasised by, for example, Graeber and Sahlins 2017.

[232] Intriguingly, Athenian thinkers arrived at a vision of supremely virtuous philosopher kings via a democratic appreciation of the illegitimacy of absolute rule (Lynette G. Mitchell 2013: 95–99). In this way too, then, 'Axial' Greece generated something akin to a 'transcendentalist' element, which later meshed with Christianity.

[233] We might put it that immanentism tames kings through ritual; transcendentalism through ethical and soteriological discipline. Confucianism, an Axial Age tradition profoundly cognate with but not strictly speaking equivalent to transcendentalism, has the same ethicising force on kingship.

[234] *Henry V* 1.2.241–3.

> The Lord of Men may be very powerful,
> But it is the Enlightened Teacher who is his guide;
> Therefore be close to gods, not men.
>   *Sutra of the Prince's Law-giving*[235]

Kings may be both righteous and emphatically human. At the very least, righteous discourses did not then depend on the divinisation of the king. But to what extent did they actually undermine it? This is to touch upon an important theme in some of the Axial Age–inspired literature and more philosophical forms of the sociology of secularisation. It is bound up with a more general theme, as conveyed for example by Charles Taylor, that the arrival of transcendentalism carries within it the beginnings of the disenchantment of the world.[236] Eisenstadt puts it baldly in relation to kingship: 'The King-God, the embodiment of the cosmic and earthly order alike, disappeared, and a secular ruler, in principle accountable to some higher order, appeared.'[237] Indeed, one outcome of an intriguing cliometric analysis of early state development by Dmitri Bondarenko and Andrey Korotayev is a clear connection between political centralisation and the sacralisation of the ruler – except for states in the 'Axial zone' where the association breaks down. In these societies, they argue, rulers were able to build the capacity of the state without paying the price of their own ceremonial dehumanisation.[238]

I shall suggest that arguments such as these must be very heavily qualified and rearranged, and certainly used with great care when

---

[235] A Tibetan treatise on statecraft by the late fourteenth-century visionary Loden Nyingpo (Ramble 2006: 137), which proceeds to emphasise the heavy contractualism of the king's position, subordinate to the higher Buddhist law. Thanks to Charles Ramble for further discussion.

[236] Taylor 2007; Gauchet 1999.

[237] Eisenstadt 1986c: 8; also Wittrock 2015: 105–108.

[238] Bondarenko and Korotayev 2003 was discovered well after I had written this chapter: I am not at all equipped to endorse the methodology they deploy (the integrity of their sample, for example), and do not rely on it here. Note that their 'sacralisation' means divinisation in the cosmic mode, which they present as inhibited in the Axial Zone, where 'political and sacral/religious authorities [were] rather sharply divided' (123), although they go awry in invoking the Indo-European heritage as the reason for this. David Graeber's comments (which alerted me to it; in Graeber and Sahlins 2017: 417) on some of the comparative problems with their argument can be resolved by understanding the particular ways in which transcendentalist and immanentist elements combined in the Indic and East Asian cases.

applied to the actual historical processes by which transcendentalism was incorporated into royal ideology. What had arrived was not the 'secular' ruler but the 'righteous' one. Moreover, the following section will be devoted to showing that righteous discourses of kingship were rarely able to develop without cleaving to forms of divinisation, especially but not only in the Indic traditions. What is left after these and further points are acknowledged is in many ways an extremely subtle point. But if we lose hold of it altogether we will fail to notice a certain novel opening in the global history of political theology that was subsequently never quite fully closed: the possibility that divinised kingship may be irrelevant and kingship itself devalued. This is surely part of any long-term story by which the divinised forms of kingship were reduced to a more metaphorical reality.[239]

As Bellah, puts it, in the Axial Age, the question may be put, 'Who is the (true) king, the one who really reflects divine justice?' The answer might now be Socrates, or Confucius, or Buddha, or Christ.[240] The continuing force of this question is most evident in the Abrahamic traditions, which only reluctantly yielded metapersonhood to any but the one God. For Bellah, indeed, the Axial breakthrough in Jewish history turns on the way the new covenant between God and the Children of Israel 'dispensed with the role of the king as mediator'.[241] The idea recurs in Jewish history that the only true king is Yaweh; in Christian history that the only true kingdom is the kingdom of God.[242] Such themes are a bequest of the struggle of the Jews against great monarchies such as Egypt, of Jesus' struggle against Rome (as when he proclaims to Pilate, 'My kingdom is not of this world'), and of the three centuries after his death which 'established an abyss between the domain of government and the domain of religion' as Fustel de Coulanges put it.[243] But even once that abyss was triumphantly bridged with Constantine's conversion, the subsequent fall of the Roman Empire served to impress again a sense of the inherent

---

[239] It may also be part of the story as to why kingship itself came to be abandoned.
[240] Bellah 2011: 267.
[241] Bellah 2011: 316, see 304–310 on the prophetic challenge to sacral kingship.
[242] Oakley 2006: 55–62; Moin 2016: 124.
[243] Oakley 2006: 55, 60–61; Price 1987: 99, on Christian hostility to deification of Roman emperors. Assmann 2010: 45, has it that this resulted in an anti-statist 'countersociety'. For an uncompromising vision of the illegitimacy of all worldly power, see Marsden 2015: 83, on nineteenth-century Russian Old Believer radicals (*beguny*).

sinfulness of the state – at least in Augustine.[244] This transcendentalist element of Christianity has even been identified as promoting the rise of the secular state in the modern era.[245]

The earlier influence of this transcendent secularisation of kingship on popular culture is manifest in the morality plays in medieval England, which 'demystify the world and its kings', for 'like Satan, the evil king is recognized ... by his self-deification', invoking the pharaohs and the Herods of the Bible.[246] In the old English story about King Cnut ('Canute' 1016–1035) and his failure to halt the tide, it is his inability to control the elements in a manner of a cosmic king that he wished to demonstrate: "Let all the world know that the power of kings is empty and worthless, and there is no king worthy of the name, save Him by whose will heaven, earth, and sea obey eternal laws.'[247] The cosmos no longer needs the ritual agency of the king, for God holds all in place. Shakespeare was at liberty to explore the humanity of kings.[248]

There is a fundamental strand of the Christian tradition, then, according to which kingship may be an institution manipulated by providence but it is not an office by which man and deity reach some kind of equivalence.[249] The king is an instrument of god or his representative – not his equal, his child, his lover, his physical host. He is king by the grace of God, by divine right and not by divine being, and his status therefore depends on his responsibility to bring his subjects to salvation.[250] This is the message then that missionaries generally

---

[244] Creppell 2010: 30; Martin 2005: 186. Hence Erik Peterson, a critic of Carl Schmitt, drew on Augustine to insist on the radical disjunction between politics and religion – in a deeply transcendentalist manner. See Geréby 2008, which also quotes Gregory of Elvira: 'Whoever would want to realize the divine monarchy on earth would be like the Antichrist, for it is him who alone will be the monarch of the whole earth.' (21–22).

[245] Katznelson and Stedman Jones 2010b: 13.

[246] Hardin 1992: 39–44. Satan had failed to tempt Christ out of the desert by the promise of worldly monarchy.

[247] In the twelfth-century account of Henry of Huntingdon 2002.

[248] *Henry V*, 4.1.102–107 has the king, in disguise, announce that 'all his senses have but human conditions; his ceremonies laid by, in his nakedness he appears but a man'.

[249] As in Paul's epistle to the Romans (13:1–7), 'Let everyone be subject to the governing authorities, for there is no authority except that which god has established,' Duindam 2016: 23.

[250] Oakley 2006: 76, 96. 'Divine right' in a more particular sense refers to more specific (and contested) claims of rather absolutist dominion over the claims of Church and community in the early modern period; see Sommerville 1991.

understood they were bringing to heathen courts. After relaying the august titles of the Siamese king in the seventeenth century, the *Missions Etrangères* priest, Jacques de Bourges, observed:

The Christian religion teaches more modest sentiments, and commanding on behalf of God that subjects obey their rulers, it teaches the same rulers to fear God and to recognize that they are men and have only received from Him the power which elevates them.[251]

Although the early years of the Islamic state are obscure, a strong core of Islamic tradition developed that also presented a check on the divinising pretensions of rulers, who were necessary to uphold the holy law (sharia), and the jurists ('ulama') who maintained it – but were above neither.[252] Their duties of piety and defence of the *umma* were paramount. For Zia al-Din Baranī (1285–1357), writing from the Delhi sultanate, 'God is the real king and earthly "kings" are the playthings of His decree and Divine Power.'[253] Armies might desert rulers who failed to observe the *Sharī'a*.[254]

In the Indic traditions, monarchical divinisation was far less problematic, as is underlined below.[255] Yet, the canonical texts of Buddhism do preserve at least a strain of disenchanted thinking about political hierarchy, as in the *Aggañña Sutta*'s account of the contractual basis upon which rulership first emerged. The 'Great Elect' or *Mahāsammata* is an office created by the people in order to restore order. It is not that kingship is singled out for demystification; this follows from the general relativisation of social convention such that the caste system and Brahmanical claims to superiority are likewise undermined.[256] However, this vision of kingship probably had little impact on how the role was subsequently conceived of in Buddhist polities. Rather than a disenchantment of kingship, then, it is better to

---

[251] Bourges 1666: 150. The book was dedicated to Louis XIV. [252] Moin [MS].
[253] Embree and Hay 1988: 410. [254] Marlow 1995: 115.
[255] Unfortunately, there is no space here to consider this theme in relation to Hinduism, which would involve reflecting on the debates between Louis Dumont and his many critics. Chinese kingship would also make for interesting comparison, given that it often combined a clearly 'cosmic' foundation with strong ethicisation and clear limits on 'theomorphic' or divinised kingship. Lastly, if Achaemenid Persia is assimilated to some narrative of 'Axialisation', then the Zoroastrian understanding of kings as rather human servants to the gods under Darius may be considered (Ehrenburg 2008).
[256] Pollock 2005: 406–408; Gombrich 1988, 63; Collins 1998: 448–451.

think of a certain dislodging or containment of it, the survival of a strand of critique.[257] This is evident in the Lankan chronicle the *Mahāvamsa*: of 'sovereignty over men' it says that 'a man of pious mind will never be attached to it like unto delicious food mixed with poison'.[258] While the *Temīya Jātaka* tells us how a Bodhisattva is reborn into a royal family but does everything he can to stop being king after overhearing the harsh sentence his father handed down to some bandits. Even royal violence would bring suffering in hell.[259] The ascetic path of the monastic will always remain, in a fundamental sense, superior.

The Inevitable Synthesis

In practice, any such disenchantment or chastisement of kingship was liable to be swallowed up during the accommodation that each transcendentalist tradition was forced to make with political power. Indeed, there are significant continuities in how kingship worked and was conceived across immanentist and transcendentalist societies. Why this should be so is explained in terms of the following five points. Underlying them all is the simple principle that in no dimension of life does transcendentalism exist without binding together with immanentism, and kingship is no exception.

(1) Both the Indic and monotheistic modes make their peace with the sphere of immanent divinity, albeit in different ways

The incorporation of forms of divinised kingship was rarely problematised in Indic traditions because the sphere of metapersonhood was not primarily the arena in which the soteriological revolution played itself out. In Buddhism, the world of the gods was encompassed and ever so subtly devalued rather than destroyed.[260] Indeed, it preserved a sense that the man–god distinction was readily overcome, for the same being could move from one category to the other through the

---

[257] This may be implicit in the superior position of the tooth relic temple in Lankan history, see above, and Obeyesekere 2017a: 178.

[258] *Mahāvamsa*, XXXVI: 133 (Guruge 1989: 733).

[259] Colllins 1998: 425–433: 'It is difficult to imagine a more explicit condemnation of kingship', but note the importance of a more accommodative strand of discourse too (448–466). Also Goh 2015: 34, 126.

[260] Duara 2015 on dialogic transcendence.

operation of *kamma*. As the notion of the Bodhisattva developed in various traditions, moreover, it provided a means for truly liberated beings to become immanent in living, breathing humans – and therefore kings. The ease with which the divinisation of kings may be both absorbed by and subordinated to Buddhism is evident in the following remarks. They were made by a 71-year-old medium for the spirit of the deceased Thai king Chulalongkorn to the anthropologist Pattana Kitiarsa:

All Thai kings are descended from Vishnu. Rama V was reborn as a god in heaven after his death. He is *thep* [deva, deity] not a mere spirit. *Thep* also follow Buddha's teachings; I can tell this from the fact that the reigning King has to pay homage to a Buddhist monk.[261]

As these comments also indicate, royal divinisation in Buddhist societies was often conveyed through the influence of 'Hindu' tradition.[262] It is notable, for example, that when the Nāyaka kings from Madurai ascended to the throne of Kandy in Buddhist Sri Lanka in the mid-eighteenth century, they brought with them what Obeyesekere refers to as a version of 'cosmic kingship' in which the king became a much more veiled and ceremonialised figure than had previously been the case.[263]

A common paradigm across much of South, East, and Southeast Asia fused cosmic and righteous kingship together such that rulers whose ethical standards and piety slipped would be punished with cosmic consequences.[264] When the *Golden Light Sutra* asserts that 'there is famine when the king is negligent', it may be taken as a most concrete expression of cosmic logic – except that negligence here is not defined by sacrificial responsibilities; it is present when the gods can say to each other, 'This king is unrighteous, he has taken the side of unrighteousness.'[265] The ethical contractualism in Buddhist and Confucian traditions has a much weaker echo in monotheism.

---

[261] Cited in Jackson 2016: 858.
[262] Holt 1996: 20; 2004. Note, however, an inscription by King Niśśankamalla (r. 1187–1196), couched in Buddhist language announcing that 'Though kings appear in human form, they are human divinities (*naradēvatā*) and must, therefore, be regarded as gods.' (Hallisey 2003: 701).
[263] Obeyesekere 2017a: 174.   [264] Cummings 2002: 175.
[265] Embree and Hay 1988: 182–184. The moral of the *Kurudhamma Jātaka* is that the righteous king will get his rain. The *Mahāvaṃsa* XXXVI: 74–79 (Guruge 1989: 703) has the notably pious king Siri Saṅgha Bodhi producing rain after a drought through an act of ascetic compassion.

On the subject of monotheism, let us listen to Shakespeare's Henry V at Agincourt. When he prays, 'O God of battles, steel my soldiers' hearts,' he finds a reply in the award of an improbable victory over the French. It is true that his celebration – 'Praised be God, and not our strength, for it!' – invokes a clear distinction between the being of the king and the being of divinity, which may be taken as a measure of the distance between the transcendent God and his earthly representative.[266] But if the king does not quite instantiate supernatural power, he has certainly found it united with his purpose. In terms of what kingship can *do*, the difference between the two may seem, from one perspective at least, rather slight.[267]

Such distinctions seem scarcely relevant, for example, in the account of the battles of King Alfred (r. 871–899) against the Danes as presented in Byrhtferth of Ramsey's *Historia regum*, completed about a hundred years later.[268] Throughout, the English have been constantly associated with angels:

Rising up, they boldly called forth their forces to battle, trusting in the kindness of the Creator, safe and fortified by the wall of the king's presence, whose countenance shone brightly like that of a gleaming angel ... The Overseer therefore, perceiving the desire of the earthly king from his sanctuary above, conceded to him the support of angelic power.[269]

This is a radiant king, both angelic and with the power of angels at his disposal. It is true that dead kings are always easier to divinise, and providence best observed in hindsight. But war was everywhere one of the clearest ways in which kings could demonstrate their harnessing of supernatural power, and from Constantine onwards, kings had a ready means of displaying this in a Christian idiom.

Christianity had already offered a resolution to the breach between the transcendent and the mundane – indeed, a model of the man-god – in Christ, a resolution that was further elaborated by apologists drawing

---

[266] *Henry V*, 4, 1; and 7, 84.
[267] This is to agree with Hocart 1941: 8, that there is 'a very fine distinction between a king who is the incarnation of the Deity and one who is only His representative', while elsewhere I might agree with David Cannadine (1987: 17) that 'kings who are divine, kings who rule by divine right, and kings who are dignified are very different things'.
[268] From 1160s: Cross 2016: 56.   [269] Cross 2016: 73.

on classical philosophy.[270] It was neither straightforward nor routine for kings to assimilate themselves to Christ, but there was a 'Christo-centric' strand of thought about kingship by which it may be done. This was most emphatically articulated by 'Anonymous of York' writing around 1100, who asserted the divinity of the king by consecration, so that like Christ he was a fusion of the divine and the human.[271]

(2) Royal magnificence, status and authority compel divinisation

Consequently it became necessary for the rulers of Islam to adopt the customs of the kings of Persia to ensure the greatness of the True Word, the supremacy of the Muslim religion.

Zia al-Din Baranī, *Fatawa-yi Jahandari.*[272]

The Delhi sultanate writer, Zia al-Din Baranī (1285–1357), had begun by reflecting on the way in which monarchy is essentially antithetical to religion. Religion is about servitude and submission to God; kingship arrogates those behaviours to itself. But 'just as the eating of carrion, though prohibited, is yet permitted in time of dire need', so Muslim kings had to adopt 'the Crown and the throne, aloofness from others, pride, rules about sitting down and getting up in the king's court, high palaces, court ceremonials, asking people to prostrate themselves before the king' and so on. In the longer term, not only such behav-ioural norms but also ancient Persian ideas of divinised kingship would come to have a significant impact on Islamic polities.

Transcendentalism offers a potentially powerful enhancement of moral legitimacy, but if this comes at the expense of a diminution of divine-like status, it may be seen as a heavy price to pay. And could not such a status be used to symbolise the righteous claims themselves? These considerations surely weighed on kings deliberating the risks and opportunities of conversion. It is no surprise then, that in the writings of Eusebius, whose task it was following the conversion of Constantine 'to hammer out the critical accommodation between

---

[270] See Oakley 2006: 71, on the influence of Hellenistic ideas vis-à-vis Christ as cosmic mediator.
[271] Oakley 2006: 101–105; Indeed, Asch 2014: 159, argues that during the reign of Louis XIV, the deficiencies and mortality of the king's body were unproblematic because God himself had taken a human form in Christ.
[272] Embree and Hay 1988: 411.

Christian belief and pagan imperial ideology', according to Francis Oakley, we also hear certain echoes of Roman and Hellenistic themes of divinisation.[273] For Eusebius, the king is both an exemplary figure of transcendentalist virtue, and yet also as such a Christ-like figure, God's creation, his friend.[274] Indeed, there are signs that worship of the emperor continued in some places, and hints that Constantine was configured as a millennial and salvific being in himself.[275] It was probably a typical feature of conversion to monotheism that kings tried to retain in some form the aura that existing forms of divinisation had generated. In short: the needs of kings and their pretensions stood as a bulwark of divinisation.[276]

(3) Divinisation follows from the broader accommodation of immanentism

The most important reason why forms of royal divinisation recur in transcendentalist settings is simply that they were sustained by much broader processes of immanentisation. The mediatory figure of Christ himself was only one of many means by which the immanent poured into the development of Christianity, as Chapter 1 briefly discussed. Gauging how far this assisted the divinisation of European kings is, however, not straightforward.[277] The *righteous* claims of kings are clearly apparent, and they only intensified during the Reformation and the wars of religion. But how much cultural weight did the theory, imagery, and language of *divinisation* carry?

If we consider a spectrum from least to most divinised forms, this book has tended to present Christian kings as clustering around the former end and to relate this in part to the inherent difficulty of articulating such norms within a monotheistic setting.[278] In Latin

---

[273] Oakley 2006: 70; and see Bardill 2012: 338–384, for a detailed analysis.

[274] Al-Azmeh 1997: 33–34.

[275] Bardill 2012: 338–384, who argues that the Christian royalisation of Christ in turn allowed a Christological vision of royalty.

[276] I am grateful to Azfar Moin for insight on this point.

[277] From the outside, European historiography seems curiously isolated from the scholarship of sacred kingship globally. Still, other historiographies might learn from the attentiveness of European scholarship to the fine grain of events and play of contesting approaches.

[278] This is, however, a highly provisional suggestion: more intensive comparative analysis might instead render Christian kingship more typical, and what follows barely scratches the surface. In particular the significance of the

Christendom, this presumably also reflected the formidable authority of the papacy from the twelfth century. At any rate, there is little sense, for example, that Christian subjects saw kings as directly responsible for the fertility of their fields or the coming of the rains. But above all, the relatively unenchanted figure of the Christian monarch (at least in the West) seems conspicuous in the norms that governed interactions with him or her, which tended towards the relatively free and non-ritualised. Certainly there was no need for monarchy to split into diarchic arrangements as happened in some other regions nor did any fall into the 'ritualisation trap'.[279] The court of Louis XIV represented in some ways the most emphatic elaboration of 'divine right' Christian kingship in Europe, where the glorification of the king was such that it pushed hard against the limits of acceptability.[280] And yet when Louis's ambassadors and missionaries travelled to the court of Ayutthaya in the 1680s, they realised that they were entering into another world of sacred kingship altogether. Here they encountered kings who sat on their thrones like gods.[281] The obvious divinisation of the Thai monarch, the severity of the behavioural codes governing interactions with him was altogether different. When Thai ambassadors made the opposite journey, the relatively human inhabitant of Versailles was no less jarring to their eyes and ears, surrounded as he was by a rather loud and jostling court.[282] Indeed, it is a common feature of European reportage during their age of expansion to note how sacralised and formalised kingship was in many of the societies they encountered.[283]

Nevertheless, if European kingship seems largely undivinised that is only relative to certain other parts of the world.[284] Catholicism allowed supernatural power to seep into the world in myriad forms. Priests were receptacles for it, objects were; why not kings? This was

---

distinction between the Kings' Two Bodies, demands proper appreciation: Monod 1999: 63–64; Kantorowicz 2016.
[279] Monod 1999: 41.
[280] Bergin 2014: 6, on the seventeenth-century *religion royale*.
[281] For example, Gervaise 1688: 77–78; Tachard 1686: 375; see *CK*.
[282] Van der Cruysse 2002: 250–251.
[283] For example, West Africa: Newitt 2010: 69–71.
[284] Not *all* other parts of the world. A systematic comparative analysis of Christian and Muslim courts is much to be desired. Duindam 2016 suggests a very rough west-to-east movement across Eurasia of least to most ritualised-isolated.

effected through the rite of coronation, in which they were anointed with the holy chrism. Kings could be held to be mystically and substantively transformed by this rite, which invoked their priestlike nature for it was modelled on the long-standing method by which bishops were consecrated.[285] The clearest and most famous example of how ideas of royal access to *mana* could take concrete and popular form is the phenomenon of 'the royal touch', the capacity to heal scrofula, which was attributed to the kings of England and France from at least the fourteenth century.[286] Evidently, it emerged out of courtly agency and popular appetite both, and frequently the latter held the upper hand. The royal touch was a curiously specific power, hedged about by theological insistence that the king was but a vehicle for a higher grace, constrained by the righteous mode through the understanding that the monarch should be sexually faithful in order to wield it, and geographically limited to two countries in Europe.[287] But it did stand as a resonant symbol or indeed argument for the reality of the immanent power that the king might hold in his hands.

If the Reformation involved a strong reassertion of transcendentalist monotheism, one would expect such forms of divinisation to be strongly challenged. From a very broad perspective, this is indeed what happened, although not in any straightforward or immediate way. Indeed, both Catholic and Protestant kings were induced to clarify and rationalise what Christian sacred kingship actually was in the face of myriad arguments and interpretations. What Robin Briggs describes as the 'remarkably confused boundary between sacred and profane' of the medieval era could no longer persist untroubled.[288] Some French theorists responded by developing strong articulations of the principles on which a form of divinisation might rest, in which the king's body

---

[285] Oakley 2006: 100–101; Asch 2014: 30; Kantorowicz 2016. Note that Ridyard 1988: 72–78, sees the consecration as producing a 'desacralized' (as in non-divinised) king to the extent that it was clerically conferred and clerically conditioned; and Schnepel 1995: 89–91, drawing on Kantorowicz, insists on the relatively 'secular' or non-divine nature of the king's body mystical from the fourteenth century.

[286] Marc Bloch 1973. Prefigured in older associations between royalty and healing: Barlow 1980: 14–16. Keith Thomas 1971: 227–242, places it in the context of wider powers of healing by touch.

[287] For Boureau 2006: 29, if it made the king a conduit of grace that did not distinguish him from a priest.

[288] Briggs 2000.

and his mystical being could be intimately fused.[289] At the funeral sermon of Henry IV, André Valladier asked, 'The king is he holy?' and replied, 'There is an element of the divine and of holiness in this crown.'[290]

The royal touch continued: Louis XIV was a particularly enthusiastic healer before his extramarital affairs undermined his suitability as a vehicle of grace.[291] But it was practised by the Protestant kings of England too, a sign of the staying power of popular immanentism and the way in which providence remained the backdoor to immanence in the Protestant imagination. James I had begun unwilling 'as the age of miracles is past, and God alone can work them', but was then persuaded that its political utility was too valuable.[292] With the restoration of the monarchy following the civil war, Charles II quickly set about healing: he and James II were touching on average about 6,000 patients a year by the 1680s.[293] This may be interpreted as a reflection of how resilient conceptions of the thaumaturgic king could be, and perhaps of the need of post-interregnum monarchs to generate charismatic authority in a land where monarchy itself could be questioned.[294] There is certainly no simple story of either rationalisation or transcendentalisation to tell, therefore.[295] But in general terms, the imperatives of both Protestant and Catholic reform problematised the practices and discourses of royal divinisation as never before. Among the most fervent were voices rejecting the right of kingship to offer any mediation between God and the self.[296] More broadly, reformism contributed to a newly intense focus on the monarch's righteous qualities: could they really embody and transmit the moral discipline of the godly?[297] Did they remain true to the truth? Did they protect

---

[289] Asch 2014: 29, refers to Denis Crouzet on explicit attempts at the 'divinisation du roi.'

[290] Asch 2014: 33.   [291] Parker 2013: 40; Duindam 2016: 52.

[292] Brogan 2015: 69–72.   [293] Brogan 2015: 67.

[294] It was deployed too by Queen Anne: Hannah Smith 2009.

[295] Asch 2014: 10; and the subtle eddies analysed by Sharpe 2006. In general, many of the dynamics described by Asch and Monod 1999 could be seen in terms of the struggle between divinised ('re-enchanted', or 'sacral') and righteous ('disenchanted' or 'godly') forms. However, Monod argues more emphatically for a transition from the former to the latter and thence to a 'rational' and abstract concept of sovereignty.

[296] And kingship itself was thus questioned. See Monod 1999: chapter 4: 'No King but King Jesus, 1637–1660.'

[297] Monod 1999: 51–53; 82–87; Briggs 2000.

and advance the faith? These were now the kind of questions to tear kingdoms apart.[298]

One of the most important mechanisms of immanentisation across both Christianity and Islam was the cult of the saints, and this too promoted the possibility of divinised monarchy. In Christianity, this was mainly confined to the veneration of medieval dead kings who had become sanctified after dying as martyrs, such as Oswald of Northumbria, whose charisma generated by his victory at Heavenfield persisted in the form of healing miracles after his death.[299] Large numbers of dead Byzantine royals were sanctified in this way.[300] In Islam, however, it became an important facilitator of the divinisation of living kings too. The increasing centrality of Sufi holy men in the post-Mongol Islamic world presented new opportunities for the generation and capture of heroic charisma. The Safavids directly translated their sacred status as Sufi *pirs* into dynastic rule in Iran, and thereby opened up the possibility of new forms of divinisation, which were also exploited by their neighbours, the Mughals.[301]

The other vital source for the early modern willingness of Muslim kings to explore the possibilities of divinisation was astrological-*cum*-millenarian hopes and teachings. As Azfar Moin has shown, the post-Mongol royal embrace of astrological titles such as Lord of Conjunction 'was a return to the "compact symbolism" of the god-king.'[302] The previous chapter suggested that millenarianism commonly emerged as a powerful means of reframing soteriological urges in immanentist terms – of merging the 'kingdom of God' with the 'kingdom of man'. For a ruler or contender who could yoke its narrative to their own person, it was a bold way of claiming pre-eminence in the narrative of salvation, as a unique being with both heroic and cosmic qualities. The Ilkhanid vizier Rashīd al-Dīn helped promote the critical astrological notion of those kings who are 'Lords of Auspicious Conjunction (*ṣāḥibqirān*), that is, kings who are not only "just, perfect, and wise," but are also "have a further, intimate relationship (*khuṣūṣiyyat*) and closeness to God"'.[303] (Note the shift here from ethical to ontological proximity.) This was part of the

[298] Burgess 2016.
[299] Higham 1997: 222; Fuglestad 2006 185; Behr 2002. See Rowe 2017 for living Habsburgs associating with saints.
[300] Monod 1999: 44.   [301] Babayan 1994.   [302] Moin 2016: 127; 2012.
[303] Brack 2018.

process by which court intellectuals attempted to drag the recently converted Mongol Chinggisid dynasty towards an Islamic framework of sacred kingship.[304] And yet it could only be done by incorporating both pre-Islamic Iranian conceptions and finding equivalences for the Chinggisid *mana* concept (*suu*, special good fortune/charisma). In this way, for example, a direct link between Allah and the Chingissid khans could be established, quite surpassing the mediatory role of the clerisy, much as the Mongol khans had always insisted on their unique connection to Heaven. And for Rashīd al-Dīn, the ruler Öljeitü (r. 1304–1316) could be credited with extraordinary feats (*karāmāt*) such as protecting the realm from drought or reading people's minds. This process thus stands as another example of the way that the accommodation of divinisation was promoted by the conversion of immanentist rulers.

(4) Divinisation is associated with attempts to consolidate the religious field under royal control

This point has been prefigured several times in this chapter and the previous one. Chapter 2 showed how frequently in an immanentist context ambitious rulers such as Chinggis Khan sought to place themselves at the head of priestly hierarchies as a concomitant of establishing political control. Although the arrival of transcendentalism reshaped and limited that dynamic, it certainly did not obstruct it altogether: ruler and clerisy continued to steal each other's clothes. The success of the church or ulema or sangha in establishing their independent institutional and moral authority stimulated temporal princes to capture such reserves of social power for their own ends.

This is the place to add a further observation: that rather often rulers concluded that the project of asserting their dominance over the priestly groups entailed a more emphatic assertion of their divinised qualities. In essence, the institutional struggle was paralleled by a struggle in the domain of cosmic kingship: who would take centre stage in the drama of mediation with the divine?[305] The efforts of

---

[304] Brack 2018. Rashid was writing about Öljeitü, who was experimenting with many religions.

[305] The first Mesopotamian ruler to assert his divinity in unequivocal terms, Shulgi, was also involved in instituting 'the subjugation of large temple estates under some form of state supervision'. Michalowski 2008: 37–38;

Kamehameha of Hawaii to facilitate political centralisation by subjecting priestly orders to his will coincided with the strongest clear evidence of the application of the term *akua* (divine) to living chiefs as opposed to deceased ones.[306]

Once again, this dynamic continued within settings where transcendentalist traditions had been established, and where rulers seem to have felt that they needed to sidestep the moral authority of the clerisy by instead finding some source of it within their very being. It is no coincidence then that when Emperor Wu sought to establish himself as the 'great helmsman' of Chinese Buddhism by imposing state control over an increasingly powerful sangha in southern China, he devised a special ordination ritual to have himself established as a Bodhisattva in 519 CE, so that he would 'would unite the worlds of the secular and the sacred under his all-encompassing rule'.[307]

This helps to explain why we can find a certain tendency to assert divinised kingship among the early modern states of Eurasia that were otherwise also dealing with movements of resurgent transcendentalism. Their new feats of imperial expansion and centralisation presented them with the need to stamp their authority on unruly or divisive clerisies. Pamela Kyle Crossley has identified a new tendency for 'self-legitimisation' in a comparison of Ottoman, Byzantine, Russian, and Central Asian rulers. Peter the Great 'acted the role not of a prince of the church but of a living, self-contained god'.[308]

The Mughal emperor Akbar (r. 1556–1605) was not only a great empire builder with a vast reservoir of charisma to draw upon but a centraliser and administrative innovator too. It is no surprise then that he was evidently involved in a bid to free himself from the authority of the ulema, especially since the elites clustering around him were drawn from many non-Muslim groups too. In 1579, for example, he issued an imperial decree in which he was declared the imam and *mujtahid* of the age, with the authority to decide on questions of religious doctrine.[309] The status of any one clerisy was relativised by the way they were set to debate with others – Jesuits,

---

[306] Charlot 1987: 138. The counterargument of Valeri (1987: 201), that this kind of innovation could not come 'when traditional religious concepts were undergoing a crisis', is not convincing; elsewhere, religious crises might push kings towards innovations that make divinisation more explicit.

[307] Janousch 1999: 113; Palumbo 2015: 97.   [308] Crossley 1999: 39–40.

[309] Moin 2012: 139.

Brahmans, Sunni and Shi'i scholars, Zoroastrians, Jains – in a late echo of long-standing Mongol claims to sublime superiority over the squabbling clerics of their diverse populations.[310] It is no coincidence, surely, that Akbar pushed Islam as far as – or indeed perhaps further than – it would go in yielding a personal divinisation. Given that his reign coincided with the marking of 1,000 years after Muhammad's death, he was identified as the *mujaddid* or 'renewer' of Islam as it entered its second millennium. Drawing on solar Iranian themes, astrological concepts such as 'Lord of Conjunction', Alid messianism, and Sufi (particularly Chishti) models of saintly veneration and discipleship, he and his vizier Abu'l-Fazl created a new 'Divine Religion' (*Dīn-i Ilāhī*) for his elite vassals focused on himself as the sunlike being at his centre. His disciples saluted each other with '*Allahu Akbar*': 'God is great', but also 'Akbar is God'.[311] And he too was a healer. The Jesuit Jerome Xavier noted: 'He works miracles through healing of the sick by means of water in which he washes his feet. Women make vows to him for the restoration of health to their children.'[312] Unlike the English and French kings, he was not the vehicle for a very specific power, but radiated a much more general sense of his supernatural potency.[313]

Oda Nobunaga, the first of the sixteenth-century unifiers of Japan, did not attempt to unify and control the Buddhist monastic orders and temples – that possibility was left to his Tokugawa successors – but he opened the door to this possibility by his shocking willingness to grind them beneath his heel when he needed to. And he too may have been involved in an attempt at self-divinisation.[314] The great general and first reunifier of Thai royal power in the eighteenth century, Taksin, mentioned previously, who sought the 'white blood of the gods' and the ability to fly, was also embroiled in a conflict with the sangha. Indeed, he came unstuck while trying to overcome a foundational behavioural principle of Thai society by which transcendentalist hegemony was most categorically maintained: that kings must bow

---

[310] Moin 2012: 133.   [311] Moin 2012:144.
[312] Mukhia 2004: 49; Moin 2012: 142–143.
[313] Compare, too, the *karamat* (supernatural potency) of Prince Dipanagara (1785–1855), who led opposition to the Dutch in Java 1825–1830, and whose leftovers were credited with the power to cure sickness: Carey 2007: 121–122.
[314] *CK.*

to monks. Instead he demanded that high-ranking monks prostrate themselves before him.[315]

In European Christendom, an equivalent struggle over the mediatory functions seems to take place in the register of the 'priestliness' of the king, an argument between Eusebius and Gelasius (492–496), constantly replayed.[316] Somewhat ironically, although the papacy denied the model of the priestly king following the 'papal revolution' of Pope Gregory VII (1073–1085), it went on to acquire some rather secular powers, thus becoming a kind of kingly priesthood. (This is the other route to divinised kingship, of course.) But the argument was never settled conclusively. And among early modern kings, James I, for example, tried to assume a position as 'a *persona mixta cum sacerdote* [a person half secular, half priest]', for 'to some extent the king has to be both secular ruler and priest if he wants to maintain his position in a potential conflict with the power of clergymen', as Ronald G. Asch put it.[317]

It is probably no coincidence that for the best example in Christian history we would have to look further east, to areas outside Rome's purview, and to the 'caesaropapist' elaboration of the Byzantine emperorship, in which the distinction between church and state was often submerged under the emperor's authority.[318] And so too we find the discourse of kingship more openly divinised than in the West, associating the emperor with the trinity, with *logos*, the divine word, and with Christ himself. If dominance of the clerical sphere and relative divinisation go together, it is no more surprising to find unusually elaborate palace protocol and the practice of proskynesis (prostration) in place.[319]

---

[315] Gesick 1983c: 100; Reynolds 2006: 144. The Burmese king Bò-daw-hpayà (r. 1781–1819) sought religious centralisation alongside the revelation of his nature as the Maitreya Buddha but was resisted by the reformist Sudhamma monks: Charney 2006: 90–94, 101.

[316] Oakley 2006: 112, 74.

[317] Asch 2014: 50, in turn citing Andreas Pečar. This claim appeared as early as the 1490s. (My thanks to John Watts.)

[318] Michael Humphreys 2015: 267; Dagron 2003: 173–181, on the use of the Biblical figure of Melchizedek as a model for claims to be both emperor and priest. Monod 1999: 44, 'The divine element in the Byzantine imperial body was to be found in its animate or physical nature, not in mystical dignitas.'

[319] Al-Azmeh 1997: 28; Shepard 2014: 236; Monod 1999: 44.

(5) All ideologies of royal legitimation must make peace with the realities of human politics

You've got it all wrong, General! It's often said that 'the Kingdom does not belong to one person; it's owned by all.' The will of Heaven is subject to change, and it always favours the virtuous.

Creation of the Gods, a seventeenth-century Chinese novel[320]

Ideologies thrive in dialogue with political action, and if they are too inflexible and unrealistic in their assertions they will simply go unheeded. Whatever cultural inheritance is drawn on, somehow all means of understanding kingship must contend with the realities of rebellion, contestation, and usurpation. Almost as strong as the need to legitimise the incumbent is the need to provide some mechanism for legitimising his supersession. This means that when it comes to how different ideologies of kingship work in practice, the similarities can be more visible than the differences. In other contexts, it will be important to register the differences between the concepts of *mana*, providence, the mandate of heaven, and Buddhist merit. For example, it is true that *mana* functions as an index of power rather than morality, while providence, the heavenly mandate, and merit all seek to establish political failure in ethical failure. This reflects, indeed, the Axial Age origins of monotheism, Confucianism, and Buddhism, and perhaps the Eurasian circulations by which these various traditions cross-fertilised each other. But here let us pause to note what all four concepts have in common. Each remain ways of articulating and formalising the operation of charisma, as accomplishment is translated directly into authority. They speak: what has come to pass was meant to come to pass.

Conclusion

This chapter has proceed through the exploration of paradox. Immanentism facilitates the 'divinisation' of kings, but it very rarely cancels out their humanity entirely, leaving them suspended in cultivated ambiguity. It is a project of mystification and will to power; and

---

[320] Cited in van Leeuwen 2017: 73. See also passim for the way in which stories about heroes and kings may mediate the relationship between de facto and de jure authority.

it is a prison into which society places its ambitious individuals. Transcendentalist traditions arrive: they attain the authority to describe kingship by their ability to rubbish it. They are grasped by kings, even though they must thereby let go of their centrality to the task of mediation with the divine, ceding that privilege to a newly authoritative priestly class. And still, transcendentalism itself must be subverted in order to speak to the urges that produced divinised kingship in the first place. The insistent melody of immanentism is never drowned out. Exactly what tune rulers thought they were playing when they converted to a transcendentalist tradition is, however, another question entirely, and one for later chapters to address.

4 | *The Economy of Ritual Efficacy and the Empirical Reception of Christianity*

How do transcendentalist traditions spread? This is a quite different question from that of how they arise. Expanding into virgin territory, their progress takes place under the conditions of immanentism itself.[1] This means that a tradition such as Christianity must show that it can provide the tangible benefits of supernatural power before it will win allegiance – a theme explored in detail in Chapter 5. This apparently simple argument brings in its train some significant theoretical implications, however. Throwing a sharp light on the means by which ritual systems may be abandoned and adopted turns out to be an excellent way of testing scholarly understandings of what, ultimately, they are for. That the ritual vehicles of immanentism are, on some level, an attempt to control the material world becomes undeniable. Yet this in turn immediately raises the question as to how impressions of achieving such control ('efficacy') are established. And how might Christian missionaries in particular ever come to seem more effective at providing prosperity, healing, or victory than any other group of priests or shamans or sorcerers? Even where they were successful, conversion per se was not necessarily the result: the energy created at the frontier where transcendentalism expanded into immanentism was typically discharged in the spectacular forms of supernatural utopianism: prophetic, cargo, and millenarian movements.

Some Reflections on the Function of Ritual

The question most insistently asked of shamans is, 'Has it worked?'

Caroline Humphrey and James Laidlaw[2]

---

[1] By 'virgin territory' I mean societies where immanentist traditions form the entirety of religious life. Of course, in some ways, transcendentalism can shape the ground it fights on too.

[2] Humphrey and Laidlaw 1994: 11. On the pragmatic/instrumentalist qualities of shamanic ritual: Willerslev 2013; Lindquist 2017.

What does it mean to say a religious ritual has worked?[3] The idea that ritual is primarily a means of attempting to control reality, a species of science before science itself arrived and rendered it obsolete, has been contested since the origins of anthropology. Associated with some of the earliest thinkers in the discipline such as Edward B. Tylor and James Frazer, this 'intellectualist' approach has been repeatedly criticised by 'symbolists' (amongst others) who argued that ritual must be understood as means of performing a range of much more subtle social, aesthetic, and expressive functions.[4] Critics took inspiration from Durkheimian emphases on religion as the essential medium of societal construction, Weberian or Geertzian insights into culture as the production of meaning and communal self-understanding, and Wittgensteinian attention to the operation of language games.

These developments helped clear the ground for a much fuller appreciation of the complexity of ritual behaviour. The Durkheimian insight that religious ritual undertakes a great range of social 'work' is to be found everywhere in this book.[5] Much of this work is accomplished by what J. L. Austin referred to as ritual's power of 'illocutionary' utterance, which creates universally acknowledged social facts.[6] Initiation ceremonies, for example, such as the Christian rites of marriage or baptism, are conceded by everyone to transform the status of the participants by the very act of performance.

The problem arises when these insights are used to deny the instrumentalist dimension to ritual activity altogether.[7] This tendency owes something to the enduring respect accorded to a commentary on

---

[3] In this book, 'ritual' normally means 'religious ritual'.
[4] Tambiah 1990; Sharot 2001: 2–5, 33–35; Peel 2003: 5.
[5] For example, by establishing group identity, mobilising and regulating group activity, inducing sensations of communitas, maintaining morale, forming hierarchy, establishing orderly dispositions, imprinting group norms and values, generating symbolic saliency.
[6] Lambek 2013b:145.
[7] I use instrumentalism in preference to intellectualism, as the latter can take on two different emphases. Intellectualism is often associated with the arguments of Robin Horton (1975a, 1975b), which focussed on religion's function in both comprehending and controlling the world. If the former is emphasized, it can come close to symbolism, if the latter, then it signals rather the performance of ritual as a pragmatic rather than meaning-making device. Moreover, 'intellectualism' fails to grasp the bodily, performed, and emotional qualities of much religious ritual, which may not engage conscious reflection in an explicit way. Thanks to Azfar Moin and Joel Robbins for discussion.

Frazer's *Golden Bough* by Wittgenstein in his late phase. Wittgenstein may have helped push theorists away from evolutionist reflections on erring 'primitives' towards a more sophisticated understanding of human beings in general as 'ceremonial animals'. But he could be understood as exhibiting a certain lapse of cultural relativism himself, an unwillingness to credit behaviour that the philosopher considered irrational: the subjects of rain-kings 'don't really think that he could make rain otherwise they would do this in the *dry periods* of the year'.[8] Or, to paraphrase this line of thought: if people truly thought that rituals made crops grow, why did they not then give up farming?[9] In fact, in the rather exceptional situations of supernatural utopianism discussed later in this chapter, people may indeed give up such ordinary work and place all their hope in ritual mechanisms.[10] But more importantly, this approach simply fails to capture how the human mind works in its assumptions about the interlacing of natural and supernatural causation. It is akin to asking why someone who carries an image of St. Christopher in order to protect himself from harm during a car journey also chooses to wear a seatbelt. The realities of seatbelt fabric and the reality of the saints may both be acknowledged at the same time, without generating much anxiety as to the exact relations and proportions of causality maintaining between them.[11]

It has long been appreciated that the symbolist approach risks eliding the rationales for ritual performances given by the performers themselves insofar as they are bluntly instrumental.[12] The danger lies in assuming that on some level, people must know that their rain-maker king does not actually create rain (which anyone could see will arrive in the rainy season anyway) and that therefore the real function of such ritual must lie elsewhere. But it is enough to consider what happened when the missionary David Livingstone converted the rain-maker king of the Bakwena (in Botswana), Sechele, to see how mistaken this is. Livingstone barred the neophyte ruler from

---

[8] Tambiah 1990: 56. Wittgenstein was mocking Frazer for attributing irrationality to ritual activity.
[9] Tambiah 1990: 58–59; Connerton 1989: 44.
[10] As in the Xhosa movement of 1856–1857, where participants slaughtered their cattle and ceased to plant crops: Landes 2011: 92.
[11] See also Atran 2002: 141–143 for thoughts on causality.
[12] Quack and Tobelmann 2010 offer a strong defence of instrumentalism/ intellectualism; and also Bell 1992: 43, 175; MacGaffey 2005: 205. Thomas 1971: 27, offers a sensible compromise.

performing the ceremonies and refused, in an austerely Protestant manner, to do it himself either. He noted:

People intensely set on rain-making. The most insignificant people in the tribe talk with great insolence to Sechele. No one doubts his ability to make it. Old men come to me to allow the chief to make rain. If I only do so all will come to meeting and all will pray to God together. The people say the missionary too has medicines.[13]

Sechele's conversion was followed by a drought, his legitimacy was shaken, and he apostatised.[14] This sort of phenomenon is quite to be expected if we appreciate what Sahlins called, in a wry twist of Marxian language, the ubiquity of 'determination by the religious basis'. As Chapter 1 argued, the immanentist instinct is to place human beings in a position of precarious dependence on the agency of metapersons.[15] There is no 'nature' that can be trusted to be either regular or benign without the ritual work of people. Cosmic kingship is one of the grandest monuments erected by such endeavours: an attempt to create a being that can meet the metapersons on something like their own terms.

For our purposes, the most salient point to emerge from the critique of instrumentalism is the attempt to argue that ritual action is different from proto-science insofar as it is unfalsifiable.[16] Ritual may be seen as a means of imposing order on the inherent messiness of lived social and physical reality by placing certain postulates beyond doubt. This perspective offers us both a potential theoretical insight, and a position to test and challenge. On the one hand, it helpfully gestures towards the way that immanentist systems, in the normal course of life, are usually rather well insulated from empirical jeopardy; on the other hand, it begs the question as to how and why, in certain situations such insulation could be torn away.

Part of the problem with debates about 'ritual' lies in the broadness of the concept itself, which encompasses a great variety of schemas of action. To return to the language of speech act theory favoured by many scholars of ritual today, some of these performances may have

---

[13] Livingstone 1960: 300; we also hear (240) the argument of a rain-doctor that rainmaking was one of the few things that God had given blacks and not whites (who had gunpowder, horses, etc.)

[14] Hastings 1994: 314.

[15] See Puett 2002: 40–43, for ritual struggles with metapersons.

[16] Lambek 2013b: 146–147. Rappaport 1999: 281, defines sanctity via 'the quality of unquestionableness', instituted by ritual. In part, he refers here to 'ultimate sacred postulates', which are not subject to empirical verification.

largely 'illocutionary' functions, while others may have 'perlocution-ary' ones (that is, aiming at persuading and shaping the will of others – in this case, supernatural others), and many will combine both.[17] A large tranche of ritual activity in immanentist societies entails, then, at some level at least, a 'perlocutionary' attempt to communicate with metapersons in order to ensure their favour.

One qualification to this is worth noting: even where rituals seem to have clear 'perlocutionary' and instrumentalist objectives, people may feel compelled to perform them in order to create the *sensation* of mastery as distinct from the fact of it. Ernesto de Martino, drawing on fieldwork on the magical rites of the south of Italy, argued that they were 'impervious to experience' because their role was really to create a kind of alternative reality in which control was achieved: a person suffering a crisis is drawn into a mythic narrative which is resolved at least on the 'metahistorical' plane of the ritual itself.[18] Equally, elaborate rites or proclaimed revelations in preparation for battle may in fact serve to create the sense of morale and unified hope that will indeed help to achieve success.[19] Even if the battle is, in fact, lost, and so the ostensible objective has failed, the hidden rationale for the rite will remain intact.[20] Yet while such subconscious or semiconscious sociopsychological functions of such rituals help to explain their endurance, they do not render conscious and public representations of the instrumentalist function of ritual irrelevant. It is going too far to say that ritual and reality are ships that must always pass each other in the night.

Ritual Efficacy: Instrumentalism and Openness

The providence of the gods ... was principally displayed on the visible theatre of the present world.

Edward Gibbon[21]

---

[17] Valeri 1985: 74; Robbins 2004: 110; 2001: 593.

[18] Martino 2015: 93–94, 103–107.

[19] Hiram Bingham 1849: 238, in Hawaii: 'Heathen leaders doubtless know that the belief that success is practicable, whether that belief be encouraged by interest, experience, martial skill, astrology or prophecy is a powerful means of union, strength and success in war.' Other functions abound, naturally, e.g., Harrison 1993: 96.

[20] Durkheim made the 'moral efficacy' of rites prior to their 'physical efficacy': Sharot 2001: 31.

[21] Gibbon 1993: 510.

If religion functioned entirely as the Durkheimian vision postulates, one might expect the religious order of any society to remain largely static and closed, or rather only to change as a secondary phenomenon of social and political transformation. But that is not what we see.[22] Chapter 1 drew out the tendency of immanentism towards openness, flexibility, innovation, empiricism, experimentalism, and pluralism. Its receptivity is essentially a function of its entirely practical ends. Unlike many transcendentalist traditions, immanentism presents no pre-formed religious boundaries that must be transgressed, no scriptures to be denied, no soteriological frameworks to be jettisoned. Instead, elements of incoming cults, whether immanentist or transcendentalist, may be folded into an existing arsenal of ritual techniques and deployed to see if they help deliver results.[23] Silvie Poirer makes such openness a characteristic of the relational ontologies of hunter gatherers, but it has been observed by scholars of Mongolia, Maori New Zealand, and diverse parts of Africa.[24] J. D. Y. Peel has commented on the Yoruba of West Africa:

A further source of tolerance lies in the character of the religion for the individual – it tends to be concerned predominantly with easing the conditions of living in this world, and is seen by its adherent as having instrumental as well as expressive value. The more religion is regarded as a technique, whose effectiveness the individual may estimate for himself, the readier will the individual be to try out other techniques which seem promising'[25]

A missionary of the Ngaju Dyaks of Borneo reported:

Dayaks play politics with supernatural beings ... Their religion is a matter of tactics. The more a man knows about ritual, the more he can do for his own and his family's welfare. A person's wealth is proof of his

---

[22] I read some of Ando's (2013) and Rüpke's (2010) criticisms of the 'polis religion' paradigm of Roman scholarship as a rebalancing away from a purely Durkheimian approach to an acknowledgement of the empirical and instrumental qualities of religion. Ando 2008: 13: 'Roman religion was thus founded on an empiricist epistemology: cult addressed problems in the real world, and the effectiveness of rituals – their tangible results – determined whether they were repeated, modified, or abandoned.'

[23] Rus: Shepard 2014: 235; Mongols: Jackson 2009: 115; sixteenth-century Angola: Francisco de Gouveia, 1 January 1564, MMA XV: 228–235; Amazonia: Pollock 1993: 172.

[24] Poirier 2015: 62; Wallace 49–50; Northrup 2002: 27; Belich 1996: 165–166; Kraft 1992: 268–269; D'Avray 2010: 97; Eaton 1993: 274.

[25] Peel 1968: 124; 2003: 227–229.

theological knowledge. They are continually changing their adherence from one set of spirits to another.[26]

This was a profoundly empirical form of religiosity. The nineteenth-century Asante even had the head of the royal priesthood, a 'proto-bureaucratic position', looking at records of the successes of both local and Muslim ritual specialists in order to establish their efficacy.[27] It follows that such empiricism would also be extended to the reception of Christianity. Joel Robbins, drawing on fieldwork from the 1990s among the Urapmin of the West Sepik region of Papua New Guinea, has described the deepening conversion of the big men from 1977 during a regional revivalist movement:

While women and younger men were busy becoming possessed and having visions and dreams, older men watched carefully to see if Christianity would visibly deliver on its promises. They watched to see if the Spirit women really did cure people and if boys ministered to by prayer and possession really did grow as strong as those who had been put through initiations in the past. ... They even designed tests in which they planted two gardens and treated one with prayer and the other with traditional ritual and magic. The proof of the stronger religion would be made visible by the garden that grew best.[28]

The more this mentality structures relations with the sphere of meta-persons, the more an 'economy of ritual efficacy' is in operation.[29] That it is to say that the value of religious practice is measured by its perceived efficacy, such that ineffective rituals, priests, and metaper-sons may lose ground to ones that are perceived to be more effective.[30] The 'Oro cult, introduced from Raiatea to Tahiti in the eighteenth century, presumably gained its associations of potency through its connection with the feats of the warrior elites who championed it. It is not surprising then that its encounter with Christianity should have been conceived as a power struggle in the most muscular terms possible. In their letters from Raiatea, the missionaries John Williams

---

[26] Miles 1976, cited in Reid 2000: 26, who makes this mentality a defining feature of Southeast Asian religion.
[27] Owasa-Ansah 2000: 479–480. See Eliis and ter Haar 2004: 72. Ando 2008: 15, notes the importance of record keeping for Roman priestly colleges.
[28] Robbins 2004: 145.
[29] To be distinguished from Scribner's 1987: 1, 'economy of the sacred', which has a more Durkheimian focus.
[30] Compare Weber 1978, I: 427, on the magician.

and Lancelot Threlkeld, report that in 1816 a priest at Opoa was inspired by 'Oro, to declaim:

Give me men, give me men. I will go and wrestle with Jehova, I will drive him to the setting sun. Who is Jehova? Did not I bring him forth? Is he not a son of mine? I will destroy him. Come let us wrestle with him, his people shall all be banished, give me men, give me men.[31]

The Christian god here is cognitively subordinated (he becomes a creation of 'Oro), but this is a function of his hopefully soon-to-be-evident subordination in terms of supernatural power: the god of war, charged with the *mana* of human sacrificial victims, will win the wrestling match.[32] Given the conditions of immanentism then, 'conversion', just as any other form of innovation, proceeds under the sign of power.[33]

Conceptual Control

The religious field is only influenced rather than dominated by the economy of ritual efficacy: it would look far more changeable and unstable otherwise. Its Durkheimian properties, for example, do indeed provide a kind of ballast against free-form innovation and fluidity. Moreover, the ritual economy – like all economies perhaps – is one in which the information available to participants is neither self-evident nor clear-cut. Empirical religiosity is not simply driven by observation of events (ritual outcomes): it is how such events are perceived and interpreted and successfully communicated that matters. Such cogitation is, of course, subject to all the frailties of the human mind and temperament that make us less than objective assessors of plausibility and probability.

It is presumably the case that certain kinds of ritual acts and indeed systems are easier to shield from the harsh glare of empirical failure than others. This is what the cognitive scientists Robert N. McCauley and E. Thomas Lawson referred to as 'conceptual control'. The more specific, and easily measurable the result aimed at, for example, the less

---

[31] Sissons 2014: 53.
[32] Compare Hugh-Jones 1996: 56 (Amazonia); or with a trial of divine strength in the Andes: Salomon and Urioste 1991:110; Mumford 1998: 151.
[33] See Peel 1977: 128–129; Seaton 1974: 202, citing Redfield 1953: 129; Hefner 1993b: 29–30; Berend 2007b: 21; Fuglestad 2006: 190; Cohen 1991: 130.

conceptual control there is over its interpretation.[34] The riddling ambiguity of the Delphic oracle may be considered to provide a form of conceptual control by diminishing its falsifiability.[35] Rituals aimed at events which may well come about naturally anyway – such as victory in battle or recovery from illness – are likely to prove more durable than those aimed at more improbable outcomes. It is, on the face of it, peculiar that the thaumaturgic powers of the kings and queens of England and France should have become confined to the healing of just one condition, scrofula. But it must have been assisted by the tendency of the disease to go into remission.[36]

It is vital to note that the economy of ritual efficacy normally only pertains to the relatively superficial level of particular spirits, cult sites, holy men, and ritualists. Rarely does it impinge upon the deeper assumptions and norms on which all such activity rests.[37] In the words of a study of cult in mid-twentieth-century Mount Hagen (Papua New Guinea): 'Particular experiments may fail but they are not designed by participants to test the assumptions of the framework.'[38] The Incas kept a careful track record of the predictions of the oracles in order to ascertain those that proved to be false or uncertain – with deities losing or gaining status as a result – but without the oracular method itself being impugned.[39] The president of Sri Lanka, Mahinda Rajapaksa, was moved to sign a decree calling an early election at the precise time of 1:04 p.m. on 20 November 2014, on the advice of his astrologer, Sumanadasa Abeygunawardena, who had also performed rituals to secure the correct outcome. After Rajapaksa lost, it was primarily the astrologer himself, rather than astrology per se, who lost status (he complained, 'You have to give us at least a 5 per cent margin of error').[40]

---

[34] McCauley and Lawson 2002: 205; Barrett in Laidlaw and Whitehouse 2007: 202.

[35] Larson 2016: 95–101; Lane Fox 1986: 215, on Egyptian oracles; 576–579, on conceptual control more generally.

[36] Marc Bloch 1973: 242; Brogan 2015:15, expresses reservations. Bloch 1973: 238–241, and Thomas 1971: 243–251, also refer to more general forms of conceptual control.

[37] See, for example, Thomas 1971: 767–769.

[38] Andrew Strathern, 1979: 92; 1980: 169–170.

[39] Gose 1996a: 6. Pachacuti Inca was said to have put a son in charge of weeding out the false oracles on the imperial roster. Also Rostworowski and Morris 1999: 794.

[40] www.theguardian.com/world/2015/jan/13/nostradamus-wrong-astrologer-advised-sri-lankas-president-election, accessed 13 January 2015.

Astrology is a highly technical and instrumentalist technology aimed at predicting effects through understanding the rules governing fundamental, though usually unrecognised, forces of the universe – just as modern science is. Its conceptual control might lie precisely in the complexity of technicalities involved. Any rites aimed at propitiating deities, however, have a particular kind of conceptual control built in: by appealing to agentive beings, the outcome of any rite becomes subject to the unknowable realm of the will.[41] The gods may be flattered, coaxed, or chastised, but they remain as unpredictable and complex in their interests as people are in general. And it is a function of their superiority that they or may not smile upon you.[42] In immanentist settings, probably the most common opportunity for conceptual control was simply to refer to an infelicity of ritual action itself – that the correct routines had not been followed, that some form of pollution had seeped in – or its contradiction by superior ritual action.[43]

Myriad conjectures, shifts of perspective, get-out clauses, and cognitive biases are usually available, therefore, to lend any form of instrumentalist–immanentist ritual activity a strong degree of conceptual control. But these processes do not preclude the functioning of the economy of ritual efficacy altogether, they just limit it to a relatively superficial dimension of religious life, slow it down, and allow various kinds of psychological, social, and political investment in the existing religious forms a measure of protection. The key question here, recall, is not the rationalist's perennial conundrum: how can people believe that instrumentalist religious or magical ritual works (when we know that it does not)? It is rather: how do people assess the *relative efficacy* of different rites or the metapersons they invoke? The purpose of using the term 'empiricism' in this context is not to suggest that ordinary pre-modern religious agents were scientists *avant la lettre* but rather that their observations of what actually happened were indeed at the heart of certain arenas of ritual activity. Ritual could only make its own reality up to a point.

---

[41] Weber 1978, 1: 428, makes the move from 'magic' to 'religion' one of greater conceptual control as priests refer ritual failure to the inadequate behaviour of the supplicants.

[42] Burridge 1960: 270–272, on rising and falling popularities of temples.

[43] See, for example, Nicholas Thomas 2010: 235; Paul Cohen 2003: 99.

It was an important element of missionary strategy to create precisely such opportunities. That is to say, missionaries sought to both boost the significance of the economy of ritual efficacy and wrest it on to a more profound epistemological level. The former was effected by heightening the sense of competition between ritual forms.[44] In immanentist systems, there are likely already to be a variety of different ritual forms available and so a degree of at least implicit competition is ever present. Presumably, this becomes more acute in times of crisis or perceived existential jeopardy. For example, Baum has argued that severe drought in the late eighteenth century allowed Djoula leaders to question the legitimacy of priest-kings at Esalau and assert the power of previously subordinated indigenous cults.[45] While in the highlands of Papua New Guinea in the mid-twentieth century, a major cult began during an epidemic that threatened the lives of the Taro Enga and their pigs. Four men, claiming revelation from their father's ancestor spirit, urged people to stop sacrificing to ancestors and instead sacrifice to the sun, for the sun and the moon were surely 'the father and mother of us all'.[46] But Christian missionaries – meaning, for present purposes, anyone interested in asserting the Christian faith – came endowed with a set of attributes that would dramatise the sense of competition, thrusting it onto a stage for all to see.

Missionaries and the Impression of Ritual Superiority

As soon as we admit that empirical outcomes could play a significant role in religious change, we are presented with a puzzle. How is value created in the economy of ritual efficacy? Given that the instrumentalist promise of ritual is a delusion, its success or failure might be expected to be entirely random. Sometimes the rain will fall; sometimes the drought will endure.

Indeed so: this is one reason why there was nothing remotely inevitable about the willingness to accept missionaries' claims to efficacy. The seventeenth-century Capuchin Giovanni Cavazzi, working in the region of present-day Angola, describes an argument with the fearsome

---

[44] In Wittgensteinian terms, we might say that they change the relevant 'language game' so as to alter what becomes falsifiable: Tambiah 1990: 64. See d'Avray 2010: 98, on conditions in which 'collision with experience can also destroy existing values'.

[45] Baum 1999: 176.   [46] Biersack 1991: 268.

Imbangala leader Kassanje, who pointed out that Christian priests died just like other men and could not act as ancestor vehicles in the manner of his ritual specialists. His recent successes at war had been won 'without this Zambi (*nzambi*, spirit) of yours called God, and without him we shall do the same in future as we have in the past'. His men applauded.[47]

There is therefore an important element of sheer contingency involved.[48] And yet, as the discussion above underlined, events only matter once they have been shaped into a meaningful narrative, which interested parties may spin this way or that. How compelling these narratives are will in turn be shaped by the hopes and sensations of plausibility aroused by the new cult. Surely, where one expects and desires efficacy, one is predisposed to discern it.[49] There are three ways in which Christian missionaries may have stimulated such expectations and thereby gained an edge over local ritualist specialists. The first is simply by virtue of their foreignness, for there seems to be a general connection between the exotic and the supernatural. The second derives from actual imbalances of wealth, health, and power between the missionising society and the missionised. The third is by virtue of the extraordinary confidence of missionaries in the powerlessness of the old order and their willingness to prove it through iconoclasm. But first, it is worth reminding ourselves that Christianity did not need to be forced into the purveyance of immanentist power; it had been in that business from the very beginning.

Christianity as a Vehicle of Immanent Power

Do not put the lord your god to the test

Luke 4:12

So he replied to the messengers, 'Go back and report to John what you have seen and heard: The blind receive sight, the lame walk, those who have leprosy are cleansed, the deaf hear, the dead are raised.'

Luke 7:22

---

[47] Cavazzi 1668: 20 (Book III, Chapter III).   [48] See Chapter 5.
[49] Compare Bloch 1973: 243, 'What created faith in the miracle was the idea that there was bound to be a miracle.'

For, as in naturall things, men of judgment require naturall signes and arguments; so in supernaturall things, they require signes supernaturall, (which are Miracles,) before they consent inwardly, and from their hearts.

Thomas Hobbes[50]

In Chapter 1 it was argued that the transcendentalist traditions incorporate immanentism *from their inception*. If Christianity can be considered, from a longer-term perspective, as a great strengthening and deepening of the logic of transcendentalism, Jesus himself can appear as a bright flash of the immanent. From a Jewish perspective he could be taken as a grotesque denial of the unique unicity of god; to ancient critics he was a wandering magician, deceiving the masses with cheap tricks and superstition, whose followers indulged in rites of blood sacrifice after his death.[51]

There are two attitudes to miracles in the Gospels.[52] The dominant message is that of their essential significance: they are present in large numbers, and they are repeatedly presented as the principal driver of Jesus' popularity: they help his followers establish his credentials as the Messiah against those of John the Baptist, as in the quotation from Luke above.[53] They have the authorities quaking.[54] They show that he is the son of God. But there is also a transcendentalist strand, which deprecates the business of producing miracles, which wants to exalt Jesus as something more than a sorcerer, which chastises those who demand them as missing the point.[55] It does not matter, for our purposes, which tradition is closer to the Jesus phenomenon in his lifetime. Morton Smith argued that some of the anti-miraculous material resulted from an apologetic desire to account for occasions in which Jesus' miracle-working power had not 'come good'.[56] If that is the case, then this strand was an attempt to provide a degree of conceptual control over empirical jeopardy through the transcendentalisation of religiosity, right from the start. But the Buddha too, it was seen, is both a miracle worker and a despiser of miracles in the tradition. Any transcendentalist tradition that aspires to popularity must, in short, have its cake and eat it.

---

[50] Hobbes 2012, II: 182 (*Leviathan* I, XII).　　[51] Smith 2014: 203.
[52] Smith 2014: 129, 145.　　[53] Smith 2014: 18–23.　　[54] Smith 2014: 23.
[55] See Matthew 12:39, for the wicked demanding a sign.
[56] Smith 2014: 19–21; 145.

Figure 4.1 Holy water in the grounds of St. Anthony's Church in Wahakotte, Sri Lanka.

No wonder, then, that missionaries in all ages subsequently found ways of presenting themselves as conduits of immanent power. They would thus be imitators of Christ and the apostles. They offered the hope of direct communication with the most powerful metaperson of all through the wish-granting medium of prayer, which readily replaced other vehicles of propitiation.[57] They were also, of course, heirs to waves of immanentisation, which had delivered diverse means of making such divine assistance more concrete and reassuring through the cult of the saints, for example, or an array of *mana*-charged objects (including beads, crosses, relics, and holy water), all of which could be transferred to good effect to the mission field.[58] (See Figure 4.1.) And lastly, they had to yield to the imperatives of the mission field itself. In a meeting with a Tupinambá tribe, the Tamoios, in 1563, the Jesuit José de Anchieta recounts that he told them that he had come so that God 'might give them an abundance of provisions, health, and victory over their enemies and other similar things, without ascending

---

[57] Robbins 2004: 317.   [58] Alberts 2013b: 15; Thomas 1971: 27–57.

any higher because this nation, without such a staircase does not want to climb to heaven.'[59]

Waves of transcendentalisation – 'reformations' – might subsequently limit the strategies for showcasing immanent power. Some Protestant groups undoubtedly had a less colourful and diverse array of such techniques to display in the mission field. But here again, the reality of the missionary predicament must have compelled a degree of flexibility and innovation. As both a scholar (trained in anthropology) and practitioner (of the Brethren Church) of Christian mission, Charles H. Kraft has been able to comment on this explicitly. While working in northern Nigeria among the Hausa and elsewhere from the 1950s, Kraft came to feel that the 'naturalism' of the Western worldview was a serious disability for missionaries insofar as it prevented them from grasping the supernaturalistic perspective of many of the people they worked amongst. In such societies it was understood that individuals' needs were primarily to be achieved through exerting influence with spiritual entities.[60] At one point, a medicine man began attending his church, having heard of the miracles of Jesus, but he stopped after a few weeks – disappointed to find that none of the Christians there exhibited such power.[61] Kraft's inherited Anabaptist theology initially left him little room to manoeuvre in response to such appetites, but subsequently he was drawn towards rites of exorcism and other techniques associated with Pentecostalism. He took to interviewing demons at length and forcing them to speak through the Holy Spirit before casting them out. According to Kraft, one of the principal barriers facing the missionary is the prevalence of group orientation (roughly what I have discussed as the Durkheimian dimension). But, he says:

There is at least one major condition that counters both religious conservatism and the expectation that ordinary people are not allowed to innovate. It is the fact that for many (probably most) of the peoples of the world, the felt need for more spiritual power seems to be more important to them than the mere perpetuating of their traditional religious practices.'[62]

There it is: revelations of immanent power may trump the traditional routines of propriety and solidarity.[63]

---

[59] Viveiros de Castro 2011: 22; Wilson 1973: 57.   [60] Kraft 1992: 265, 272.
[61] Casey 2011.   [62] Kraft 1992: 269.
[63] Compare with the Baptist missionary Edward Hudspith, working for thirty years among the Karen (Erick Cohen 1991: 133–134), who came to believe in the need for 'a battle of power at every level' between Jesus and the spirits.

The Mana of the Exotic: Hope and Threat

Jesus said to them, 'A prophet is not without honour except in his own town, among his relatives and in his own home.'

Mark 6:4

Where was the one place that Jesus' miracles would not work? Home. He mustered up a few healings but otherwise his charisma deserted him: his family found it hard to recognise the son of God in their son and brother.[64] Wandering abroad, as a stranger, the crowds flocked. In a series of works, Mary W. Helms has assembled a wide range of evidence on the tendency to attribute unusual power to the realms beyond domestic society.[65] The domestic realm is often imagined as surrounded by expanding circles of wildness, alienity, supernaturalism, and power; people and things from these outer lands must be absorbed and tamed in order to serve domestic flourishing. The evidence comes from every part of the world, but it perhaps emerges particularly clearly in the work of Africanists, who have attested to a 'readiness to import new ideas or to pay respect to an outsider who claimed spiritual power' as a feature of societies across the continent.[66] One manifestation of this general propensity is the emergence of notions of 'stranger kingship', as analysed by Marshall Sahlins, in which ruling figures from afar become the condition of flourishing, order, and civility in the host society.[67] This logic will be shown at work in the reception of Christianity in Kongo and Hawaii in the companion volume. There is perhaps an inherent glamour and promise in the strangeness of the exotic, of rare and unusual things. Hence an entirely mute towering cross left by stranded Portuguese sailors at Trañovato in Madagascar in the sixteenth century subsequently became a site of cultic devotion, as residents left offerings in the hope that it would bring sun and rain and give their cattle respite from insects.[68]

---

[64] This is rather reminiscent of Buddha's experience in the *Vessantara Jātaka*; see Chapter 1.

[65] Helms 1988, for example, on the Iraqw of East Africa (133); Andrew Strathern 1970 on the foreignness of Great Spirit cults as an index of potency. See also Taussig 1987.

[66] Ranger 1975: 9, on 'mystical geography'; Law 1991: 61; Greene 1996: 125; Ellis and ter Haar 2004: 146.

[67] Sahlins 2014; Helms 1988: 143.   [68] Larson 2007: 352.

Missionaries, with their unusual appearances, their new symbols, ceremonies, and babbling tongues – not always translated into something intelligible – were also things from afar onto which immanentist hopes could be projected.[69] In Anlonquin-speaking North America, Jesuits could be understand as shamanic beings, assimilated to the concept of *manitou* (spirit).[70] The Capuchin missionary Montesarchio wandering around the more remote peripheries of Kongo in the seventeenth century found chiefs pressing their daughters in marriage upon him; he was told that he was a '*banchita*' – 'a man returned from the other world'.[71] Indeed, Christianity found its beginning in this part of the world through its association with the life-giving powers of the world of the dead.[72] Most missionaries, wittingly or unwittingly, surely did not forgo the influence that such attributions gave them.[73]

Yet, recall that in the immanentist imagination the attribution of immanent power was not an attribution of moral status: that which might be benevolent might also be malevolent. One scholar of Vanuatu remarks that Christianity and sorcery engaged 'a shared conception of miraculous and sacred power as essentially immanent and morally undifferentiated'.[74] This had very important implications for conversion dynamics, for it meant that where Christianity was endowed with *mana* it would arouse suspicions as well as hopes. In two of the three most important states in sixteenth-century sub-Saharan Africa – Kongo and Mutapa – a sudden switch in the ethical category of Christianity occurred at a crucial point in the ruler conversion process. In Kongo it led to the apostasy of the first ruler to convert, and in Mutapa it scuppered the chances of conversion altogether.[75] The Jesuit, Gonçalo da Silveira, had been warmly welcomed by the young king of Mutapa, who seems to have become taken with an idol of Our Lady of Grace who granted to him a revelatory dream.[76] He requested baptism and had hundreds of his nobles baptised. But then his Muslim advisors – already themselves immanentised as fortune-telling sorcerers (*ngangas*) – claimed that the Jesuits were also *ngangas* who would take

---

[69] Belich 1996: 217, on Maori.
[70] Griffiths 1999: 16–17. For analogies: Hodgson 1997 (Xhosa); Elbourne 2012 (Khoekhoe and Mohawk).
[71] Graeber and Sahlins 2017: 186.   [72] As argued in *CK*.
[73] Landau 1999: 10.
[74] John Taylor 2016: 141. See Griffiths 1999: 16, for the 'double-edged power' of Jesuits in North America.
[75] *CK*.
[76] Luís Fróis, 15 December 1561, in *Documentos* (1962–1989), VIII: 42–57.

control of the king through the water of baptism. They were 'bringing the sun and famine in a dead man's bone and many other spells to take possession of the land and kill the king.'[77] That night, men were sent to the Jesuit's hut: he was strangled and his body was immediately dragged off to be cast into the river. Indeed, across Central Africa, early modern Catholic missionaries were often placed in the category of more 'magical' (instrumentalist, private-oriented) types of ritual specialists.[78]

Inequalities of Wealth and Power

Notice that the Mutapa court interpreted the imperial menace of the Portuguese in terms of the supernatural power it was presumed to be based on. This speaks to an important feature of the dynamics of religious innovation in the immanentist mode: obvious displays of special attainment may be taken as evidence of superior ritual and/or metapersonal efficacy.[79] Among the Aztecs, deities of cities on the rise assumed sunlike positions over their defeated rivals.[80] Pagan Rome claimed that its success in war related to its unique relationship with the divine: 'Their triumphs over gods as many as their nations, their booty as great as the number of surviving statues of captive gods,' as Tertullian put it.[81] History became a record of divine favour, as it did with Christian Rome. Subsequently, the imperial power, glamour, sophistication, and wealth of Rome and Byzantium, and then the Franks, were used to impress upon the surrounding 'barbarians' the power of the Christian God to aid his followers.[82] Historians of early medieval European missions are fond of quoting Bishop Daniel of Winchester's (d. 745) letter to Boniface:

If the [pagan] gods are almighty and beneficent and just, they not only reward worshippers, but also punish those who scorn them. If they do both

---

[77] António Caiado, 1561, *Documentos* (1962–1989), VIII: 5–9 (compare Fróis, 56–57).

[78] As *nganga*: MacGaffey 1994: 263.

[79] I am grateful to Marshall Sahlins for discussion of 'an indigenous anthropology of the power of alterity/the gods as the source of order and prosperity'. See also Graeber and Sahlins 2017: 5, 'Indeed, as a sign of the metahuman sources of royal power, force, notably as demonstrated in victory, can function politically as a positive means of attraction as well as a physical means of domination,' and Erick Cohen 1991: 117.

[80] Umberger 2015: 85.

[81] Cited in Ando 2008: 122, 163, though note that rival deities were more suborned than dominated. Note Woolf 1998: 231, on Roman Gaul.

[82] On Byzantium, see Shepard 2014: 236.

in the temporal world, why then do they spare the Christians who are turning almost the whole globe away from their worship and overthrowing their idols? And while they, that is, the Christians, possess fertile lands, and provinces fruitful in wine and oil and abounding in other riches, they have left to them, the pagans that is, with their gods, lands always frozen with cold, in which these, now driven from the whole globe, are falsely thought to reign. There must also often be brought before them the might of the Christian world, in comparison with which those who still continue in the ancient faith are few.[83]

The message here is that it is, ironically, the religion that promises unearthly rewards which also provides earthly delights, while those who follow gods with only worldly intentions in mind sit freezing on the benighted periphery. Displays of asceticism risked undermining this proposition: a barefoot preacher among the Pomeranians was scornfully received, for poverty was a poor indicator of divine potency.[84]

When the Portuguese arrived in west central Africa in the fifteenth century, they found Bantu societies in which the technology of iron-working was strongly associated with both ritual mastery and political lordship.[85] The coming of Christianity, carried by Europeans also bearing new kinds of swords, armour, and firearms, was in some ways a recapitulation of these themes.[86] The things brought by trade, or the blacksmith's art, or new agricultural techniques, were not disassociated from the work of ritual.[87]

The Italian explorer, Alvise Cadamosto, who tracked down the West African coast on behalf of the Portuguese crown, described an encounter with a ruler named 'Budomel' in 1455, who was happy to engage in religious discussion. He is reported as commenting, 'Our faith appeared to him to be good: for it could be no other than God that had bestowed so many good and rich gifts and so much skill and knowledge upon us.'[88] It is always wise to maintain a healthy suspicion of European self-congratulation in such evidence. But we find it again in a letter by the king of Dahomey, Agaja, to King George I, in 1726:

I much admire the white Man's Way of Speaking by Writing, the Knowledge of which, with other Things, your God has given you beyond us, by which Means you know his Ways. We think and believe him to be the greatest of

---

[83] Fletcher 1998: 243; Yorke 2016: 241.   [84] Bartlett 1985: 198.
[85] Fromont 2014: 39–47.   [86] *CK*; Fromont 2014.
[87] Helms 1988: 134–135.
[88] Tymowski 2015: 231. Compare De Marees 1987 [1602]: 72.

Gods, and that he has appointed our Gods, or Fetishes, to rule, govern, direct, kill or destroy us as we act.[89]

Like Budomel, Agaja did not convert and found other ways of conceptually incorporating the reality of the Christian metaperson – but he had taken the first step of ceding the reality of ritual efficacy to the Europeans.[90] According to Charles H. Kraft, in the modern world the association between greater wealth and greater spiritual power has been a major feature of non-Western reactions to Christianity.[91]

Marshall Sahlins refers us to a reported comment by the Fijian chief of Cakaudrove: 'True-everything is true that comes from the white man's country; muskets & gunpowder are true, and your religion must be true.'[92] This is advanced in agreement with A. M. Hocart's observation on how close, almost interchangeable, the notions of truth (*dina*) and *mana* were for Fijians.[93] This is not at all to deny that Polynesians could display vigorous scepticism towards missionary claims.[94] Indeed, note, how close scepticism and empiricism are in this mentality. The trader John Turnbull was met with incredulity when questioned by Pomare II on his Christian beliefs in 1803. His brother, Itia, was even worse, 'looking on, with a kind of haughty and disdainful indifference. It was all [*ha'avare*] or falsehood, and adding, they would not believe unless they could see; and observed, we could bring down the sun and the moon by means of our quadrant, why could we not bring down our Saviour by a similar operation?'[95] But Pomare became the first chiefly convert in Polynesia, and in the long run this empiricism told in Christianity's favour.

---

[89] Law 2002: 264.
[90] For Africa, also Southall 2004: 230; Peel 1977: 128; and Yai 1993: 262, (Western religion as a 'miraculous weapon'); for Sioux: Lindenfeld 2007: 283.
[91] Kraft 1992: 266.
[92] Sahlins 1985: 38; see also Keith Thomas 1971: 107; Nicholas Thomas 2010: 123.
[93] Hocart 1914: 98.
[94] See Tomlinson 2009. The Fijian chief Ratu Tanoa told an American lieutenant, 'To be a Christian would not make him white or give him ships, so what the good would be, he could not tell' (Sahlins 2004: 201, ft. 5). Compare Belich 1996: 110.
[95] Newbury 1980: 13; compare Niel Gunson 1978: 218, on Marquesan scepticism.

Iconoclasm: Inequalities of Scepticism and Confidence

Three converts had gone into the village and boasted openly that all the gods were dead and impotent and that they were prepared to defy them by burning all their shrines.

Chinua Achebe, *Things Fall Apart*[96]

Missionaries and their local converts had the capacity to stimulate and transform the economy of ritual efficacy because of the unusually stark and uncompromising challenge they put before the old order. To some extent, they shared this curious confidence in the superiority of the system they represented with the emissaries of other transcendentalisms: recall Buddhist monks setting out to tame local deities as if they were merely troublesome animals. But monotheistic missionaries were so much more aggressive in their attack on the uselessness of the old order. They did not set out merely to show that their god was better but that any alternatives were mere frauds. There was a chance that some of the typical techniques of conceptual control would weaken under this punishing glare, shrivelling into mere excuses.

Missionaries did not need to push the question of ritual efficacy from the particularistic to the systemic in order to force an opening for their new cult. The new god merely needed to show his strength in order to get a foothold as a favoured deity among others, without breaching the habitual terms of immanentist thought too severely. However, missionaries were also unusual in trying to draw the more deep-lying structures of religious behaviour into competitions of ritual efficacy. The suggestion that such structures are normally shielded from empiricism might be assimilated to the argument that religion pertains to that which is 'empirically indeterminate' – axiomatic and untestable.[97] Typically, it may indeed be the case that core religious principles are not subject to scrutiny in this way, but missionaries attempted very directly to do just that, and surprisingly often they were successful.

Immanentist societies, it was suggested, are loosely universalist, insofar as the deities of all and sundry might readily be granted existence. Monotheist missionaries had stepped outside of this world and were thus liberated to turn a withering scepticism upon it: they

---

[96] Achebe 2001: 114. The novel is eloquent on several themes advanced here.
[97] Southwold 1979.

functioned, indeed as de facto atheists with regard to the powers of all other metapersons. Indeed, their discourse of idolatry, by which agentive and sacred object–subjects ('idols') were turned into dumb stone or unthinking wood, rendered missionaries (selective) 'naturalists' or materialists. In November 866, the newly converted khan of the Bulgars, Boris, received a long letter from Pope Nicholas, addressing a series of anxieties:

You say that a stone was found among you before you had accepted Christianity, and if someone took some of this rock on account of some illness, it used sometimes to offer a remedy to his body, but at other times to remain without benefit. But surely this is certain to happen even to those who never consume some of that stone, namely that some will in fact receive the remedy of health from their illness, while others waste away in theirs. Therefore, when you ask whether this should be done or rejected from now on, we respond and judge that every use of this rock should be completely forbidden.[98]

He goes on to refer to the Biblical conceit of Christ as the cornerstone and refers to Peter's exhortation: 'Approach that living stone, rejected to be sure by men, but elected and honoured by God, and you yourselves shall be built as living stones into a spiritual house.'[99] This passage begins by noting that the Bulgars had already taken an empirically informed and potentially sceptical approach to their ritual deployment of the stone, which is intriguing in itself. But then the far more corrosive scepticism enabled by monotheism is applied in order to conclusively strip the stone of *mana* and agency. And lastly, an attempt is made to turn the neophyte king's mind from all hope in particular objects and discrete attempts at ritual remedy, towards a totally different system of religious thought, in which all become part of a vaulting project of ultimate salvation, and in which actual stones became symbols for metaphorical imaginings.

The most dramatic and public way in which missionaries might hope to place their cult in competition with the pre-existing forms was through staging violent repudiations of their physical vehicles. The deliberate destruction of ritual sites and objects was not quite unknown in immanentism. It came in two principal forms, which I shall refer to here as 'auto-iconoclasm' and 'warrior iconoclasm'.

---

[98] North 1998: chapter LXII.   [99] A version of I Peter 2:4–5.

Auto-iconoclasm, perhaps particularly visible in the literature on Africa, occurs when a collective understanding emerges that the effects of ritual activity have become useless or harmful, as when the spirits in question are deemed malevolent. (It is, in other words, a function of the ethical ambiguity of supernatural power.)[100]

Warrior iconoclasm occurs when the temples of defeated enemies are deliberately destroyed.[101] Burning down the principal temple of the enemy city was the standard expression of victory for the Aztecs; indeed, a burning temple was the glyph that signified conquest in their painted histories.[102] In many Polynesian societies it was customary to destroy the temples of the defeated, which would customarily be rebuilt the following season.[103] Such practices were partly driven, no doubt, by a logic that was not specifically religious: to attack a temple was to seize its wealth, perhaps to tear down a fortified stronghold, certainly to wipe out a potent symbol of enemy authority, a source of status, pride, and morale. But where an immanentist worldview was in place, this was also likely to have resonance for the question of relative ritual efficacy. It indicated that the metapersonal alliances of the invading people were conclusively stronger than those of the enemy. After they had burned down the temple of their enemies, the Aztecs took its idol back to their capital of Tenochtitlan, where it was held in a 'god captive house'.[104] Meanwhile the tutelary god-slaying god of the Aztecs, Huitzilopochtli, was installed in its place in the defeated city.[105] Where the pantheon was essentially shared between victor and vanquished, it was not the gods themselves that were belittled but merely the particular claims to be able to represent the gods, or access their power.

To some extent, then, the sacred violence wielded by Christians – let us call it righteous iconoclasm – lent itself to be understood in terms analogous to both these pre-existing forms where they existed. In common with warrior iconoclasm, Christian violence was also a means of demonstrating superior supernatural power.[106] A late sixteenth-century Spanish observer of the Andes recommended the public

---

[100] Chapter 5 for more.
[101] Palmer 1928: 100, for a Sudanese example; Moin 2015, South Asia.
[102] Clendinnen 1991a: 78.   [103] Sissons 2014: 42.
[104] Clendinnen 1991b: 78.   [105] Clendinnen 1985: 57.
[106] Meanwhile, Mughal temple destruction of Hindu structures (Eaton 2000; Moin 2015) might be described as warrior iconoclasm surrounded by some of the rhetoric of righteous iconoclasm.

destruction of *huaca*s (idols/gods), 'because the community pays little respect to a *huaca* once it is defeated'.[107]

Christian iconoclasm, however, did not only occur as the conclusion to a successful war which had already demonstrated the inferiority of the defeated god or ritual centre. It was also undertaken by missionaries and converts stepping up to humble unhumbled gods as a matter of principle.[108] More importantly, the missionaries staged the violence as a *challenge* to the metapersons, and indeed to the entire cosmology they represented, by so fearlessly discounting the possibility of their revenge while violating their most sacred precincts and taboos at will.[109] Such extreme offensiveness placed a rare onus on the ancestors, spirits, or gods to rise to the challenge: if they could not show their power, when their power itself was on trial, when would they show it?

Normally, this was a tactic that came into play after the ruler had already decided on converting, because it required the protection of political authority, but before the mass of his subjects had been convinced.[110] For what is the most significant anxiety that the prospect of a ruler conversion will arouse among his or her unconverted subjects? It is that their ancestors, or spirits, or gods – whose emotions had always been a matter of grave concern – would turn on them in anger at their wilful abandonment. Acts of iconoclasm deliberately created precisely this scenario – provoking these metapersons, jabbing them in the ribs – to show that such fears were baseless. The missionary took upon himself all the jeopardy of this venture – and walked away unscathed. Otto of Bamberg, in his mission to the Pomeranians of the 1120s, purportedly gave a speech in which he presented the implications of smashing the idols and dragging them out of the town, inducing the pagans to wonder: 'If they had any

---

[107] Stern 1982: 16, citing Cristóbal de Albornoz in 1582.

[108] See also Assmann 2008: 30–31, on intrasystemic versus extrasystemic violence.

[109] Similar confidence was exhibited by the Christian-inspired Taiping rebels (1850–1864), who 'defeated one local Chinese god after another in displays of ritual combat' and tore down all other representations of gods in the areas they conquered (Dean 2017). Where 'the idols proved no match for the Taiping forces, it graphically illustrated the powerlessness of these gods against the Taiping deity' (Reilly 2004: 137–138).

[110] Or, of course, in regions conquered by Christians. See Marcelo de Ribadeneira 1970 [1601] I: 356 on the Philippines.

divine power ... they would defend themselves. But if they cannot defend themselves, how can they defend us?'[111]

Typically, as missionaries predicted, the observable outcome was indeed an echoing silence from the heavens, especially in the immediate aftermath. This was a result that could be relied upon when other attempts to prove the superiority of the new god were undone by contingent reversals. In the 1560s, two Augustinian friars travelling to the Inca rump state at Vilcabamba found the recently converted Christians at Puquiura deeply anxious about the setbacks to their prosperity that had afflicted them since their conversion, and which were attributed to neglect of the shrine to the sun of Yurac Rumi. They were teetering on apostasy. The tactic adopted by the missionaries was to ask the people to bring firewood and observe the fiery destruction of the shrine. This was an exorcism, and it succeeded: the commitment of the people was restored.[112]

In other contexts, the mere continuation of the natural order post-iconoclasm might speak volumes – for there is no 'natural order' in the immanentist ontology: every bounty requires ritual work.[113] The selective atheism of the missionaries brutally exposed the falsity of that ubiquitously assumed premise. Among the Urapmin described by Robbins, the iconoclastic stage was undertaken with more than a trace of experimentalism still lingering. 'Wagering that God was strong enough to protect them from the anger they were sure to inspire,' they removed the bones of their ancestors from their dwellings and watched to see the results. And sure enough, the taro still grew. As one inform-ant put it:

As time went on people observed, 'Oh! We do have pigs, we do have gardens, we have [so much taro] that it is rotting because we can't eat [all] of it Oh! We were just wrong in the past.[114]

That is not to say that the iconoclastic manoeuvre could find no reply at all. One of the most important forms of conceptual control available

[111] Bartlett 2007: 67. Whether he said this matters less than that it was seen as a plausible piece of missionary rhetoric.
[112] Redden 2016: 50–51.
[113] Analogously, the arrival of foreigners who flourish while cheerfully flouting all local taboos may weaken the taboos' power: Biersack 1991: 272, for Papua New Guinea; *CK* for Hawaii.
[114] Robbins 2004: 148–149.

to any ritual system is simply the ambiguity of timing. How far after the event the expected reaction may occur is often indeterminate. For those committed to the old order or politically associated with it, a calamity or sign appearing months or years after iconoclastic activity could be attributed to the anger of the gods. This point will be an important feature of the 'pushbacks' against ruler conversion discussed in Chapter 5.

In the sixteenth century the use of iconoclasm as a means of discon-firming religious claims was given particular salience in a Europe falling prey to confessional conflict. It became a tactic of Protestant communal violence: the elevated host could be snatched from a priest and crumbled to dust; relics cast into the street to show that they were mere animal bones.[115] In February 1529 in Basel, a crucifix was taunted: 'If you are God, defend yourself!' before it was burned.[116] As Alexandra Walsham notes:

> To see a great abbey reduced to rubble or to cast an image on to a pyre without disaster striking was to be convinced that these structures and artefacts were indeed lifeless and vacuous and that acts against them were not, in fact, forms of sacrilege.[117]

This was then an intra-Christian manifestation of the way that transcendentalist-inspired scepticism could seize upon a vulnerability of immanentism.[118] But both Catholics and Protestants felt empowered to deploy precisely these tactics abroad.

Healing and Exorcism

And the people all tried to touch him, because power was coming from him and healing them all.

Luke 6:19

They told us that if we joined their god he would protect us and heal my uncle... we were afraid of the sickness. The Christians came to pray in the

---

[115] Davis 1973: 56.   [116] Scribner 1987: 76.
[117] Walsham 2008: 507; Walsham 2010.
[118] Yet the logic of their actions also speak of the continuing influence of immanentism. Where reformers, just like Lollards in earlier centuries, 'tested' images of saints, their actions suggest a lingering attribution of personhood: images were tried and punished as if for breach of contract; and attacked as if they had perpetrated a colossal act of betrayal: Graves 2008.

morning and the same evening my uncle was healed. God healed him and we converted to Christianity.

Catherine Scheer, 'When the Spirits are Angry...'[119]

Physical healing has always been a primary function of religious activity.[120] The possibilities of conceptual control are here enhanced by feedback mechanisms between mind and body that have been revealed as ever more complex and significant in recent decades. Conditions that tend to be temporary, episodic, or susceptible to psychosomatic factors and the placebo effect presumably helped establish sensations of ritual efficacy.[121] There is a strong association between Buddhist monasticism and the curative arts; the Buddha himself may be invoked as a healer.[122] Healing is certainly a remarkably enduring and coherent theme of the expansion of Christianity.[123] In early medieval Europe, missionaries left a trail of healing stories, miracles, and magic stones in their hagiographies.[124] In their global early modern expansion, from Panama and New France to Madagascar, South India, Tonkin-china, China, Japan, and the Philippines, everywhere missionaries went they profited from their perceived association with healing expertise.[125]

In some cases, Christian missionaries were readily slotted into this role because of their willingness to provide care for the sick: thus a transcendentalist impulse towards ethical display and selfless love was interpreted in terms of an immanentist specialism in ritual efficacy. Particularly in the period of modern medicine, albeit much less reliably before that, their impact was enhanced by a genuine superiority in the efficacy of the non-ritual treatments missionaries offered.[126] In 1905, for example, the missionary Vincent Briggs working among the Lahu living along the Meking River reported:

We administered to their sick, and the effects of our medicines were simply miraculous to those people. In one village eight adults took a stand for Christ

---

[119] Scheer 2011: 59.   [120] Bellah 2011: 135, 157–165.
[121] Porterfield 2005 explores some of these themes.
[122] Zysk 2015; Salguero 2017; Liyanaratne 1999: 14–17; 112.
[123] Porterfield 2005.   [124] Compare among Picts: Fletcher 1998: 246–248.
[125] Deslandres 2018: 133; Larson 2009: 76–84; Županov 2008; Alberts 2013b: 89; Restall 2003: 133; Laven 2012: 8; Ribadeneira 1970 [1601] I: 344. See missionaries being tested in North Molucccas: Platenkamp 2017: 239.
[126] Paredes 2006: 545; Jordan 1993: 293; Erick Cohen 1991: 131–132, particularly on the rush to baptism during epidemics in northern Thailand.

and cut loose from devil worship. The rest of the village and one or two other villages are waiting to see how these eight Christians get along. If Jesus can help and protect them, they too will seek him next year.[127]

A Baptist missionary working among the Kengtung Lahu revealed another way in which hopes may have been raised: an immanentisation of the Christian discourse of personal resurrection.[128] 'When baptized many [of the Lahu] felt they were getting eternal life – that is their body would never die. This is the great longing of the lahus, so they flocked to be baptized.'[129]

More ubiquitously, the self-presentation of missionaries as spiritual warriors doing combat with the diabolical meant that they were frequently received as effective exorcists. The late sixteenth and seventeenth centuries formed a 'golden age of the demoniac' in Europe, in which cases of possession and exorcism ratcheted up as part of the Catholic war against Protestantism.[130] Yet, it was not merely a European concern that missionaries brought with them as they travelled into the wider world. Roughly comparable notions of spirit possession and exorcism appear to have been surprisingly widespread across the globe. In the 1660s, the king of Allada, on the slave coast of Africa, summoned missionaries to his presence so that he could throw holy water over his head, which he had been advised would protect him against the 'demons'.[131] The appeal vaulted over all religious boundaries: in 1570s Kyushu (Japan), many were caught up in atmosphere of possession that sprung up around the Jesuits.[132] In 1970s Sri Lanka, successful exorcists such as Father Jayamanne at Kudagama drew crowds of thousands.[133] In such scenarios, missionaries were taking on a major feature of Christ's charisma. But through the vehicle of healing they were also providing a visible and affecting drama of the act of defeating local metapersons, which their evangelism turned upon.[134] This was enabled by the existing ethical ambiguity of

---

[127] Walker 2003: 567; Biersack 1991: 272, penicillin injections among the Paiela chase away spirits so effectively they do not return.
[128] Although the image of resurrection is already rather corporeal. Porterfield 2005: 7–8.
[129] Walker 2003: 581.   [130] Levack 2013.
[131] *Relation of the Kingdom of Arda*, 7 July 1662, MMA XII: 381; Law 1991: 64.
[132] See *CK* on Japan; also Central Africa.
[133] Stirrat 1992; Gunaratne 2017: 139–140, for Jayamanne's appearance in a memoir.
[134] Fletcher 1998: 244, for early medieval material.

metapersons in immanentism: with a little twist of the mind, gods could be reduced to hunted and malevolent entities dominated by a commanding benevolence.[135] As the anecdote about the shrine to the sun of Yurac Rumi indicates so nicely, exorcism and iconoclasm worked via the same immanentist logic of supernatural warfare.

The observable efficacy of Christianity as a ritual facilitator of bodily health was also shaped by global variations in disease vulnerability. Daniel T. Reff has argued that Christianity expanded so strongly in early medieval Europe and the early modern New World because in both cases it was moving among societies ravaged by disease, coping with unprecedented suffering and social chaos, and open to the imagery of miraculous cures offered by Christianity.[136] If the missionary accounts from these two far-distant episodes often seems similar, then, it was not only because Jesuits were immersed in the texts of their forefathers, but because they were immersed in a similar historical context.[137] In the case of the New World, of course, the disease had been brought by the Christians themselves. In such cases, the fact that Europeans enjoyed relative immunity from the diseases could be attributed to a discrepancy in ritual efficacy.[138] A similar scenario played out much later in the Pacific, where populations lacking immunity were hit hard by the arrival of Old World pathogens, and the old gods of healing seemed powerless to stop them.[139] In sub-Saharan Africa, by contrast, it was Europeans who were vulnerable until the nineteenth century.

One way in which we can tell that missionary reports of the role of healing reflect a genuine empiricism amongst their host populations (and not just a genre stereotype) is the unpredictability of the results they disclose. Where missionaries rushed to baptise the dying, imbued with a transcendentalist concern for their otherworldly salvation, their coincidence with death might instead indicate ritual malignancy.[140] A Spanish official in sixteenth-century Guatemala, where baptism had thus become associated with disease, complained of local elites who prevented commoner children from exposure to its deadly *mana* while trying to be baptised themselves repeatedly. Clendinnen wonders

---

[135] Japan in *CK*.   [136] Reff, 2005: 4–6, 25–27.   [137] Reff 2005: 4–5.
[138] Keary 2011: 254.   [139] *CK*.
[140] See apostasies among the Maori: Sissons 2015: 131, 143. On associations between missionary arrival and plague in Amazonia: Viveiros de Castro 2011: 23–24; also Fausto 2012: 275; Donald Pollock 1993: 169.

if they were sorcerer-priests, attempting to 'test and augment their own spiritual force'.[141] To return to the Augustinians in the neo-Inca state of Vilcabamba, in 1571 the ruler, Titu Cusi Yupanqui, died a few years after his baptism.[142] One of his wives in her wrath commanded Friar Diego Ortiz to celebrate a Mass and resurrect him – taking quite literally, as surely many societies were wont to do, the imagery of Christ's resurrection. When this failed, Ortiz was tied to a cross and killed as a wooden stick was pushed through his body.

Prophetic, Millenarian, and Cargoist Responses to the Missionary Stimulus

> My brother, do you think as I do,
> My brother, do you see what I see?
> I look up, and behold
> The world bank breaks open and comes to us.
> Song of a Kawelka leader, Papua New Guinea, participating in the red box money cult 1968–1971[143]

In his narrative account of the early progress of the Church in the Philippines, the Jesuit Pedro Chirino relates three instances where local female ritual specialists had been involved in corruptions of the faith. The first woman was a priestess who claimed that her deity was a great friend of the Christian one.[144] The second had received visions of Jesus Christ and preached to her people in the manner of the former priest-esses. The third woman believed that she had died and gone to heaven, where she had read about healing herbs and been sent back to earth to heal people. The Jesuit chastised and tried to silence each.

Thus the openness of immanentist traditions: their willingness to grant authority and sense to incoming cults. The result was that where Christianity succeeded in establishing plausible claims to superior ritual efficacy it did not follow that 'conversion', as the missionaries understood it, would have to be the result. Naturally, the host society would not immediately abide by the transcendentalist attempt to limit the significance of continuing revelation, and nor would it immediately

---

[141] Clendinnen 2003: 164–165.   [142] Redden 2016: 68.
[143] Andrew Strathern 1980: 166.
[144] Chirino 2000: 236, 286–287. I owe this information to an unpublished manuscript by Natalie Cobo.

abide by the monotheistic sense of identity. Rather, indigenous ritual specialists could seize ownership of the ritual promise of the new cult for themselves, thereby creating new syncretic forms with remarkable swiftness.[145] Local visionaries everywhere claimed that they too had effective access to the Christian god, who might only be something indigenous in origin anyway.[146]

Most striking are those movements, found in all regions of the globe, which scholarship has described as prophetic, millenarian, or cargo cults, but which are united by their common expression of supernatural utopianism as a response to culture contact. They may be seen as the product of two dynamics in particular. The primary dynamic is produced by immanentist cognition in situations where the inequalities of wealth, health, and power referred to above are experienced as painfully severe, above all in encounters between indigenous peoples and agents of Western modernity in the nineteenth and twentieth centuries.[147] The second dynamic is what happens when the startling message of otherworldly salvation is interpreted in immanentist terms: it is likely to be understood as a form of supercharged immanentism, in which this-worldly fortune could be granted in a truly miraculous, all-encompassing and ultimate form.

Immanentist traditions may already contain an inherent strain of utopianism. Again this follows from the principle that all that is worth having in life is produced by labour in the field of the supernatural. What if a ritual performance could be discovered that yielded a much more transformative and permanent solution? If nothing is 'natural', nothing is impossible. A people's sense of their past, in their mythic tellings of it, may be discontinuous and episodic, in which fundamental features of existence, such as gender, were suddenly created.[148] What if a great discontinuity lay too in the future? As when, for the late twentieth-century Paiela, in Papua New Guinea, the sky

---

[145] The term 'syncretism' is now often criticised. Used as a hard 'taxonomic' distinction, i.e., a means of distinguishing the syncretic from the non-syncretic, it is indeed problematic given that all traditions have absorbed influences from outside; used as a means of highlighting a distinctive phase and quality of religious genesis, it is, however, perfectly acceptable. Gruzinski 1989 for Mexico; Kimpasi cults in Kongo, see Fromont 2014: 78–79.

[146] See Newbury 1980: 62; Chowning 1990 on a Fijian claim that Jehovah and Jesus were the banished twin grandsons of the local god Degei.

[147] Adas 1979: 150–166. Wilson 1973: 220.   [148] Marilyn Strathern [MS].

and the ground will meet and, 'All men will be brothers and we will marry our sisters.'[149]

Chapter 2 referred to the existence of prophets in immanentist contexts, who may be distinguished from other ritualist specialists by virtue of their estrangement from the daily round of social and ritual activity, and by their capacity to articulate more startling and comprehensive solutions to suffering. The greater the sense of crisis the more traction their voice tends to have. Oona Paredes describes the typical form of a revitalisation movement among the Higaunon in the Philippines, centred on a *baylan*, the spirit medium:

During a time of great crisis or stress, a baylan receives a message from supernatural beings that soon the world would be turned upside down and the chosen people will be delivered from their hardship. Instructions are given to abandon settlements and crops, kill all domestic animals, and proceed to a distant location to await further instruction. The reason for these instructions is that, when the world ends as we know it, the order of things will be reversed, e.g., domestic animals will devour their owners, and those experiencing sickness and hardship will become perpetually healthy and prosperous. With this prophecy, the baylan leads his followers to paradise.[150]

From one perspective, there is a direct analogy to be made between figures such as these, the longing for deliverance they speak to, and the prophets of Ancient Israel searching for succour amidst imperial subjection.[151] If such abrupt transformations are already possible in immanentism, of course, then the radicalism involved in Christian conversion no longer seems so implausible or unprecedented. Both involve a decisive repudiation of the status quo in favour of a more complete solution to human need. The taboos and ritual responsibilities of normal life may then be viewed as a burden, given up with some relief, as the world is turned upside down. Indeed this latent awareness of the onerousness of ritual labour and subjection to the lordship of metapersons, may be a clue to the mysteries of auto-iconoclasm mentioned previously.

There is, however, a significant problem with establishing how deeply and widely such movements are inherent to immanentism

---

[149] Biersack 1991: 266. Connecting to interpretations of the technology of white foreigners: Biersack 2011b: 233.

[150] Paredes 2006: 523.

[151] On closeness/distance between pagan and Judaic prophets, see James Davidson 2004.

because nearly all our evidence comes from societies that have already been thrust into contact with a transcendentalist tradition such as Christianity, Islam, or Buddhism.[152] In any case, it is a reasonable assumption that the sudden visibility of such cults is not just a function of societies emerging into the historical record but of the dynamics of the encounter itself – and one dimension of that encounter is the sudden exposure to salvationist teaching.[153]

The first cargo cult in Melanesia emerged in 1857, and although on the face of it the ideological content seems essentially indigenous, it is difficult not to note that the first mission had arrived in the region in 1855.[154] Such 'cargo cults' erupted spontaneously, independently, and repeatedly in different parts of Melanesia and Polynesia through the nineteenth and twentieth centuries.[155] More than any other phenomenon, they make plain how directly, concretely, and literally the immanentist mind attributes prosperity to ritual action.[156] To those reared in transcendentalism or naturalism, they can be uncomfortable to behold. But the logic is difficult to resist: if Westerners seem to have extraordinary wealth (and often appear to do little work) then they must have arrived at superior ritual mechanisms. This can be a painful realisation. Why are the spirits or ancestors assisting these men in this way, and not us?[157]

In Mount Hagen, Papua New Guinea, for example, spirit cults had already claimed to provide more extraordinary benefits than the normal interactions with ancestors. But the introduction of money made Hageners dependent on a new medium of wealth that was apparently entirely in the gift of outsiders. In 1968 a young man named Makla became a medium for spirits, who 'whistled in his throat' and demanded money and moral strictures from adherents. The money was placed in red boxes: it was promised that when they were finally opened, the money would have multiplied many times.[158] As one big man participant put it,

---

[152] The Paiela, for example, are an arguable case; see Biersack 1991: 268–270 and 2011b: 238–239. See Wilson 1973: 197; Adas 1979: 104.
[153] For example, among the Maori: Belich 1996: 220–222.
[154] Worsley 1957: 126–131.
[155] The term has been problematised for its pejorative associations: Hermann 1992.
[156] Compare Trompf 2000: 117.   [157] Leavitt 2000: 307.
[158] Andrew Strathern 1979: 98.

Money, knowledge and wealth lie along a line. We people do not know their source, only you white men who have power know this. We do not know, and simply bump into these things from an angle, at one point along the line.[159]

It is true, as always, that such cults may also be the vehicle for the management of all manner of political, social, moral, and psychological matters.[160] But there is no reason to discount the significance of the consciously held objectives, which derive straightforwardly from the immanentist premise. In that case, the position of the cult leader is akin to that of the divinised king. As Burridge puts it: 'He is taken to have communication with the divine, and in the context of Cargo he stands in relation to the community as, or like a divine king.'[161]

Indeed, the prophets of supernatural utopianism more generally may be taken as sudden surges of something like divinised kingship in the heroic mode, as leaders establish their charisma on the battlefield or through healing powers, for example, and quickly translate it into social power.[162] They are unusually vivid illustrations of the role of popular need in fashioning such leadership, especially where the prophets emerge from lower status groups. Where they flare up against colonial authorities, of course, they also represent a rejection of the essentially disenchanted forms of colonial government, which had refused to adopt the traditional forms of sacred rule.[163]

Equally, however, cargo cults in particular may read the logic of divinised kingship onto the procedures of colonial government, adopting their forms as if they were rituals.[164] One district officer visiting Iwa in the Louisiade archipelago in Papua in 1946 discovered 'a fully indigenous organization there headed by a king, a second king, governor, boss, doctor, sergeant, eighteen policemen [etc]... in open imitation of the prewar structure of the administration' – all due to a prophecy by a local leader three years earlier.[165]

Frequently, such movements also drew upon explicitly Christian themes.[166] During the 'Vailala Madness' among the Elema of the Papuan Gulf of 1919–1922, taboos and initiation ceremonies were abandoned, idols were destroyed – the ancestors were 'bloody fools,

---

[159] Andrew Strathern 1979: 97.
[160] See Burridge 1960; Leavitt 2000: 312; Hefner 1993b: 25.
[161] Burridge 1960: 282.   [162] Adas 1979: 120.   [163] Adas 1979: 113
[164] Adas 1979: 157.   [165] Rollason 2014: 49.
[166] Andrew Strathern 1979: 93, 97.

no savvy anything' – and new ritual forms, involving European-style feasts, flagpoles, and parade-ground marching were taken up.[167] It seems to have been triggered by an apocalyptic sermon delivered by a member of the London Missionary Society (LMS).[168] Indeed, the LMS missionaries themselves initially viewed it as a movement of the Holy Spirit. To be sure, some great societal renewal was expected, but it would take the form of ancestors returning to them from across the seas in ships laden with European goods.[169]

That is not to say that the goods themselves represented the *summum bonum* of cargo cult. They tended to represent a more general reformation of relations between people and with metapeople; they were valued as an index of a more general condition of powerfulness. Incoming outsiders had already attained that state of grace, and by 'a reverse anthropology', their methods could be discerned and recreated.[170] Still, otherworldly salvation became this-worldly salvation in the process. Great hope and rupture are readily grasped, but in an essentially concrete and imminent form.[171] By pushing the implications of the immanentist premise as far as they will go, cargo cults, along with other forms of supernatural utopianism focusing on immanent and imminent end points, gain a great enhancement of social power, but at the cost of a significant loss of conceptual control.[172] If most instrumentalist ritual confines itself to outcomes that could conceivably come about anyway, utopianist ones reach for the impossible. This is why such movements may repeatedly flare up but must at some point die down. Of the *baylan*, Paredes says, 'Invariably, the movement fails.' No less invariably the red boxes of Hagen turned out to contain junk; the whole affair lasted three years.[173] As Richard Landes notes, such vulnerability to empirical disconfirmation makes these movements intense, brief, and subject to certain typical patterns of evolution.[174] In the beginning, the very swiftness of their rise and the communal enthusiasm they generate seem proof enough of their

---

[167] Nicholas Thomas 2012a: 142–145.   [168] Landes 2011: 124.
[169] Swain and Trompf 1995:176–177.   [170] Wagner 1975: 31–34.
[171] Gray 1990: 68.
[172] One option was to switch focus to more immediate immanentist ends, which Wilson 1973: 359–373, refers to as tacking between the 'revolutionist' and 'thaumaturgical'.
[173] Andrew Strathern 1979: 97.   [174] Landes 2015: 1094.

assertions. They make their own reality for a while, then – until reality proper comes crushing in.[175]

At the same time, the social power of these movements rendered them irresistible vehicles for political projects. Indeed, supernatural utopianism remained almost the only ideological force in the pre-modern world capable of generating popular participation in movements with radical sociopolitical objectives. It was therefore ubiquitous in rallying opposition to the encroachment of Western imperial power, as with the *Santidade* movement among the Tupi of the Amazon, which prophesied that God was about to inaugurate the millennium, and the native people would soon become masters of the Portuguese.[176]

There is a sense in which it will not do to draw too tight a distinction between the utopian or millenarian movements that sprung up on the frontier of an expanding Christianity and the core of Christian tradition itself. Jewish and Christian interpretations of the import of their message have fluctuated between the concretely and imminently millennial and the more transcendent and deferred.[177] Jesus was supposed to return … until he did not. With the conversion of Constantine inaugurating Christian dominance of the Roman Empire, the millennium could be imagined as at hand; a hundred years later, and the sack of Rome by Alaric and his army of Goths in 410 fuelled arguments among the remaining pagans and even some Christians that this calamity was attributable to the spurned pagan gods who had withdrawn their protection. A bishop in North Africa, Augustine of Hippo, watched with dismay. He was moved to argue that the City of Men was ever unreliable, and only the City of God could be trusted.[178] What is now often taken as the standard Christian vision of the end of the world is a transcendentalised version, a remarkably successful item of engineered conceptual control, in which the final proof is ever held in suspension.

---

[175] Landes 2011: 96; Donald Pollock 1993: 175.
[176] Lee 2017: 66–67. Hugh-Jones 1996 for later movements in the region. See Stern 1982: 51, and Mumford 1998 on the Taki Onqoy cult (1560s), which claimed a pan-Andean alliance of deities would defeat the Christian god and wipe out the Spanish through disease.
[177] Thereby balancing social power and conceptual control. See Landes 2011: 6–7.
[178] Thanks to Robin Whelan for discussions on Augustine.

5 | The Conversion of Kings under the Conditions of Immanentism: Constantine to Cakobau

What I would like you to beware is the doctrine of the Manifestation of the Primary Noumenon. That teaching had the natives of this land think of the Sun Goddess as identical to the Great Sun Buddha. Was that the Sun Goddess' victory? Or was it the victory of the Great Sun Buddha? ... Ours is not the power that destroys. It is the power that recreates.

Akutagawa Ryūnosuke, *The Faint Smiles of the Gods*[1]

A prevalent theme of Japanese self-understanding has been the extent to which their country has not so much been converted to immigrant forms, as those forms have been converted by their arrival in Japan. In the sphere of religion, much of what writers describe of this process might well be understood as immanentisation.[2] Therefore, in the struggle between the deities referred to in Akutagawa's short story, the Buddha has collapsed into the sun goddess. In fact, this everywhere represents the reality of transcendentalism at the point of its introduction: it obeys the logic of immanentism and is stretched to contain it.

The task of this chapter is to elucidate both the underlying persistence of immanentism and specific qualities of its vulnerability. Most of the chapter dwells on the importance of the empirical assessment of supernatural power – as particularly evident in existential dramas of military conflict and medical healing – in stimulating and enabling rulers to take a decisive step towards conversion. Only towards the very end of the chapter will we approach the means by which this logic was finally subjugated.

---

[1] Akutagawa 1989 [1922]: 18. My thanks to James Raeside for this reference and our discussions.
[2] Eisenstadt 1996; Higashibaba 2001: 84; Kitagawa 1987: xii.

A Model of Ruler Conversion

Christian writers – and indeed Muslim and Buddhist too – liked to tell stories about the conversion of kings. They provided a simple and dramatic way of envisaging an invariably messier and longer process of religious transformation.[3] In this vision of top–down conversion, the ruler first submits to the faith himself and then submits his people to his decision. We do not need to be credulous readers of these stories, however, to recognise that ruler conversion was, indeed, a fundamental element of the expansion of the transcendentalist traditions.[4] Before the modern era, for example, the substantial Christianisation of any society only occurred once its ruling elite were either decapitated through conquest (as in the Americas), or won over through conversion. Where missionaries were not following in the footsteps of European empires, the conversion of the ruler was usually a crucial objective.[5] This was essentially the way in which Europe itself had become Christian, after all.[6]

One measure of the significance of the ruler's role in societal conversion is how often it aroused opposition. Insofar as they ruled over elites and masses who were by and large not yet affiliated to the new cult, their moves to adopt and promote the new faith tended to produce a legitimacy crisis. Why were rulers induced to take such a risk, and how they could possibly overcome the ructions it caused?

As in the preceding chapter, the advance of transcendentalism is represented here only by Christianity, and only its arrival *into immanentist societies* – that is, where no other transcendentalist tradition had already established dominance. This means particularly late antique and early medieval Europe, from the conversion of Constantine to that of Vladimir I of Rus, and the chiefly conversions that spread across the Pacific in the early nineteenth century, from that of the Tahitian chief, Pomare II (1812), to Cakobau of Fiji (1854), although other material, from Africa and elsewhere, is also woven in at times.

---

[3] It also conformed to a broadly 'feudal' logic: see in Angola, Francisco de Gouveia, 1563, MMA, II, 519–520.

[4] Such stories may overlook the existence of an already-Christian section of the population, for example. See Haas 2008: 106; Alan Strathern 2017a; Melville 1990.

[5] Brockey 2008.

[6] See Berend 2007b: 12; Higham 1997: 28; Fletcher 1998: 236. Ditchfield 2015: 157.

What emerges from a consideration of these cases together with those of the companion volume – and indeed still further examples – is a model isolating three principal modes by which rulers were drawn to Christianity. These modes may also be thought of as stages to the extent that they often followed chronologically.[7] (1) *Religious diplomacy*. Rulers are first induced to tolerate and favour Christianity through enticements of diplomatic advantage, military assistance, and commercial profit. (2) *Accessing immanent power*. The breakthrough to a more substantial incorporation of the new cult is often connected to perceptions about its ability to provide supernatural assistance. (3) *Enhancing authority*. The Christianisation of the realm may then be seized upon as a means of enhancing the authority of the ruling dynasty.

These are the elements that I have found to be the most consistent and decisive features of *ruler* conversions.[8] They are not intended, in the first instance, to apply to the conversion of people in general. Even in relation to rulers, they do not form an exhaustive list, and two further issues – of cultural glamour and intellectual force – are also considered in the companion volume. That is also where the question of what happened when Christianity encountered fellow transcendentalisms is addressed, in particular through the case studies of Japan and Ayutthaya (Thailand).[9] And it is where the extremely important first mode, religious diplomacy, is explained at length – unfortunately, there is no space here in which to explain it. The present chapter is rather focused on the second mode, which examines how an immanentist logic of supernatural contest shaped the ruler conversion process.

Conversion and Group Identity

But first we must briefly address what is to be understood by 'conversion' at all. That is not to say that establishing when, exactly, conversion happened is a principal concern here. The model of ruler conversion focuses on certain moments within a broad spectrum of engagement with the new religion, starting with its toleration, moving to its patronage, then to a decisive expression of commitment,

---

[7] Each mode does not necessarily apply in each case.

[8] Indeed, they also apply to rulers in transcendentalist societies, although such conversions were much rarer, as I argue in *CK*.

[9] These cases are referred to occasionally in what follows, however.

and ending with an attempt to unroll it across their realm. There is certainly little attempt to consider conversion as a theologian might see it, as an intellectual–emotional transformation of the self. This would be to view the matter through a transcendentalist – and more specifically monotheistic – discourse of truth recognition, emotional sincerity, and interior reconstruction. In the immanentist vision, for example, there is obviously nothing 'irreligious' or 'false' about experimenting with new ritual practices in order to obtain worldly benefits.

Nevertheless, for many analytical purposes, conversion is best conceived in terms of 'the moral economy of self-identification' as Hefner puts it: it is when a ruler announces to the world that he or she has assumed a Christian identity that the most significant line in the sand has been crossed.[10] Missionaries normally presented baptism as the ritual expression of this transformation, and many neophyte rulers understood that it signalled some kind of change in group affiliation. To be sure, the consequences for subsequent religious behaviour varied considerably. No doubt, 'converting' rulers often did incorporate transcendentalist understandings into their inner lives at some point in their careers. At times, it may be worth speculating as to whether they arrived at a more intense and personal commitment.[11] But much more often than one may think, making distinctions between 'genuine' and 'insincere' conversions turns out to be an analytical dead end. Rulers who seem to accept baptism for the most contingent, instrumental, and calculated of reasons may end up as the most stalwart proponents of the faith.[12] Moreover, interiority rarely leaves much imprint on the historical evidence at our disposal, and is not straightforwardly perceptible to the individuals themselves. All selves, and surely royal selves above all, are constructed in dialogue with what is publicly necessary and privately convenient. Inner movements must often follow where the performance of rulership leads. The focus here, then, is less on individual motivation – itself a most obscure matter – than on the power of religious claims, images, and institutions to shape and legitimise political activity.

However, the language of 'identity' needs to be handled with care when we step outside of monotheistic settings. As Chapter 1 argued, it

---

[10] Hefner 1993b: 25, 17.
[11] As in the case of Ōtomo Sōrin of Bungo (*CK*); compare Khan Boris: Shepard 1995.
[12] Compare Robbins 2004: 85.

was the eruption of transcendentalism that allowed the field of 'religion' to become something truly separable from society in general, and to act, therefore, as the basis for a realm of identity creation distinct from other forms of social membership. And it was the monotheisms which made such identities most salient insofar as they were conceived in exclusivist terms. The process of adopting Christianity from a purely immanentist system may often be seen as less a matter of *switching identities* as *learning what it is to have a religious identity in the first place*. This is an important point to bear in mind. At the same time, it is also insufficient as an expression of what it meant to abandon an immanentist religious culture. In *all societies*, a prospective ruler conversion was a matter of communal concern and invited political risk.[13] In other words, the prospect of a ruler conversion stimulated and revealed boundaries that might otherwise be invisible.

It is typically not the adoption of a new cult per se that tends to be problematic but rather the attack on the old cults which might follow.[14] Exclusivist transcendentalisms like Christianity may therefore be considered 'universal irritants' for their capacity to stimulate reactive hardening of boundaries among host societies which had otherwise practiced de facto religious tolerance. That some vague and latent quality of identity construction may lurk within any kind of religious system is implied by the Durkheimian vision of its social function. Given that religion plays a fundamental part in establishing sensations of community, shared norms, acquiescence in social roles and so on, refusing to take part in or actively attacking communal religious activity may be identified as a species of social subversion or self-alienation. This was surely more likely to arouse the concern of political authorities in societies where the religious field was more strongly 'geared up' or consolidated to serve the purposes of the state. In these contexts, refusal to honour the local gods might even be tantamount to treason.

But here the focus is on the potential conversions of rulers themselves and how to conceptualise sources of resistance among the subjects of societies with immanentist traditions. If ruler conversion was felt as a threat to an 'identity', the latter may not have a name or any

---

[13] See Dumézil 2005: 175.

[14] Except, of course, when Christian proselytisation takes place in other monotheistic societies.

prior history of self-conscious realisation. Indeed it need not pertain to a distinctly 'religious' sphere at all, for it is essentially coterminous with society. It was typically simply 'our traditions' or, as it was so often expressed, the 'traditions of our ancestors', which become a rallying point. In the context of facing down a monotheistic attack, these could become a more consciously borne badge of distinction.[15]

War and Healing as Turning Points

Far from men fighting for the Gods, it was, as in Homer, the Gods who fought for men.

Jean-Jacques Rousseau, *The Social Contract*[16]

This chapter touches upon many forms of the revelation of supernatural superiority: longer-term developments that gradually disclose the potency of the Christian god; decisive events such as the failed healing of a family member or the loss of a crucial battle, which plant the seeds of doubt about the existing ritual order; classic Constantinian wagers in which the new god is deliberately put to the test; post-conversion victories against the inevitable pushback in the name of the abandoned cults; iconoclastic actions against the pre-existing religious symbols in order to undermine the credibility of the older panoply of spirits and deities; and the legendary stories that subsequently accreted in popular culture and pious chronicles, providing lasting reassurance that the new god has entirely outclassed all previous and rival metapersons in his ability to provide succour in the here and now.

At the level of each case, it is important to attempt to distinguish between these different phenomena – between, for example, the motivations of a ruler and their subsequent rhetoric of legitimation, or between events that actually happened and those that were fashioned out of the mythic imagination. On another level, however, such distinctions are less analytically significant than the observation that all conform to the same logic of empirical verification of immanent superiority.

---

[15] Pagan reactions in early medieval Eastern Europe: Bartlett 2007: 65–66; 1985: 90; nineteenth-century Africa: Hastings 1994: 332, 379.
[16] Rousseau [1762] 1968: 178.

This focus on phenomena that are often bundled under the category of the magical or the miraculous should serve to indicate how far the analysis has moved away from a legalistic and intellectualist approach to legitimisation; and how far it moves beyond the language of legitimacy altogether in order to acknowledge the direct appeal of supernatural power in and of itself. Once we begin to take seriously these phenomena in the historical record, a number of aspects of the typical dynamics of conversion move more clearly into focus. What follows should be read in the light of the theoretical exploration in Chapter 4, which showed how missionaries sought to enhance a sense of competition between ritual systems in terms of their capacity to effect results. This amounted to an attack on the possibilities of 'conceptual control' held by the old system and its capacity to rationalise misfortune so that it is not attributed to a failure of the system itself. But neither missionaries nor their opponents ever enjoyed complete conceptual control over events. Happenings in the real world could decisively enhance or undermine the persuasive power of religious arguments. It is therefore most important to register the role of sheer contingency in determining both ruler conversions and apostasies. The fact that they turned on twists of fortune to some extent is one way of ascertaining that empiricism – observations of the perceived results of ritual performance and religious affiliation – really mattered.

Interpretation was vital too, of course: over the long run, it would be the capacity to formulate a compelling narrative of supernatural intervention that mattered. Rulers may embrace a religion in order to advance a vehicle for their own political objectives, or even as the fruition of some private religious experience, but they need a story to tell their subjects that all will find compelling and one framed in terms that are already well understood.

Source Criticism and the Problem of the Miraculous

This opens up some important questions of source criticism, however. When presented with an apparent revelation of supernatural power in our sources, there are at least four different ways of explaining how it was generated: (1) because the principal actors did indeed perceive events unfolding as the sources insist; (2) because the principal actors and their ideologues presented it as part of a retrospective narrative they wished to disseminate in the aftermath of the alleged event – perhaps weeks, perhaps years; (3) because, over the longer term, the story was shaped by the mythicising propensities of oral transmission, which tends towards the generation of miraculous content; and (4) because later chronicles, hagiographies, and missionary texts deliberately inserted such elements in order to make the narrative conform to genre norms and pious objectives.[17]

The more ancient the events in question, and the more chronologically distant they are from our sources, the more reasonable it will seem to discount the first possibility and instead to seek answers by recourse to the third and fourth. The material on the Christianisation of early medieval Europe, for example, is notably vulnerable to this mode of interpretation – especially because of the dearth of any non-Christian evidence.[18] It is not unreasonable to consider, for example, that the story of Constantine's conversion at the battle of Milvian Bridge provided a literary template for how ruler conversions should happen, which churchmen and chroniclers subsequently used to shape their narratives.[19] And yet, it is no less important to note that such topoi were not just stereotypes for textual production; they were also templates for missionary action.[20] That is to say, they informed the arguments and strategies deployed by missionaries in approaching pagan lords, and therefore also shaped, potentially, the expectations of the lords themselves.

This is where the comparative method proves most helpful. When similar themes are found in early modern material, and indeed in much more abundant and contemporary letters and reports from the nineteenth century, then we are obliged to think again about their presence in the earlier evidence. Indeed, the comparative method could be extended much further than this – to take in Islamic ruler conversion stories, for example, as I have attempted elsewhere – in order to show that we are dealing here with something more general than specifically Christian traditions of representation.[21] In the companion volume, the significance of the themes of victory in battle and healing crises are

---

[17] On the role of the miraculous in textual strategies, see Mesley and Wilson 2014.
[18] Fletcher 1998: 12, 19, on topoi.
[19] However, Kendall in Kendall 2009 notes that the story may also be uncomfortable for churchmen such as Bede for the way it empties conversion of its 'spiritual' (aka transcendentalist) qualities.
[20] Yorke 2006: 236.   [21] See Alan Strathern 2017a.

explored in detail for each of the cases: Kongo, Hawaii, Ayutthaya, and Japan. Here, they are sketched out in cases drawn from two areas: late antique and early medieval Europe and nineteenth-century Oceania.[22]

By considering such an array of different cases from across the world and across time, it becomes possible to argue that the recurrence of these themes reflects a real phenomenon of the frontier of Christianisation rather than merely an illusion of Christian textuality.[23] It is the ubiquity of immanentism as a structuring principle of religious encounter that gives rise to the sensation of déjà vu.

Nearly all the forms of supernatural invention in these cases conform to one type: they are manifest in events which are essentially realistic in themselves. It is entirely plausible that a battle was won by the party that offered a Christian prayer or that a medical recovery followed the application of holy water. It is the typically impossible form of intervention that some missionaries had in mind when they lamented the fact the age of miracles (the apostolic church) had long since passed. Evidently, it was their lot to toil in the mission field without the gift of raising the dead or walking on water.[24] But even where missionaries bemoaned the absence of miracles in the strict sense, they were by and large all too ready to see the wondrous hand of the divine at work in the more inherently 'realistic' events.

The distinction between the two types is not always clear cut: a narrative of a battle won by a Christian prince may also contain references to heavenly hosts appearing in the sky. Can we isolate those details or entire events which have to be retrospectively imagined due to their essential impossibility?[25] One reason for caution in applying this approach is that rumours and even purported eyewitness accounts of extraordinary elements may well spring up instantaneously or very quickly afterwards and go on to become the collectively accepted

---

[22] I had to exclude African material for lack of space. Healing miracles and rulers: in South India, Susan Bayly, 1989: 399–400, and in the Amazon: Viveiros de Castro 2011: 20.

[23] See Fowden 1993: 182, for a similar methodological stance; Fernandez-Armesto 2009: 16–17, for scepticism with regard to source material for conversion.

[24] For example, La Loubère 1987 [1691]: 418. Early modern categorisations of prodigies and miracles was, however, much more complex than this: Daston 1991.

[25] That is, deduce that they must fall into interpretative options 2, and especially 3 and 4.

version of what happened.[26] Contemporaneous testimonies to miraculous happenings are reported to this day.

The Religious Meaning of Survival, in War and Healing

If you go to war with anyone you will defeat him, because your relations to the deity are perfect.

A Hawaiian priest, after the successful consecration of a *luakini* temple.[27]

Victory in personal combat was taken as a sign of ancestral support, so that challenging a feared *ramo* was like drawing on a famous gunman who had God on his side.

On the *ramo,* the warrior leaders of Malaita, the Solomon Islands.[28]

Before battle was joined, he noticed that their priests were assembled apart in a safer place to pray for their soldiers, and he enquired who they were and what they had come there to do. As soon as King Ethelfrid was informed of their purpose, he said: 'If they are crying to their God against us, they are fighting against us even if they do not bear arms.' He therefore directed the first attack against them...

Bede, on the pagan king Æthelfrith, confronted with the prayers of
British monks[29]

What characterises the most critical events that spurred ruler conversions is their *existential import* – in the basic rather than philosophical sense. Under this heading could be placed concerns about fertility and control of the elements.[30] But the most acute sensations of jeopardy attended the prospects of battle and healing crises.[31] The ritual systems deployed to achieve positive outcomes in these circumstances certainly

---

[26] Smith 2014: 13; on Sai Baba, Srinivas 2008: 18, 57; Alan Strathern 2017a: 31, for conjuring tricks; www.bbc.com/news/world-africa-38063882, on deliberate hoaxes.

[27] Malo 1951: 172.   [28] Keesing and Corris 1980: 18

[29] Bede 1988: 103 (II, 3).

[30] Fertility played its part in the conversions of the warlords of Ōmura and Ōtomo in late sixteenth-century Japan: see *CK*. On the association between missionaries and weather magic, see Thornton 2001: 87, on a Mbundu ruler, and the Capuchin report on Allada (Arda), 17 July 1662, MMA XII: 381; Law 1991: 64; and Alberts 2013a: 76, 83; Alberts, 2013b: 90–92; Halikowski-Smith: 164. Compare Fletcher 1998: 197, 243–234, for early medieval examples.

[31] Fernandez Armesto 2009: 24, on battle; Stark 2001: 111–112.

had reserves of conceptual control to draw on. Still, in relative terms, they were unusually vulnerable to the implications of observed outcomes: the end result was so critical, and specific, and expected to follow closely from ritual performance. When different ritual methods, and the metapersons they invoked, were placed in an explicit framework of competition, conclusions about their respective efficacies might be drawn rather readily.

In every pre-modern society, war was a profoundly enchanted arena of action.[32] The prospect of battle tended to produce a particularly results-focused, flexible, and omnivorous appetite for supernatural assistance.[33] It is important to grasp how concretely and directly ritual efforts were supposed to provide this. This was not a matter of vague prayers and morale boosting homilies but rather instruments for delivering specific forms of protection and potency. The timing of battles was often determined by calculations of propitiousness.[34] Warriors could become convinced of their actual invulnerability to bullets or spears – as with fighters in the Indonesian revolution rushing recklessly into battle protected by headband amulets.[35] Kings in early nineteenth-century Nepal were urged to donate lands to Brahmans to ensure victory against the East India Company.[36] Priests in fourteenth-century Japan could argue that they deserved more war booty than soldiers since it was their deity petitions which had really achieved victory.[37]

This theme is most explicit in the politics of the Inca civil war into which Francisco Pizarro and his men arrived in 1531 and 1532. One of the candidates for the throne, Huascar, had been making animal sacrifices to the god Viracocha to weaken the *huacas* of his rival. According to Susan E. Ramírez, the Spanish were taken as the reply of the sky god, dispatched to ensure victory to Huascar's faction.[38] A consecrated Inca only personally engaged in battle as a last resort

---

[32] Papua New Guinea: Biersack 1991: 257; Andrew Strathern 1970: 573; 1979: 9. Some African examples: MacGaffey 1986: 178; Ravenstein 1901: 28; Bay 1998: 65 (Dahomey); Byzantium: White 2013; Islamic world: Moin 2012: 101–102.

[33] Conlan 2003: 181.

[34] Ayutthaya: Cushman 2000: 278; Amazon: Viveiros de Castro 2011.

[35] And being mown down in shocking numbers: Fogg [MS]. Also see Comaroff and Comaroff 1992: 3, on Mozambique; Cohen 1997: 112, on the 'red lanterns' in the Boxer rebellion; Adas 1979: 147–156.

[36] Burghart 1987: 255.   [37] Conlan 2003: 166, 171, 79–81.

[38] Ramírez 2005: 1–4; Lamana 2005: 19.

given that it was a 'public test of his semi-divine condition, of his *camac* – energy or power'.[39] Not then until his final battle did Huascar himself engage, promising that he would 'turn into fire and water against his enemies'.[40] Huascar was, however, defeated by his rival Atahualpa, who was in turn defeated by the small force of Spanish at Cajamarca in November 1532. The result was that the major gods of the state were discredited; having risen in authority with the Inca Empire, they now sank with its defeat.[41]

In short, war raises the stakes of the economy of ritual efficacy.[42] The state of physiological–psychological arousal induced by battle may also be relevant to its potential for religious seminality, that is to say, its capacity to overturn received patterns of interaction with the super-natural sphere. These patterns are not a matter cognition alone, they are shaped by group experience and are held too in the body memory. Hypothetically, the intensity of the subjective experience of survival and victory in battle, the sharp peaks of emotion, and the sensations of *communitas* will make it unusually effective in reshaping the dispos-itions of those involved. In other words, it might act as the stimulus for what Harvey Whitehouse referred to the imagistic form of religiosity, which operates by the triggering of episodic (as opposed to semantic) memory. The paradigmatic event for this is the initiation ritual, but many experiences of violent conflict must create the same condi-tions of group jeopardy, terror, and sensory overload.[43] For Nietzsche, at least, the association between religion and violence 'has its origins in the instinct that realized that pain is the most powerful aid to mnemonics'.[44] The enduring memories of dramatic battle compel the application of meaning, forming a peg from which a religious narrative may be hung. Lastly, and speculatively, the strain and chaos of battle

---

[39] Lamana 2005: 29.

[40] Lamana 2005: 29, quoting Pedro Sarmiento de Gamboa's *Historia* of 1571.

[41] Stern 1982: 57–58. Compare the Spanish conquest of the Aztecs: Elliott 2009: 220.

[42] It has been argued that fledgling monotheism among the Jews only survived thanks to this logic: when the all-conquering Assyrian king Sennacherib failed to take Jerusalem in 701 BCE because his besieging army was suddenly struck down by disease, it was taken as a sign that the God of Israel really was omnipotent as the prophets insisted. For even Assur, the god of their mighty enemies, was rendered impotent. See McNeill 1999; Levine 2005: 414.

[43] Whitehouse 2000; Xygalatas 2012.

[44] Cited in Assmann 2008: 32; note Lane Fox 1986: 617.

might also enhance the possibility of abnormal patterns of perception and projections of fantasy.

If that is what war might mean to warriors, what does it mean for their kings? It is, of course, one of their definitive functions; it is often their jealous preserve and the cause of their greatest glories and most complete failures.[45] Its outcome is plain to see. The battlefield is the generator par excellence of charisma, and therefore the quintessential condition of heroic divinisation; it is where supernatural potency, the will of the gods, and the approval of heaven are loudly announced.[46] War is, in short, a crucible of kingship itself. Much might be risked in order to ensure that it is served by the most powerful ritual apparatus possible. And victory yielded a fund of charisma that might be expended on intervening in and transforming the religious field.

The healing crisis is no less existential a matter, of course, whether it pertains to the ruler themselves or their family members.[47] Any concerns of the longer term, about the implications for legitimacy, for example, or intellectual doubts, are liable to suddenly seem trivial when set against the unforgiving imperatives of the sickbed. The tendency in such situations (as for many people facing them today) will be to explore *all* ritual and medical options, to try any means of succour no matter its provenance.[48] Again, if healing does follow, the ritual performance will be associated with a vivid set of memories saturated with emotion.

Constantine

The conversion of the Roman emperor Constantine was a development of world-historical importance, triggering the archetypal rapprochement between the Christian faith and power, yet even a brief analysis opens up complicated questions of source criticism and scholarly debate. One story familiar to many later medieval and early modern

---

[45] See Hocart 1970: 1; McCormick 1986: 12, on Rome; Lamana 2005: 29, on Inca rulers and their *'atao*, or warlike luck.'

[46] See some germane comments in Hocart 1941: 15–18.

[47] For the conversion of a *babalawo* priest after the death of his son: Peel 1990: 52; compare Bolton 2012: 222.

[48] See Strathern and Strathern 1968: 181, on the Mbowamb on Papua New Guinea. Following the influence of Lutheran missions in the 1960s, while traditional rituals for the likes of crop growth were largely suppressed, 'at sickness crises traditional causal beliefs persist'.

missionaries is readily attributable to the accretion of legendary think-ing. It tells us that he was afflicted with a mysterious disease and fled to a cave; pagan priests advised him to sacrifice 3,000 children, but Saints Peter and Paul appeared to him in a dream and ushered him instead to the baptismal font of Bishop Sylvester.[49]

But by far the most influential story, still famous today, originated much closer in time to the event. It is that told in *Life of Constantine* by Eusebius (c. 260–340), in which the contender received a vision of a cross formed by light in the sky inscribed with the words 'in this sign, conquer', before joining battle with his rival Maxentius at Milvian Bridge in 312 CE.[50] The prophecy proved true and Constantine's victory opened up to him the gates of Rome and the rule of the entire Western Roman Empire from Scotland to North Africa. This story as it stands is a later confection of the bishop and the emperor in the mid-320s, which condenses into a single pivotal moment a longer and subtler evolution towards Christian commitment. In its entirety, then, it is best seen by means of interpretative choice (2) [51]: as a *post hoc* retelling formed roughly within the lifetime of the main protagonist and probably with his connivance. But how far does the story falsify the actual logic of the conversion process?

It is widely acknowledged that the battle of Milvian Bridge was indeed a decisive moment, after which Constantine 'favoured Chris-tianity with his imperial power, and became the first emperor to make common cause with the Christians', even if he was not actually bap-tised until his deathbed in 337.[52] He was also receiving revelations from the heavens at the time. Much scholarly dispute focuses on exactly when and how these happened. One reading of the evidence has it that Constantine experienced a profound vision of a radiant Apollo in 310 while he was in northern France and that this was the basis for the vision that Eusebius describes as taking place before the battle of Milvian bridge. Some scholars, indeed, now consider that the experience of 310 was genuine in an entirely straightforward sense:

---

[49] Brockey 2008: 150.
[50] Eusebius's *Life of Constantine* (1999: 79–81); a shorter version is in his *History of the Church* (1989: 292–293). My thanks to Jonathan Bardill for his comments.
[51] As described in the section 'Source Criticism and the Problem of the Miraculous'.
[52] Weiss 2003: 237; Averil Cameron 2008: 543. Constantine probably considered imperial office to be incompatible with a Christian life: Bardill 2012: 304–305.

for what he had witnessed was a solar halo, which can sometimes be perceived in a cross-like shape.[53]

At this point, however, Constantine's understanding of the being who had revealed itself to him in this way was neither fixed nor unambiguously public. His vision came within a period of searching experimentalism and political jeopardy, in which he sought an intimate relationship with a deity who might fulfil his hopes of world conquest. This in itself was not new, reverberating with the long-standing Roman theme of providential destiny expressed in military glory.[54] His predecessor Aurelian had created a new cult of the Syrian deity Elagabal, identified with Sol Invictus, after his men were fortified by a divine apparition at a battle in Emesa.[55] His father, Constantius, had also associated himself with the god.[56] There is an intriguing combination of the personal and the epic in this developing mode of imperial religiosity. But note that on one level it amounts quite simply to a desire to capture immanent power to achieve political ends, rather than, in the first instance, a strategy for establishing popular legitimacy.[57] The two previous attempts to march on Rome had led to death or shame for the leaders.[58] According to Eusebius:

Knowing well that he would need more powerful aid than an army can supply because of the mischievous magical devices practised by the tyrant, he sought a god to aid him ... and while he thought, a clear impression came to him, that of the many who had in the past aspired to government, those who had attached their personal hopes to many gods, and had cultivated them with drink-offerings, sacrifices and dedications, had first been deceived by favourable predictions and oracles which promised welcome things, but then met an unwelcome end, nor did any god stand at their side to protect them from divinely directed disaster.[59]

This no doubt served Eusebius's own rhetorical aims, harping on paganism's false claims to immanent power in the manner of later missionaries. But it may also reflect a genuinely empirical quality to Constantine's sense of mission: he needed to find a new god because

---

[53] Weiss 2003, and Barnes 2011: 75–76.   [54] Potter 2013: 152.
[55] Potter 2013: 21–22. Aurelian created 'a new priesthood into which senior members of the Senate could be (and were) recruited as a sign of imperial favour' – reminiscent of Akbar.
[56] Bardill 2012: 89–91.   [57] Potter 2013: 36.   [58] Drake 2000: 178.
[59] Eusebius 1999: 79–80; Drake 2000: 178. See also Lane Fox 1986: 614, whose overall discussion is compelling.

others had failed, or, perhaps, find a way of conceptualising and accessing the supreme deity he felt must exist. Apollo was one such way and was readily conflated with Sol Invictus, whose images appear on Constantine's coin around this time.[60] Another was the deity Mens Divina (Divine Mind), a world-governing force who appears in panegyrics to Constantine in these years – though that may simply reflect a cultivated ambiguity on Constantine's part so as not to challenge his pagan subjects too severely.[61] Intellectually (rather than politically), it was not too great a leap from such entities to the Christian god. Indeed, rather than picturing Constantine 'becoming Christian' in a simple sense in the years around 312, it may be better to conceive of the Christian deity both being assimilated to and yet also transforming these other attempts to conceptualise an ultimate divinity.[62]

Still, if we are looking for a turning point with which to dignify the term 'conversion', there is no doubt that it will be found in the period leading up to and climaxing with the battle. It is most likely that Constantine had begun to interpret his vision of 310 in terms of the Christian god well before the battle itself.[63] Three bishops accompanied him on his campaign, and they would have been at hand to encourage precisely that understanding.[64] At Milvian Bridge, according to Lactantius, Constantine had his men inscribe a new symbol onto their shields, combining the Greek letter *Chi* with the letter *rho*, which was probably a reference to Christ.[65] He was, the account goes, thus following instructions from 'the Highest god' received in a dream. Constantine was indeed, then, engaged in an act of ritual innovation, a direct invocation of his new god to bring his powers to bear. The resulting victory was proof of a reply.

Together with Licinius, who was now Augustus in the east, he issued a letter formally extending freedom of worship across the empire, 'in order that whatever divinity there is in the seat of heaven may be

[60] Potter 2013: 128.   [61] Potter 2013: 136.
[62] Bardill 2012; Drake 2000: 181–183.
[63] Though possibly conflated with the other sun deities of Apollo and Sol Invictus.
[64] Barnes 2011: 80, and Scheid 2016: 134.
[65] Weiss 2003, followed by Barnes 2011: 79, argues that this was a reference to the symbol Constantine had seen in 310. It could also mean *chrestos*, 'good luck' (Potter 2013: 142), but the fact that it was later used as a symbol of imperial Christianity is telling. See Bardill 2012: 192–193, on the *chi-rho* monogram on what may be his sarcophagus.

appeased and made propitious.'[66] This great shift in imperial policy was facilitated by the fact that, as David Potter remarks, 'Christianity is now associated with the very substance that holds the empire together: the ideology of imperial victory.'[67] By this time it was widely understood that Constantine attributed his empire-winning feats to divine intervention.[68] Constantine quickly demonstrated a newfound favour towards Christianity, granting privileges and subsidies for the church, restituting property that had been seized during persecution, building the church of St. John Lateran on imperial land, and in August of 314 convoking the first-ever council of bishops.[69]

Strangely enough, what we are left with then is the same of logic of empirical religiosity that is expressed by the story told by Eusebius. Both the actual process of conversion and its later retelling turn on the demonstration of the new god's military power. Indeed, in this case, that logic would appear to be the primary form of motivation.[70] Moreover, the newness of the new god was part of its appeal: it was not associated with the failures and turmoil of the past, and especially once it had again granted Constantine victory when he became sole emperor in 324, its protective capacity was enduringly confirmed.[71]

Constantine was not the first ruler to convert to Christianity, nor was he alone in converting when he did.[72] Around the time that Constantine became sole emperor of Rome, Ezana, the ruler of the kingdom of Aksum in Ethiopia, permanently changed the iconography of the coinage of his realm: a cross appeared, where before there had been a crescent. Thus was signalled a shift in divine patrons akin to that effected by Constantine. The kings of Aksum had previously been

---

[66] Bardill 2012: 133; Potter 2013: 149. [67] Potter 2013: 149.
[68] Drake 2000: 181; Brown 2003: 60. [69] Barnes 2011: 84; Potter 2013: 145.
[70] McCormick 1990: 101. No doubt there were other considerations; some political motives are mentioned in Chapter 6, and see Potter 2013: 145. He also needed to find some solution to the problem of what to do with Christian recalcitrance: there was a growing tendency among the Tetrarchy to appreciate that persecution was not working.
[71] The logic of supernatural warfare is also emphasised in Eusebius's account (1999: 95–97) of Constantine's battle with Licinius in 324.
[72] Haas 2008: 103: 'The Syriac kingdom of Osrhoëne probably was the first to embrace the new religion, perhaps as early as the reign of King Abgar VIII in the third century.' King Trdat of Armenia (298–330) converted before 314: Binns 2002: 30, referring to a healing miracle according to the much later account of Agathangelos.

divinised as the sons 'of the invincible god Mahrem.'[73] As for how they conceived of their new patron, let us evade the scanty textual evidence from Latin writers and consider an inscription from Ezana's reign. It is brutally repetitive on the successful violence that he was able to wield after conversion:

> May the might of the Lord of Heaven, who has made me king, who reigns for all eternity, invincible, cause that no enemy can resist me, that no enemy may follow me!
> By the might of the Lord of All I campaigned against the Noba when the Noba peoples revolted.[74]

It proceeds to boast of the people he had slaughtered, the villages burned, the great numbers of prisoners captured, all under the protection of the new Lord of Heaven. 'My people took their cereals, bronze, iron and copper and overthrew the idols in their dwellings,' casting them into the Blue Nile.

Early Medieval Europe

Was it any different in Europe? According to Bruno Dumézil:

> The Germanic ruler did not consider that he had the power of altering the sacred unless it meant an improvement, obtaining an extra magical efficacy of his person, from which his subjects would benefit in an immediate and tangible way.[75]

It was 'prosperity and military glory', which allowed rulers to innovate in the sphere of the supernatural.[76] Missionaries were happy to assure Germanic kings that conversion would mean 'victory, wide dominion, fame and riches', drawing on the careers of Constantine, or the Israelite king David to that end.[77] In its embrace of the unabashedly martial, thus was Christianity 'Germanised' or even 'barbarised' as some historians have put it – although in the light of the material gathered in this book, it is better to simply say 'immanentised'.[78]

---

[73] Haas 2008: 103; Iliffe 1995: 41; Munro-Hay 1991, chapter 6.1; Phillipson 2012: 95–99, estimating conversion between 337 and 350.
[74] Munro-Hay 1991, chapter 11.5.   [75] Dumézil 2005: 175 (my translation).
[76] Dumézil 2005: 176.
[77] Fletcher 1998: 122; Berend 2007b: 19; McCormick 1990: 342.
[78] Russell 1994; Sullivan 1994: 30, refers to 'barbarization'. Brown 2003: 18–19, argues that late antique Christianity was already filled with such features.

According to Gregory, Bishop of Tours (573–594), the Frankish king Clovis was introduced to Catholicism through his queen Clotilde, who had her first-born son baptised. When the son then died, Clovis judged it a failure on the part of her god. But when the next son fell ill, the queen prayed and this time the son survived. However, his turning point took the form of a Constantinian wager when he was close to defeat against the Alamans and in desperation called upon Christ, saying that if he was granted victory, he would believe.[79] Gregory's narrative, written so long after the events, is naturally open to doubt, and so the themes of healing and war that come through it so clearly may be interpreted in terms of options (3) and (4)[80]: the result of either popular or authorial mythmaking.[81] Yet, it has been argued that he was actually baptised in 508 CE following a mighty victory over Alaric II, for there are signs that en route to battle he went 'out of his way to appease the God of the Catholics'.[82] There is nothing implausible about the suggestion that the military implications of cultic choice were at the forefront of the mind of the great conquering king of the Franks.[83]

Gregory's narrative, like the accounts of Constantine, entered into the bloodstream of Christian literati – and their missionary tactics.[84] One of the earliest ruler conversions among the Anglo-Saxon kings also seems to involve military wager, although the source criticism problems are equivalent to that of Clovis. This time it is Bede who is our much later narrator. The story of the conversion of Edwin of Northumbria once again combines fertility magic, healing, and war. In 626 Edwin was wounded by an assassin wielding a poisoned-dipped dagger. The same night his queen had given birth to a daughter. Bishop Paulinus informed Edwin that this was due to his prayers to the Christian god, and Edwin is moved to promise that if that god would ensure that he survived his wound and overcame the enemy who had caused it, he would renounce his idols. As a pledge, his baby daughter

---

[79] Fletcher 1998: 104.
[80] As noted in the section 'Source Criticism and the Problem of the Miraculous'.
[81] Although the inclusion of a failed healing attempt here seems superfluous in rhetorical and mythical terms.
[82] Ian N. Wood 1985: 270.
[83] Dumézil 2005: 175, 219–220, gives credence to the idea.
[84] See Pope Gregory's letter to Æthelbert, King of Kent, on Constantine – far surpassing his predecessors in fame after conversion: Higham 1997: 99.

would receive baptism immediately. Edwin went to war, killed five chieftains of the West Saxons, and returned victorious.[85] He privately took to Christianity at this point (the public declaration would have to wait).[86]

In Nick Higham's analysis of these decades of British history, the back-and-forth of military fortune was interpreted in terms of the supernatural struggle between the gods, and therefore shadowed by the ebb and flow of the faith.[87] Edwin's death in battle in 633 damaged the credibility of the Christian deity, but then the tide turned again: the apostate king Eanfrith died, while the star of the British Christian King Cadwallon waxed strong. Thus when a young Oswald asserted his claim to a Northumbrian throne, he did so as a Christian appealing to this same evidently effective deity.[88] Just before the battle with Cadwallon in 634, Bede reports that Oswald set up a cross and knelt before it in prayer. He was victorious, and Cadwallon was killed: the deity had chosen him. The cross he set up at 'Heavenfield' became a site of pilgrimage.[89] Although this is not, strictly speaking, a story of ruler conversion, it is a story of how a nascent royal Christianity may win popular legitimacy. According to the somewhat earlier account of Adomnán of Iona, most of his men were pagan but promised to be baptised if they were victorious.[90] The tide turned again: the military victories of Penda, the pagan king of Mercia, who then killed and dismembered Oswald (probably offering him up for sacrifice) in 642, acted as a bulwark for the reputation of the indigenous deities.[91] But when Penda was in turn defeated and killed in 655, it 'sounded

[85] Bede 1988: 115–7 (II, 9). Fletcher 1998: 4–5, Dumézil 2005: 175, and Higham 1997: 167–168, are prepared to take this story seriously; the latter suggests that Edwin may have been wearing a magic shirt sent by the Pope during the assassination attempt.

[86] See the section 'The Immanentist Priesthood'.

[87] Although Higham consistently interprets ruler conversions in term of empirical religiosity, he also notes that Christian kings were not especially successful on the battlefield, which causes him to pull back, arguing that the victory-giving powers of the new faith must have been secondary to its organisational and ideological attractions (1997: 41). However, what this really reflects is the way that Christianity both profits from but is, over time, relatively insulated from empirical religiosity – see the section 'Transcendentalisation and the Containment of the Economy of Ritual Efficacy'.

[88] Higham 1997: 189, 201–208.   [89] Bede 1988: 142–143 (III, 2).

[90] Adomnán, *Life of Columba*, 1991: 15.

[91] Higham 1997: 220; Yorke 2006: 109.

the death-knell of English paganism as a political ideology and public religion.[92] His opponent, Oswiu, had propitiated the Christian deity before the battle, and afterwards had his daughter Aelfflaed take holy orders in keeping with his pledge.[93]

Khan Boris of the Bulgars was already prepared to tout his baptism for diplomatic advantage in the early 860s, but he finally accepted it after defeat at the hands of a Byzantine force in 864 and the experience of famine.[94] Thus he accepted the lordship of a wrathful deity that had visited hunger and defeat upon him.[95] But defeat need not be so complete in order to stimulate innovation, if we agree with Jonathan Shepard on the context for the conversion of Vladimir of Rus. It was 'only when Vladimir's run of victories came to an end with his failure to subjugate the Volga Bulgars in the mid-980s, and the pantheon of gods was seen publicly to be failing to deliver, that Vladimir began his quest for a better guarantor of victory, sometimes termed his "Investigation of the Faiths"', engaging the representatives of all the principal monotheisms.[96] He had previously sought to reorganise the local form of public cult founded upon military victory and fuelled by human sacrifice, much like the chiefly cults of many parts of Oceania, but now sought more radical answers.[97]

Nineteenth-Century Oceania

The progress of Christianity among the island societies of the Pacific in the early nineteenth century represents a greatly accelerated process

---

[92] Higham 1997: 241.   [93] Higham 1997: 250. Yorke 2006: 232.

[94] The chronology is ambiguous, here, however: see Shepard 1995: 239–241.

[95] Sullivan 1994: 72, sees in his long list of concerns about the niceties of Christian conduct (including much detail on points about ritual procedures before battle), a great anxiety not to provoke that anger any further.

[96] Shepard 2007: 381–382.

[97] Shepard 2009: 208–209, drawing here on the *Russian Primary Chronicle*, which took its present form more than 100 years afterwards, and which is therefore open to interpretation in terms of modes (3) and (4) (for example, DeWeese 1999: 169–170). But the chronicle's account of Vladimir exploring the religious marketplace receives some surprising support in the independent testimony of Marwazi, who refers to Vladimir's dispatch of four envoys to obtain instruction in Islam (Minorsky 1942: 36; Shepard 1992). Shepard 2009: 213–214, also notes that the chronicle's claims of destroying pagan sites have received some archaeological corroboration. The *Primary Chronicle* relates another story about Vladimir's conversion, connecting it to victory in battle at Cherson and a sudden attack of blindness cured by baptism – presumably to be filed under options (3) or (4).

among much more far-flung but largely small-scale communities: the faith traversed the vast, watery spaces of the ocean like a contagion. It began with the decision to ask for baptism by the chief contender for the paramount authority in Tahiti, Pomare II, in 1812. In 1825, Ka'ahumanu of Hawaii was baptised along with other ruling chiefs, although the real breakthrough had happened in 1819 when Liholiho had begun his reign by breaking the eating tabu and consigning the traditional form of sacred kingship to oblivion. Then in Tonga, the high chiefs Aleamotu'a and Taufa'ahau were baptised in 1830–1831. Taufa'ahau, did so en route to his acknowledged supremacy and subsequently took the title King George Tupou I. He was quickly followed in 1832 by Malietoa Vainu'upo, the pre-eminent chief in Samoa, and then in 1854 by Cakobau, the aggressive war chief of Bau in Fiji.

The speed of this process in the Pacific often surprised observers. Religion had been identified as an inveterate quality of the social and political order: missionaries were surely on a hiding to nothing. And then suddenly they were whispering in the chief's ear and dousing him with the baptismal waters. The Russian naval explorer, Otto von Kotzebue, was appalled at the results in Hawaii: 'That a people so lively should readily submit to such gloomy restrictions at the command of their rulers.'[98]

Our sources for these events are not only more abundant and far more contemporary than those for early medieval equivalents but also produced by Protestant missionary groups with rather different attitudes to ritual, magic, and 'superstition'.[99] And yet the central theme – of existential crisis and the salience of ritual efficacy – emerges even more readily. Defeat in war prompted experimentation with Christianity; enemies were stimulated to frame their opposition as antagonism to the new faith, and the victors were able to describe the result in terms of a triumphalist religious narrative.[100] The role of healing, meanwhile, was ever present. Not long after their arrival, the missionaries began to record the quite devastating impact of new diseases on the populations of Polynesia as they moved among people increasingly broken and ailing with sickness.[101] It meant that the

---

[98] Kotzebue 1821, II: 259.
[99] Although the movements of providence fulfilled the same function.
[100] Also see Alan Strathern 2017a.
[101] Thomas 2010: 72, 96; D'Arcy 2003: 551; Sissons 2014: 47, 50, 62.

credibility or benignancy of the old ritual system was arguably damaged independently of missionary concerns to shine the spotlight on its failure.[102]

It was in Tahiti where Christianity first moved from being a hopeless project on the fringes of society to a vehicle for elite ambition – and which therefore set off, in a sense, equivalent moves by high chiefs across Polynesia over the next forty years. Pomare had been fighting and manoeuvring himself into a position of supremacy for years before he finally turned to baptism. The turning point came in around 1811 when his advance had been firmly checked and he was languishing in the island of Mo'orea off the northwest coast of Tahiti. Missionaries were all but absent by this time. Pomare had been subject to periodic bouts of ill-health in the previous decade, for which missionaries and local ritualists competed to provide supernatural explanations.[103] But in 1811, his half-sister was suddenly taken ill. Every means within the traditional system were deployed to assist her recovery but she died. Her parents were inconsolable, and 'the chiefs were alike vexed and angry with the gods'. Pomare summoned them to his house and declared that the old gods were false and foolish, and he was going to worship Jehovah.[104] He continued to fall ill.[105] By November he was floating the idea of his baptism to the one remaining missionary, Henry Nott.[106]

He began to challenge the sacred tabus and dispense with the traditional ceremonies at certain occasions, culminating in a meeting of chiefs in March 1815 at which the food was blessed in the name of the Christian god.[107] By this time, then, the movement to bring Pomare back to assert his claims in Tahiti was assuming an unmistakable association with the cause of the Church. A violent pushback mounted in the name of 'Oro.[108] Pomare's Constantine moment came with his victory over recalcitrant chiefs at the battle of Fei Pei in circa November 1815.[109] The source criticism issues around this important event in the national history of Tahiti must be addressed elsewhere,[110] but there

---

[102] Thomas 2010: 102–103, 115; Barker 2005: 89; Davies 1961: 156.
[103] Davies 1961: 58, 86, 103, 111.   [104] Thomson (n.d.): 30–31.
[105] Oliver 1974: 1326.   [106] Davies 1961: 153, ft. 2; Thomson (n.d.): 32–33.
[107] Davies 1961: 186.   [108] Davies 1961: 185.
[109] Tyerman and Bennet 1831, I: 158–162; Davies 1961: 191–192; Oliver 1974: 1343–1349. The date is contested.
[110] Hopefully, in *CK*.

is little doubt that it was readily understood as an act of disconfirmation.[111] This is what gave Pomare the authority to publicly enforce the rejection of the old religion, though it seems most temples were burned down as voluntary acts of allegiance to him.[112] The following year, the high chief of Raiatea, Tamatoa, fell extremely ill and destroyed the cult centre to 'Oro in order to avert the wrath of Jehovah – in effect, sacrificing the old god to appease the new.[113] The Protestant missionaries, however, demonstrating from the first that their severe baptismal standards would not be relaxed for royal candidates, did not deign to baptise Pomare until May 1819.[114]

In Tonga, missionaries initially struggled as their prayers were associated with a period of violence, and their attempts at high-profile healing backfired.[115] As in Tahiti, it was a reversal of fortunes for an ambitious faction that provided the most important entry point.[116] One of the leading rulers Taufa'ahau, had begun to express an intriguingly experimentalist attitude to testing the contrasting powers of the new cult and the old. One time, for example, he threw a spear at a shark from a canoe and then cast overboard a Tongan convert teacher, Pita Vi, to fetch it to see if Jehovah would come to his aid – which, apparently, he did.[117] But the crucial turning point came in July 1830, when Taufa'ahau fell victim to a poison plot. Pita Vi called on two missionaries to come, who applied an emetic and said prayers throughout the night. The following morning a cry of joy broke out as the king recovered.[118] On 7 August 1831, he was baptised with the name King George, after George III of England.

Shortly after the conversion of Taufa'ahau, the most powerful chief in Samoa, Malietoa Vainu'upo, embraced Christianity, also against a backdrop of healing episodes and wars taking on the hue of religious allegiance.[119] John Williams reports a speech made by Malietoa to his family in 1832, which bears quoting for the exquisitely empirical mentality evoked:

---

[111] See, for example, the report by John Davies, March 1816, in Newbury 1980: 41.
[112] Sissons 2014: 51; Gunson 1969: 81.   [113] Sissons 2014: 53.
[114] Newbury 1980: 52.   [115] Thomas 2010: 42; Latukefu 1974: 45.
[116] Latukefu 1974: 59–60.
[117] For more disconfirmatory actions of Pita Vi: Harold Wood 1975: 47.
[118] Harold Wood 1975, I: 49, citing Pita Vi's narrative in West 1865: 367–368.
[119] Robson 2009: 21, 29.

'Do you not know', he said, 'that the gods will be enraged with me for abandoning them, and endeavour to destroy me? And perhaps Jehovah may not have the power to protect me against the effects of their anger! My proposition, therefore, is, that I should try the experiment of becoming his worshipper, and then, if he can protect me, you may with safety follow my example; but if not, I only shall fall a victim to their vengeance — you will be safe.'[120]

In Fiji, Cakobau, the king of Bau, tolerated missionaries for diplomatic reasons but remained sceptical and unyielding for more than twenty years. Again, he was given pause to rethink the matter during a series of military setbacks. Some of his own men rebelled and went over to his opponents now gathering at Kaba.[121] In early March 1854, the temple to his war-god Cagawalu was destroyed by fire.[122] Later that month, Cagawalu was invoked and predicted victory in an attempted assault on the stronghold of Kaba.[123] The missionary Joseph Waterhouse, according to his own report at least, instead predicted defeat, and when the attack was repulsed it made a deep impression on the chief.[124] A close friend of Cakobau, the chief Varani, explained to him that he had converted after two of his children had died, each time following the construction of a temple: 'I then began to think that the gods of Fiji were lying gods.'[125] Cakobau himself was suffering an anal fistula, and the chief went to seek medical aid from the missionaries on the Good Friday just before the announcement of his conversion in the last few days of April 1854.[126]

A major element in Cakobau's thinking remained essentially diplomatic: he needed to win the support of the Christian king of Tonga, George Tupou, in particular, as well as Christian factions.[127] But it is important to recognise that Tupou's conversion had had consequences

---

[120] Williams 1837: 435; see Weir 1998.
[121] Thornley and Vulaono, 2002: 68–70.   [122] Derrick 1950: 110.
[123] Waterhouse 1866: 236 (the priests claim that the gods announce, 'You have not served me faithfully but tomorrow your unbelief ceases. Ye shall destroy Kaba!'), 239–240.
[124] At least, according to Waterhouse 1866: 255–256.
[125] Waterhouse 1866: 107.
[126] He publicly announced his commitment to Christianity on 30 April and received instruction from this time but was not finally baptised till January 1857. Sahlins 2004: 164; Thornley and Vulaono 2002: 69–70, 171.
[127] Waterhouse 1866: 243–234; Thornley and Vulaono 2002: 69–70; Sahlins 1985: 39–40, 2004: 164.

for the regional economy of ritual efficacy as well as the field of religious diplomacy. The paramount chief Qaraniqio of the island of Rewa had reportedly acknowledged to the missionary William Cross in 1838 that the gods of Fiji had somehow also suffered from the failure of the gods of Tonga, for these were 'not gods; those who trusted them have been destroyed, and those who attended to the religion of the foreigners are prosperous'.[128] When the fleet from Tonga arrived and Cakobau launched a new attack on Kaba in April 1855, both sides represented it as a power clash between the gods.[129] In the 'one great pitched encounter in the whole history of Fijian warfare', the forces of Cakobau and George Tupou broke through the defences of Kaba and were victorious.[130] Afterwards, one chief observed that 'the *lotu* [the Christian cult] is true or Kaba would not have been taken'.[131] The Christianisation of Cakobau, and Fiji, was secure.

In this case, then, we see how smaller moments of empirical evaluation – an unpleasant medical condition, the death of two children of a friend, a fire consuming a temple – the kind of details that may well fall out of the historical record for earlier ruler conversions, cumulatively assisted the conviction that it was worth taking the risk of adopting the new deity. The great battle was most significant for its effect on the public arena, confirming to rivals and subordinates that the deity had proved its worth.

Overcoming Resistance: Immanentism Recreated and Destroyed

Around these decisive moments, however, immanentism shaped the possibility of conversion in more subtle ways. Rarely can the historian undertake the task of tracking the nature of cultural change following elite conversion with the analytical depth of an anthropologist – while the global historian must forgo that ambition entirely.[132] We obtain

---

[128] Sahlins 1985: 38, quoting from William Cross's unpublished diary: 2 October 1838. There is always a question mark hovering over this sort of reported conversation by a missionary.
[129] Derrick 1950: 114–116; Sahlins 2004: 19; Thornley and Vulaono 2002: 79–80.
[130] Routledge 1985: 86.   [131] Thornley and Vulaono 2002: 80.
[132] As in, for example, Robbins 2004. Still, to adopt Robbins's schema (6–13) of cultural change, the underlying progression described here is from an experimental phase of 'assimilation' to the more wholesale 'adoption' of

at best a shallow skim of turbid movements. Taking a very broad perspective on so many different cases of ruler conversion does at least allow us to discern some distinct patterns: that the priesthoods of immanentist societies rather often failed to obstruct the passage of Christianity with the obduracy expected of them; that converted rulers regularly deployed the technique of iconoclasm in order to enhance their legitimacy in immanentist terms; that ruler conversions were normally vulnerable to reversal for a generation or two under the conditions of empiricism; and finally, that, in the longer term, transcendentalist traditions subordinated the relevance of ritual efficacy.

The Immanentist Priesthood: A Wall or a Gateway?

If converting rulers typically face crises of legitimacy, it would be natural to expect the strongest articulation of grievance to emanate from the existing bodies of ritual specialists. They had more invested in the religious status quo than anyone else; their very *raison d'être* was at stake. Such was certainly the assumption of the missionaries, who expected to face local priesthoods as implacable enemies, like the magi of old, the very servants of the devil.[133] By no means were they always mistaken. Often, of course, priests did resist, and perhaps the more strongly organised and institutionalised they were, the more this mattered.[134] And yet their opposition was less consistent than one might expect.[135] Terence Ranger, for example, refers to 'a stream of instances in which African prophets advised a sympathetic hearing for the missionaries'.[136]

As we shall see, in some cases, high priests even acted as facilitators of ruler conversions, as bridges over the rupture of legitimacy.[137] It is easier to understand this once we put to one side a transcendentalist vision of religion as a matter of identity formation, truth commitment, and salvation. Instead, the ritual specialists of immanentist societies

---

Christianity, in which the nature and structure of the value system itself changes.

[133] Reff 2005: 27; Hastings 1994: 314.

[134] Early medieval Europe: Dumézil 2005: 177; Bartlett 1985: 190. Early modern Paraguay: Wilde 2018: 85–86; Nineteenth-century Africa: Robinson 2004: 165–166. Oceania: Latukefu 1974: 119; Sissons 2014: 63, 87.

[135] Higham 1997: 168; Viveiros de Castro 2011: 36–37.

[136] Ranger 1975: 8. See also Janzen 1982: 86.

[137] In early sixteenth-century Sierra Leone: Gonçalves 1996: 138.

were – just like anyone else – susceptible to arguments based on relative efficacy.[138] The arrival of a brashly self-confident new cult certainly presented a deeply awkward challenge, but that challenge could be met in various ways apart from sheer resistance. One response was already explored in Chapter 4: to incorporate aspects of Christianity within an indigenous or syncretic framework so as to create a new locally owned cult which promised access to the same source of power. Another answer was to throw in their lot with the conversion drive itself. To some extent, the willingness of immanentist ritual specialists to countenance the latter option was a function of their relative lack of institutional autonomy and strength. But they were also enabled by the flexibility and continuity of streams of revelation, the constant possibility that new kinds of metaperson might have important information to divulge.

In some cases, the old metapersons themselves were called upon to bear to witness to the authority of the new: a perfect image of how immanentism may consume itself. Peel noted that among the Yoruba a surprising number of the *babalawo*, priests of the high-status Ifa cult, converted to Christianity following prophetic information about the new faith coming from Ifa itself.[139] This was a particularly satisfying means of containing a legitimacy crisis. Queen Njinga of Ndongo, for example, could not take the decisive step towards baptism without staging a public meeting in which she called upon the five most powerful *xingulas* to offer their verdict. The *xingulas* were ritual specialists possessed by the spirits of illustrious ancestors – four dead imbangala captains and her own dead brother Ngola Mbande. The question was acute: accepting the 'God of the Sky and of the land' worshipped by the Christians would mean setting aside the very reliquaries of ancestral bones used by the *xingulas*; it would mean ceasing all sacrifices to them. A lively debate followed, but all five spirits ended by endorsing Njinga's plans. After this, Njinga was thus authorised to take Capuchin missionaries as her advisors on matters supernatural, and mass baptisms followed, overseen by the queen.[140]

But revelation was not confined to priestly groups. Political elites themselves could have dreams or visions, which were open to

---

[138] The Jesuit Cristovão Ribeiro in Central Africa reported a conversation with 'the son of a sorcerer and sorceress', who remarked that 'only the white men had good sorcery': Ribeiro, 1 August 1548: MMA XV: 163.
[139] Peel 1990.   [140] Heywood 2017: 197–199.

interpretation in ways that testified to the new opportunities brought by the missionaries.[141] This was the case for the two noblemen who helped facilitate the baptism of the king of Kongo in 1491 by dreaming of visitations by a power-giving handsome woman – confidently identified as the Virgin Mary by the Portuguese.[142] The young king of Mutapa spent the night with an image of Mary, and was also dazzled by dreams of her before signalling his willingness to convert.[143]

Among the Urapmin of Papua New Guinea in the 1970s, there was no established class of ritual specialist; instead it was the community leaders, the 'big men', who had most invested in the cult of ancestral bones and who looked after them and sacrificed to them. But they were also quick to effect their abandonment. Some reported that they had already spoken with the Holy Spirit who had ordered them to throw out the bones.[144] In the Amazon, after the Franciscan Padre Coppi in the 1880s installed himself in a Tariana village and exposed the sacred masks of the god Jurupary to the women and children, different shamans had competing visions as to the most appropriate response to such dreadful iconoclasm. One reported the anger of the god Jurupary but another announced that the people should submit to the priests and renounce their traditional feasts.[145]

The converting queen of Hawaii, Ka'ahumanu, told the American missionary Hiram Bingham that in the generation before the arrival of Christianity, the prophet Kalaikuahulu had proclaimed that 'a communication would be made to them from Heaven (the residence of 'Ke Akua maoli', the real God) entirely different from anything they had known, and that the tabus of the country would be subverted'.[146] It matters little when in reality this prophecy had been conjured up; more that it could be imagined as having been uttered at all. When the abolition of the tabus was enacted in 1819 following the succession of Liholiho, it was presented as a fulfilment of this prophecy. Moreover, Liholiho had apparently been influenced by the promptings of the high priest of the war god Ku, Hewahewa. This conductor of human

---

[141] Thornton 1992: 242, on the King of Allada.
[142] Rui de Pina in MMA I: 124; *CK*.
[143] In the account by António Caiado, in *Documentos* 1962–69, VIII: 42–43.
[144] Robbins 2004: 27, 147.
[145] Hugh-Jones 1996: 56. Compare Walker 2003: 573–574.
[146] Bingham 1849: 28. There were in fact many prophecies of rupture and millennial change around this time.

sacrifice, the pinnacle of chiefly religion, was indeed the first to apply the torch to the wooden gods.[147]

Indeed, the material on the conversion of the high chiefs and kings of Oceania is most explicit on the way that important priests acted in partnership with rulers (or even as initiators) in the elite conversion dynamic.[148] Hewahewa's story is prefigured in that of the first ruler conversion of Polynesia, Pomare of Tahiti, and the role played by Pati'i, the *ariori* priest of Papeto'ai on Mo'orea. On 14 February 1815, the month before Pomare made a dramatic public announcement to the other chiefs of his Christianity at a feast, Pati'i attended an evening meeting held by the missionaries and pronounced that he had examined the old religion thoroughly and could find no good in it. Afterwards he took the effigy of his god and cast it into the flames.[149] He was, indeed, one of several important priests who had converted around this time.[150] The case of Pati'i also indicates what such men might hope to gain: he became a chief judge in Pomare's new order.[151]

On the same day as the baptism of Aleamotu'a in Tonga, 'a man who had been a magician or a kind of god and of so high rank that the king used to pray to him was baptized: so in the same day we have baptized both the king and his god'.[152] For Fiji, an unpublished account by Joseph Waterhouse gives an illuminating report of how the elite of Rewa managed their accommodation to Cakobau's *lotu* after the sudden death of their paramount chief and the defeat at Kaba in 1855:

The two principal ministers of state bowed in worship to the true God and their partisans endeavoured to help forward a change in the national religion. One of the chief priests publicly announced a dream which he had had. In his vision he saw the Rewa deities sitting together low down, and he saw, also, the true God, very great and high—so high that he saw only the lower parts: His head was hidden in the clouds. "This," said he, "is the only true God." Thus did this heathen priest endeavour to lead his people to the truth, and the population apparently attached more importance to his words than to the more rational instructions of the Christian missionary. Another priest

---

[147] Thurston 1882: 26; Bingham 1849: 71.
[148] Emphasised in Sissons 2014: 43–49, 65.   [149] Davies 1961: 184.
[150] Davies 1961: 173, 198, 201–202; Tyerman and Bennet 1831, II: 32; Driessen 1982: 6.
[151] Sissons 2014: 136.
[152] Harold Wood 1975: 43, citing the missionary involved, Nathaniel Turner.

declared that the gods had held a conference respecting the wonderful and startling spread of Christianity. "It grows and grows, and rises and rises," said some: "what must we do?" The majority of the gods decided that they could not hinder it; and that they must await a more favourable season for their interference. The destruction of Kaba, the safety and invincibility of which had been pledged by the gods and their priests, decided the question in the minds of thousands.[153]

After pondering such diverse material on priest–chief alliances in the orchestration of public acts of conversion, we may turn to Bede's famous story of the pagan priest Coifi and the conversion of Edwin of Northumbria with fresh eyes. Just like Njinga, Edwin was not able to make the move to an official conversion before holding a council in 627 to deliberate the merits of the new cult. At the meeting, Bede tells us, his chief priest Coifi took the initiative in announcing that the old rites had failed to be as effective as would be expected, as measured by his personal fortune as well as that of the people as a whole. He advised burning down the temples, and broke his status as a priest by mounting a stallion and taking up arms; riding to the temple of Godmunddingaham he desecrated it by casting his spear into it, thus triggering its destruction.[154] This story is often quoted because it offers a vivid splash of imagery about such matters in an otherwise information-less desert, but just as often it is referred to as a mirage, a Christian simulacrum of pagan behaviour for rhetorical effect.[155] That, of course, it may yet be. But in the light of the foregoing discussion, it is not at all implausible; indeed it represents an important element of the way that legitimacy crises were defused or overcome in immanentist societies.

---

[153] Tomlinson 2009: 70–71 (and compare 81–82) citing an unpublished manuscript ('History of Fiji'). Also see Thornley and Vulaono 2002: 231–232. On the qualities of Waterhouse as a source, see Brantlinger 2002: 35–44. His account cannot be assumed to be unproblematic, but he was in many ways well placed to receive the two Fijian reports mentioned here and note the thrust of this anecdote rather tells against missionary conceits.

[154] Bede 1988: 126–128 (II, 12).

[155] See, for example, Wickham 2016: 21; Kendall et al. 2009. Yorke 2016: 247–248, refers to further examples of 'textualist' readings but also offers the other side of the picture, as does Higham 1997: 168–169. Walls 1995: 10, affirms general logic.

Iconoclasm as a Strategy of Rulers and Auto-iconoclasm as a Movement of People

It may seem as if to acknowledge that rulers and their subjects under-took iconoclastic attacks is to concede that they swiftly took on the implications of an exclusive Christian identity and the abhorrence of heathen abominations. In which case, it may seem more realistic to suspect that such acts were invented or exaggerated by Christian writers and missionaries intent on reproducing the image of the good neophyte prince. There is, however a third option, which is to consider the way that iconoclasm may be driven by a potential lurking within immanentism itself and explicable in terms of its own logic. This was referred to in Chapter 4 as 'auto-iconoclasm': internally validated violence against ritual structures. That validation essentially derived from empirical outcomes, which might suddenly render cult objects, and the forces they invoked, useless or malignant.[156]

Yet 'outcomes' may be the product of paranoiac and manipulated perceptions too. A world saturated by immanent powers is one in which people may come to feel surrounded by destructive forces. Movements of social cleansing might arise that set out to abolish the objects and practices of sorcery, the incessant arms race between ritual means of defence and ritual means of attack.[157] It is possible, though difficult to be sure, that these developed quite apart from any transcen-dentalist influence. They are particularly noticeable in Central African history.[158] MacGaffey tells us, 'In 1900, in the coastal region near Moanda, the people responded to a drought by joining a movement to destroy magical charms. Europeans assumed at the time that this rejection of magic was a product of their own civilizing influence, but it soon appeared that the leader of the movement had established a strong new loyalty to the cult of the spirit Bunzi.'[159] It was often

---

[156] See Peel 2003: 113, on the eradication of smallpox healing cults following an outbreak in 1884, involving a Christian-sympathising Yoruba chief – but 'hardly any' of the participants were Christian.

[157] Thornton 2001: 81. Adas 1979: 104–105, on German East Africa.

[158] Ranger 1993: 79. See, for example, Douglas 2003: 245–250, on the 1950s Belgian Congo.

[159] A territorial spirit, associated with rainmaking: MacGaffey 1977: 190. See also Ranger 1975: 7.

popular movements of indigenised Christianity that fully grasped the means to tap the appeal of fetish destruction.[160]

The kinds of iconoclasm ordered by converting kings were likely to be more encompassing and often permanent – although that may also be a function of our evidence. But the point is that the missionary attempt to compel communities to see their metapersons as harmful was not entirely outlandish. It rested rather upon the same immanentist capacity to swiftly reclassify the moral categories of those beings wielding immanent power. This process of moral reclassification was precisely what the missionary discourse of local metapersons as 'devils' attempted to do. Indeed, the radical quality of monotheism may be appealing insofar as it promised a kind of universal disarmament of all techniques of private ritual one-upmanship, and an enduring freedom from the whims and exactions of innumerable spirits. All this may help explain some cases of popular acquiescence or participation in iconoclastic movements, although it does not exhaust the rationale behind it. There is something mysterious about the way in which communities may turn on the very symbols and entities that have been placed at the heart of their communal life, seizing what had been exalted so high in order to bring it so low, as if suddenly experiencing their Durkheimian power as an intolerable burden – a process witnessed also in Europe in the popular iconoclasms of the Reformation.[161] At any rate, the idea that iconoclasm was something undertaken only under either elite duress and the missionary harangue on the one hand or the compulsion of newly minted piety on the other must be set aside.[162]

For converting rulers, it was just as important to showcase the relative powerlessness of the old cults: they adopted, in effect, the stratagems of the missionary.[163] And just like missionaries, that also meant taking on the lion's share of the jeopardy. This was perhaps what Vladimir of Rus was doing when he ordered the thunder god Perun to be dragged to the Dneiper and beaten with sticks.[164] It was certainly what the Samoan chief Malietoa Vainu'upo, quoted in

---

[160] For example, William Wade Harris's evangelisations in the Ivory Coast: Hastings 1994: 444.

[161] See Sheehan 2006 (and other contributions there) for early modern reflections on idolatry.

[162] For example, Nicholas Thomas 2012a: 134–140; 2012b: 282–283.

[163] See Chapter 4.

[164] Cross and Sherbowitz-Wetzor 1953: 116 (thanks to Jonathan Shepard).

Chapter 4, was intent upon by offering himself as an experimental conversion and waiting for supernatural displeasure. His sons were eager for the experiment to be over so that they too could try their hand at disconfirmation. As in Tahiti and Hawaii, this was achieved by a rite of consumption. They feasted upon a certain species of bird, which was held to be their *etu*, the vehicle of a particular god, and yet survived unharmed.[165] In Tahiti, Pomare ate a turtle earmarked as a sacrificial offering.[166] Soon after he announced his conversion he gathered up his 'family idols' and dispatched them to the missionaries, saying they could do what they wanted with them.[167] In Hawaii, Liholiho risked the wrath of the gods by breaking the food taboo, and sitting down to eat with Ka'hamunu and other high-ranking women. In the years leading up to her baptism in 1825, Ka'ahumanu took tours of the islands burning hundreds of 'wooden gods'.[168] In Tonga, Taufa'ahau's (King George) series of experiments to show the inactivity of the existing gods gave him the confidence to embark on comprehensive spree of idol destruction in his own lands and in Vava'u.[169] In Fiji, shortly after his baptism, Cakobau set about destroying the old sacred sites and humiliating the priests.[170] Those priests still prophesying divine displeasure were summoned to sit in a circle around him, were challenged, and then whipped.[171] These were all acts of creative transgression, clearing a space for a new structure of legitimacy to be built. But they only worked because they exploited the promise of real-world efficacy that immanentist ritual had at its heart.

Pushback: Post-Conversion Instability

Particularly where the existing ritual system had not been cognitively undermined, rulers could anticipate that their conversion would

---

[165] Williams 1837: 437.
[166] Ellis 1832: 75, who only suggests some time before July 1812. For equivalent moves in New Zealand: Sissons 2015.
[167] Davies 1961: 198.   [168] Bingham 1849: 162.
[169] Latukefu 1974: 63–65.
[170] Waterhouse 1866: 261; Thornley and Vulaono 2002: 71.
[171] Waterhouse 1866: 265: 'This public action gave evidence that Thakombau no longer feared the gods of Bau.'

provoke a legitimacy crisis on immanentist grounds.[172] Opponents of the baptism of the Wydah king Agbangla in the 1680s argued that it would place his subjects 'in danger of perishing, by abandoning their worship of the Gods to whom he owed the good fortune of his Kingdom'.[173] Indeed, just along the coast in the kingdom of Allada (or Arda) a Spanish Capuchin mission has been met by similar arguments in 1660–1661:

> We spoke to him of the charms he was making, and he replied that it was not possible to abandon them because it was a custom of the land, just as he cannot quit the idols, because the captains would not come round to it nor want to give permission. He said that it was a thing his ancestors and his father had observed, and that it was due all attention and respect; that each one of those things had its office and its minister; that if he abandoned them he would die instantly, that his enemies would enter through the doors and he would have no forces with which to resist them.[174]

Ruler conversions not only take place under the conditions of immanentism, they tend to remain subject to those conditions for a certain period afterwards – which is to say, such conversions were reversible. The economy of ritual efficacy remained, to some extent, intact and lingeringly salient. None of the tactics deployed by missionaries, or neophyte priests and princes produced inarguable conclusions. Iconoclasm left a troubling psychological legacy: who could say when and where the anger of the old gods might make itself felt?[175] The old cults still retained, in other words, certain reserves of conceptual control, which could be exploited by factions antagonistic to the ruling party. Since political legitimacy still depended to some extent upon demonstrations of supernatural efficacy, obvious misfortune might lead to apostasies. Whenever the very survival of the community was placed at risk, another throw of the dice in ritual affairs remained a tempting option.

Typically, the first determined act of resistance happened shortly after the ruler had publicly announced his commitment to the new faith – and it was therefore usually in the resulting battle that the faith

---

[172] See Sissons 2015: 139–140, for despairing receptions of the conversion of a ruler as akin to his death in parts of Polynesia.
[173] Law 1991: 60; Hastings 1994: 309–311.
[174] Report on Allada (Arda), 17 July 1662, MMA XII, 385.
[175] See, for example, Firth 1970: 309–311; Mayr-Harting 1994: 13, or among the Maori: Sissons 2015: 130.

proved its military credentials rather than in a classic Constantinian wager. The resistance often fought explicitly in the name of the old religion but also in the preservation of oligarchic principles that many converting kings sought to overcome.[176] All these elements are present, for example, in the conversion of Khan Boris of the Bulgars. His ordered baptism of the elites (boyars) stimulated them to rise up against him in 865.[177] One chronicle relates that Boris and a small number of local Christians defeated the insurrection assisted by divine signs and support.[178] In this instance, the revelation of the deity's power in war was not conclusive in the longer term given the continuing military insecurity of the Bulgars.[179] After Boris retired to the monastery in 889, his son Vladimir cooperated with the boyars to briefly restore paganism.[180]

This sort of reversal was common among early medieval European royal conversions, as historians have widely understood.[181] Some peoples switched several times between paganism, Arianism, and Catholicism. It was perhaps akin to a politician promising contrast with the previous incumbent: if you have been dissatisfied with achievements under the previous leader, I can promise a better metaperson to solicit as our patron. It was promoted by the experience of military ambitions stalled or reversed, or sudden threats to communal health. After the initial breakthrough of Christianity among the East Saxons, a severe outbreak of the plague in the 660s ushered in a return to paganism and the restoration of derelict temples.[182] A thousand years later, in the Philippines, an incursion of disease in 1599 led people to return to their previous rites, saying that the god of the Castilians had been beaten by their old deities, who had come now to punish those who had abandoned them.[183]

This febrile quality to the first generations of ruler conversion is not particular to Christianity; it may be found in the early career of transcendentalism in any new terrain, necessarily taking root in

---

[176] See Chapter 6.   [177] Sullivan 1994.   [178] Sullivan 1994: 73.
[179] Emphasised by Mayr-Harting 1994: 18.
[180] Sullivan 1994: 74. Boris was forced to have him blinded.
[181] Dumézil 2005: 193–195, referring to the contractualism of Germanic conversion; Bartlett 2007: 45, 66; Higham 1997: 36–37; Tyler 2007: 157; Wickham 2016: 23.
[182] Bede 1988: 201 (III, 30); Higham 1997: 38; Yorke 2016: 246. For one of several healing miracles, see Bede 1988: 101 (II, 2).
[183] Chirino 2000: 283–284. My thanks to Natalie Cobo for this reference.

immanentist soil. In Japan, the Heavenly Sovereign Kinmei cautiously allowed the Soga clan to import the cult of the Buddha in the 550s, but when the city was struck by plague they were ordered to stop and their statue was dumped in the canal. Thereafter, however, the Soga clan, still loyal to the Buddha, flourished, and their new divine patron was accepted by the imperial family.[184] The Kano chronicle's account of the introduction of Islam to the Hausa presents a long period in which continuing empiricism kept attitudes to the new cult seesawing. Although the new god brought victory to Yaji, King of Kano (r. 1349–1385), when his son Kanajeji (r. 1390–1410) failed to win a war he turned back to the traditional priest, whose traditional remedies helped him secure victory.[185]

And yet, in Japan, Buddhism was never dislodged after this point; in the Sahel, Islam gained ground and remained secure, just as in Europe the march of Christianity was inexorable, as it was in the Philippines, and in the Pacific.

Transcendentalisation and the Containment of the Economy of Ritual Efficacy

Providence seems to take delight in testing the confidence we should place in it, given the vicissitudes of pleasant and unpleasant events.

Marcel Le Blanc, *History of Siam in 1688*[186]

The persistence of the economy of ritual efficacy is not so surprising. It chimes with a long-standing appreciation among scholars of how enduring the pre-existing religious sensibility may be in populations long after they have accepted a Christian identity in some sense. This is nicely expressed in the exasperated comment of the Jesuit António Vieira (1608–1697) bemoaning the inconstancy of the Tupinambá: 'Other peoples are unbelieving until they believe; the Brazilians, even after they have come to believe, are unbelieving.'[187] The monotheistic

---

[184] DuBois 2011: 57–58. Moreover, 'In 741, to put a stop to a series of poor harvests and rampant disease, the Emperor Shomu (701–56) required each province to build at least one major Buddhist temple'. Compare also the reversion to Shamanic rituals among Mahayana Buddhists in Mongolia after a three-year drought in the Gobi: Wallace 2015: 50.

[185] Palmer 1928: 104–108; Levtzion 2000: 82–83.   [186] Le Blanc 2003: 189.

[187] Viveiros de Castro 2011: 4.

notion of belief itself, as missionaries understood it, was often a long time coming in many societies worldwide.[188]

What is more intriguing is why the febrile, experimental stage explored in the previous pages should come to a halt. And why, so often, should it end with transcendentalism triumphant? Once again, the historian's instincts may be to recoil from any suggestion of the latter, as if it would involve a naïve capitulation to the grand narratives of our Christian sources. But, from a long-term perspective, is this not what so often the outcome looks like – frankly, bizarrely teleological?[189] The only explanation is that something fundamental about the conceptualisation of the religious field in its entirety is transformed. What happens, eventually, is not the election of a new party; it is a rewriting of the constitution.

Sometimes the imperviousness to reversal took some generations; sometimes it was rather swift. There were no great reversions by chiefs in nineteenth-century Oceania equivalent to those of first millennium Europe, partly because these island societies were subject to such rapid and all-embracing forms of sociopolitical change in subsequent generations, and partly also, perhaps, because the church infrastructure was unrolled quite quickly among them. Indeed one way of understanding the peculiar intransigence of transcendentalist traditions is through the strength and focus of the institutional systems they bring with them. Another very simple reason why monotheism proved ineradicable in the long run is its determination to eradicate rivals. Where this did not happen, and a degree of ritual pluralism or syncretism was maintained, then reversions were obviously much more likely. But when rulers unrolled programmes that redesigned the sacred landscape and persecuted the priesthoods of rival cults, the consequences were obvious. Especially in societies where religious knowledge was essentially preserved orally, the old cults would be badly damaged by the loss of high-status individuals tasked with their preservation and comprehension. This meant that the persistence and recrudescence of immanentist urges would have to take the form of new rites and objects, either

---

[188] Not always: Robbins 2004 challenges the universality of this principle. But for examples, see Barker 1993; Landau 1999: 11.

[189] Berend 2007b: 2, refers to Northern, Central, and Eastern European ruler conversions which 'turned out to be the point of no return, after which, despite pagan revolts in some of the areas, religious change progressed in one direction only, towards Christianization'.

loosely contained by an expanding Christianity or existing in a shadowy world of private ritual practice ('magic' and 'superstition').[190]

The peculiarly comprehensive form of iconoclasms spurred by the missionaries also contained within it a psychological mechanism that hindered return. When the anthropologist Joel Robbins undertook field work among the Urapmin in the 1990s he expected them to retain the option of return on some level, even after many sacra had been destroyed in sacred bonfires. 'But the answer to my questions was clear and firm: after how we treated those ancestors, there is no way they would have us back.'[191] The old metapersons have been spurned; bridges have been burned.

Yet, more importantly, as Robbins himself has argued, there is danger in failing to grasp that the arrival of a religion such as Christianity has the capacity to profoundly alter not just the form of the ritual life but the values and metaphysical understandings which give it meaning. In terms of the analytical language used here, that change also amounted to a great enhancement of the possibilities of conceptual control. The central rituals of Christianity were not ones with perlucionary import; they were not directed at immediate practical ends.[192] What the whole system was now geared towards – on an official level, at least – were rewards placed in the afterlife, firmly out of reach of empirical jeopardy.[193] This, then, is the vital difference: it amounted to a distinct containment of the significance of the economy of ritual efficacy. If the purpose of religious action was salvation, it could never be shown to be misguided in this life.

Providence was still expected to be at work in this world. But, set within this encompassing narrative frame, its actions were now conceded to be surpassingly mysterious. The writings of the Jesuits from late sixteenth-century Japan are full of appeals to this mystery. If an awful shipwreck occurred, the leader of the mission might comment: 'But since the reasons of God cannot be understood, and His secrets

---

[190] The economy of ritual efficacy is thus contained by Christianity, being reserved for different saints or shrines or amulets, or is displaced outside it.

[191] Robbins 2004: 150.   [192] Barrett 2007: 202.

[193] See Peel 2003: 229: 'The world religions also had an intrinsic doctrinal advantage, in that they could offer rewards in the next life, which were not susceptible to empirical disconfirmation in this one.' Compare Viveiros de Castro 2011: 34.

are so profound there is nobody who can reach them.'[194] Indeed, the Jesuit mission in Japan had to endure the most galling turns in fortune. It is extraordinary to see how readily they were able to rationalise this, but the same cognitive slippage will be found daily in any Christian life: successes are attributed readily to God and one's prayers; failures are never attributed to his impotence or malevolence. They are taken as tests, or divine judgement, as temporary narrative twists, or as small beer when set alongside the deep draught of the everlasting. Even the fall of Christian empires may be explained in this way, as when the Jesuit Fernão de Queirós claimed that the Portuguese losses to the Dutch in seventeenth-century Asia were punishment for their failure to make their dominion truly godly.[195] Thus empirical failure could stimulate arguments for the intensification of transcendentalist commitment.[196]

All this is connected to the construction of the religious field as a primary site of *identity* construction, which is particularly a feature of the monotheisms. But no less profoundly, it is the product of precisely its transcendentalisation: now *ultimate truths* are at stake (rather than practical effects); the principal metaperson has been rendered exceedingly *ineffable* (he moves in mysterious ways); religious action has been thoroughly *ethicised* (so that misfortune may be taken as a comment less on the metaperson's efficacy than on one's own sinfulness); and it has been restructured by the new norm of *salvation* (whatever injustice is endured in this life will be more than made up for in the next). Indeed, suffering may be welcomed as a mark of the truly devout or even as the tumult of a millenarian narrative. The first Anglo-Saxon king to convert, Æthelbert of Kent, was promised this-worldly glory, but Pope Gregory also had an argument to deploy in the face of what looked like disasters:

As the ending of the world approaches, many things threaten which have not occurred before ... wars, famines, pestilences ... do not be at all troubled in mind; because these portents of the ending of the world are sent in advance that we should be heedful of our souls.[197]

---

[194] Zampol D'Ortia 2017: 256.   [195] Queyroz 1992: 1003–1004.
[196] As in Byzantium challenged by the rise of Islam: Michael Humphreys 2015: 269.
[197] Higham 1997: 100.

Perhaps the most resonant symbol of this shift of mentality is the ideal of martyrdom. Turning the defeat of death into the victory of salvific heroism represents conceptual control of the highest order. It was noted earlier that King Oswald's victory at Heavenfield was taken as a confirmation of the Christian god's potency. But notice what happened when Oswald was in turn killed, and possibly also ritually sacrificed, by his pagan rival Penda of Mercia.[198] He became the focus of a popular cult of the martyred king; he became, in the end, a saint.[199] The hagiographic treatment of Christians who died in battle and suffered for their faith became a means of ensuring glory and status even in the face of defeat.[200] Among the Picts to the north, meanwhile, as elsewhere, the Old Testament David appears as a model king in their art. David was not only a great warrior leader, he was also a ruler who failed – but as a consequence of his own sin rather than divine impotence.[201] Thus was empirical failure grounded in ethical–salvific interiority rather than metaphysical inferiority, becoming something that might tighten rather than unravel the bonds of conviction. This is only to touch on some of the ways in which the transcendentalisation of religious life occurred. How and when that was achieved was of course subject to huge variation across many different dimensions of life, and may be conceptualised in many different ways. Perhaps it was only when ascetic norms seeped out of the monasteries and began to influence lay life that it was truly underway in Europe.[202] But that a dimension of some such transformation had already begun in the generations after royal conversions must be a principal reason why once Christianity had sunk in its claws it was almost impossible to shake off.

---

[198] On sacrifice, see Chaney 1970: 40.

[199] Meanwhile, the sons of Vladimir of Rus, Boris and Gleb, eliminated by their brother in a succession battle, were both venerated as saints for their 'Christlike non-resistance' after death and yet also propitiated as potent agents of military success, 'likened to weapons and fortresses': White 2013: 135, 142.

[200] Bede 1988: 156 (III, 9); Dumézil 2005: 176; compare Reid 1993: 153, on 'the doctrine of martyrdom to sanctify failures – something animists could never do'.

[201] Yorke 2006: 231, 237.   [202] Markus 1990.

6 | Dreams of State: Conversion as the Making of Kings and Subjects

The conversion of rulers did not automatically entail the Christianisation of their subjects. But very often, and often at considerable risk, rulers did begin the task of inducing their subjects to abandon the ingrained behaviours, taboos, and matrices of meaning that had governed their lives hitherto. This was, indeed, the third mode in the model of ruler conversion, and often the final stage.[1] What was the nature of its political appeal?[2]

Viewed from a Durkheimian or functionalist perspective – in which society is a contraption held together by the constant whirring of religious machinery – this move is initially puzzling. Why pull this machinery apart? This puzzle is partly a trick of the light created by the Durkheimian perspective itself, which occludes the extent to which religion is a vehicle of world manipulation as well as society-making. But it also prompts an intriguing thesis: that Christianising rulers were able to appreciate that new and better engines of society-making may be assembled. The existing apparatus may be found to be dysfunctional or somehow anachronistic for new ambitions and circumstances. What if, for example, 'society' was in fact a collection of distinct communities recently brought under a single ruler? There is always new work to be done – and sometimes new tools will begin to seem appealing.

It would follow that the greatest opportunities for ruler conversion will occur when the order of society and polity is already warping under the strain of change. For example, consider what is involved in moving from a roughly egalitarian society in which 'big men' do not pass on their office, to one in which an elite is accorded special political and ritual privileges due to their genealogy; or in the emergence of an

---

[1] See p. 257 for model.
[2] For note that longer-term political transformations cannot be equated with what a converting king actually had in mind, as Berend 2007b: 15–16, points out. See also D'Avray 2010: 95, on not confusing functionalism and motivation.

office of kingship whose incumbent must set aside certain claims of kinship in order to rule impartially; or when an empire suddenly rises above various defeated kingdoms. Such transitions have a convulsive quality, arising out of and generating conflict – less like the maturation of a mammal, for instance, and more like the liquidation of a caterpillar within a chrysalis in order to create a butterfly – and could therefore be expected to precipitate significant transformations in the religious field.[3] So for Webb surveying the conversion of the high chiefs of the Pacific in the early nineteenth century, it is telling that the great religious changes in the principal island chains happened 'in the generation *following* the first significant attempts at state formation'.[4] In all the main cases, the primary converts were ambitious chiefs attempting to overcome not only the rivalry of other individual chiefs but a general property of the existing system to pull back on the authority of would-be centralisers: in Tahiti, Pomare was overcoming a conscious restoration of oligarchic principle; in Tonga, Aleamotu'a and Taufa'ahau sought to resurrect and solidify the monarchy; while in Fiji, Cakobau struggled less successfully with the same sorts of problems.[5] (Most of the empirical material in this chapter comes from the Pacific.)[6] Equally, periods of state meltdown and re-formation, in which new kinds of rulers were given to experiment with new forms of political authority – as in *sengoku* Japan – would also be expected to provide relatively fertile grounds for conversion.[7]

It does not follow that such attempts would proceed smoothly or successfully. Indeed, one of the more predictable consequences of ruler conversion, as Chapter 5 indicated, was a violent 'pushback' of some sort. If that was in part a product of the continuing grip of a profoundly empiricist religious sensibility, arguably it was also because the Christian project was understood as a centralising move in some manner, which powerful vassals would instinctively resent. In other words, conversion was potentially transgressive in a political as well as a religious sense: it produced crises of legitimacy in the hope of

---

[3] Grinin 2011: 251; Webb 1965: 31.   [4] Webb 1965: 35; Newbury 1967.
[5] And see *CK* for Hawaii; Routledge 1985: 87; Oliver 1974: 1326. More generally, see Pierre Clastres 1989 on the structural inhibitiors of the emergence of the state from chiefship.
[6] And some from early medieval Europe, with African material largely cut due to pressures of space.
[7] Massarella 2000: 235.

ultimately placing legitimisation on a new footing. These propositions, and others put forward in this chapter, are offered in an experimental spirit. The first two stages of the model of ruler conversion rest on fairly robust generalisations; the themes explored in this chapter tend to splay out into diverse implications.

The Consolidation of the Religious Field

Tupou has behaved as though he wished to be a Pope.

> John Thomas complaining of King George of Tonga
> (Taufaʻahau), 1833[8]

The slow expansion of Christianity among the barbarian peoples of early medieval Europe after the fall of Rome is a story of both ruler conversion and the crystallisation of monarchy.[9] Following a systematic comparison of many ruler conversions from early medieval Northern and Central Europe, Nora Berend concluded that in all cases 'rulers who succeeded in promoting Christianity also further consolidated their power' whether that meant extending centralisation or establishing it for the first time.[10] Or, as Richard Fletcher put it, 'The benefits to kings did not happen all at once, but they were visible for those who had eyes to see.'[11]

But what kinds of benefits were they? Chapter 2 considered a hypothesis: the dispersal of supernatural power in an immanentist ecology could also lead to a certain dispersal of the social energies of religion. These were liable to be captured by communities clustering around the village ancestors, the spirits of the place, or a particular lineage of shrine priests, for example. The task for would-be kings was to overlay these local forms with a state cult, which often associated the ruler with a high god or overarching pantheon. But religious fields are not 'consolidated' in this way inevitably, instantaneously, or completely. A transcendentalist tradition such as Christianity may appear as an 'off-the-peg' mechanism of consolidation, by which the older concentrations of supernatural (and therefore social) power were undermined, reframed, or appropriated.

---

[8] Harold Wood 1975: 51   [9] Berend 2007b: 12; Blair 2005: 49.
[10] Berend 2007b: 14–15; Haas 2008. Bartlett 2007: 66–67.
[11] Fletcher 1998: 237; Haour 2007: 118–122.

There is, however, something distinctly paradoxical about the deployment of a transcendentalist tradition for the purposes of religious consolidation. By installing the Christian church in their lands were not kings taking control over the religious sphere only to hand it over to a clerisy who were yet more insistent on their autonomous guardianship of it?[12] Sometimes this may indeed have put off potential converts, as when its missionaries were seen as the agents of powers located in faraway Rome, Madrid, or Lisbon.[13] Converting rulers may have been surprised too by how much power they had in fact ceded to the Church. But at the point of conversion, we must envisage a ruler or contender attempting to establish a unique association with a new religious order, and deliberately delegitimising alternative sources of ritual power available to subordinates and rivals who are not prepared to submit. The latter may convert too, but they are now converting to a dispensation associated with the ruler as 'first mover'.[14]

Moreover, there were ways in which the potential autonomy of the Church was muffled or obscured in the first generations of ruler conversion. Firstly, the ruler could anticipate gaining powers of patronage over a relatively unified system.[15] In early medieval England, kings could appoint bishops to dioceses which were often coterminous with the boundaries of kingdoms, and unroll a novel hierarchical network of churches and monasteries over their lands.[16] Chiefs in the Pacific also used the church bodies and missions to exercise their own forms of patronage and political oversight.[17]

Secondly, in some cases converting rulers developed, partly out of necessity but also out of choice, a strong reliance on indigenous teachers and catechists who were subject to royal patronage rather

---

[12] Dumézil 2005: 175–177.   [13] *CK.*
[14] Hence disgruntled rivals could feel compelled to identify with the threatened traditional cultic practices.
[15] According to Drake 2000, Constantine sought allies among the bishops in order to effect certain reforms without working through the obstreperous imperial administration (though he underestimated the disunities and potential dissension of churchmen in the process).
[16] Tyler 2007: 147: 'The monopolization of the power of religion by a centralized, hierarchic institution dependent on and allied with the king increased his influence over society'; Higham 1997: 10: the 'fundamental sylloge between royal and episcopal interests'; Yorke 2006: 238–239.
[17] Derrick 1950: 129; Barker 2005: 90–91.

than the formal hierarchy of the Church.[18] This is a strong feature of early sixteenth-century Kongo under its convert king Afonso, but is even more evident in the rapid extension of schools and churches across early nineteenth-century Hawaii, which also drafted in native teachers, and was dominated by chiefs and their entourages in the first instance.[19] As Sahlins put it, they formed 'the privileged mode of disseminating the new Ka'ahumanu regime'.[20]

Third, whatever their official status in the eyes of the Church, converting rulers usually sought to establish themselves as the head of the new religion in some form – by dictating its affairs and by becoming the focus of attention. This was presumably how in one sense Constantine saw himself. The Nicene Creed was issued in 325 as a kind of imperial edict, for 'in Constantine's world power flowed from the top and it would be in heaven as it was on earth'.[21] Converted Anglo-Saxon kings assumed the role of leaders of the Church.[22] King Afonso of Kongo took a spiritual centrality in his mission to his people,[23] and chiefs in the Pacific no less.[24] John Thomas in Tonga, quoted at the beginning of the chapter, wrote again in 1834, describing the various ways in which Aleamotu'a sought to influence Church appointments and the like: 'Tongan chiefs wish to be gods to their people and not only to govern their bodies but their consciences. I have made a firm stand and would sooner be ordered out of the chapel than allow him to govern in the house of God.'[25] In Hawaii, Ka'ahumanu, even before her actual baptism, toured the islands, dedicating churches, displaying the new learning, and proclaiming the gospel as 'a mother to all of her people', according to 'Ī'ī.[26] It is as if converting rulers are able to recapitulate the prophetic role in becoming the fount of a new dispensation.

---

[18] This could amount to some vision of a 'national church': on Khan Boris: Sullivan 1994: 96; Shepard 1995: 241–245.

[19] Sahlins 1992: 91–93. These soon covered a third of the population: Bingham 1849: 215, 256–258, 272, 298. In Kongo, the king's brother was installed as a bishop (*CK*). In many early medieval European cases, royal kinsmen were deployed in the church (my thanks to Jonathan Shepard).

[20] Sahlins 1981; Mykkänen 2003: 53–56.   [21] Potter 2013: 235.

[22] Yorke 2006: 127.   [23] *CK*.

[24] Davies 1961: xlviii; Webb 1965: 32; Linnekin 2008: 195.

[25] Harold Wood 1975: 51. Taufa'ahau's desire to establish a truly independent Wesleyan church was finally accomplished in the form of the Free Church of Tonga in 1875: Swain and Trompf 1995: 183.

[26] 'Ī'ī 1959: 157–158. Bingham 1849: 293–295, for the first tour in July and August 1826. Also Sahlins 1992: 71, 172; Fish-Kashay 2008: 29–30.

Loyalty, Governability, and Pacification

If anyone of you speak against my new God Jehova, I will extract that man's rectum while he is yet alive, and then extirpate his race.

Pomare, Tahiti.[27]

[I am] glad indeed that the Norman race, which once delighted in running riot in human blood, has been converted to the faith by the inspiration of divine mercy, and now, by your exhortations and with the Lord's help, rejoices that it will have been redeemed by and drink of the divine blood of Christ.

Pope John X to Archbishop Hervé of Reims[28]

Christianity provided a new language of power that rulers might command their vassals and rivals to speak, with baptism functioning as a ritual expression of political submission.[29] Some scholars of early medieval Europe have been willing to attribute the appeal of Christianity as a discourse of hierarchy to its inherent qualities: the imagery of the transcendent deity, the single dynasty of father and son, the uniformity of cult.[30] In sixteenth-century Japan, Jesuits were quick to depict the relationship between God and man as a model of perfect vassalage, and this seems to have proved attractive to some warlords in the conditions of civil war when principles of hierarchical obedience and honest oath keeping were at a premium.[31]

Christianity also provided a discourse of unity and social reformation. Constantine did not try to convert his subjects, but he did provide a language of obedience to the 'Highest God' to which all might subscribe, and his overriding concern for pan-imperial unity and harmony is clear in his own communications on religion.[32] In his *Oration*

---

[27] Gunson 1962: 81.
[28] Migne (1996) cxxxi, cols 27–29. Thanks to Lesley Abrams for providing the text, and Lucy Hennings and Natalie Cobo for translation from Latin.
[29] Berend 2007b: 9–10, 23–25; Bartlett 2007: 65–68; Fletcher 1998: 195–223; Tymowski 2011.
[30] As suggested in Chapter 2. On early medieval Europe: Higham 1997: 41; Tyler 2007: 146, and thanks to Lesley Abrams for discussion.
[31] CK.
[32] Bardill 2012: 272, 292. Whitmarsh 2016: 236, points to the 'alliance between absolute power and religious absolutism' entailed by the Christianisation of the empire, although this was a project which stretched over a much longer term than the reign of Constantine himself.

to the Assembly of the Saints his role is implicitly aligned with that of the deity who is the 'one overseer for all existent things and that everything is subject to his sole rulership, both things in heaven and on earth'.[33] (Of course, in Rome, as in other cases, the most pressing crisis of religious unity was created by the small minority of Christians themselves. Christian intransigence is always liable to frustrate non-Christian rulers intent on consolidation, and once a section of the population has converted, the options available to a ruler begin to narrow.)[34] The Byzantine patriarch Photius advised Khan Boris, who had to unite Bulgars and Slavs, on the relevance of Durkheimian sociology: for his people, while 'propitiating the Divinity in common, and offering praise in common ... may be drawn together more and more into common unanimity'.[35] The princes of early medieval Europe needed to create kingdoms out of diverse populations, and Bruno Dumézil speculates that conversion was a means of returning to the state of ethnogenesis, in which all other social distinctions would be lost within a new focus for identity formation.[36]

In regions which had not yet developed literacy or written laws, the arrival of Christianity carried a particularly revolutionary potential for state construction. Admittedly, the association between Christianity and a broader package of statehood including education, law codes, modes of civility, calendars, and ecclesiastical advisors may be seen as rather contingent – because these could have been bequeathed by any number of traditions of high culture.[37] Yet qualities inherent to transcendentalism per se also underpinned the association. The autonomous organisational capacity and orientation to the text of the transcendentalist clerisy made them exceptionally strong guardians of learning even where political structures faltered. The lawmaking mentality of monotheism has an affinity with the transcendentalist esteem for the authority of the text, explicitly codified injunctions, and the internalisation of ethical principles. For the Christian tradition in particular, the Old Testament presented the king as a lawmaker, and

---

[33] Bardilll 2012: 305.
[34] This applies particularly to the Japan case in *CK*. See also Mayr-Harting 1994: 15.
[35] Photius 1982: 59.   [36] Dumézil 2005: 180, 461.
[37] Berend 2007b: 14–15; Arnason and Wittrock 2004: 6. There are analogies with the role of Brahmans (Kulke 1993: 257) and Buddhist monks (Piggott 1997: 98, 123, 152–153).

converting rulers in medieval Europe were not slow to see the advantages. 'The coming of Christianity gave the first impulse to the process by which the custom of the folk became the king's law,' according to Fletcher.[38] The first Frankish ruler to convert, Clovis, became a law-making king, while the first Anglo-Saxon king to convert, Æthelbert of Kent, also set down laws in writing for the first time. This was bound up with a new emphasis on the king's role in overseeing the moral development of his people.[39]

More than 1,200 years later, the American missionary Hiram Bingham in Hawaii put it to the neophyte chiefs that God's laws should become the foundation of the actual laws of the land.[40] In the mission circular it was asserted:

We have also endeavoured, from the same authority, to inculcate on the people, their duties as subjects. We have taught them that they must needs be subject "not only for wrath, but also for conscience's sake, rendering to all their due." To all we have insisted on the obedience to the precepts of the Bible, which teach justice, honesty, integrity, punctuality, truth, purity, good order, union and peace.[41]

In Tahiti, too, missionaries had been central to composing the new law codes that sought to replace the old system of tabu as the basis for social order. The missionary Henry Nott became the main author of the 1824 constitution of Tahiti and was chosen as the first president of its parliament of male chiefs.[42] This was of a piece with the common missionary conceit that conversion ought to be part of a much more total reformation of life.[43] Yet, this urge sat uneasily with a Protestant insistence on the proper distance between church and state and the explicit injunctions against political meddling in the missionary charters.[44] It was therefore the desire on the part of indigenous rulers

---

[38] Fletcher 1998: 118; Dumézil 2005: 180.

[39] On Khan Boris, Sullivan 1994: 104, concludes that conversion amounted to 'a vast expansion of the power of the khan', endowing him with the responsibility and opportunity to intervene in his subjects' lives in novel ways in order to effect their Christianisation; compare Shepard 1995: 247.

[40] Bingham 1849: 278–282, 295; see Mykkänen 2003: 91–94; Fish-Kashay 2008: 30–32.

[41] Bingham 1849: 300.   [42] Linnekin 2008: 210.

[43] Gunson 1978: 269, on a sermon of 1819: 'Religion is strictly and essentially a civilizing process.'

[44] Linnekin 2008: 194; Gunson 1978: 281.

to make conversion the centrepiece of a more wholesale transformation that was critical.[45]

Looking back with some bitterness, the missionary J. M. Orsmond commented of Pomare that 'the King changed his Gods, but he had no other reason but that of consolidating his Government'.[46] There is no need to assume that this accelerated push for nation-state making in Tahiti smoothly placed ever more power in the hands of the monarch.[47] Christianity was not a kind of magic powder of instant statehood, and it appeared most to strengthen the hand of the centre where it was already strong.[48] But in terms of converting rulers' intentions and stratagems, the evidence from the Pacific is compelling.[49]

There are intriguing clues from the Pacific material, too, that Christianity was credited with an unprecedented capacity to achieve the monopolisation and stabilisation of violence. For Hawaiian chiefs, no longer would insurrection be assisted by the respect accorded to the *mana*-filled rebel, and in their victories over pagan rulers they were induced to abide by a new moral value accorded to restraint in warfare.[50] The same effect may be found in Tonga and Tahiti and other parts of the Pacific, where missionaries also carried with them a discourse of peace.[51] To ambitious centralisers, who had fought for decades and suffered deep reverses before their success, there was surely something appealing about the opportunity offered by the new religion to escape some of the structures of social life that had always

---

[45] Linnekin 2008: 205–206, on Vanuatu; Barker 2005: 99.

[46] Newbury 1967: 498.

[47] Gunson 1969: 66–68; 1978: 282; Newbury 1980: 49–52; 1967: 500; Davies 1961: 203.

[48] Barker 2005: 91.

[49] Afonso of Kongo is Ka'ahumanu-like in his zeal for learning, literacy, and societal reformation but was unusual among early modern African rulers in this regard and even he did not adopt European law codes. Why other African rulers were apparently more indifferent to Christian literacy in this period deserves further thought.

[50] Ellis, 26 October 1824, South Seas, box 4 CWM/LMS; Ellis 1827: 162; Bingham 1849: 238, 243, 249, 303; Ralston 1984: 38–39. Compare Christianisation of warfare among Anglo-Saxons: Yorke 2006: 232–234.

[51] Latukefu 1974: 97, 110; Davies 1961: 192; Gunson 1978: 215, 296. In Fiji, there are signs that this message hindered chiefs from 'going lotu' when they were intent on violence: Tomlinson 2009: 73; Swain and Trompf 1995: 198, 210.

generated conflict.[52] Christianity never made a pacifist of any ruler, and rather lent its own form of respectability to attacks on political enemies within and without.[53] Still, in Fiji, Cakobau addressed the chiefs of Rewa: 'War with us is now ended; any party that again causes evil to spring up shall be subdued by our united attack on that place. All must *lotu*, that peace may be permanent and that we may give up that which is so injurious.'[54]

In a rare surviving scrap of his journal, Pomare describes a journey he took to Raivavae in the Austral islands to the south of Tahiti in August 1819, which was then at war.[55] This is what he reports of his words to the assembled islanders:

This is my mission in sailing hither to you here ... This is the word of God: Do not fight. Do not kill people. Do not steal. Do not lie. Do not pray to those evil spirits (*varua 'ino*) in your keeping, give them up; do not keep them up, they are false.

Pomare had used every ritual resource in the existing system to elevate his own rank, but these had neither won him popularity nor been rendered superfluous by the development of institutional means for establishing authority.[56] Nor did the misery of internecine violence abate when his opponents were victorious.[57] Christianity presented an opportunity for a new kind of political settlement, in which older forms of life and the competitive behaviours they generated were dissolved into a larger sense of allegiance.[58] Righteous kingship might therefore make sense as a way of modelling the new virtues that statehood demanded of subjects: Photius's advice to Boris is again

---

[52] See Nicholas Thomas, 2012b: 283; 2010: 122; Webb 1965: 32; and Brantlinger 2006: 33. The end of the Musket wars coincided with the expansion of Christianity in nineteenth-century New Zealand: Sissons 2015: 132–133; Belich 1996: 164–168.

[53] Gunson 1978: 297.

[54] Cited in Thornley and Vulaono 2002: 81; compare Sahlins 1985: 39.

[55] The scrap was copied down by the missionary J. M. Orsmond. Gunson, 1966: 199–203, gives the translation by Ralph Gardiner White from a Tahitian transcript in the Orsmond Papers, Mitchell Library, Sydney.

[56] Oliver 1974: 1328.   [57] Oliver 1974: 1324, 1344.

[58] What Newbury 1980: 38, says of Pomare could surely stand for others: 'But there is also a certain war-weariness with the futility of ritual sacrifices, raid and counterraid, and a search for the answer to the predicament of Tahitian politics-namely, how to exercise power in a hierarchical and tribal society without continually alienating status rivals at one level and suppliers of produce and manpower at another.'

apposite. He urged that Boris's new moral conduct would exalt him in the eyes of his subjects (that is, enhance his legitimacy) but also shape his subjects in his image (that is, enhance their governability), for 'the ways of a ruler become law to those who are under him'.[59] Crime and dishonesty would diminish among his subjects once they were induced to love one another.

However, this raises the question of what was lost once the old traditions had been discarded. Would it not make sense that the more divinised the form of kingship the more absurd the conversion of the king? Should not the tremendous capacity of immanentist traditions to exalt the being of the ruler stand as a great world historical obstacle to the advance of proselytising transcendentalisms?

Conversion and Dilemmas of Sacred Kingship

The divinisation of kingship attempted to assert the centrality of kings to every dimension of existence. The more seriously these claims were taken – that is, the more cultural weight they carried – the more difficult it becomes to understand how their abandonment would be countenanced by king or subject. The consequences could be imagined as taking place imminently and immanently, after all – not in the dim obscurity of the afterlife. What follows is not an attempt to show why Christianity was likely to seem a superior choice in terms of ruler sacralisation. It is rather to begin to explain why it was ever considered an acceptable replacement – through six lines of approach.

One response to the conundrum is to offer a partial agreement with the premise. It is a reasonable hypothesis that rulers were more likely to convert where their office had not been elaborated in terms of their divinisation or even subject to sacralisation in general.[60] This may apply to some of the barbarian kingdoms of early medieval Europe.[61] It certainly applies to the Japanese daimyo whose own position in the mid-sixteenth century was undersacralised and certainly

---

[59] Photius 1982: 65.
[60] As with opportunistic princes in Sri Lanka, not yet incumbents of throne, for example, Strathern 2007a.
[61] Where the ritual splendour and righteous sanctification of royal office brought by the Church evoked a uniquely sacral quality for the first time. On twelfth-century Denmark: Gelting 2007: 88–89.

non-divinised.[62] Equally, entrenched modes of divinisation may have formed a kind of obstacle to conversion as some scholars of Africa have suggested.[63] Peel has compared the king (Awujale) of late nineteenth-century Ijebu, as a sacralised figure with cosmic functions, who did not convert, with that of the apparently more secular figure of the ruler (or Kabaka) of Buganda, who did.[64] This may help explain why certain kings in early modern Africa who had strong contemporary reputations as highly ritualised and magical figures, such as the obas of Benin and the kings of Loango, in the end, did not turn an interest in Christianity into conversion.[65]

Nevertheless, the explanatory power of this principle is ultimately limited. Divinised rulers have undoubtedly converted.[66] Constantine himself stood at the end of centuries of experimentation with imperial divinisation, expressed in both the heroic and cosmic modes.[67] These were expressed, for example, in a panegyric of 289, which hailed Maximian as the new Hercules, with a unique ability to provide this-worldly salvation – as reflected directly in the bounties of the harvest.[68] Yet after 312, Constantine increasingly saw fit to articulate his sacrality in a Christian register. In the 1660s the king of Bissau took a leading role in fertility and sea-placation ceremonies; in 1696 he was baptised.[69]

---

[62] *CK*. Their position contrasted with that of the over-ritualised and politically impotent emperor.

[63] Hastings 1994: 312.

[64] Peel 1977: 118–119; Graeber and Sahlins 2017: 400–401. Note the resistance of Lubosi Lewanika (1842–1916), who was, in the words of one ritual specialist, 'the son of the divinity, a God himself': Mainga, 1976: 104.

[65] De Heusch 2000: 39–57, emphasises the magical powers of the king of Loango, but downplays their extensive contact with missionaries, on which see Alan Strathern 2018: 162–163. Also see Heywood and Thornton 2007: 106. Recall Livingstone's problems with Sechele (Chapter 4).

[66] For divinisation of Central African rulers, many of whom converted: MacGaffey 2005. Note Hastings 1994: 312–314, on rainmakers converting.

[67] Price 1987: 97–98. However, for important qualification see below (footnote 72).

[68] Bardill 2012: 68. 'And truly, most sacred Emperor, we all know, before you restored soundness to the State, what great scarcity there was of crops and what a harvest of deaths, when hunger and diseases ranged everywhere. But from the time when you brought forth light for the nations a healthy atmosphere immediately spread about. No field fails its farmer expectations unless its abundance exceeds his hope. The life expectancies and numbers of men increase.' On divinisation themes in the time of Diocletian (emperor 284–305): Bardill 2012: 65–66, 339–340.

[69] Hair 1982: 24–25.

The point is particularly clear in the cases of African rulers converting to Islam. Among the first to do so were the rulers of Kanem in the thirteenth century.[70] A tenth-century Egyptian report on Kanem provides a perfect expression of cosmic divinised kingship:

> They exalt their king and worship him instead of Allah. They imagine that he does not eat any food. He has unlimited authority over his subjects. Their religion is the worship of kings, for they believe that they bring life and death, sickness and health.[71]

A second answer complicates the premise by recalling that the cultural weight of royal divinisation cannot be taken for granted. If there is an affinity between assertions of royal divinisation and attempts to consolidate the religious field, then it is worth noting that significance of the former will depend to some extent on the efficacy of the latter. State cults focusing on the king may play a relatively minor part in people's lives and their ritual attempts to secure human flourishing. This is a genuine weakness of immanentist consolidation – that state cults may leave too much of the religious life distinct from the ruler at the centre. Perhaps the more imperial the polity – that is, the more culturally diverse its subjects – the more likely that is to be the case. A second look at the case of Constantine indicates some debate about the significance of the imperial cult.[72] But even in much smaller scale societies, there may be a disconnect between chiefly cult and popular religion, especially where the immanentist theme of ritual secrecy has come to predominate.[73] In Tahiti and Fiji, for example, the preferred cult of the warrior elite may have focused too much on exalting their status and will to power rather than establishing more inclusive forms of popular legitimacy.[74] Lastly, as a much more general principle, we must be alert to the possibility of scepticism and indifference with

---

[70] Though retained earlier forms of royal divinisation (Haour 2007: 62) in keeping with an argument of Chapter 3.
[71] Levtzion 2000: 80.
[72] For Gradel 2002: 349–371, the state cult had been crumbling over the third century, *in part* under the pressure of rationalist scepticism. Bardill 2012: 58, suggests the cult to the emperor's numen was damaged by the loss of dynastic continuity during the ructions of the mid-third century. Note Rüpke 2010: 762, on the lack of centralisation of religion.
[73] See *CK* for Hawaii.
[74] Oliver 1974: 1330; Newbury 1961: xliii; 1967: 492; Thomas 2010: 97. The war god Tu/Ku may have been in the ascendant across Polynesia. On New Zealand, see Belich 1996: 109.

regard to rulers and their religious claims among some sections of the population, a 'hidden transcript' which may yet be shaping the course of events.[75] In other words, the extent to which themes of royal divinisation mattered to the religious lives and objectives of subjects is culturally and temporally variable.

A third response takes note of certain tensions within the immanentist sacralisation of kingship itself – but it only applies in select cases. Where the king's daily life became defined by isolation and ritualisation, there were two consequences for the prospect of conversion. It meant that the office itself might start to be diminished in its political capacity – this is the ritualisation trap – and that the onerous lifestyle itself might be experienced as a burden.[76] It is possible that this induced some incumbents to reach for a system that reimagined sacrality in different terms. This may be what lay behind the attempts of the kings of Benin to make contact with missionaries in 1651, 1691, and 1710. By this time they were increasingly beleaguered and ritually isolated figures, having ceded much political efficacy to officials and military commanders.[77] The obas tried periodically to fight against this state of affairs, which broke out into a rumbling civil war from the 1640s. However, the problem is that the further a ruler has sunk into the ritualisation trap the less capacity he or she has to push through such a radical approach.[78] Moreover, normally the status (if not the power) sustained by the old system was still difficult to give up.

The other consequence followed from the emergence of 'diarchical' forms of kingship, split between a ceremonial cosmic form and a more active and executive office.[79] The point here is that those occupying the less divinised role seem to have felt less invested in the traditional framework, and more ready to countenance conversion to an entirely new system that would condense sacral and political power into one office. At least this seems the case in the Pacific instances. In both Fiji and Tonga it was the war leaders who adopted Christianity. In Tonga, the more sacred king had long been more dormant; in Fiji it was only in

---

[75] Scott 1985; nuanced discussion in Andy Wood 2006.

[76] See the case of the Narai, king of Ayutthaya, in *CK*. Although he did not convert, Narai was increasingly restless within his highly protocol-governed role in the capital.

[77] Ryder 1969: 256; Ben-Amos 1999: 38–45.

[78] This might also apply to the case of Loango.   [79] See Chapter 4.

expansionist Bau that the sacred king (the Roko Tui Bau) had become more subordinate.[80] But these titular positions represented a limitation on the accumulation of status by the war leaders.[81] The case of Pomare is different in that he pursued his ambitions through the sacred status conferred by the dominant 'Oro cult (although he was ritually subordinate to the rulers of Raiatea and still faced resistance to the 'Oro cult among adherents to older gods).[82] But then he faced the opposite problem of over-ritualisation. Pomare remained an effective politician, but the way in which the tabus surrounding his person affected relations with Europeans or his freedom of movement may just have begun to weigh heavy.[83]

In Hawaii, the exploits of the great conquering unifier, Kamehameha, were assisted, ironically, by the fact that he was not of the highest genealogical rank. The charisma generated by military expansion more than made up for this deficit. But, very much in tune with the suggestions made in Chapter 3, once the work of conquest was done, he seems to have found the need to assert a more cosmic, ritualised status. He retired to Hawaii Island in 1812, leaving the bulk of the defiling activities of day-to-day commerce and government to the relatives of his wife, Ka'ahumanu, in O'ahu.[84] The latter promptly usurped some of his executive function.[85] His other move was to exalt his son and heir, Liholiho, into a more ceremonialised and divinised position – but this too backfired, when it became apparent that his son could not perform with the ritual decorum that was required.

Thus it was Ka'ahumanu, with a number of other high-ranking female chiefs, who largely took advantage of the power vacuum and seized the initiative in abolishing the old state cult and converting to Christianity. In one sense, the position of powerful female chiefs had been analogous to that of the 'more secular' partner in a diarchy: they could attain very real power and influence, and even a divinised status thanks to their 'divine descent', but they were denied the ability to participate in the highest rites that were associated with kingship itself. Their investment in this system was therefore crucially limited, and they were prepared to dismantle it even before being baptised.[86] Once again, it would surely be worthwhile to consider whether gender

---

[80] Sahlins 2004: 198; Linnekin 2008: 191–192. Philips 2007: 198.
[81] Latukefu 1974: 23, 84.   [82] Newbury 1967: 492.
[83] Gunson 1969: 72–73; compare Newbury 1967: 488.
[84] Sahlins 1981: 58–60.   [85] CK.   [86] Also Linnekin 2008: 196.

functioned in this way in earlier cases – and again Njinga of Ndongo springs to mind. It is true that she had succeeded in establishing great authority for herself before conversion – and like Ka'ahumanu also set a precedent for female rule – but it seems that earlier she had only been able to reign as an Imbangala leader through a striking manipulation of gender norms. In the 1640s she turned herself symbolically into a man, taking several husbands and transforming them into concubines who dressed in women's clothing and slept chastely among her maids in waiting.[87] Was Christianity, when it finally came, then finally a shift out of an ultimately restrictive gendering of political theology?[88]

Nevertheless, let us return to the point that even kings occupying the most divinised of offices have converted. If it was an obstacle, it was not an insurmountable one. Indeed, in the case of Roman emperors no less than that of the high chiefs of Hawaii, explicit attempts to assert the divinised status of rulers might presage their embrace of Christianity; in an immanentist setting, it seems, the need to innovate may take the form of what comes to be seen as 'conversion'. A fourth answer, then, shifts the perspective from incentives to opportunity, by considering the relative lack of institutional and moral autonomy on the part of the immanentist religious specialists. Chapter 5 has shown that they could give way quite easily before – or even help – promote royal conversions. Divinised kings, particularly those standing at the head of priestly hierarchies, as a class may have had less reason to convert on that score – but, paradoxically, more opportunity!

Somehow, in an immanentist setting, the religious authority granted to the king by the old system may become the means of transforming the nature of the religion on which it is based.[89] It was partly by reflecting on this fact that Sahlins conceived the societies of the Polynesia as operating according to a 'hierarchical solidarity', by which collective action depends on the chief or king at its pinnacle.[90] Missionaries had often been frustrated by the way that chiefs would

---

[87] Thornton 1991: 38.

[88] Although both Mbundu and Imbangala traditions had ancestral founder figures who were female – and associated with violent, gender-reversed, and transgressive acts (Heywood 2017: 120–121).

[89] Heywood and Thornton 2007: 60, 'The power that the kings had over religious practices could readily be transferred to other religious traditions like Christianity.' Also Dumézil 2005: 175.

[90] Sahlins 1985: 41–45.

tend to make the question of their conversion dependent on the deci-
sions of their superiors, as if such matters were really just like any other
kind of political business and had to be referred up to the highest
authority.[91] They subsequently discovered that this this was no mere
excuse but an expression of a very real principle of society, which then
miraculously began to operate in their favour. A century after their
conversion, Fijians could still refer to Christianity as 'the religion of
Thakombau' (Cakobau), the ruling chief of the Mbau confederacy
who had finally accepted baptism.[92] The divinised king of an immanentist society stands at the centre of what the entire state-sanctioned
religious project is about – rather than as an interlocutor with a salvific
enterprise that far transcends the kingdom or its people.

A fifth answer queries the premise again by recognising that converting rulers were not necessarily given to recognise that they would have
to accept a diminution of their divinised status.[93] In part, this was
because Christianity, and particularly Catholicism, had incorporated
some divinising tendencies as part of its general immanentisation. This
was particularly apparent precisely at moments of ruler conversion,
when transcendentalist traditions were stretched through processes of
translation, misunderstanding, substitution, and de facto syncretism,
as Chapter 3 argued.[94] In founding her new kingdom of Ndongo-
Matamba, Queen Njinga drew upon Mbundu traditions of kingship
as well as Christianity. She continued to distribute her *mana* in a very
immediate way, appearing in the courtyard at a certain time of the day
to give out the *lunene royal* (royal word), which was believed to be the
'best luck in the world'.[95] Surely her reputation as a warrior lent her an
element of heroic divinisation that Christianity was not allowed to
diminish. Her axe was reputed to be invincible, the bows dispensed
from her hand unerring in use. Indeed, now she had lived to an unusual
age, she encouraged the Mbundu belief that rulers were literally
immortal – a striking disavowal of the Christian teaching of earthly
death. The very notion of her death was a forbidden topic. No surprise
then, that Njinga insisted that the traditional postures and attitudes of

---

[91] Davies 1961: 60–61; Thomas 2010: 123; Tomlinson 2009: 72–73; Latukefu,
    1974: 82–83.
[92] Sahlins 1985: 37.   [93] Discussion in Chapter 3.
[94] Note Firth 1970: 309, on Tikopia.
[95] Heywood 2017: 196, quoting Giovanni Antonio Cavazzi.

respect and deference be accorded to her person.[96] The sheer habitus of reverence may well be something that survives – temporarily at least – ideological change.

But even where kings moved into a more exclusively Christian mode of kingship, the very novelty of their status created a certain opportunity to convey a vaguely divinised intimacy with the sacred. As 'first movers' of a kind themselves they were able to establish their special closeness to the divine through the providential significance of their agency; they were, after all, truly akin to apostles, even prophets, to their people. This was arguably the position of Afonso of Kongo and Ka'ahamanu of Hawaii.[97] If ruler conversion can function as a recapitulation of ethnogenesis, then the ruler appears as a kind of founder-hero (also often associated with radical transgression): an image which is explicit in the public memory of Afonso.[98] Crucially, they were often associated too with the displays of *mana*, particularly on the battlefield, as described in Chapter 5. Whatever the niceties of official political theology, such access to the life-bestowing powers of metapersons was thereby confirmed. Rulers found ways, then, of placing themselves at the symbolic centre of the new dispensation, and intimating, therefore, their centrality in relations to the divine.[99] In the main chapel that King George of Tonga had constructed, a platform was raised so that he could sit higher than the pulpit.[100]

Plus ça change, plus c'est la même chose? Only initially, and in a limited sense. After the influence of the revival of 1834, King George tore down the platform and subsequently sat on the floor with everyone else. There were means of masking and slowing down the select disenchantment of the monarchy, but in many cases it proved to be real enough nonetheless.[101] A sense of the genuine ambivalence of Christianity on this point must therefore be preserved, even in its earliest expansion. It is perceptible, for example, once again, in the

---

[96] Heywood 2017: 227–229.

[97] See the glamorous role suggested by Patriarch Photius to Khan Boris: Mayr-Harting 1994: 24. Vladimir of Rus was eventually worshipped as a saint, an 'apostle among rulers', according to Shepard 2007: 383. In his lifetime, Christianity brought to Rus 'a better organized cult, more sharply focused on the ruler's authority than previous ones had been'.

[98] *CK.*   [99] Thomas 2010: 104–105; Swain and Trompf 1995: 174.

[100] Latekefu 1974: 72.

[101] The effects of descralisation undermined chiefly authority in Samoa according to Meleisa 1987: 12–13.

illuminating responses from the Pope to Khan Boris of the Bulgars in 866, as to how he should live as a Christian king:

> You say that you wish to know, if in a time of drought you are allowed to command all of your people to pray and fast to summon the rain. Of course you are allowed to do this, because prayer and fasting are great virtues, and your exhortation has a great effect by having these performed constantly.[102]

This alludes to a communal focus on the king as figure with cosmic responsibilities – and the way in which that focus may be maintained. Boris might still command the ritual obligations of his people through the immanentist Christian practice of prayer. But note the next line:

> It is more fitting, however, if these things are done by the decision of the bishops, for they are the ones who receive the power of binding and loosing, and it is at the sound of their voice that the camps of the people of God are moved and come to rest.

This indicates, no less clearly, a subtle shift of focus in the intercessory role from the king to the transcendent clerisy: it is at the voice of the bishops that the people move or rest. Another chapter in the long letter addresses what ought to be done about the protocol of royal mealtimes. It would appear that the Bulgarian king – in common with many other kings worldwide and in keeping with the tendency towards dehumanisation – had to take meals unaccompanied. The pope admits that this does not contradict doctrine per se, but does not suit the spirit of Christianity: sainted kings of the past had learned to be 'meek and humble in heart' and lived together with their friends, while the king of kings, Christ, had 'reclined and eaten with publicans and sinners'.[103]

There will be, of course, much variety on this theme to be explored from case to case, but the capacity of Christianity to quietly suppress the divinisation of the ruler in favour of a righteous mode of sacrality was not then completely blunted. Roman Catholic and Protestant Christianity was – relative to Buddhism or even Islam – less prepared to concede too much in this respect. This may be one reason why it was

---

[102] North 1998: 568–600, chapter LVI. However, we know little of how pagan kingship had worked hitherto.
[103] North 1998: chapter XLII.

Islam rather than Christianity which made greater advances in converting rulers in sub-Saharan Africa and Southeast Asia, for it was both better able to translate indigenous forms of divinisation into a new idiom and to allow longer periods of plural cohabitation.[104] Thomas Gibson has argued that the king of Sulawesi only converted when a form of Islam arrived into maritime Southeast Asia that placed the ruler at the apex of the religious hierarchy and maintained a focus on his divine centrality.[105] Pluralism is a notable feature of West African courts, as they were slowly incorporated into Muslim commercial networks over the second millennium CE. Sunjata, the founder of the huge Mali empire in the thirteenth century, was a great magician and hunter, and yet also apparently a Muslim.[106] Two hundred years later, Sonni 'Alī, who claimed descent from Sunjata and turned Songhay into a large empire, was recognised as a Muslim king while also drawing on the ancestral practices of his mother's family. No doubt the heroic charisma generated by his vast conquest also propelled his reputation as 'one of the most powerful and gifted magicians that the Sudan has ever known'.[107] It is true that this created unrest among the more Islamised elements in urban centres and that his successor Askia Muhammad had to turn to a more righteous form of Islamic state cult, appealing to the Abbasid caliph in Cairo for legitimisation as 'Commander of the Faithful' in 1496. Indeed, this move has also been interpreted as a result of the lack of heroic charisma on the part of Askia.[108] But the chief point is that it is difficult to imagine baptised Christian kings so openly claiming the immanent powers of ancestral cult.

And yet. Does a king need to be godlike to access the power of the god? If rulers may be guaranteed access to thamaturgical efficacy through their role as servants and appointees of God, in some ways the result may look rather similar to their subjects. This is what lies behind the sixth answer, which may be the most important, and has already been revealed. The promise that divinised kings hold within their being is that of advancing the worldly lives of their subjects. If a convincing public narrative of dramatic divine intervention can be

---

[104] Reid 2015: 113. Moin 2016: 126, relates this capacity to the absence of a Church and the consequences of the Mongol destruction of the Caliphate. Islam developed over a longer chronology in both regions of course.

[105] Gibson 2007: 38–39.   [106] Levtzion 2000: 66.

[107] Rouch 1953: 181, cited in Kaba 1984: 250.   [108] Levtzion 1977: 428.

spun, of the kind described in Chapter 5, then the converting monarch can demonstrate that he or she has not in fact forfeited his or her cosmic function but advanced it in a different register. Then the slow work may begin of inducing subjects to see that the ruler is in fact the representative of something much more important than the arrival of the rains or victory over their neighbours.

Conclusion

Momentarily setting aside various important nuances and reservations, it may be possible to force the discussion into a single abstract argument: the less consolidated (unified, centralised, instrumentalised) the religious field, and the less divinised the ruler, the stronger the incentive to convert. It was not that Christianity (or Islam or Buddhism) necessarily delivered an unproblematic religious consolidation to political elites; certainly, over the longer term, their clerisies might fragment into sectarian conflict or thwart monarchy in distressing ways. It is rather because at the point of its introduction conversion offered a way of radically clearing or reframing the religious field and installing a new cult with which the converting ruler enjoyed a unique relationship.

To some extent, ruling figures who were accorded a less divinised status for whatever reason (because kingship simply had not been elaborated in that fashion; because they occupied a less cosmic role in a diarchy; because they were internal rebels, parvenus, or warlords; because they were women rather than men) did indeed show a greater readiness to convert. But divinised kingship had some internal fragilities of its own: it was never a simple matter to sustain the argument of the ruler's godlike status. Over time, it risked sliding into the ritualisation trap – which the kind of legitimacy offered by the transcendentalist model deftly sidestepped. Moreover, paradoxically, the very concentration of religious authority that divinised kings held in their person might also enable them to impose radical forms of religious innovation and conversion.

If there is a tendency then, for more deeply divinised kings to resist conversion, it is not strong enough to present us with a particularly clear pattern, or produce real predictive power for any given case. More striking, indeed, is the long-term vulnerability of the class of divinised kingship as a whole.[109] Ultimately, then, this chapter has not sought to marshal the material into a single line of argument. It has rather identified some of the different ways in which the more visionary rulers of immanentist societies might have been able to perceive political opportunities in attempting to Christianise their realms, outweighing the obvious risks.[110] Still, more significant – in providing both means and motivation to rewriting the rules of legitimacy – was the charisma generated by demonstrations of immanent power. The power grab on the level of the supernatural was typically primary to the power grab on the level of politics.

---

[109] That is, the systems of political theology created by societies adhering only to immanentist religious traditions.

[110] Explored in more depth in *CK*.

Conclusion

Transcendentalism allowed the emergence, for the first time in history, of a governing ideology that did not have as its telos the observable conditions of existence. A higher purpose was conceived in the realm of the unobservable and almost inconceivable kind of existence that would follow the death and liberation of the individual. The project of ameliorating the human condition yielded to the ambition to escape it altogether.

This leap of the imagination mattered to rulers, for it is in the imagination of their subjects that rulers live and die. In the immanentist ontology, the supernatural is not only invoked to legitimise political power; it is held to create such power and to be embodied in the human beings who wield it. If rulers professed a centrality in the political sphere they were liable to be regarded as pivotal to the religious and cosmological dimensions of existence too. The arrival of transcendentalism, however, forced a breach between the ends of life and the ends of politics: sometimes no more than a tiny fracture, at other times a chasm.

It is easy to see why rulers would hasten after subjects who had already converted in significant numbers, thereby gaining ownership of a religious movement whose obvious social power otherwise threatened their position. But kings were often first movers themselves. Thus, long after the brief life of a Jewish troublemaker had expired, the Roman Empire itself succumbed to the radical vision he and his followers had given voice to. Long after the Buddha lay down and passed away under a full moon, kings across Sri Lanka and Southeast Asia could only describe their authority in relation to his teachings and physical remains. They poured their wealth into huge statues of him lying down, his eyes half-closed: a graceful rebuke to the assertion of power.

Most of the world now identifies with traditions that combine the transcendentalist and immanentist modes – to the extent that some may wonder why they need to be conceptually distinguished. The answer is that for most of human history, particularly, but not only, as lived outside the great Eurasian circulations of the post-Axial traditions, religious activity took place in terms of immanentism alone. Some might argue – depending on a strong version of the 'popular religion' thesis – that most of human religious activity essentially remained in that mode long after those traditions arrived. But even if that is granted, it only becomes more puzzling why so many societies had to pay lip service to the hegemony of transcendentalist forms, to texts and truths and the clerisies that maintain them, to universal ethics, identities, and salvation quests. Moreover, the result of such combinations took a specific tension-filled form that shaped the societies generating them.

The modal hybridity of traditions such as Christianity and Buddhism was a vital element of their capacity to expand, just as the imperatives of expansion always served to produce modal hybridity. Monks and missionaries became the purveyors of supernatural power, as revealed on the battlefield and the sickbed in particular. Such concrete demonstrations have an inherent capacity to cross religious boundaries.[1] When Paul cured a cripple at Lystra, the crowd cried, 'The gods are come down to us in the likeness of men,' and the priest of Jupiter brought him oxen and garlands.[2]

For the imagery of the *transcendence* of supernatural power was easily interpreted in terms of the *mastery* of it. Christian missionaries and their leading converts were empowered to take one step outside the universal assumptions of immanentism into a form of culturally selective disenchantment, waging war on the ritual order, defeating the legions of metapersons, destroying the homes that people had built for them, driving them from people's minds through exorcism. Buddhists, meanwhile, did not attack the realm of metapersons in so direct a manner, but overmastered it no less surely, taming its inhabitants and redescribing them according to its sublime narrative. Thus was already begun the process by which immanentism was transformed into something else.

---

[1] In transcendentalist systems supernatural power still mattered, of course (and is considered at length in the Japanese and Thai cases), but it was no longer the entire *raison d'être* of the system.

[2] Acts 14:8–13. This principle also applies, to a lesser extent, in transcendentalist religions.

In effect, this was the strategy of monotheism on the march: first to enhance the salience of the economy of ritual efficacy, by making competition explicit and unavoidable; secondly, by achieving premium value in that economy; and thirdly, by subsequently undermining its significance, so that the vicissitudes of worldly existence could never again challenge the fundamental structures of the tradition. This was the point at which a gleaming new engine of conceptual control was wheeled into action. Promises of immanent assistance were offered with one hand, but rendered insignificant by a flourish of the other: the real reward was always yet to come and had to be conceived in quite different terms.

Immanentism was open to this strategy because it was open tout court; it was not a site of explicit identity construction, it did not found itself upon a closed canon, guarded by a caste of exegetes and gate-keepers; it rarely developed continuous traditions of intellectualised self-defence. Immanentist systems were not, by any means, a pushover, and different forms of it long held out. After all, they spoke to humanity's most immediate needs and harmonised with evolved or universal traits of human cognition. Particularly where they had already been 'consolidated' and overlain with state cult, they tapped the social power of religion with great efficiency, helping communities and even vast empires to hold together in some form. Indeed, the deployment of religion as the basis for social order always served to constrain the reach of the economy of ritual efficacy, to entrench a degree of stability, and to ensure that any ruler who dared abandon and attack traditional rites was liable to face a serious legitimacy crisis. Yet such crises were usually overcome.

Converting kings who survived early ructions gained a particularly compelling language though which to insist upon the monopolisation of violence and to construe their moral authority. This was generated by the gap between the purpose of life and the purpose of politics that transcendentalism opened up. This was the logic of legitimation: the repudiation of power sucked in power. Over the longer term, rulers did not necessarily benefit in any smooth and consistent fashion; transcendentalism created its own forms of dissension and fragmentation. But once it had struck roots in society, it proved notably resistant to being dislodged.[3]

---

[3] The encounter with other transcendentalist religions is dealt with in *CK*.

Divinised kingship, in its 'pure' form, was less resilient. But kingship never ceased resenting its surrender of intercessory centrality. Kings attempted to clutch on to the forms of divinisation at the point of conversion; they turned to them when they sought to assert their authority over the institutions of religion; they generated them through the force of charisma won on the battlefield; they yielded to them when popular hopes demanded it; and, in the case of some of the sprawling land empires of Asia at least, they recognised in them a means of appealing to all religious communities regardless of the identities and commitments promoted by quarrelsome transcendentalist clerisies. Yes, all this had to proceed now in a hybrid form under the aegis of some such transcendentalist tradition, but nothing suggests that the attractions of divinised kingship ceased to make sense across much of the world until perhaps the nineteenth century and beyond. It was only with the arrival of certain secularising tendencies in modernity that divinised kingship was put to the sword, and even then it returned in the ghostly simulacra of the transgressive and utopianist strongmen of the twentieth century, fascist dictators, and chiliastic communist leaders.

Glossary of Theoretical Terms

The Foundational Concepts of Religion

Immanentism – a form of religiosity oriented towards the presence of supernatural forces and agents in the world around us, which are attributed with the power to help or thwart human aspirations. It is found in every society and religious system, and is defined here by 10 features. An *immanentist tradition* or system is solely defined by immanentism.

Transcendentalism – a form of religiosity oriented towards the transcendence of mundane existence and the imperative of salvation or liberation from the human condition. It is characterised here by 15 features. A *transcendentalist tradition* is one in which transcendentalism has achieved a certain hegemony, albeit always in dialogue with immanentism – as in Buddhism or Christianity.

An immanentist tradition

> Immamentism

A transcendentalist tradition

> Transcendentalism
>
> Immamentism

The Foundational Concepts of Kingship

Divinised Kingship
— kings are divinised when they are regarded as godlike and treated as if they were metapersons. As the mode of ruler sacralisation promoted by immanentist religiosity, it locates that sacrality in the being and capacities of the ruler.

Righteous Kingship
— kings are righteous when they are idealised in moral terms and assigned a special role in the quest for salvation. As the mode of ruler sacralisation promoted by transcendentalist religiosity, it locates that sacrality in his or her relationship with the imperatives of a transcendentalist tradition.

Heroic Kingship
— a form of divinised kingship that focuses on the inherent supernatural power or charisma of the ruler, and which is revealed through observable achievements, especially on the battlefield.

Cosmic Kingship
— a form of divinised kingship that makes the king a crucial intermediary between human society and the divine forces that govern its affairs, ensuring the reproduction of order and flourishing. It is revealed through ritual performance.

Sacred Kingship
— Any form kingship which is conceived, performed, and legitimised in terms of immanentism and/or transcendentalism. It is therefore an umbrella term encompassing both divinised and righteous kingship.

Sacred kingship

Divinised Kingship   Righteous Kingship

Cosmic Kingship   Heroic Kingship

Further Concepts Defined

Auto-iconoclasm	– occurs when people destroy the ritual objects and images they had previously held as sacred in a way that is consistent with the internal assumptions of their own religious tradition, as when a collective understanding emerges that the metapersons invoked by the objects have become useless or malevolent.
Charisma	– the social power available to individuals who are attributed with supernatural qualities and potencies, especially where these are revealed through heroic accomplishment.
Conceptual Control	– the capacity of a religious group or tradition to maintain control over the terms in which the success or failure of ritual activity is interpreted, such that unwanted outcomes do not cast doubt on the efficacy of that activity.
Consolidation	– the process by which the ruler or the state gains control over religious activity, centralising and instrumentalising its social power.
Diarchy	– occurs when kingship is split into two offices, usually where one takes on a more active role and the other a more ritualised role (or the heroic and cosmic roles).
Durkheimian	– evokes a long tradition of the interpretation of religion expressed most completely by Emile Durkheim, in which the capacity of religion to produce social order and cohesion is emphasised.

Economy of Ritual Efficacy	– is evident in situations where the value of a religious practice is associated with its perceived efficacy, such that new rituals, ritual specialists, metapersons, or entire systems may be adopted if they are perceived to be more effective than old ones.
Empirical Religiosity	– religious behaviour focused on outcomes that are realised in – and therefore assessed in terms of – lived, observable reality.
Intellectualisation	– the process by which a religious tradition is shaped by a class of high-status literate intellectuals, who value textual authority, systematisation, abstraction, self-reflexive thinking, offensiveness, and debate.
Legitimation	– the establishment of the mental, cultural, and behavioural norms which allow power to be exercised with consent, such that it is assumed to be natural, inevitable, beneficial, moral, just, divinely sanctioned, or soteriologically vital.
Mana	– originally a Polynesian term, it is also used here to refer to supernatural potency or efficacy made immanent in the world.
Metapersons	– supernatural agents who have some of the characteristics of people but are not present to the senses in the way that ordinary people are, and who have diverse powers to influence human well-being, for good or ill: ancestors, spirits, deities.
Moral Community	– a group that shares a common set of moral understandings, values, and norms, and is conscious of doing so.

Non-Euphemised   – a form of sacred kingship in which
Kingship   the amoral, violent, terrifying, and
transgressive dimensions to the
exercise of power are expressed. It is
allowed but not necessitated by
immanentist religious systems.

Offensiveness   – a tradition has an offensive quality
when it is predicated on the existence
of alternative worldviews, which it is
oriented towards challenging. Ernest
Gellner saw it as a feature of
'ideology', but it is also a defining
feature of transcendentalism.

Relativisation   – the relegation of a given cultural
feature or system to secondary
importance through an awareness of
its merely customary and
contingent basis.

Righteous   – the targeted destruction of religious
Iconoclasm   sites and images in accordance with
soteriological imperatives. It is
usually a function of the monotheistic
sensibility of abomination.

Ritualisation Trap   – occurs where the ritualisation and
isolation of the ruler diminishes their
political power and freedom.

Social Power   – the capacity to shape, cohere,
motivate, and discipline groups of
people.

Soteriology   – relating to salvation or liberation.

State   – 'A coercion-wielding organization
that is distinct from household and
kinship groups and that exercises
priority over all other organizations
within a substantial territory'
(Charles Tilly).

Supernatural   – refers to beings and forces that
modern science does not recognise in
its account of the natural world.

Supernatural Utopianism	– refers to visions of an imminent transformation of society through the agency of supernatural forces and beings such that it is lifted into a permanent, idealised, utopic state. Exhibited by prophetic and cargo cults, and also 'millenarian' movements (although in this book the latter term is reserved for transcendentalist variants).
Warrior Iconoclasm	– the targeted destruction of the religious sites and images of the enemy for both religious and political reasons. In immanentist settings it will often imply the subordination of enemy claims to supernatural power.

Bibliography

Abbreviations

CK   Alan Strathern, *Converting Kings: Kongo, Thailand, Japan and Hawaii Compared, 1450-1850*. Cambridge University Press, forthcoming.

CWM/   Council for World Mission/London Missionary Society
LMS   archives, School of Oriental and Asian Studies, London.

MMA   António Brásio (ed.), *Monumenta Missionaria Africana: África Occidental* (1st series, 15 Vols., Lisbon: Agência Geral do Ultramar, 1952–).

Bibliography

Achebe, Chinua (2001) *Things Fall Apart*. London.
  (2010) *Arrow of God*. London.
Adas, Michael (1979) *Prophets of Rebellion: Millenarian Protest Movements against the European Colonial Order*. Chapel Hill.
Adolphs, Ralph (2009) 'The Social Brain: Neural Basis of Social Knowledge', *Annual Review of Psychology* 60(1): 693–716.
Adomnán (1991) *Life of Columba*, Alan Orr Anderson and Marjorie Ogilvie, eds. Oxford.
Akutagawa, Ryūnosuke (1989) 'The Faint Smiles of the Gods' in *The Kyoto Collection, Stories from the Japanese*, Tomoyoshi Genkawa and Bernard Susser, trans. Osaka.
Al-Azmeh, Aziz (1997) *Muslim Kingship: Power and the Sacred in Muslim, Christian and Pagan Polities*. London.
Alberts, Tara (2012) 'Catholic Communities and Their Festivities in the Portuguese Padroado' in *Portuguese and Luso-Asian Legacies in Southeast Asia, 1511–2011: Volume 2. Culture and Identity in the Luso-Asian World: Tenacities and Plasticities*, Laura Jarnagin, ed. Singapore: 21–43.
  (2013a) *Conflict and Conversion: Catholicism in Southeast Asia, c. 1500– c. 1700*. Oxford.

(2013b) 'Priests of a Foreign God: Catholic Religious Leadership and Sacral Authority in Seventeenth-Century Tonkin and Cochinchina' in *Intercultural Exchange in Southeast Asia: History and Society in the Early Modern World*, Tara Alberts and D. R. M. Irving, eds. London: 84–117.

Amitai, Reuven (2013) 'Hülegü and His Wise Men: Topos or Reality?' in *Politics, Patronage and the Transmission of Knowledge in 13th–15th Century Tabriz*, Judith Pfeiffer, ed. Leiden: 15–34.

Ando, Clifford (2008) *The Matter of the Gods: Religion and the Roman Empire*. Berkeley.

(2013) 'Subjects, Gods and Empire, or Monarchism as a Theological Problem' in *The Individual in the Religions of the Ancient Mediterranean*, Jörg Rüpke, ed. Oxford: 85–111.

App, Urs (2012) *The Cult of Emptiness: The Western Discovery of Buddhist Thought and the Invention of Oriental Philosophy*. Kyoto.

Aquinas, Thomas (1949) *On Kingship, To the King of Cyprus*, Gerald Phelan, trans., revised by I. Th. Eschmann. Toronto.

Armstrong, Karen (2006) *The Great Transformation: The Beginning of Our Religious Traditions*. New York.

Arnason, Johann P. (2012) 'Rehistoricizing the Axial Age' in *The Axial Age and Its Consequences*, Robert N. Bellah and Hans Joas, eds. Cambridge, MA: 337–365.

Arnason, Johann P. and Björn Wittrock, eds. (2004) *Eurasian Transformations, Tenth to Thirteenth Centuries: Crystallisations, Divergences, Renaissances*. Leiden.

Arnason, Johann P. and S. N. Eisenstadt, and Björn Wittrock, eds. (2005) *Axial Civilizations and World History*. Leiden.

Asad, Talal (1993) *Genealogies of Religion*. Baltimore.

(2003) *Formations of the Secular: Christianity, Islam, Modernity*. Stanford.

Asch, Ronald G. (2014) *Sacral Kingship between Disenchantment and Re-Enchantment: The French and English Monarchies, 1587–1688*. New York.

Assmann, Jan (2008) *Of God and Gods: Egypt, Israel, and the Rise of Monotheism*. Madison, WI.

(2010) *The Price of Monotheism*. Stanford.

(2012) 'Cultural Memory and the Myth of the Axial Age' in Bellah and Joas (2012): 366–408.

Astuti, Rita and Maurice Bloch (2013) 'Are Ancestors Dead?' in Boddy and Lambek (2013): 101–117.

Atran, Scott (2002) *In Gods We Trust: The Evolutionary Landscape of Religion*. Oxford.

Auge, Marc (1982) *Genie du paganisme*. Bibliotheque des Sciences Humaines. Paris.

Babayan, Kathryn (1994) 'The Safavid Synthesis from Qizilbash Islam to imamate Shi'ism', *Iranian Studies* 27: 135–161.

Baker, Chris and Pasuk Phongpaichit (2014) *A History of Thailand*, 3rd ed. Cambridge.

Baker, Chris and Pasuk Phongpaichit trans. and eds. (2016) *The Palace Law of Ayutthaya and the Thammasat: Law and Kingship in Siam*. Ithaca.

    trans. (2017) *Yuan Phai, the Defeat of Lanna. A Fifteenth-Century Thai Epic Poem*. Washington.

Balandier, Georges (1968) *Daily Life in the Kingdom of the Kongo from the Sixteenth to the Eighteenth Century*, Helen Weaver, trans. London.

Bandaranayake, Senake (2012) 'The God-King and the Cloud-Maiden: Royal Ritual and Urban Form in Sigiriya' in *Continuities and Transformations: Studies in Sri Lankan Archaeology and History*. Colombo: 249–262.

Bardill, Jonathon (2012) *Constantine, Divine Emperor of the Christian Golden Age*. Cambridge.

Barker, John (1993) '"We are Ekelesia": Conversion in Uiaku, Papua New Guinea' in Hefner (1993a): 199–230.

    (2005) 'Where the Missionary Frontier Ran Ahead of Empire' in *Missions and Empires*, Norman Etherington, ed. Oxford: 86–106.

Barlow, Frank (1980) 'The King's Evil', *English Historical Review* 95: 3–27.

Barnes, Timothy D. (2011) *Constantine. Dynasty, Religion and Power in the Later Roman Empire*. Chichester.

Barrett, Justin L. (2007) 'Gods' in *Religion, Anthropology and Cognitive Science*, Harvey Whitehouse and James Laidlaw, eds. Durham, NC: 179–210.

Barrett, Tim (2000) 'Shinto and Taoism in Early Japan' in Breen and Teuwen (2000): 13–31.

Bartlett, Robert (1985) 'Conversion of a Pagan Society', *History* 70: 185–201.

    (2007) 'From Paganism to Christianity in Medieval Europe' in Berend (2007a): 47–71.

Barton, Tamsyn (1996) 'Astrology and the State in Imperial Rome' in Thomas and Humphrey (1996): 146–163.

Baum, Robert M. (1999) *Shrines of the Slave Trade: Diola Religion and Society in Precolonial Senegambia*. Oxford.

Bay, Edna G. (1998) *Wives of the Leopard: Gender, Politics and Culture in the Kingdom of Dahomey*. Charlottesville.

Bayly, Christopher (2004) *Birth of the Modern World, 1780–1914. Global Connections and Comparisons*. Oxford.

Bayly, Susan (1989) *Saints, Goddesses and Kings. Muslims and Christians in South-Indian Society, 1700–1900*. Cambridge.

Baumann, Brian (2013) 'By the Power of Eternal Heaven: The Meaning of *Tenggeri* to the Government of the pre-Buddhist Mongols', *Extrême-Orient Extrême-Occident* 35: 233–284.

Beard, Mary (1996) 'The Roman and the Foreign: The Cult of the "Great Mother" in Imperial Rome' in Thomas and Humphrey (1996): 164–190.

Beattie, John (1971) *The Nyoro State*. Oxford.

Bede (1988) *A History of the English Church and People*, Leo Shirley-Price, trans. London.

Behr, Charlotte (2002) 'The Origins of Kingship in Medieval Kent', *Early Medieval Europe* 9: 25–52.

Belich, James (1996) *Making Peoples: A History of New Zealanders from Polynesian Settlement to the End of the Nineteenth Century*. Honolulu.

Bell, Catherine (1992) *Ritual Theory, Ritual Practice*. Oxford.

Bellah, Robert N. (1964) 'Religious Evolution', *American Sociological Review* 29: 358–374.

(2005) 'What is Axial about the Axial Age?', *European Journal of Sociology* 46: 69–89.

(2011) *Religion in Human Evolution*, Cambridge, MA.

Bellah, Robert N. and Hans Joas, eds. (2012) *The Axial Age and Its Consequences*. Cambridge, MA.

Ben-Amos, Paula (1999) *Art, Innovation, and Politics in Eighteenth-Century Benin*. Bloomington.

Ben-Amos Girshick, Paula and John Thornton (2001) 'Civil War in the Kingdom of Benin 1689–1721', *Journal of African History* 42: 353–376.

Berend, Nora ed. (2007a) *Christianization and the Rise of Christian Monarchy: Scandinavia, Central Europe and Rus' c. 900–1200*. Cambridge.

Berend, Nora (2007b) 'Introduction' in Berend (2007a): 1–46.

Berger, Peter L (1967) *The Sacred Canopy: Elements of a Sociological Theory of Religion*. Garden City.

Bergin, Joseph (2014) *The Politics of Religion in Early Modern France*. New Haven.

Berkwitz, Stephen C. (2016) 'Reimagining Buddhist Kingship in a Sinhala Praśasti', *Journal of the American Oriental Society* 136(2): 325–341.

(2017) 'Sinhala *Sandēśa* Poetry in a Cosmopolitan Context' in Biedermann and Strathern (2017): 94–112.

Bernbeck, Reinhard (2008) 'Royal Deification: An Ambiguation Mechanism for the Creation of Courtier Subjectivities' in Brisch (2008): 157–169.

Betanzos, Juan de (1996) *Narrative of the Incas*, R. Hamilton and D. Buchanan, eds. and trans. Austin.

Biersack, Aletta (1991) 'Prisoners of Time. Millenarian Praxis in a Melanesian Valley' in *Clio in Oceania: Toward a Historical Anthropology*, A. Biersack, ed. Washington, DC.

(2011a) 'The Sun and the Shakers, Again: Enga, Ipili, and Somaip Perspectives on the Cult of Ain Part One', *Oceania* 81(2): 113–136.

(2011b) 'The Sun and the Shakers, Again: Enga, Ipili, and Somaip Perspectives on the Cult of Ain, Part Two', *Oceania* 81(3): 225–243.

Biedermann, Zoltán, and Alan Strathern, eds. (2017) *Sri Lanka at the Crossroads of History*. London.

Bingham, Hiram (1849) *A Residence of Twenty-one Years in the Sandwich Islands*, 3rd ed. Hartford.

Binns, John (2002) *An Introduction to the Christian Orthodox Churches*. Cambridge.

Bosman, Willem (1705) *A New and Accurate Description of the Coast of Guinea, Divided Into the Gold, the Slave, and the Ivory Coasts*. London.

Blackburn, Anne M. (2001) *Buddhist Learning and Textual Practice in Eighteenth Century Lankan Monastic Culture*. Princeton.

Blair, John (2005) *The Church in Anglo-Saxon Society*. Oxford.

Blake, John Ballard (1942) *European Beginnings in West Africa, 1454–1578: A Survey of the First Century of White Enterprise in West Africa, with Special Emphasis Upon the Rivalry of the Great Powers*. London.

Blanning, Timothy (2002) *The Culture of Power and the Power of Culture: Old Regime Europe, 1660–1789*. Oxford.

Bloch, Marc (1973) *The Royal Touch: Sacred Monarchy and Scrofula in England and France*, J. E. Anderson, trans. London.

Bloch, Maurice (1974) 'Symbols, Song, Dance and Features of Articulation: Is Religion an Extreme Form of Traditional Authority?', *European Journal of Sociology / Archives Européennes de Sociologie / Europäisches Archiv für Soziologie* 15(1): 54–81.

(1987) 'The Ritual of the Royal Bath in Madagascar: The Dissolution of Death, Birth and Fertility into Authority' in Cannadine and Price (1987): 271–297.

Boahen, Albert A. (1992) 'The States and Cultures of the Lower Guinean Coast', Ogot (1992): 399–433.

Bodhi, Bikkhu (1978) *The Discourse on the All-Embracing Net of Views: The Brahmajala Sutta and Its Commentarial Exegesis*. Kandy.

(2000) *The Connected Discourses of the Buddha: A New Translation of the Saṃyutta Nikāya*, Vol. II. Boston.

Boddy, Janice, and Michael Lambek, eds. (2013) *A Companion to the Anthropology of Religion*. Oxford.

Bolton, Lissant (2012) 'Transformations 1890–1940', in Brunt and Thomas (2012): 218–241.

Bolotta, Giuseppe (2018) 'Development Missionaries in the Slums of Bangkok: From the Thaification to the De-Thaification of Catholicism' in *The Mission of Development: Techno-Politics of Religion in Asia*, C. Scheer, Philip Fountain, and R. Michael Feener, eds. Leiden: 135–164.

Bondarenko, Dmitri M., and Andrey V. Korotayev (2003) "Early State' in Cross-Cultural Perspective: A Statistical Reanalysis of Henri J. M. Claessen's Database', *Cross-Cultural Research* 37(1): 105–132.

Bossy, John (1982) 'Some Elementary Forms of Durkheim', *Past & Present* 95: 3–18.

(1985) *Christianity in the West 1400–1700*. Oxford.

Bourdieu, Pierre (1977) *Outline of a Theory of Practice*. Cambridge.

(1987) 'Legitimation and Structured Interests in Weber's Sociology of Religion', Chris Turner, trans., in *Max Weber: Rationality and Modernity*, S. Whimster and S. Lasch, eds. London: 119–136.

Boureau, Alain (2006) 'How Christian was the Sacralization of Monarchy in Western Europe (Twelfth-Fifteenth Centuries)?' in *Mystifying the Monarch: Studies on Discourse, Power and History*, Jeroen Deploige and Gita Deneckere, eds. Amsterdam: 25–34.

Bourges, Jacques de (1666) *Relation du voyage de Monseigneur l'Evêque de Béryte, vicaire apostolique du royaume de la Cochinchine, par la Turquie, la Perse, les Indes, &c. jusqu'au royaume de Siam & autres lieux*. Paris.

Boxer, Charles R. (1959) *The Great Ship from Amacon: Annals of Macao and the Old Japan Trade, 1555–1640*. Lisbon.

Bowring, Richard (2005) *The Religious Traditions of Japan, 500–1600*. Oxford.

Boyer, Pascal (2001) *Religion Explained. The Human Instincts that Fashion Gods, Spirits and Ancestors*. London.

(2010) 'Why Evolved Cognition Matters to Understanding Cultural Cognitive Variations', *Interdisciplinary Science Reviews* 35: 377–387.

Brack, Jonathan (2018) 'Theologies of Auspicious Kingship: The Islamization of Chinggisid Sacral Kingship in the Islamic World', *Comparative Studies in Society and History* 35(4): 1143–1171. doi:10.1017/S0010417518000415.

Brantlinger, Patrick (2002), *Taming Cannibals: Race and the Victorians*. Ithaca.

(2006) 'Missionaries and Cannibals in Nineteenth-century Fiji', *History and Anthropology* 17(1): 21–38.

Breen, John and Mark Teeuwen, eds. (2000) *Shinto in History: Ways of the Kami*. Richmond.

Breen, John and Mark Teeuwen (2010) *A New History of Shinto*. Oxford.

Brekke, Torkell (2002) *Religious Motivation and the Origins of Buddhism: A Social-Psychological Exploration of the Origins of a World Religion*. London.

Bremmer, Jan N. ed. (2007a) *The Strange World of Human Sacrifice*. Leuven and Dudley.

Bremmer, Jan N. (2007b) 'Introduction' in Bremmer (2007a): 1–8.

Brereton, Joel P. (2004) 'Dhárman in the Rg Veda', *Journal of Indian Philosophy*, 32: 449–489.

Briggs, Robin (1996) *Witches and Neighbours:* The Social and Cultural Context of European Witchcraft. London.

(2000) 'Review of Paul Kleber Monod: *The Power of Kings: Monarchy and Religion in Europe, 1589–1715*, New Haven, CT, Yale University Press, 1999' in *Reviews in History*, np. 127 Thursday, 1 June 2000.

(2007) *The Witches of Lorraine*. Oxford.

Brisch, Nicole, ed. (2008a) *Religion and Power: Divine Kingship in the Ancient World and Beyond*. Chicago.

Brisch, Nicole (2008b) 'Introduction' in Brisch (2008a): 1–11.

Brockey, Liam (2008) 'Surpassing Sylvester: Jesuit Missionaries and Asian Rulers in the Early Modern Period' in *Encompassing the Globe: Portugal and the World in the 16th and 17th Centuries*, Jay Levenson, ed. 3 Vols. Washington, DC: ii, 150–167.

Brogan, Stephen (2015) *The Royal Touch in Early Modern England: Politics, Medicine and Sin*. Woodbridge.

Brook, Timothy (2005) *The Chinese State in Ming Society*. London.

(2010) *The Troubled Empire: China in the Yuan and Ming Dynasties*. Cambridge, MA.

Brooks, George (1996) *Landlords and Strangers: Ecology, Society and Trade, in West Africa 1000–1630*. Oxford.

Brown, Peter (1975) 'Society and the Supernatural: A Medieval Change', *Daedalus* 104(2): 133–151.

(2003) *The Rise of Western Christendom: Triumph and Diversity, AD 200–1000*, 2nd ed. Oxford.

Brunt, Peter and Nicholas Thomas, eds. (2012) *Art in Oceania: A New History*. New Haven.

Buhl, F., A. T. Welch, Annemarie Schimmel, A. Noth, and Trude Ehlert (2017) 'Muḥammad' in *Encyclopaedia of Islam*, 2nd ed., P. Bearman, Th. Bianquis, C.E. Bosworth, E. van Donzel and W.P. Heinrichs, eds. Leiden. Consulted online on 06 March 2017. http://dx.doi.org/10.1163/1573-3912_islam_COM_0780.

Burbank, Jane and Frederick Cooper (2010) *Empires in World History: Power and the Politics of Difference*. Princeton.

Burgess, Glenn (2016) 'Political Obedience' in *The Oxford Handbook of the Protestant Reformations*, Ulinka Rublack, ed. Oxford: 83–102.

Burke, Peter (1992) *The Fabrication of Louis XIV*. New Haven.

Burghart, Richard (1987) 'Gifts to the Gods: Power, Property and Ceremonial in Nepal' in Cannadine and Price (1987): 237–270.

Burridge, Kenelm (1960) *Mambu: A Melanesian Millennium*. London.

Bynum, Caroline Walker (2007) *Wonderful Blood: Theology and Practice in Late Medieval Northern Germany and Beyond*. Philadelphia.

Byron, George A. (1826) *Voyage of H. M. S. Blonde to the Sandwich Islands, in the Years 1824–1825*, Maria Callcott, ed. London.

Cameron, Averil (2008) 'Constantine and the Peace of the Church' in *The Cambridge History of Christianity, Volume I: Origins to Constantine*, Margaret M. Mitchell and Frances M. Young, eds. Cambridge: 538–551.

Cameron, Euan (1991) *The European Reformation*. Oxford.

(2004) 'Dissent and Heresy' in *A Companion to the Reformation World*, Ronnie Po-Chia Hsia, ed. Oxford: 3–21.

(2010) *Enchanted Europe. Superstition, Reason, and Religion, 1250–1750*. Oxford.

Cannadine, David (1987) 'Introduction: Divine Rites of Kings' in Cannadine and Price (1987): 1–19.

Cannadine, David and Simon Price, eds. (1987) *Rituals of Royalty: Power and Ceremonial in Traditional Societies*. Cambridge.

Cannell, Fenella (2005) 'The Christianity of Anthropology', *The Journal of the Royal Anthropological Institute* 11(2): 335–356.

(2006) 'Introduction: The Anthropology of Christianity' in *The Anthropology of Christianity*, F. Cannell, ed. Durham.

(2013) 'Ghosts and Ancestors in the Modern West' in *A Companion to the Anthropology of Religion*, Janice Boddy and Michael Lambek, eds. Hoboken, NJ: 202–222.

Carey, Peter (2008) *The Power of Prophecy: Prince Dipanagara and the End of an Old Order in Java, 1785–1855*. Leiden.

Carrasco, David (2008) 'Human Sacrifice/Debt Payments from the Aztec Point of View' in Díaz (2008): 458–465.

(2011) *The Aztecs. A Very Short Introduction*. Oxford.

Carrithers, Michael (1983) *Buddha: A Very Short Introduction*. Oxford.

(2000) 'On Polytropy: Or the Natural Condition of Spiritual Cosmopolitanism in India: The Digambar Jain Case', *Modern Asian Studies* 34(4): 831–861.

Carrithers, Michael Steven Collins, and Steven Lukes, eds. (1985) *The Category of the Person: Anthropology, Philosophy, History*. Cambridge.

Carroll, Michael P. (1992) *Madonnas That Maim: Popular Catholicism in Italy Since the Fifteenth Century*. Baltimore.

Casanova, José (2012) 'Religion, the Axial Age, and Secular Modernity in Bellah's Theory of Religious Evolution' in Bellah and Joas (2012): 191–221.

Casey, Anthony (2011) 'A New Reality: Charles Kraft's View of Spiritual Warfare' https://culturnicity.files.wordpress.com/2011/04/kraft-on-spiritual-warfare.pdf. Accessed 12 April 2018.

Castiglione, Baldesar (1967) *The Book of the Courtier*, George Bull, trans. London.

Cavazzi da Montecuccolo, Giovanni Antonio (1668) *Missione evangelica nel Regno de Congo*. MSS Araldi, Modena. Vol. A., John K. Thornton, ed., trans. Available at www.bu.edu/afam/faculty/john-thornton/john-thorntons-african-texts/.

Chaney, William A. (1970) *The Cult of Kingship in Anglo-Saxon England: The Transition from Paganism to Christianity*. Berkeley.

Charlot, John (1987) 'Review of Valerio Valeri: Kingship and Sacrifice: Ritual and Society in Ancient Hawaii', *Pacific Studies* 10(2): 107–147.

Charney, Michael W. (2006) *Powerful Learning: Buddhist Literati and the Throne in Burma's Last Dynasty, 1752–1885*. Ann Arbor.

Chau, Adam Yuet (2011) 'Modalities of Doing Religion and Ritual Polytropy: Evaluating the Religious Market Model from the Perspective of Chinese Religious History', *Religion* 41(4): 547–568.

Chirino, Pedro (2000) *Història De La Província De Filipines De La Companyia De Jesús 1581–1696*. P. Miquel Batllori and Jaume Gorriz i Abella, eds. Barcelona.

Chrétien, Jean-Pierre ed. (1993) *L' invention religieuse en Afrique. Histoire et religion en Afrique noire*. Paris.

Christian, William A. (1981) *Apparitions in Late-Medieval and Renaissance Spain, 1400–1700*. Princeton.

Chowning, Ann (1990) 'God and Ghosts in Kove' in *Christianity in Oceania: Ethnographic Perspectives*, John Barker, ed. Lanham: 33–58.

Clarke, Shayne Neil (2014) *Family Matters in Indian Buddhist Monasticisms*. Honolulu.

Clastres, Pierre (1989) *Society against the State*. New York.

Clendinnen, Inga (1985) 'The Cost of Courage in Aztec Society', *Past & Present* 107(1): 44–89.

(1987) 'Franciscan Missionaries in Sixteenth Century Mexico' in *Disciplines of Faith. Studies in Religion, Politics and Patriarchy*, Jim Obelkevich, Lyndal Roper, and Raphael Samuel, eds. London: 229–245.

(1991a) *Aztecs: An Interpretation*. New York.

(1991b) '"Fierce and Unnatural Cruelty": Cortés and the Conquest of Mexico', *Representations* 33: 65–100.

(2003) *Ambivalent Conquests: Maya and Spaniard in Yucatan, 1517–1570*, 2nd ed. Cambridge.

Clodore, Jean de, ed. (1671) *Relation de ce qui s'est passe dans les Isles et Terre-ferme de l'Amerique*. 2 Vols. Paris.

Clossey, Luke, Kyle Jackson, Brandon Marriott, Andrew Redden, and Karin Vélez (2016) 'The Unbelieved and Historians, Part I: A Challenge', in *History Compass* 15: 594–602.

Clossey, Luke (2007) 'From the Mission to the Classroom: The Global Perspective and the History of Teaching Religion' in *World History Association Bulletin* 23: 18–21.

Coe, Michael D. (2003) *Angkor and the Khmer Civilization*. New York.

Cohen, Erick (1991) 'Christianity and Buddhism in Thailand: The "Battle of the Axes" and the "Contest of Power"', *Social Compass* 38(2): 115–140.

Cohen, Paul A. (1997) *History in Three Keys: The Boxers as Event, Experience and Myth*. New York.

(2003) *China Unbound: Evolving Perspectives on the Chinese Past*. London.

Collier, George A. Renato I. Rosaldo and John D. Wirth eds. (1982) *The Inca and Aztec States, 1400–1800: Anthropology and History*. New York.

Collins, Andrew (2014) 'Alexander's Visit to Siwah: A New Analysis', *Phoenix* 68(1/2): 62–77.

Collins, Steven (1982) *Selfless Persons: Imagery and Thought in Theravada Buddhism*. Cambridge.

(1990) 'On the Very Idea of the Pāli Canon', *Journal of the Pāli Text Society* 15: 89–126.

(1998) *Nirvana and Other Buddhist Felicities*. Cambridge.

Collins, Steven, ed. (2016) *Readings of the Vessantara Jātaka*. New York.

Cohn, Norman (1970) *The Pursuit of the Millenium: Revolutionary Millenarians and Mystical Anarchists of the Middle Ages*. London.

Comaroff, Jean and Comaroff, Jean L. (1992) *Ethnography & the Historical Imagination*. Boulder.

(2002) 'Millennial Capitalism: First Thoughts on a Second Coming', *Public Culture* 12(2): 291–343.

Coningham, Robin et al. (2017) 'Archaeology and Cosmopolitanism in Early Historic and Medieval Sri Lanka' in Biedermann and Strathern (2017): 19–43.

Conlan, Thomas David (2003) *State of War: The Violent Order of Fourteenth-Century Japan*. Ann Arbor.

Connerton, Paul (1989) *How Societies Remember*. Cambridge.

Corney, Peter (1896) *Early Voyages in the Northern Pacific: Narrative of Several Trading Voyages from 1813–18*. Honolulu.

Crone, Patricia (2003) *Pre-Industrial Societies: Anatomy of the Pre-Modern World*. Oxford.

Cross, Katherine (2016) 'Byrhtferth's Historia Regum and the Transformation of the Alfredian Past', *The Haskins Society Journal* 27: 55–78.

Cross, Samuel H. and Olgerd P. Sherbowitz-Wetzor, eds. and trans. (1953) *The Russian Primary Chronicle*. Cambridge, MA.

Crossley, Pamela Kyle (1999) *A Translucent Mirror: History and Identity in Qing Imperial Ideology*. Ann Arbor.

Crouzet, Denis (2011) 'Violence and the State in Sixteenth-Century France' in *Religious Conflict and Accomodation in the Early Modern World*, Marguerite Ragnow and William D. Philipps, eds. Minneapolis: 83–99.

Creppell, Ingrid (2010) 'Secularisation: Religion and the Roots of Innovation in the Public Sphere' in Katznelson and Stedman Jones (2010): 23–45.

Cummings, William (2002) *Making Blood White: Historical Transformations in Early Modern Makassar*. Honolulu.

Cushman, Richard D., trans. and David K. Wyatt, ed. (2000) *The Royal Chronicles of Ayutthaya*, 2nd ed. Bangkok.

Da Col, Giovanni (2011) 'Foreword: The Return of Ethnographic Theory', *Hau: Journal of Ethnographic Theory* 1: vi–xxxv.

Dagron, Gilbert (2003) *Emperor and Priest: The Imperial Office in Byzantium*. Cambridge.

D'Altroy, Terence N. (2003) *The Incas*. Malden.

D'Arcy, Paul (2003) 'Warfare and State Formation in Hawai'i: The Limits on Violence as a Means of Political Consolidation', *Journal of Pacific History* 38: 29–52.

Daston, Lorraine (1991) 'Marvelous Facts and Miraculous Evidence in Early Modern Europe', *Critical Inquiry* 18(1): 93–124.

Daguan, Zhou (2016) *Customs of Cambodia*, Solang Uk and Beling Uk, trans. Sarasota.

Davidson, James (1998) 'Domesticating Dido: History and Historicity' in *A Woman Scorn'd: Responses to the Dido Myth*, Michael Burden, ed. London: 65–88.

(2004) 'I Told You So!' in *London Review of Books* 26: 12–18.

(2007) 'Time and Greek Religion' in *Companion to Greek Religion*, Daniel Ogden, ed. Wiley Blackwell. Oxford: 204–218.

Davidson, Ronald (2002) *Indian Esoteric Buddhism: A Social History of the Tantric Movement*. New York.

(2015) 'Review of Christian K. Wedemeyer: *Making Sense of Tantric Buddhism: History, Semiology, and Transgression in the Indian Traditions*', *History of Religion* 54(3): 371–375.

D'Avray, David (2010) *Rationalities in History. A Weberian Essay in Comparison*. Cambridge.

Davies, John (1961) *The History of the Tahitian Mission, 1799–1830*, Colin W. Newbury, ed. London.

Davis, Natalie Zemon (1973) 'The Rites of Violence: Religious Riot in Sixteenth-Century France', *Past & Present* 59: 51–91.

(1974) 'Some Tasks and Themes in the Study of Popular Religion', in *The Pursuit of Holiness in Late Medieval and Renaissance Religion*, C. Trinkaus and H. Oberman, eds. Leiden: 307–336.

Davis, Richard H. (1997) *Lives of Indian Images*. Princeton.

De Heusch, Luc (2000) *Le Roi de Kongo et les monstres sacrés. Mythes et rites bantous III*. Paris.

De Marees, Pieter. (1987) *Description and Historical Account of the Gold Kingdom of Guinea*, Albert van Dantzig and Adam Jones, eds. and trans. Oxford.

Deal, William E. and Brian Ruppert (2015) *A Cultural History of Japanese Buddhism*. Chichester.

Dean, Kenneth (2017) 'Underworld Rising: The Fragmented Syncretic Ritual Field of Singapore' paper given at conference *Political Theologies and Development in Asia*, 21 February 2017, Asia Research Institute, Singapore.

DeCaroli, Robert (2004) *Haunting the Buddha: Indian Popular Religions and the Formation of Buddhism*. Oxford.

(2015) *Image Problems: The Origin and Development of the Buddha's Image in Early South Asia*. Seattle.

Deeg, Max (2015) 'Conversion and Environment in East Asia – The Case of Buddhism' in Papaconstantinou et al., eds. (2015): 267–279.

D'Elbée, François (1671) 'Journal du Voyage du Sieur Delbée' in Clodore (1671): 347–558.

(2005) 'Forms of Sacralized Power in Africa' in Quigley (2005): 25–37.

Delumeau, Jean (1977) *Catholicism between Luther and Voltaire: A New View of the Counter-Reformation*, introd. by John Bossy. London.

Dempsey, Corinne G. (2011) *Bringing the Sacred Down to Earth: Adventures in Comparative Religion*. Oxford.

Derrick, R. A. (1950) *A History of Fiji*. Suva.

Descola, Philippe (2013a.) *Beyond Nature and Culture*, Janet Lloyd, trans. Chicago.

(2013b) 'Presence, Attachment, Origin: Ontologies of "Incarnates"' in Boddy and Lambek (2013): 35–49.

Deslandres, Dominique (2018) 'New France', Po-chia Hsia (2018): 124–147.

DeWeese, Devin (1994) *Islamization and Native Religion in the Golden Horde*. University Park.

Diamond, Stanley (1996) 'Dahomey: The Development of a Proto-state', *Dialectical Anthropology* 21(2):121–216.

Díaz del Castillo, Bernal (2008) *The History of the Conquest of New Spain*, David Carrasco, ed. Albuquerque.

Dibble, Sheldon (1839) *History and General Views of the Sandwich Islands' Mission*. New York.

(1843) *History of the Sandwich Islands*. Lahainaluna.

Digby, Simon (1990) 'The Sufi Shaykh and the Sultan: A Conflict of Claims to Authority in Medieval India', *Iran* 28: 71–81.

Dirks, Nicholas B. (1987) *The Hollow Crown: Ethnohistory of an Indian Kingdom*. Cambridge.

Ditchfield, Simon (2015) 'Catholic Reformation and Renewal' in *The Oxford Illustrated History of the Reformation*, Peter Marshall, ed. Oxford: 152–185.

Dixon, C. Scott (1996) *The Reformation and Rural Society: The Parishes of Brandenburg-Ansbach-Kulmbach, 1528–1603*. Cambridge.

Dixon, Leif (2011) 'William Perkins, "Atheisme", and the Cries of England's Long Reformation', *Journal of British Studies* 50: 790–812.

Documentos sobre os portugueses em Mocambique e na Africa central, 1497–1840 (1962–89) Vols. 1–9. Lisbon.

Dodds Pennock, Caroline (2008) *Bonds of Blood: Gender, Lifecycle and Sacrifice in Aztec Culture*. Basingstoke.

(2012) 'Mass Murder or Religious Homicide? Rethinking Human Sacrifice and Interpersonal Violence in Aztec Society', *Historical Research* 37(3): 276–302.

Donald, Merlin (1991) *Origins of the Modern Mind: Three Stages in the Evolution of Culture and Cognition*. Cambridge, MA.

Douglas, Mary (2003) *The Lele of the Kasai*. London.

Drake, Harold A. (2000) *Constantine and the Bishops: The Politics of Intolerance*. Baltimore.

DuBois, Thomas David (2011) *Religion and the Making of Modern East Asia*. Cambridge.

Doak, Brian R. (2015) *Phoenician Aniconism in Its Mediterranean and Ancient Near Eastern Contexts*. Atlanta.

Driessen, H. A. H. (1982) 'Outriggerless Canoes and Glorious Beings: Pre-Contact Prophecies in the Society Islands', *The Journal of Pacific History* 17(1): 3–28.

Duara, Prasenjit (2015) *The Crisis of Global Modernity: Asian Traditions and a Sustainable Future*. Cambridge.

Duindam, Jeroen (2016) *Dynasties: A Global History of Power, 1300–1800*. Cambridge.

Dumézil, Bruno (2005) *Les racines chrétiennes de l'Europe: conversion et liberté dans les royaumes barbares, Ve-VIIIe siècle*. Paris.

Dumont, Louis (1986) *Essays on Individualism: Modern Ideology in Anthropological Perspective*. Chicago.

Durán, Diego (1994) *The History of the Indies of New Spain*, Doris Heyden, ed. and trans. Oklahoma.

Easwaran, Eknath, trans. (2007) *The Dhammapada*, 2nd ed. Tomales.

Eaton, Richard M. (1993) *The Rise of Islam and the Bengal Frontier, 1204–1760*. New Delhi.

(1997) 'Comparative History as World History: Religious Conversion in Modern India', *Journal of World History* 8(2): 243–271.

(1999) 'Islamization in Late Medieval Bengal: The Relevance of Max Weber' in *Max Weber and Islam*, Toby E. Huff and Wolfgang Schluchter, eds. New Brunswick: 163–181.

(2000) 'Temple Desecration and Indo-Muslim States' in *Beyond Turk and Hindu: Shaping Indo-Muslim Identity in Pre-modern India*, David Gilmartin and Bruce B. Lawrence eds. Gainesville: 254–260.

Ehrenberg, Erica (2008) '*Dieu et Mon Droit*: Kingship in Late Babylonian and Early Persian Times' in Brisch (2008): 103–131.

Ehrenreich, Barbara (2014) *Living with a Wild God: A Non-Believer's Search for the Truth About Everything*. London.

Eire, Carlos M. N. (1986) *War against the Idols: The Reformation of Worship from Erasmus to Calvin*. Cambridge.

(2016) *Reformations: The Early Modern World, 1450–1650*. New Haven.

Eisenstadt, Shmuel N. (1962) 'Religious Organizations and Political Process in Centralized Empires', *The Journal of Asian Studies* 21(3): 271–294.

Eisenstadt, Shmuel N., ed. (1986a) *The Origins and Diversity of Axial Civilization*. Albany.

(1986b) 'The Secondary Breakthrough in Ancient Israelite Civilization – The Second Commonwealth and Christianity' in Eisenstadt (1986a): 227–241.

(1986c) 'Introduction: The Axial Age Breakthroughs—Their Characteristics and Origins' in Eisenstadt (1986a): 1–28.

(1992) *Jewish Civilization: The Jewish Historical Experience in a Comparative Perspective*. Albany.

(1996) *Japanese Civilization: A Comparative View*. Chicago.

Elbourne, Elizabeth (2012) 'Christian Soldiers, Christian Allies: Coercion and Conversion in Southern Africa and Northeastern America at the Turn of the Nineteenth Century' in *Beyond Syncretism and Conversion:*

Indigenous Encounters with Mission Christianity, 1800–2000, David Lindenfeld and Miles Richardson, eds. New York: 79–109.

Elkana, Yehuda (1986) 'The Emergence of Second Order Thinking in Classical Greece' in Eisenstadt (1986a): 40–64.

Elliott, John H. (2009) 'The Overthrow of Moctezuma and His Empire' in *Moctezuma: Aztec Ruler*, Colin McEwan and Leonardo López-Luhán eds. London: 218–235.

Ellis, Stephen and Gerrie ter Haar (2004) *Worlds of Power: Religious Thought and Political Practice in Africa*. London.

    (2007) 'Religion and Politics: Taking African Epistemologies Seriously', *The Journal of Modern African Studies* 45(3): 385–401.

Ellis, William (1827) *Narrative of a Tour History Through Hawaii, or Owhyhee; with Observations on the Natural of the Sandwich Islands, and Remarks on the Manners, Customs, Traditions, History, and Language of their Inhabitants*, 2nd ed. London.

    (1832) *Polynesian Researches, During a Residence of Nearly Eight Years in the Society and Sandwich Islands*, 2nd ed. London.

Elverskog, Johan (2010) *Buddhism and Islam on the Silk Road*. Philadelphia.

Embree, Ainslie Thomas and Stephen N. Hay, eds. (1988) *Sources of Indian Tradition. Vol. 1: From the Beginning to 1800*. New York.

Emonds III, Radcliffe G. (2015) 'Imagining the Afterlife in Greek Religion' in *The Oxford Handbook of Ancient Greek Religion*, Esther Eidinow and Julia Kindt, eds. Oxford: 551–563.

Erickson, Kyle (2013) 'Seleucus I, Zeus and Alexander' in Mitchell and Melville (2013): 109–128.

Eusebius (1989) *History of the Church from Christ to Constantine*, Geoffrey A. Williamson and Andrew Louth, trans. Revised Edition. London.

    (1999) *Life of Constantine*, Averil Cameron and Stuart Hall, trans. Oxford.

Evans-Pritchard, Edward (1956) *Nuer Religion*. Oxford.

    (1976) *Witchcraft, Oracles and Magic Among the Azande*. Abridged edition, with an introduction by Eva Gillies. Oxford.

    (2011) 'The Divine Kingship of the Shilluk of the Nilotic Sudan. The Frazer Lecture, 1948', *Hau: Journal of Ethnographic Theory* 1(1): 407–422.

Faubion, James D. (2006) 'Paranomics: On the Semiotics of Sacral Action' in Tomlinson and Engelke (2006): 189–210.

Fausto, Carlos (2012) *Warfare and Shamanism in Amazonia*. Cambridge.

Feeley-Harnik, Gillian (1985) 'Issues in Divine Kingship', *Annual Review of Anthropology* 14: 273–313.

Ferme, Mariane Conchita (2001) *The Underneath of Things: Violence, History, and the Everyday in Sierra Leone*. Oxford.

Fernandez-Armesto, Felipe (2009) 'Conceptualizing Conversion in Global Perspective: From Late Antique to Early Modern' in Kendall et al. (2009): 13–44.

Firth, Raymond (1970) *Rank and Religion in Tikopia: A Study in Polynesian Paganism and Conversion to Christianity*. London.

(1996) *Religion: A Humanist Interpretation*. London.

Fish-Kashay, Jennifer (2008) 'From *Kapus* to Christianity: The Disestablishment of the Hawaiian Religion and Chiefly Appropriation of Calvinist Christianity', *The Western Historical Quarterly* 39: 17–39.

Fisher, Humphrey J. (1973) 'Conversion Reconsidered: Some Historical Aspects of Religious Conversion in Black Africa' *Africa*, 43: 27–40.

(1994) 'Many Deep Baptisms: Reflections on Religious, Chiefly Muslim, Conversion in Black Africa', *Bulletin of the School of Oriental and African Studies* 57: 68–81.

Flechner, Roy and Máir Ní Mhaonaigh, eds. (2016) *The Introduction of Christianity into the Early Medieval Insular World. 1, Converting the Isles*. Turnhout.

Fletcher, Joseph (1986) 'Mongols: Ecological and Social Perspectives', *Harvard Journal of Asiatic Studies* 46(1): 11–50.

Fletcher, Richard (1998) *The Conversion of Europe: From Paganism to Christianity, 371–1386 AD*. London.

Forest, Alain (1998) *Les missionaires francais au Tonkin at au Siam (XVIIe-XVIIe siècles). Analyse comparée d'un relatif succès et d'un échec total.* 3 Vols. Paris.

Frandsen, Paul John (2008) 'Aspects of Kingship in Ancient Egypt' in Brisch (2008): 47–73.

Frankfort, Henri, Henriette A. Groenewegen-Frankfort, John A. Wilson, and Thorkild Jacobsen (1946) *Before Philosophy: The Intellectual Adventure of Ancient Man*. Chicago.

Frasch, Tilman (2017) 'A Pāli Cosmopolis? Sri Lanka and the Theravāda Buddhist Ecumene, c. 500–1500' in Biedermann and Strathern (2017): 66–76.

Frazer, James George (1927) *The Devil's Advocate: A Plea for Superstition*, 2nd ed. London.

(1994) *The Golden Bough*, Robert Fraser, ed. Oxford.

Friedel, David (2008) 'Maya Divine Kingship' in Brisch (2008): 191–201.

Friedman, Kasja Ekholm (1985) 'Sad Stories of the Death of Kings: The Involution of Divine Kingship', *Ethnos* 50: 248–272.

Fromont, Cécile (2014) *The Art of Conversion: Christian Visual Culture in the Kingdom of Kongo*. Chapel Hill.

Fogg, Kevin [MS] *Indonesia's Islamic Revolution*.

Foucault, Michel (1991) 'Governmentality' in *The Foucault Effect*, Burchell et al., eds. Chicago: 1–51.

Fowden, Garth (1993) *Empire to Commonwealth, Consequences of Monotheism in Late Antiquity*. Princeton.

Fuglestad, Finn (2006) 'Precolonial Sub-Saharan Africa and the Ancient Norse World: Looking for Similarities', *History in Africa* 33: 179–203.

Garnett, Jane and Gervaise Rosser (2013) *Spectacular Miracles Transforming Images in Italy from the Renaissance to the Present*. London.

Garrett, Mary M. (1997) 'Chinese Buddhist Religious Disputation', *Argumentation* 11(2): 195–209.

Gauchet, Marcel (1999) *The Disenchantment of the World: A Political History of Religion*. Oscar Burge, trans. Princeton.

Gaster, Theodor H. (1955) 'Mythic Thought in the Ancient Near East. A Review of: *Before Philosophy: The Intellectual Adventure of Ancient Man* by H. Frankfort, Henri, H. A. Grocnewegen-Frankfort, John A. Wilson, and Thorkild Jacobsen (1946). Chicago', *Journal of the History of Ideas* 16: 422–426.

Geary, Patrick (1994) *Living with the Dead in the Middle Ages*. Ithaca.

Geertz, Clifford (1973) '"Internal Conversion" in Contemporary Bali' in *Interpretation of Cultures: Selected Essays*, by Clifford Geertz. New York: 170–192.

(1983) *Local Knowledge: Further Essays in Interpretive Anthropology*. New York.

(1988) *Negara: The Theatre State in Nineteenth-Century Bali*. Princeton.

Gell, Alfred (1997) 'Exalting the King and Obstructing the State: A Political Interpretation of Royal Ritual in Bastar District, Central India', *The Journal of the Royal Anthropological Institute* 3(3): 433–450.

(1998) *Art and Agency: An Anthropological Theory*. Oxford.

Gellner, Ernest (1979) 'Notes Towards a Theory of Ideology' in *Spectacles and Predicaments: Essays in Social Theory*, Ernest Gellner, ed. Cambridge: 117–132.

(1991) *Plough, Sword and Book: The Structure of Human History*. London.

Gelting, Michael H. (2007) 'The Kingdom of Denmark' in Berend (2007a): 73–120.

Gentilcore, David (1992) *From Bishop to Witch. The System of the Sacred in Early Modern d'Otranto*. Manchester.

Geréby, György (2008) 'Political Theology versus Theological Politics: Erik Peterson and Carl Schmitt', *New German Critique* 105: 7–33.

Gernet, Jacques (1985) *China and the Christian Impact: A Conflict of Cultures*, Janet Lloyd, trans. Cambridge.

Gervaise, Nicolas (1688) *Histoire naturelle et politique du Royaume du Siam*. Paris.

Geschiere, Peter (1997) *The Modernity of Witchcraft: Politics and the Occult in Postcolonial Africa*. Charlottesville.

Gesick, Lorraine, ed. (1983a) *Centers, Symbols, and Hierarchies: Essays on the Classical States of Southeast Asia*. New Haven.

Gesick, Lorraine (1983b) 'Introduction' to Gesick (1983a): 1–8.

(1983c) 'The Rise and Fall of King Taksin: A Drama of Buddhist Kingship' in Gesick (1983a): 87–105.

Ghosh, Peter (2014) *Max Weber and the Protestant Ethic, Twin Histories*. Oxford.

Gibbon, Edward (1993) *The History of the Decline and Fall of the Roman Empire*, with an introduction by Hugh Trevor-Roper. 6 Vols. London.

Gibson, Thomas (2007) *Islamic Narrative and Authority in Southeast Asia: From the Sixteenth to the Twentieth Century*. New York.

Gilbert, Michelle (1987) 'The Person of the King: Ritual and Power in a Ghanaian state' in Cannadine and Price (1987): 298–330.

(2008) 'The Sacralized Body of the Akwapim King' in Brisch (2008): 171–190.

Gilman, Neill (1997) *The Death of Death: Resurrection and Immortality in Jewish Thought*. Woodstock, VT.

Gilmartin, David (2017) 'Imperial Sovereignty, Total Religion and Total Politics', *History and Theory* (56): 89–97.

Gluckman, Max (1963) 'Rituals of Rebellion in Southeast Africa' in *Readings for a History of Anthropological Theory*, Paul A. Erickson and Liam Donat Murphy, eds. Toronto: 197–216.

Goh, Geok Yian (2015) *The Wheel-Turner and His House: Kingship in a Buddhist Ecumene*. DeKalb.

Golden, Peter B. (2011) *Central Asia in World History*. Oxford.

Gombrich, Richard F. (1971) *Precept and Practice: Traditional Buddhism in the Rural Highlands of Ceylon*. Oxford.

(1988) *Theravada Buddhism: A Social History from Ancient Benares to Modern Colombo*. London.

(1996) *How Buddhism Began: The Conditioned Genesis of the Early Teachings*. London.

Gombrich, Richard F. and Gananath Obeyesekere (1988) *Buddhism Transformed: Religious Change in Sri Lanka*. Princeton.

Gonçalves, Nuno da Silva (1996) *Jesuítas e a Missão de Cabo Verde (1604–42)*. Lisbon.

Goody, Esther N. (1995) 'Social intelligence and Prayer as Dialogue', in *Social Intelligence and Interaction*, Esther Goody, ed. Cambridge: 206–220.

Goody, Jack (1997) 'A Kernel of Doubt: Agnosticism in Cross-Cultural Perspective (Huxley Lecture)', *Journal of the Royal Anthropological Institute* (2): 667–681.

Gornall, Alastair (forthcoming). *Rewriting Buddhism: Monastic Reform and Pali Literature in Sri Lanka, 1153–1270.* London.

Gornall, Alastair and Justin Henry (2017) 'Beautifully Moral: Cosmopolitan Issues in Medieval Pāli Literary Theory' in Biedermann and Strathern (2017): 77–93.

Gose, Peter (1996a) 'Oracles, Divine Kingship, and Political Representation in the Inka State', *Ethnohistory* 43(1): 1–32.

(1996b) 'The Past is a Lower Moiety: Diarchy, History, and Divine Kingship in the Inka Empire', *History and Anthropology* 9(4): 383–414.

(2008) *Invaders as Ancestors: On the Intercultural Making and Unmaking of Spanish Colonialism in the Andes.* Toronto.

Grabačić, Milena (2010) 'Multiple and Fluid: Religious and Diasporic Belonging in Venice's Maritime State in the Late Medieval and Early Modern Period', *Diaspora: A Journal of Transnational Studies* 19(1): 74–96.

Grabowsky, Volker (2007) 'Buddhism, Power and Political Order in Pre-Twentieth Century Laos' in Harris (2007): 121–142.

Gradel, Ittai (2002) *Emperor Worship and Roman Religion.* Oxford.

Graeber, David (2005) 'Fetishism and Social Creativity, or Fetishes are Gods in the Process of Construction', *Anthropological Theory* 5(4): 407–438.

(2011a) *Debt: The First 5,000 Years.* New York.

(2011b) 'The Divine Kingship of the Shilluk: On Violence, Utopia, and the Human Condition, or, Elements for an Archaeology of Sovereignty', *Hau: Journal of Ethnographic Theory* 1(1): 1–62.

(2015) 'Radical Alterity is Just Another Way of Saying "Reality": A Reply to Eduardo Viveiros de Castro', *Hau: Journal of Ethnographic Theory* 5(2): 1–41.

Graeber, David and Marshall Sahlins (2017) *On Kings.* Chicago.

Graulich, Michel (2007) 'Aztec Human Sacrifice as Expiation' in Bremmer (2007): 9–30.

Graves, C. Pamela (2008) 'From an Archaeology of Iconoclasm to an Anthropology of the Body: Images, Punishment, and Personhood in England 1500–1660', *Current Anthropology* 49(1): 35–60.

Gray, David B. (2016) 'Tantra and the Tantric Traditions of Hinduism and Buddhism' in *Oxford Research Encyclopaedia of Religion* http://religion.oxfordre.com/view/10.1093/acrefore/9780199340378.001.0001/acrefore-9780199340378-e-59.

Gray, Richard (1990) *Black Christians and White Missionaries*. New Haven, CT.

Greenblatt, Stephen (1985) 'Invisible Bullets: Renaissance Authority and Its Subversion, Henry IV and Henry V' in *Political Shakespeare: New Essays in Cultural Materialism*, Jonathon Dollimore and Alan Sinfield, eds. Manchester: 18–48.

Greene, Sandra E. (1996) 'Religion, History and the Supreme Gods of Africa: A Contribution to the Debate', *Journal of Religion in Africa* 26(2): 122–138.

Griffiths, Nicholas (1999) 'Introduction' in *Spiritual Encounters: Interactions between Christianity and Native Religions in Colonial America*, Nicholas Griffiths and Fernando Cervantes eds., Birmingham: 1–42.

Grinin, Leonid (2011) 'Complex Chiefdom: Precursor of the State or Its Analogue?', *Social Evolution & History* 10(1): 234–273.

Groslier, Bernard Philippe (2006) *Angkor and Cambodia in the Sixteenth and Seventeenth Centuries*, Michael Smithies, trans. Bangkok.

Gruzinski, Serge (1989) *Man-Gods in the Mexican Highlands: Indian Power and Colonial Society, 1520–1800*. Stanford.

Gunaratne, Herman (2017) *God's Secret Agent: A Battle Against Dark Forces*. Galle.

Gunawardana, Raṇavīra A. L. H. (1979) *Robe and Plough: Monasticism and Economic Interest in Early Medieval Sri Lanka*. Tuscon.

Gunn, Steven (1999) 'War, Religion and the State' in *Early Modern Europe: An Oxford History*, Euan Cameron, ed. Oxford: 102–133.

Gunson, W. Niel (1962) 'An Account of the Mamaia or Visionary Heresy of Tahiti, 1826 – 1841', *Journal of the Polynesian Society* 71(2): 209–243.

(1966) 'Journal of a Visit to Raivavae in October 1819 by Pomare II, King of Tahiti', *The Journal of Pacific History* 1: 199–203.

(1969) 'Pomare II of Tahiti and Polynesian Imperialism', *Journal of Pacific History* 4: 65–82.

(1978) *Messengers of Grace: Evangelical Missionaries in the South Seas*. Oxford.

Guruge, Ananda W. P., trans (1989) *Mahāvaṃsa: The Great Chronicle of Sri Lanka*. Colombo.

Haas, Christopher (2008) 'Mountain Constantines: The Christianization of Aksum and Iberia', *Journal of Late Antiquity* 1(1): 101–126.

Hair, Paul E. H. ed. and trans. (1982) *Andre de Faro's Missionary Journey to Sierra Leone in 1663–1664*. Freetown.

Halikowski-Smith, Stefan (2011) *Creolization and Diaspora in the Portuguese Indies: The Social World of Ayutthaya, 1640–1720*. Brill.

Hall, Kenneth R. (2001) 'Upstream and Downstream Unification in Southeast Asia's First Islamic Polity: The Changing Sense of Community in the Fifteenth Century *Hikayat Raja-Raja Pasai* Court Chronicle', *Journal of the Economic and Social History of the Orient* 44(2): 198–229.

Hallisey, Charles (1995) 'Roads Taken and Not Taken in the Study of Theravada Buddhism' in *Curators of the Buddha: The Study of Buddhism under Colonialism*, Donald S. Lopez Jr., ed. Chicago: 31–61.

(2003) 'Works and Persons in Sinhala Literary Culture' in *Literary Cultures in History: Reconstructions from South Asia*, Sheldon Pollock, ed. Berkeley: 689–746.

Halton, Eugene (2014) *Axial Age to the Moral Revolution: John Stuart-Glennie, Karl Jaspers, and a New Understanding of the Idea*. New York.

Handelman, Don (2008) 'Returning to Cosmology: Thoughts on the Positioning of Belief', *Social Analysis* 52(1): 181–195.

Hardin, Richard F. (1992) *Civil Idolatry: Desacralizing and Monarchy in Spenser, Shakespeare, and Milton*. Newark.

Harris, Ian ed. (2007) *Buddhism, Power and Political Order*. London.

Harris, Olivia (1995) '"The Coming of the White People". Reflections on the Mythologisation of History in Latin America', *Bulletin of Latin American Research* 14(1): 9–24.

Harrison, Regina (2014) *Sin and Confession in Colonial Peru: Spanish-Quechua Penitential Texts, 1560–1650*. Austin.

Harrison, Simon (1993). *The Mask of War: Violence, Ritual, and the Self in Melanesia*. Manchester.

Hastings, Adrian (1994) *The Church in Africa 1450–1950*. Oxford.

Haour, Anne (2007) *Rulers, Warriors, Traders and Clerics: The Central Sahel and the North Sea*. Oxford.

Hefner, Robert, ed. (1993a) *Christian Conversion: Historical and Anthropological Perspectives on a Great Transformation*. Berkeley.

Hefner, Robert (1993b) 'Introduction: World Building and the Rationality of Conversion' in Hefner (1993a): 3–46.

Helms, Mary W. (1988) *Ulysses' Sail: An Ethnographic Odyssey of Power, Knowledge, and Geographical Distance*. Princeton.

Hendrix, Scott (2000) 'Rerooting the Faith: Reformation as Re-Christianisation', *Church History* 69(3): 558–577.

Henry, John (2002) *The Scientific Revolution and the Origins of Modern Science*, 2nd ed. Basingstoke.

Henry of Huntingdon (2002) *The History of the English People 1000–1154*, Diana Greenaway, trans. Oxford.

Henry, Teuira (1928) *Ancient Tahiti*, based on material recorded by J. M. Orsmond. Honolulu.

Hermann, Elfriede (1992) 'The Yali Movement in Retrospect: Rewriting History, Redefining 'Cargo Cult'", *Oceania* 63(1): 55–71.

Herskovits, Melville J. (1938) *Dahomey. An Ancient West African Kingdom.* 2 Vols. New York.

Heyes, Cecilia M. (2012) 'New Thinking about the Evolution of Human Cognition', *Philosophical Transactions of the Royal Society B* 367: 2091–2096.

(2018) *Cognitive Gadgets. The Cultural Evolution of Thinking.* Cambridge, MA.

Heywood, Linda M. (2017) *Njinga of Angola: Africa's Warrior Queen.* Cambridge, MA.

Heywood, Linda M. and John K. Thornton (2007) *Central Africans, Atlantic Creoles and the Foundation of the Americas.* Cambridge.

(2009) 'Kongo and Dahomey, 1660–1815: African Political Leadership in the Era of the Slave Trade and Its Impact on the Formation of African Identity in Brazil' in *Soundings in Atlantic History: Latent Structures and Intellectual Currents, 1500– 1825,* Bernard Bailyn, ed. Cambridge, MA: 86–111.

Higashibaba, Ikuo (2001) *Christianity in Early Modern Japan: Kirishitan Belief and Practice.* Leiden.

Higham, Nick J. (1997) *The Convert Kings; Power and Religious Affiliation in Early Anglo-Saxon England.* Manchester.

Hill, A. H. (1960) 'The Chronicles of the Kings of Pasai', *Journal of the Malaysian Branch of the Royal Asiatic Society* 33(2): 1–215.

Hilton, Anne (1985) *The Kingdom of Kongo.* Oxford.

Hiroo, Satō (2003) 'Wrathful and Saving Deities' in Rambelli and Teeuwen (2003a): 95–114.

Hobbes, Thomas (2012) *Leviathan,* Noel Malcolm, ed. 3 Vols. Oxford.

Hocart, Arthur Maurice (1914) 'Mana', *Man* 14: 97–101.

(1924–8) 'The Coronation Ceremony', *Ceylon Journal of Science. Section G, Archaeology, Ethnology etc.* Vol 1: 27–42.

(1941) *Kingship.* Abridged Edition. London.

(1952) *The Northern States of Fiji.* London.

(1970) *Kings and Councillors: An Essay in the Comparative Anatomy of Human Society,* Rodney Needham, ed. Chicago.

Hodgson, Janet (1997) 'A Battle for Sacred Power: Christian beginnings among the Xhosa' in *Christianity in South Africa: A Political, Social, and Cultural History,* Richard Elphick and Rodney Davenport, eds. Berkeley: 68–88.

Hodgson, Marshall G. S. (1974) *The Venture of Islam: Volume I, The Classical Age of Islam.* Chicago.

Hölbl, Günther (2000) *A History of the Ptolemaic Empire,* Tina Saavedra, trans. London.

Holbraad, Martin and Morten Axel Pedersen (2017) *The Ontological Turn: An Anthropological Exposition.* Cambridge.

Holt, John Clifford (1991) *Buddha in the Crown: Avalokitesvara in the Buddhist Traditions of Sri Lanka*. Oxford.

(1996) *The Religious World of Kīrti Śrī: Buddhism, Art and Politics in Late Medieval Sri Lanka*. Oxford.

(2004) *The Buddhist Visnu: Religious Transformation, Politics and Culture*. New York.

Hooper, Steven (2006) *Pacific Encounters: Art & Divinity in Polynesia 1760–1860*. London.

Horton, Robin (1971) 'African Conversion', *Africa: Journal of the International African Institute* 41(2): 85–108.

(1975a) 'On the Rationality of Conversion. Part I', *Africa: Journal of the International African Institute* 45(3): 219–235.

(1975b) 'On the Rationality of Conversion. Part II', *Africa: Journal of the International African Institute* 45(4): 373–399.

Howe, Leo (1996) 'Kings and Priests in Bali', *Social Anthropology* 4(3): 265–280.

Hugh-Jones, Stephen (1996) 'Shamans, Prophets, Priests, and Pastors' in Thomas and Humphrey (1996): 32–75.

Hughes-Freeland, Felicia (1991) 'A Throne for the People: Observations on the Jumenengen of Sultan Hamengku Buwono X', *Indonesia* 51: 129–152.

Hume, David (1987) *Essays Moral, Political and Literary*, Eugene F. Miller, ed. Indianapolis.

(2007) *The Clarendon Edition of the Works of David Hume: A Dissertation on the Passions; The Natural History of Religion*, Tom L. Beauchamp, ed. Oxford.

Humphrey, Caroline (2006) 'Shamanic Practices and the State in Northern Asia: Views from the Centre and Periphery' in Thomas and Humphrey (1996): 191–228.

Humphrey, Caroline and James Laidlaw, eds. (1994) *The Archetypal Actions of Ritual*. Oxford.

Humphreys, Michael T. G. (2015) *Law, Power, and Imperial Ideology in the Iconoclast Era: c. 680–850*. Oxford.

Humphreys, Sarah C. (1975) 'Transcendence and Intellectual Roles: The Ancient Greek Case', *Daedalus* 104(2): 91–118.

(1986) 'Dynamic of the Greek Breakthrough' in Eisenstadt (1986a): 92–110.

Hunwick, John O. (1993) 'Not Yet the Kano Chronicle: King-Lists With and Without Narrative Elaboration from Nineteenth-Century Kano', *Sudanic Africa* 4: 95–130.

Hutton, Ronald (2004) 'Anthropological and Historical Approaches to Witchcraft: Potential for a New Collaboration', *The Historical Journal* 47: 413–434.

'Ī'ī, John Papa (1959) *Fragments of Hawaiian History*, Dorothy B. Barrere, ed., Mary Kawena Pukui, trans. Honolulu.

Ilangasinha, H. B. M. (1992) *Buddhism in Medieval Sri Lanka*. Delhi.

Iliffe, John (1995) *Africans: The History of a Continent*. Cambridge.

Insole, Christopher (2001) 'Anthropomorphism and the Apophatic God', *Modern Theology* 17(4): 475–483.

Iogna-Prat, Dominique (2002) *Order and Exclusion: Cluny and Christendom Face Heresy, Judaism, and Islam (1000–1150)*, Graham Robert Edwards, trans. London.

Janzen, John M. (1982) *Lemba, 1650–1930: A Drum of Affliction in Africa and the New World*. New York.

Jackson, Peter (2006) 'World Conquest and Local Accommodation: Threat and Blandishment in Mongol Diplomacy' in *History and Historiography of Post-Mongol Central Asia and the Middle East: Studies in Honor of John E. Woods*, Judith Pfeiffer and Sholeh A. Quinn, eds. Wiesbaden: 3–22.

——— (2009) 'Mongol Khans and Religious Allegiance: The Problems Confronting a Minister-Historian in Ilkhanid Iran', *Iran (Journal of the British Institute of Persian Studies)* 47: 109–122.

Jackson, Peter A. (2016) 'The Supernaturalization of Thai Political Culture: Thailand's Magical Stamps of Approval at the Nexus of Media, Market and State', *Sojourn: Journal of Social Issues in Southeast Asia* 31(3): 826–879.

Janousch, Andreas (1999) 'The Emperor as Bodhisattva: The Bodhisattva Ordination and Ritual Assemblies of Emperor Wu of The Liang Dynasty' in *State and Court Ritual in China*, Joseph P. McDermott, ed. Cambridge: 112–149.

Jaspers, Karl (1953) *The Origin and Goal of History*. New Haven.

Jayatilleke, Kulatissa Nanda (1963) *Early Buddhist Theory of Knowledge*. Delhi.

Johnson, Trevor (2006) '"Everyone Should Be Like the People": Elite and Popular Religion and the Counter Reformation', *Studies in Church History* 42: 206–224.

Jordan, David K. (1993) 'The Glyphomancy Factor: Observations on Chinese Conversion' in Hefner (1993a): 285–304.

Josephson, Jason Ānanda (2012) *The Invention of Religion in Japan*. Chicago.

Juneja, Monica (2011) 'Translating the Body into Image: The Body Politics and Visual Practice at the Mughal Court during the Sixteenth and Seventeenth Centuries' in *Images of the Body in India*, Axel Michaels and Christoph Wulf, eds. New Delhi: 235–260.

Kaba, Lansiné (1984) 'The Pen, the Sword, and the Crown: Islam and Revolution in Songhay Reconsidered, 1464–1493', *The Journal of African History* 25: 241–256.

Kalupahana, David J. (1992) *A History of Buddhist Philosophy: Continuities and Discontinuities*. Honolulu.

Kame'elehiwa, Lilikalā (1992) *Native land and foreign desires: a history of land tenure change in Hawai'i from traditional times until the 1848 Māhele, including an analysis of Hawaiian ali'i nui and American Calvinists*. Honolulu.

Kantorowicz, Ernst (2016) *The King's Two Bodies: A Study in Medieval Political Theology*, with a New Introduction by Conrad Leyser. Princeton.

Katzenstein, Peter (2010) *Civilizations in World Politics: Plural and Pluralist Perspectives*. London.

Katznelson, Ira and Gareth Stedman Jones, eds. (2010a) *Religion and the Political Imagination*. Cambridge.

Katznelson, Ira and Gareth Stedman Jones (2010b) 'Introduction: Multiple Secularities' in Katznelson and Stedman Jones (2010a): 1–22.

Keane, Webb (2006) *Christian Moderns: Freedom and Fetish in the Mission Encounter*. Berkeley.

Keary, Anne (2011) 'Colonial Constructs and Cross-Cultural Interaction: Comparing Missionary/Indigenous Encounters in Northwestern America and Eastern Australia' in Lindenfeld and Richardson (2011): 243–298.

Kee, Howard Clark (1993) 'From Jesus Movement to Institutional Church' in Hefner (1993a): 47–64.

Keesing, Roger M. and Peter Corris (1980) *Lightning Meets the West Wind: The Malaita Massacre*. Melbourne.

Kendall, Calvin B. et al., eds. (2009) *Conversion to Christianity from Late Antiquity to the Modern Age: Considering the Process in Europe, Asia, and the Americas*. Minneapolis.

Keyes, Charles F. (1993) 'Why the Thai are not Christians; Buddhist and Christian Conversion in Thailand' in Hefner (1993a): 259–284.

  (2002) 'Weber and Anthropology', *Annual Review of Anthropology* 31: 233–255.

Kim, Chin-Tai (1987) 'Transcendence and Immanance', *Journal of the American Academy of Religion* 55(3): 537–549.

Kim, Hyung-Jun (2007) *Reformist Muslims in a Yogyakarta Village: The Islamic Transformation of Contemporary Socio-Religious Life*. Canberra.

Kinberg, Leah (1993) 'Literal Dreams and Prophetic Hadith in Classical Islam —A Comparison of two ways of legitimation', *Der Islam* 70(2): 279–300.

Kippenberg, H. G. (1986) 'The Role of Christianity in the Depoliticization of the Roman Empire' in Eisenstadt 1986: 261–279.

Kirch, Patrick Vinton (2010) *How Chiefs Became Kings: Divine Kingship and the Rise of Archaic States in Ancient Hawaii*. Berkeley.

Kitagawa, Joseph M. (1987) *On Understanding Japanese Religion*. Princeton.

Kitiarsa, Pattana (2012) *Mediums, Monks and Amulets: Thai Popular Buddhism Today*. Chiang Mai.

Korvela, Paul-Erik (2012) 'Sources of Governmentality: Two Notes on Foucault's Lecture', *History of the Human Sciences* 25(4): 73–89.

Kotzebue, Otto von (1821) *A Voyage of Discovery into the South Seas... in the Years 1815–18*. 3 Vols. London.

Kraft, Charles H. (1992) 'Conversion in Group Settings', in *Handbook of Religious Conversion*, H. Newton Malony and Samuel Southard, eds. Birmingham, AL: 259–275.

Krech, Volkhard and Marion Steinicke, eds. (2011) *Dynamics in the History of Religions between Asia and Europe: Encounters, Notions and Comparative Perspectives*. Leiden.

Kuhrt, Amélie (1987) 'Usurpation, Conquest and Ceremonial: From Babylon to Persia', *Cannadine and Price* (1987): 20–55.

Kulke, Hermann (1993) *Kings and Cults:* State Formation and Legitimation in India and Southeast Asia. New Delhi.

Kümin, Beat (2016) 'Rural Society' in Rublack 2016. Accessed online: DOI: 10.1093/oxfordhb/9780199646920.013.11.

Kuroda, Toshio (1996) 'The Discourse on the "Land of the Kami" (Shinkoku) in Medieval Japan: National Consciousness and International Awareness', Fabio Rambelli, trans., *Japanese Journal of Religious Studies* 23: 353–385.

Laidlaw, James (2007) 'A Well-Disposed Anthropologist's Problems with the 'Cognitive Science of Religion' in Whitehouse and Laidlaw (2007): 211–246.

 and Whitehouse (2007) 'Introduction' to Whitehouse and Laidlaw (2007): 3–36.

La Loubère, Simon de (1987) *Étude historique et critique du livre de* Simon de La Loubère "Du Royaume de Siam", Michel Jacq-Hergoualc'h, ed. Paris.

Lamana, Gonzalo (2005) 'Beyond Exoticization and Likeness: Alterity and the Production of Sense in a Colonial Encounter', *Comparative Studies of Society and History* 47(1): 4–39.

Lambek, Michael (2013a) 'What is "Religion" for Anthropology? And What Has Anthropology Brought to Religion?' in Boddy and Lambek (2013): 1–31.

 (2013b) 'Varieties of Semiotic Ideology in the Interpretation of Religion' in Boddy and Lambek (2013): 137–153.

Landau, Paul (1999) '"Religion" and Christian Conversion in African History: A New Model', *Journal of Religious History* 23(1): 8–30.

Landes, Richard (2011) *Heaven on Earth: The Varieties of the Millennial Experience*. Oxford.

(2015) 'Millenarianism/Millennialism, Eschatology, Apocalyptic, Utopianism' in *Handbook of Medieval Culture: Fundamental Aspects and Conditions of the European Middle Ages*, Albert Classen, ed. 3 Vols. Berlin: ii, 1093–1113.

Lane Fox, Robin (1973) *Alexander the Great*. London.

(1986) *Pagans and Christians*. Harmondsworth.

Lannstrom, Anna (2010) 'A Religious Revolution? How Socrates' Theology Undermined the Practice of Sacrifice', *The Society for Ancient Greek Philosophy Newsletter*. 460. https://orb.binghamton.edu/sagp/460.

Larson, Jennifer (2016) *Understanding Greek Religion*. London.

Larson, Pier M. (2007) 'Colonies Lost: God, Hunger, and Conflict in Anosy (Madagascar) to 1674', *Comparative Studies of South Asia, Africa and the Middle East* 27(2): 345–366.

(2009) *Ocean of Letters: Language and Creolization in an Indian Ocean Diaspora*. Cambridge.

Last, Murray (1980) 'Historical Metaphors in the Kano Chronicle', *History in Africa* 7: 161–178.

Latour, Brunto (2010) *On the Modern Cult of the Factish Gods*. Durham, NC.

Latourette, Kenneth Scott (1939) *A History of the Expansion of Christianity. Volume III Three Centuries of Advance A D 1500 A D 1800*. London.

Latukefu, Sione (1974) *Church and State in Tonga: The Wesleyan Methodist Missionaries and Political Development, 1822–1875*. Honolulu.

Laven, Mary (2012) *Mission to China: Matteo Ricci and the Jesuit Encounter with the East*. London.

Law, Robin (1991) 'Religion, Trade and Politics on the 'Slave Coast': Roman Catholic Missions in Allada and Whydah in the Seventeenth Century', *Journal of Religion in Africa* 21: 42–77.

(2002) 'An Alternative Text of King Agaja of Dahomey's Letter to King George I of England, 1726', *History in Africa* 29: 257–271.

Le Blanc, Marcel (2003) *History of Siam in 1688*, M. Smithies, trans. Chiang Mai.

Leavitt, Stephen C. (2000) 'The Apotheosis of White Men?: A Reexamination of Beliefs about Europeans as Ancestral Spirits', *Oceania* 70: 304–323.

Lee, M. Kittiya (2017) 'Cannibal Theologies in Colonial Portuguese America (1549–1759): Translating the Christian Eucharist as the Tupinambá Pledge of Vengeance', *Journal of Early Modern History* 21: 64–90.

Levack, Brian P. (2013) *The Devil Within: Possession and Exorcism in the Christian West*. New Haven.

Levenda, Peter (2011) *Tantric Temples: Eros and Magic in Java*. Lake Worth.

Levine, Baruch A. (2005) 'Assyrian Ideology and Israelite Monotheism', *Iraq* 67(1): 411–427.

Levtzion, Nehemia (1977) 'Western Maghrib and Sudan' in Oliver (1977): 331–462.

(2000) 'Islam in the Bilad al-Sudan to 1800' in Levtzion and Pouwels (2000): 63–91.

Levtzion, Nehemia and Randall L. Pouwels, eds. (2000) *The History of Islam in Africa*. Athens, OH.

Lieberman, Victor (2003) *Strange Parallels: Southeast Asia in Global Context, c. 800–1830, Vol. 1: Integration on the Mainland*. Cambridge.

(2009) *Strange Parallels: Southeast Asia in Global Context, c. 800–1830, Vol. 2, Mainland Mirrors: Europe, Japan, China, South Asia, and the Islands*. Cambridge.

Lilla, Mark (2007) *The Stillborn God: Religion, Politics, and the Modern West*. New York.

Lin, Irene H. (2003) 'From Thunder Child to Dharma-Protector. Dōjō hōshi and the Buddhist Appropriation of Japanese Local Deities' in Rambelli and Teeuwen (2003a): 54–76.

Lindenfeld, David (2007) 'The Varieties of Sioux Christianity, 1860–1980, in International Perspective', *Journal of Global History* 2(3): 281–302.

Lindquist, Galina (2017) 'Loyalty and Command: Shamans, Lamas, and Spirits in a Siberian Ritual', *Social Analysis* 61: 111–126.

Linnekin, Joceyln (2008) 'New Political Orders' in *Cambridge History of the Pacific Islanders*, Donald Denoon, Malama Meleisea, Stewart Firth, Jocelyn Linnekin, and Karen Nero, eds. Cambridge: 185–217.

Livingstone, David (1960) *Livingstone's Private Journals, 1851–1853*, Isaac Schapera, ed. London.

Liyanagamage, Amaradasa (2008) *State, Society and Religion in Premodern Sri Lanka*. Colombo.

Liyanaratne, Jindasa (1999) *Buddhism and Traditional Medicine in Sri Lanka*. Kelaniya.

Lotz-Heumann, Ute (2016) 'The Natural and Supernatural' in Rublack (2017): 688–707.

Lovins, Christopher (2015) 'Shangdi Is Watching You: Tasan and Big Moralizing Gods', *Journal of the American Academy of Religion* 83(2): 464–489.

Lyon, Jeffrey (2013) 'Malo's Moʻolelo Hawaiʻi: The Lost Translation', *The Hawaiian Journal of History* 47: 27–60.

Lukes, Steven (1979) 'Power and Authority' in *A History of Sociological Analysis*, Tom Bottomore and Robert Nisbet, eds. London: 633–676.

Machiavelli, Niccolò (1970) *The Discourses*. Leslie J. Walker, trans. Introduction by Bernard Crick. London.

MacCormack, Sabine (1991) *Religion in the Andes: Vision and Imagination in Early Colonial Peru*. Princeton.

MacCulloch, Diarmaid (2003) *The Reformation: Europe's House Divided, 1490–1700*. London.

MacGaffey, Wyatt (1977) 'Cultural Roots of Kongo Prophetism', *History of Religions* 17(2): 177–193.

(1986) *Religion and Society in Central Africa: The BaKongo of Lower Zaire*. Chicago.

(1994) 'Dialogues of the Deaf: Europeans on the Atlantic Coast of Africa' in *Implicit Understandings: Observing, Reporting, and Reflecting on the Encounters between Europeans and Other Peoples in the Early Modern Era*, Stuart B. Schwarz, ed. Cambridge: 249–267.

(2005) 'Changing Representations in Central African History', *The Journal of African History* 46(2):189–207.

Maffie, James (2014) *Aztec Philosophy: Understanding a World in Motion*. Boulder.

Mainga, Mutumba (1976) 'A History of Lozi Religion to the End of the Nineteenth Century' in *The Historical Study of African Religion*, Terence O. Ranger and Isaria N. Kimambo, eds. London: 95–107.

Mair, Victor H. (2011) 'Religious Formations and Intercultural Contacts in Early China' in Krech and Steinicke (2011): 85–110.

Malalgoda, Kitsiri (1976) *Buddhism in Sinhalese Society, 1750–1900: A Study of Religious Revival and Change*. Berkeley.

Malcolm, Noel (1998) 'The Titlepage of Leviathan, Seen in a Curious Perspective', *The Seventeenth Century* 13(2): 124–155.

Malo, David (1951) *Hawaiian Antiquities*, Nathaniel B. Emerson, trans. Honolulu.

Mandelbaum, David G. (1966) 'Transcendental and Pragmatic Aspects of Religion', *American Anthropologist* 68(5): 1174–1191.

Mann, Michael (2012–2013) *The Sources of Social Power*. Cambridge.

Marchant, Alicia (2008) 'Cosmos and History: Shakespeare's Representation of Nature and Rebellion in *Henry IV Part One*' in *Renaissance Poetry and Drama in Context: Essays for Christopher Wortham*, Andrew Lynch and Anne Scott, eds. Newcastle: 41–59.

Mark, Peter (1999) 'Religion, Identity and Slavery in the Casamance', *African Studies Review* 42(3): 75–80.

Markus, Robert A. (1990) *The End of Ancient Christianity*. Cambridge.

Marlow, Louise (1995) 'Kings, Prophets and the 'Ulamā' in Mediaeval Islamic Advice Literature', *Studia Islamica* 81: 101–120.

Marsden, Thomas (2015) *The Crisis of Religious Toleration in Imperial Russia: Bibikov's System for the Old Believers, 1841–1855*. Oxford.

Martin, David (2005) *On Secularization: Towards a Revised General Theory*. Aldershot.

Martino, Ernesto de (2015) *Magic: A Theory from the South*, Dorothy Louise Zinn, ed. and trans. Chicago.

Massarella, Derek (2000) 'The Jesuits and Japan' in *Vasco da Gama and the Linking of Europe and Asia*, Anthony Disney and Emily Booth, eds. Oxford.

Masuzawa, Tomoko (2005) *The Invention of World Religions*. Chicago.

Mathison, Gilbert Farquhar (1825) *Narrative of a Visit to Brazil, Chile, Peru and the Sandwich Isles, during the Years 1821 and 1822*. London.

Matthee, Rudi (2010) 'The Politics of Protection. Iberian Missionaries in Safavid Iran under Shāh 'Abbās I (*1587–1629*)' in *Contacts and Controversies between Muslims, Jews and Christians in Ottoman Empire and Pre-Modern Iran*, Camilla Adang and Sabine Schmidtke, eds. Würzburg: 245–271.

Mayo, Christopher M. (2015) 'Tachibana Dōsetsu's Thoughts on Warrior Society and Religion in Sixteenth-Century Japan', *Kōgakkan Shigaku* 30: 64–32.

Mayr-Harting, Henry (1994) *Two Conversions to Christianity: The Bulgarians and the Anglo-Saxons*. Reading.

McCauley, Robert N. and E. Thomas Lawson (2002) *Bringing Ritual to Mind: Psychological Foundations of Cultural Forms*. Cambridge.

McCormick, Michael (1990) *Eternal Victory: Triumphal Rulership in Late Antiquity, Byzantium and the Early Medieval West*. Cambridge.

McCoy, Alfred W. (1982) 'Baylan: Animist Religion and Philippine Peasant Ideology', *Philippine Quarterly of Culture and Society* 10(3): 141–194.

McKay, Ryan and Harvey Whitehouse (2015) 'Religion and Morality', *Psychological Bulletin* 141(2): 447–473.

McKeown, Adam (2012) 'What are the Units of World History' in *A Companion to World History*, Douglas Northrop ed. Chichester: 79–94.

McKinley, Alex (2016) 'The Sacred Second: Religious Moments in a Colombo Marketplace', *Culture and Religion* 17(2): 1–21.

McMullen, David (1987) 'Bureaucrats and Cosmology: The Ritual Code of T'ang China' in Cannadine and Price (1987): 181–236.

McMullin, Neil (1989) 'Historical and Historiographical Issues in the Study of Pre-Modern Japanese Religions', *Japanese Journal of Religious Studies* 16(1): 3–40.

McNeill, William H. (1999) 'Infectious Alternatives: The Plague That Saved Jerusalem, 701 BC' in *The Collected What If? Eminent Historians Imagine What Might have Been*, Robert Crowley, ed. New York: 1–14.

Meleisa, Malama (1987) *The Making of Modern Samoa: Traditional Authority and Colonial Administration in the History of Western Samoa*. Suva.

Melville, Charles (1990) 'Padshah-i Islam: The Conversion of Sultan Mahmud Ghazan Khan', *Pembroke Papers* 1: 159–177.

Melvin-Koushki, Matthew S. (2016) 'Astrology, Lettrism, Geomancy: The Occult-Scientific Methods of Post-Mongol Islamicate Imperialism', *Medieval History Journal* 19(1): 142–150.

Merolla, Girolamo (1814) 'A Voyage to Congo and Several Other Countries Chiefly in Southern Africa' in *Voyages and Travels in All Parts of the World*, John Pinkerton, ed. London: 195–316.

Mesley, Matthew M. and Louise E. Wilson, eds. (2014) *Contextualizing Miracles in the Christian West, 1100–1500: New Historical Approaches*. Oxford.

Meyer, Birgit (2013) 'Mediation and Intimacy: Sensational forms, Semiotic Ideologies and the Question of the Medium' in Boddy and Lambek (2013): 309–326.

Michalowski, Piotr (2008) 'Mortal Kings of Ur: A Short Century of Divine Rule in Ancient Mesopotamia' in Brisch (2008): 33–45.

Miles, Douglas (1976) *Cutlass & Crescent Moon: A Case Study of Social and Political Change in Outer Indonesia*. Sydney.

Migne, J.-P. (1996) *Patrologia Latina*. Online Edition, *Patrologia Latina Database*, http://pld.chadwyck.co.uk/.

Miller, Christopher L. (1985) *Blank Darkness, Africanist Discourses in French*. Chicago.

Minorsky, Vladimir (1942) *Sharaf al-Zaman Tahir Marvazi on China, the Turks and India*. London.

Mitchell, Jon P. (2006) 'Performance' in *Handbook of Material Culture*, Chris Tilley et al., eds. London: 384–401.

Mitchell, Jon P. and Hildi J. Mitchell (2008) 'For Belief: Embodiment and Immanence in Catholicism and Mormonism', *Social Analysis* 52(1): 79–94.

Mitchell, Lynette G. (2013) 'Alexander the Great: Divinity and the Rule of Law' in Mitchell and Melville (2013a): 91–108.

[MS] 'Keeping Oneself to Oneself: Royal Inaccessibility at the Achaemenid Court'.

Mitchell, Lynette G. and Charles Melville, eds. (2013a.) *Every Inch a King. Comparative Studies on Kings and Kingship in the Ancient and Medieval Worlds*. Leiden.

(2013b) 'Every Inch a King: Kings and Kingship in the Ancient and Medieval Worlds' in Mitchell and Melville (2013a): 1–22.

Moeller, Bernd (1972) 'Religious Life in Germany on the Eve of the Reformation' in *Pre-Reformation Germany*, Gerald Strauss, ed. New York: 13–42.

Moin, A. Azfar (2012) *Millennial Sovereign: Sacred Kingship and Sainthood in Islam*. Oxford.

(2015) 'Sovereign Violence: Temple Destruction in India and Shrine Desecration in Iran and Central Asia', *Comparative Studies in Society and History* 57: 467–496.

(2016) 'Cosmos and Power: A Comparative Dialogue on Astrology, Divination and Politics in Pre-Modern Eurasia', *The Medieval History Journal* 19: 122–129.

[MS] 'Why did Muslim Kings Worship the Sun? Islam and Cosmotheism' paper given at *Nodes, Networks, Orders: Three Global History Workshops on Transformative Connectivity*, *Itinerario* 40th anniversary, University of Leiden, Netherlands, 20–22 April 2017.

Momigliano, Arnaldo (1986) 'The Disadvantages of Monotheism for a Universal State', *Classical Philology* 81(4): 285–297.

(1990) *Alien Wisdom: The Limits of Hellenization*. Cambridge.

Monod, Paul (1999) *The Power of Kings: Monarchy and Religion in Europe, 1589–1715*, New Haven, CT.

Moran, Arik (2007) 'From Mountain Trade to Jungle Politics: The Transformation of Kingship in Bashahr, 1815–1914', *Indian Economic and Social History Review* 4(2): 147–177.

Morris, Brian (2005) *Religion and Anthropology*. Cambridge.

Morrison, Kathleen D. (2008) 'When Gods Ruled: Comments on Divine Kingship' in Brisch (2008): 267–271.

Monius, Anne E. (2002) *Imagining a Place for Buddhism: Literary Culture and Religious Community in Tamil-Speaking South India*. Oxford.

Moore, Robert I. (1999) 'The Birth of Europe as a Eurasian Phenomenon' in *Beyond Binary Histories: Re-imagining Eurasia to c. 1830*, Victor B. Lieberman, ed. Ann Arbor: 139–159.

(2003) 'The Eleventh Century in Eurasian History: A Comparative Approach to the Convergence and Divergence of Medieval Civilizations', *Journal of Medieval and Early Modern Studies* 33: 1–21.

(2004) 'The Transformation of Europe as a Eurasian Phenomenon', *Medieval Encounters* 10: 77–98.

(2007) *The Formation of a Persecuting Society: Authority and Deviance in Western Europe, 950–1250*, 2nd ed. Oxford.

Mukhia, Harbans (2004) *The Mughals of India*. Oxford.

Mumford, Jeremy (1998) 'The Taki Onqoy and the Andean Nation: Sources and Interpretations', *Latin American Research Review* 33(1): 150–165.

Munro-Hay, Stuart (1991) *Aksum: An African Civilisation of Late Antiquity*. Edinburgh.

Mykkänen, Juri (2003) *Inventing Politics: A new Political Anthropology of the Hawaiian Kingdom*. Honolulu.

Naumann, Nelly (2000) 'The State Cult of the Nara and Early Heian Periods' in Breen and Teeuwen (2000): 47–67.

Needham, Rodney (1972) *Belief, Language and Experience*. Oxford.

Newbury, Colin (1961) 'Introduction' in *The History of the Tahitian Mission, 1799–1830,* Written by John Davies, Colin Newbury, ed. Cambridge: xxvii–liv.

  (1967) 'Te Hau Pahu Rahi: Pomare II and the Concept of Inter-Island Government in Eastern Polynesia', *Journal of the Polynesian Society* 76: 477–514.

  (1980) *Tahiti Nui: Change and Survival in French Polynesia, 1767–1945.* Honolulu.

Newitt, Malyn (2010) *The Portuguese in West Africa, 1415–1670: A Documentary History*. Cambridge.

Newman, John Henry (1890) *Apologia Pro Vita Sua: Being a History of His Religious Opinions*. London.

Nietzsche, Friedrich (1968) *Twilight of the Idols* and *the Anti-Christ*, R. J. Hollingdale, trans. Harmondsworth.

Niumeitolu, Heneli T. (2007) '*The State and the Church, the State of the Church in Tonga*'. PhD diss., The University of Edinburgh.

Nongbri, Brent (2013) *Before Religion: A History of a Modern Concept*. New Haven.

North, William L., trans. (1998) *The Responses of Pope Nicholas I to the Questions of the Bulgars A.D. 866 (Letter 99)*, trans. from the edition of Ernest Perels, in *Monumenta Germaniae Historica Epistolae* VI, Berlin, 1925, 568–600. www.pravoslavieto.com/history/09/866_responce_pope_Nicholas_I.htm.

Northrup, David (2002) *Africa's Discovery of Europe 1450–1850*. Oxford.

Nowakowska, Natalia (2018) *King Sigismund of Poland and Martin Luther: The Reformation before Confessionalization*. Oxford.

Oakley, Francis (2006) *Kingship. The Politics of Enchantment*. Oxford.

Obeyesekere, Gananath (1995) 'On Buddhist Identity in Sri Lanka' in *Ethnic Identity: Creation, Conflict and Accommodation*, Lola Romanucci-Rossi and George A. de Vos, eds. London: 222–241.

  (1997) 'The Myth of the Human Sacrifice: History, Story and Debate in a Buddhist Chronicle' in *Identity, Consciousness and the Past: Forging of*

Caste and Community in India and Sri Lanka, H. L. Seneviratne, ed. Delhi: 70–93.

(2002) *Imagining Karma: Ethical Transformation in Amerindian, Buddhist, and Greek Rebirth*, Berkeley.

(2005) *Cannibal Talk: The Man-Eating Myth and Human Sacrifice in the South Seas*. Berkeley.

(2012) 'The Buddha's Meditative Trance: Visionary Knowledge, Aphoristic Thinking, and Axial Age Rationality in Early Buddhism' in Bellah and Joas (2012): 126–145.

(2017a) 'Between the Portuguese and the Nāyakas: The Many Faces of the Kandyan Kingdom, 1591–1765' in Biedermann and Strathern (2017): 161–177.

(2017b) *The Doomed King. Requiem for Sri Vikrama Rājasinha*. Colombo.

Ogilby, John (1670) *Africa. Being an Accurate Description of the Regions of Aegypt, Barbary, Lybia and Billedulgerid.* 2 Vols. London.

Ogot, Bethwell A., ed. (1992) *Africa from the Sixteenth to the Eighteenth Century*. Oxford.

Ohnuki-Tierney, Emiko (1991) 'The Emperor of Japan as Deity (Kami)', *Ethnology* 30: 199–215.

Okuyama, Michiaki (2000) 'Approaches East and West to the History of Religions: Four Japanese Thinkers', *Japanese Journal of Religious Studies* 27: 99–114.

Oliver, Douglas L. (1974) *Ancient Tahitian Society*. Honolulu.

Oliver, Roland, ed. (1977) *The Cambridge History of Africa, Volume 3: From c.1050 to c.1600*. Cambridge.

Olivier, Guilhem (2016) 'Humans and Gods in the Mexica Universe' in *The Oxford Handbook of the Aztecs*, Deborah L. Nichols and Enrique Rodríguez-Alegría, eds. Online edition: www.oxfordhandbooks .com/view/10.1093/oxfordhb/9780199341962.001.0001/oxfordhb-9780199341962-e-46.

Ooms, Herman (1985) *Tokugawa Ideology: Early Constructs, 1570–1680*. Princeton.

Orii, Yoshimi (2015) 'The Dispersion of Jesuit Books Printed in Japan: Trends in Bibliographical Research and in Intellectual History', *Journal of Jesuit Studies* 2: 189–207.

Ortner, Sherry B. (1984) 'Theory in Anthropology since the Sixties', *Comparative Studies in Society and History* 26(1): 126–166.

(2016) 'Historical Contexts, Internal Debates, and Ethical Practice', *Hau: Journal of Ethnographic Theory* 6(2): 29–39.

Owasa-Ansah, David (2000) 'Prayer, Amulets, and Healing', in Levtzion and Pouwels (2000): 477–488.

Palmer, Herbert R., ed. and trans. (1928) *Sudanese Memoirs: Being Mainly Translations of a Number of Arabic Manuscripts Relating to the Western and Central Sudan.* 3 Vols. Lagos.

Palumbo, Antonello (2015) 'From Constantine the Great to Emperor Wu of the Liang: The Rhetoric of Imperial Conversion and the Divisive Emergence of Religious Identities in Late Antique Eurasia' in Papaconstantinou, McLynn, and Schwartz (2015): 95–122.

Pande, Govind Chandra (1995) *Studies in the Origin of Buddhism*, 4th ed. Delhi.

Panoplist (1820) *The Panoplist, and Missionary Herald for the Year 1820, Vol. XVI.* Boston.

Papaconstantinou, Arietta (2015) 'Introduction' in Papaconstantinou, McLynn, and Schwartz (2015): xv–xxxvii.

Papaconstantinou, Arietta and Neil McLynn and Daniel L. Schwartz, eds. (2015) *Conversion in Late Antiquity: Christianity, Islam, and Beyond*, Farnham.

Paramore, Kiri (2016) 'Confucian Ritual and Sacred Kingship: Why the Emperors Did Not Rule Japan', *Comparative Studies in Society and History* 58(3): 694–716.

(2017) 'Premodern Secularism', *Japan Review* 30: 21–37.

Paredes, Oona Thommes (2006) 'True Believers: Higaunon and Manobo Evangelical Protestant Conversion in Historical and Anthropological Perspective', *Philippine Studies* 54(4): 521–559.

Parker, Geoffrey (1992) 'Success and Failure in the Reformation', *Past & Present* 136(1): 43–82.

(2013) *Global Crisis: War, Climate Change and Catastrophe in the Seventeenth Century.* New Haven.

Parry, Jonathan P. (1986) 'The Gift, the Indian Gift and the "Indian Gift"', *Man* 21(3): 453–73.

(1998) 'Mauss, Dumont, and the Distinction between Status and Power' in *Marcel Mauss, A Centenary Tribute.* Wendy James and N. J. Allen, eds, New York: 151–172.

Peacock, Andrew C. S., ed. (2017) *Islamisation: Comparative Perspectives from History.* Edinburgh.

(2018) 'Sufi Cosmopolitanism in the Seventeenth-Century Indian Ocean: Shari'a, Lineage and Royal Power in Southeast Asia and the Maldives' in *Challenging Cosmopolitanism. Coercion, Mobility and Displacement in Islamic Asia*, R. Michael Feener and Joshua Gedacht, eds. Edinburgh.

Peel, John D. Y. (1968) 'Syncretism and Religious Change', *Comparative Studies in Society and History* 10(2): 121–141.

(1977) 'Conversion and Tradition in Two African Societies: Ijebu and Buganda', *Past & Present* 77(1): 108–141.

(1987) 'History, Culture and the Comparative Method: A West African Puzzle' in *Comparative Anthropology*, Ladislav Holy, ed. New York: 88–119.

(1990) 'The Pastor and the Babalawo', *Africa* 60: 339–369.

(2003) *Religion and the Making of the Yoruba*. Bloomington.

(2016) *Christianity, Islam, and Orisa-Religion: Three Traditions in Comparison and Interaction*. Oakland, CA.

Perkins, William (1608) 'How to Live, and That Well' in *The Workes of … William Perkins, Newly Corrected*. 3 Vols. Cambridge: i: 473–484.

Pew Research Center (2017) *The Changing Global Religious Landscape*. http://assets.pewresearch.org/wp-content/uploads/sites/11/2017/04/07092755/FULL-REPORT-WITH-APPENDIXES-A-AND-B-APRIL-3.pdf

Philips, Susan U. (2007) 'Changing Scholarly Representations of the Tongan Honorific Lexicon' in *Consequences of Contact: Language Ideologies and Sociocultural Transformations in Pacific Societies*, Miki Makihara and Bambi Schieffelin, eds. Oxford: 189–215.

Phillipson, David W. (2012) *Foundations of an African Civilisation: Aksum & the Northern Horn 1000 BC–AD 1300*. Woodbridge.

Photius I, Patriarch of Constantinople (1982) *The Patriarch and the Prince. The Letter of Patriarch Photios of Constantinople to Khan Boris of Bulgaria*, D. S. White and J. Berrigan, trans. Brookline, MA.

Pietz, William (1985) 'The Problem of the Fetish, I', *RES: Anthropology and Aesthetics* 9: 5–17.

(1987) 'The Problem of the Fetish, II: The Origin of the Fetish' in *RES: Anthropology and Aesthetics* 13: 23–45.

Piggott, Joan R. (1997) *The Emergence of Japanese Kingship*. Stanford.

Pina-Cabral, João de (1992) 'The Gods of the Gentiles are Demons: The Problem of Pagan Survivals in European Culture' in *Other Histories*, Kirsten Hastrup, ed. London: 45–61.

Platenkamp, Jos D. M. (2017) 'Encounters with Christianity in the North Moluccas (Sixteenth-Nineteenth centuries)' in *The Appropriation of Religion in Southeast Asia*, Michel Picard ed. Cham: 217–249.

Poirier, Sylvie (2013) 'The Dynamic Reproduction of Hunter-Gatherers' Ontologies and Values' in Lambek (2013): 50–68.

Pollock, Donald K. (1993) 'Conversion and "Community" in Amazonia' in Hefner (1993a): 165–197.

Pollock, Sheldon (2005) 'Axialism and Empire' in Arnason et al. (2005): 397–450.

(2006) *The Language of the Gods in the World of Men: Sanskrit, Culture, and Power in Premodern India*. Ranikhet.

Porterfield, Amanda (2005) *Healing in the History of Christianity*. Oxford.

Potter, David (2013) *Constantine the Emperor*. Oxford.

Prazniak, Roxann (2014) 'Ilkhanid Buddhism: Traces of a Passage in Eurasian History', *Comparative Studies in Society and History* 56(3): 650–680.

Price, Simon (1987) 'From Noble Funerals to Divine Cult: The Consecration of Roman Emperors' in Cannadine and Price (1987): 56–105.

Puett, Michael (2002) *To Become a God: Cosmology, Sacrifice, and Self-Divinization in Early China*. Cambridge, MA.

(2013) 'Critical Approaches to Religion in China', *Critical Research on Religion* 1(1): 95–101.

(2015) 'Ghosts, Gods, and the Coming Apocalypse: Empire and Religion in Early China and Ancient Rome' in *State Power in Ancient China and Rome*, Walter Scheidel, ed. Oxford: 230–259.

Pyysiäinen, Ilkka (2004) *Magic, Miracles, and Religion: A Scientist's Perspective*. Walnut Creek, CA.

Quack, Johannes and Paul Tobelmann (2010) 'Questioning "Ritual Efficacy"', *Journal of Ritual Studies* 24(1): 13–28.

Queyroz, Fernão de (1992). *The Temporal and Spiritual Conquest of Ceylon*, S. G. Perera, trans. 3 Vols. New Delhi.

Quigley, Declan, ed. (2005a) *The Character of Kingship*. Oxford.

Quigley, Declan (2005b) 'Introduction: The Character of Kingship' in Quigley (2005a): 1–23.

Ralston, Caroline (1984) 'Hawaii 1778-1854: Some Aspects of *Maka'ainana* Response to Rapid Cultural Change', *The Journal of Pacific History* 19: 21–40.

Rambelli, Fabio and Eric Reinders (2012) *Buddhism and Iconoclasm in East Asia: A History*. London.

Rambelli, Fabio and Mark Teeuwen, eds. (2003a) *Buddhas and Kami in Japan: Honji Suijaku as a Combinatory Paradigm*. London.

Rambelli, Fabio and Mark Teeuwen (2003b) 'Introduction: Combinatory Religion and the *Honji Suijaku* Paradigm in Pre-modern Japan' in Rambelli and Teeuwen (2003a): 1–53.

Ramble, Charles (2006) 'Sacral Kings and Divine Sovereigns: Principles of Tibetan Monarchy in Theory and Practice' in *States of Mind: Power, Place and the Subject in Inner Asia*, David Sneath, ed. Bellingham: 129–149.

Ramírez, Susan Elizabeth (2005) *To Feed and Be Fed: The Cosmological Bases of Authority and Identity in the Andes*. Stanford.

Ranger, Terence (1975) 'Introduction' in *Themes in the Christian History of Central Africa*, Terence Ranger and John Weller, eds. London: 3–13.

(1993) 'The Local and the Global in Southern African Religious History' in Hefner (1993a): 65–98.

Rapp, Francis (1998) 'Religious Belief and Practice' in *The New Cambridge Medieval History. Vol. VI. c. 1415 - c. 1500*, C. Allmand, ed. Cambridge: 203–219.

Rappaport, Roy A. (1999) *Ritual and Religion in the Making of Humanity*. Cambridge.

Ravenstein, Ernst G., ed. (1901) *The Strange Adventures of Andrew Battell of Leigh*. London.

Ravina, Mark (1999) *Land and Lordship in Early Modern Japan*. Stanford.

Rawcliffe, Carole (2006) *Leprosy in Medieval England*. Woodbridge.

Read, Kay (1994) 'Sacred Commoners: The Motion of Cosmic Powers in Mexica Rulership', *History of Religions* 34(1): 39–69.

Redden, Andrew (2016) *The Collapse of Time. The Martyrdom of Diego Ortiz (1571) by Antonio de la Calancha*. Berlin.

Redfield, Robert (1953) *The Primitive World and Its Transformations*. Ithaca.

Reff, Daniel F. (2005) *Plagues, Priests, Demons: Sacred Narratives and the Rise of Christianity in the Old World and the New*. Cambridge.

Reid, Anthony (1993) *Southeast Asia in the Age of Commerce, 1450–1680, Volume II: Expansion and Crisis*. New Haven.

(2000) *Charting the Shape of Early Modern Southeast Asia*. Bangkok.

(2015) *A History of Southeast Asia: Critical Crossroads*. Chichester.

Reilly, Thomas H. (2004) *The Taiping Heavenly Kingdom: Rebellion and the Blasphemy of Empire*. Washington, DC.

Reinders, Eric (2012) 'Situated on the Rock of Ages: Western Iconoclasm and Chinese Modernity' in Rambelli and Reinders (2012): 89–133.

Restall, Matthew (2003) *Seven Myths of the Spanish Conquest*. Oxford.

Reynolds, Craig J. (2005) 'Power' in *Critical Terms for the Study of Buddhism*, Donald S. Lopez Jr., ed. Chicago: 211–228.

(2006) *Seditious Histories, Contesting Thai and Southeast Asian Pasts*. Seattle.

Ribadeneira, Marcelo de (1970) *History of the Philippines and other Kingdoms by Marcelo de Ribadeneira, O.F.M.*, Pacita Guevara Fernandez, trans. 2 Vols. Manila.

Ridyard, Susan J. (1988) *The Royal Saints of Anglo-Saxon England: A Study of West Saxon and East Anglian Cults*. Cambridge.

Riesebrodt, Martin (2010) *The Promise of Salvation: A Theory of Religion*, Steven Rendall, trans. Chicago.

Robbins, Joel (2001) 'Ritual Communication and Linguistic ideology: A Reading and Partial Reformulation of Rappaport's Theory of Ritual' in *Current Anthropology* 42(5): 591–614.

(2004) *Becoming Sinners: Christianity and Moral Torment in a Papua New Guinea Society*. Berkeley.

(2009) 'Is the Trans- in Transnational the same as the Trans- in Transcendent: On Alterity and the Sacred in the Age of Globalization' in *Transnational Transcendence: Essays on Religion and Globalization*, Thomas J. Csordas, ed. Berkeley: 55–72.

(2012) 'Transcendence and the Anthropology of Christianity: Language, Change, and Individualism (Edward Westermarck Memorial Lecture)', *Journal of the Finnish Anthropological Society* 37: 5–23.

Robbins, Joel with B. Schieffelin and A. Vilaça (2014) 'Evangelical Conversion and the Transformation of the Self in Amazonia and Melanesia: Christianity and the Revival of Anthropological Comparison', *Comparative Studies in Society and History* 56: 559–90.

Robinson, David (2004) *Muslim Societies in African History*. Cambridge.

Robson, Andrew E. (2009) 'Malietoa, Williams and Samoa's Embrace of Christianity', *Journal of Pacific History* 44(1): 21–39.

Roetz, Heiner (2012) 'The Axial Age Theory: A Challenge to Historism or an Explanatory Device of Civilization Analysis? With a Look at the Normative Discourse in Axial Age China' in Bellah and Joas (2012): 248–274.

Rollason, William (2014) 'The Hanging of Buliga: A History of the Future in the Louisiade Archipelago, Papua New Guinea' in *Pacific futures: Projects, Politics and Interests*, William Rollason, ed. Oxford: 48–70.

Root, Margaret Cool (2013) 'Defining the Divine in Achaemenid Persian Kingship: The View from Bisitun' in Mitchell and Melville (2013): 23–65.

Roper, Lyndal (2016) *Martin Luther: Renegade and Prophet*. London.

Rostworowski, María and Craig Morris (1999) 'The Fourfold Domain: Inka Power and Its Social Foundations' in *The Cambridge History of the Native Peoples of the Americas, Vol. 3: South America, Part 1*, Frank Salomon and Stuart B. Schwartz, eds., Cambridge: 769–863.

Rouch, Jean (1953) *Contribution a 1'histoire du Songhay*. Dakar.

Rousseau, Jean-Jacques (1968) *The Social Contract*, Maurice Cranston, trans. London.

Routledge, David (1985) *Matanitu: The Struggle for Power in Early Fiji*. Suva.

Rowe, Erin K. (2017) 'The King, the City, and the Saints: Performing Sacred Kingship in the Royal Capital' in *The Early Modern Hispanic World: Transnational and Interdisciplinary Approaches*, Kimberly Lynn and Erin K. Rowe eds. Cambridge: 62–88.

Rowe, John Howland (1982) 'Inca Policies and Institutions Relating to the Cultural Unification of the Empire' in Collier et al. (1982): 93–118.

Rubiés, Joan-Pau (2000) *Travel and Ethnology in the Renaissance: South India through European Eyes, 1250–1625*. Cambridge.

Rublack, Ulinka (2005) *Reformation Europe*. Cambridge.

(2010) 'Grapho-Relics: Lutheranism and the Materialization of the Word' in *Relics and Remains, Past & Present Supplement 5*, Alexandra Walsham, ed. Oxford: 144–166.

Rublack, Ulinka, ed. (2016) *The Oxford Handbook of the Protestant Reformations*. Oxford.

Ruddick, Andrea (2013) *English Identity and Political Culture in the Fourteenth Century*. Cambridge.

Runciman, W. Garry (2012) 'Righteous Rebels: When, Where, and Why?' in Bellah and Joas (2012): 317–334.

Rüpke, Jörg (2010) 'Religious Pluralism' in *The Oxford Handbook of Roman Studies*, Alessandro Barchiesi and Walter Scheidel eds. Oxford: 748–766.

(2013) 'Individualization and Individuation as Concepts for Historical Research' in *The Individual in the Religions of the Ancient Mediterranean*, Jörg Rüpke ed. Oxford: 3–40.

Ruppert, Brian (2000) *Jewel in the Ashes: Buddha Relics and Power in Early Medieval Japan*. Cambridge, MA.

Russell, James C. (1994) *The Germanization of Early Medieval Christianity: A Sociohistorical Approach to Religious Transformation*. New York.

Ryan, Michael T. (1981) 'Assimilating New Worlds in the Sixteenth and Seventeenth Centuries', *Comparative Studies in Society and History* 23: 519–538.

Ryder, Alan F. C. (1969) *Benin and the Europeans: 1485–1897*. Harlow.

Sahlins, Marshall (1981) *Historical Metaphors and Mythical Realities: Structure in the Early History of the Sandwich Islands Kingdom*. Ann Arbor.

(1985) *Islands of History*. Chicago.

(1992). *Anahulu: The Anthropology of History in the Kingdom of Hawai'i, Vol. 1: Historical Ethnography*. Chicago.

(1995) *How "Natives" Think: About Captain Cook, For Example*. Chicago.

(2004) *Apologies to Thucydides: Understanding History as Culture and Vice Versa*. Chicago.

(2011) 'Twin-Born with Greatness: The Dual Kingship of Sparta', *Hau: Journal of Ethnographic Theory* 1: 63–101.

(2014) 'Stranger Kings in General: The Cosmo-Logics of Power' in *Framing Cosmologies. The Anthropology of Worlds*, Allen Abramson and Martin Holbraad, eds. Manchester: 137–163.

(2016) 'Inaugural Hocart Lecture: The Original Political Society' Centre for Ethnographic Theory, SOAS, London, 29 April 2016.

Saler, Benson (2000) *Conceptualizing Religion: Immanent Anthropologists, Transcendent Natives, and Unbounded Categories*. New York.

Salguero, C. Pierce, ed. (2017) *Buddhism and Medicine: An Anthology*. New York.

Salomon, Frank and George L. Urioste, eds. and trans. (1991) *The Huarochirí Manuscript: A Testament of Ancient and Colonial Andean Religion*. Austin.

Salvatore, Armando (2016) *The Sociology of Islam: Knowledge, Power and Civility*. Chichester.

Samuels, Jeffrey (2007) 'Buddhism and Caste in India and Sri Lanka', *Religion Compass* 1(1): 120–130.

      (2008) 'Is Merit in the Milk Powder? Pursuing *Puñña* in Contemporary Sri Lanka', *Contemporary Buddhism* 9: 123–147.

Sanderson, Alexis (2006) 'Saivism and Brahmanism in the Early Medieval Period' 14th Gonda Lecture, 24 November 2006.

Sango, Asuka (2015) *The Halo of Golden Light: Imperial Authority and Buddhist Ritual in Heian Japan*. Honolulu.

Sansi, Roger (2011) 'Sorcery and Fetishism in the Modern Atlantic' in *Sorcery in the Black Atlantic*, Luis Nicolau Parés and Roger Sansi, eds. Chicago: 19–40.

Scheer, Catherine (2011) 'When the Spirits are Angry, God Gains in Popularity: Exploring the Emergence of Bunong Protestantism in the Highlands of Cambodia', *Aséanie* 28: 45–72.

Scheible, Kristin (2016) *Reading the Mahavamsa: The Literary Aims of a Theravada Buddhist History*. New York.

Scheid, John (2016) *The Gods, the State, and the Individual: Reflections on Civic Religion in Rome*, Clifford Ando, trans. Philadelphia.

Schieffelin, Edward L. and Robert Crittenden (1991) *Like People You See in a Dream: First Contact in Six Papuan Societies*. Stanford.

Schnepel. Burkhard (1995) *Twinned Beings: Kings and Effigies in Southern Sudan, East India and Renaissance France*. Göteborg.

Schoffeleers, Matthew (1992) *River of Blood: The Genesis of a Martyr Cult in Southern Malawi. c. AD 1600*. Madison.

Schonthal, Benjamin (2017) 'The Tolerations of Theravada Buddhism' in *Tolerations in Comparative Perspective*, Vicki A. Spencer, ed. Lanham, MD: 179–196.

Schopen, Gregory (1997) *Bones, Stones and Buddhist Monks: Collected Papers on the Archaeology, Epigraphy and Texts of Monastic Buddhism in India*. Honolulu.

Schurhammer, Georg and Ernst Arthur Voretzsch, eds. (1928) *Ceylon zur Zeit des Konigs Bhuvaneka Bahu und Franz Xavers, 1539 – 1552*. 2 Vols. Leipzig.

Schwarz, Benjamin I. (1975) 'The Age of Transcendence', *Daedalus* 104(2): 1–7.

Scott, James C. (1985) *Weapons of the Weak: Everyday Forms of Peasant Resistance*. New Haven.

(1990) *Domination and the Arts of Resistance: Hidden Transcripts*. New Haven.

Scribner, Robert W. (1982) 'Religion, Society and Culture: Reorienting the Reformation', *History Workshop Journal* 14: 2–22.

(1987) *Popular Culture and Popular Movements in Germany*. London.

(2001a) *Religion and Culture in Germany (1400–1800)*, Lyndal Roper, ed. Leiden.

(2001b) 'The Reformation: Popular Magic, and the "Disenchantment of the World"' in Scribner (2001a): 347–365.

Seaton, S. Lee (1974) 'The Hawaiian "Kapu" Abolition of 1819', *American Ethnologist* 1(1): 193–206.

Seckel, Dietrich (2004) *Before and Beyond the Image: Aniconic Symbolism in Buddhist Art*, Andreas Leisinger, trans., Helmut Brinker and John Rosenfield, eds. Zurich.

Selz, Gebhard J. (2008) 'The Divine Prototypes' in Brisch (2008): 13–31.

Sharot, Stephen (2001) *A Comparative Sociology of World Religions: Virtuosi, Priests, and Popular Religion*. New York.

Sharpe, Kevin (2006) 'Sacralization and Demystification. The Publicization of Monarchy in Early Modern England' in *Mystifying the Monarch: Studies on Discourse, Power, and History*, Jeroen Deploige and Gita Deneckere, eds. Amsterdam: 99–116.

Sheehan, Jonathan (2006) 'Introduction: Thinking about Idols in Early Modern Europe', *Journal of the History of Ideas* 67(4): 561–570.

Shepard, Jonathon (1995) 'Slavs and Bulgars' in *New Cambridge Medieval History, Vol. II*, R. McKitterick, ed. Cambridge: 22–48.

(2007) 'Rus' in Berend (2007a): 369–416.

(2009) 'The Coming of Christianity To Rus. Authorized and Unauthorized Versions' in Kendall et al. (2009): 185–222.

(2014) 'Byzantine Emissions, not Missions, to Rus', and the Problems of "false" Christians', in Русь в IX-X вв.: общество, государство, культура [Rus in the 9th-12th Centuries: Society, State, Culture], N. A. Makarov and A. E. Leontiev, eds. Moscow. pp. 234–242.

Shimizu, Kōichi 清水紘 (1977) 'Kirishitan kankei hōsei shiryō shū | キリシタン関係法制史料集' in *Kirishitan kenkyū* | キリシタン研究 17: 251–438.

Simonse, Simon (1992) *Kings of Disaster: Dualism, Centralism, and the Scapegoat King in Southern Sudan*. Leiden.

(2005) 'Tragedy, Ritual and Power in Nilotic Regicide. The Regicidal Dramas of the Eastern Nilotes of Sudan in Comparative Perspective' in Quigley (2005): 67–100.

Sissons, Jeffrey (2014) *The Polynesia Iconoclasm: Religious Revolution and the Seasonality of Power.* New York.

(2015) 'Personhood as History: Maori Conversion in Light of the Polynesian Iconoclasm', *Journal of the Polynesian Society* 124(2): 129–146.

Skilling, Peter (2007) 'Kings, Sangha, Brahmans: Ideology, Ritual, and Power in Premodern Siam' in Harris (2007): 182–215.

(2013) 'Vaidalya, Mahayana and Bodhisatva in India: An Essay Towards Historical Understanding' in *The Bodhisattva Ideal: Essays on the Emergence of Mahayana*, Karel Werner, Jeffrey Samuels and Bhikkhu Bodhi, eds. Kandy: 69–164.

Skinner, Quentin (1998) *Liberty before Liberalism.* Cambridge.

Smith, Bardwell L. (1978) 'Kingship, the Sangha, and Legitimation in Anuradhapura Ceylon: An Interpretive Essay' in *Religion and the Legitimation of Power in Sri Lanka*, Bardwell L. Smith, ed. Chamberburg, PA: 73–95.

Smith, Hannah (2009) '"Last of All the Heavenly Birth": Queen Anne and Sacral Queenship', *Parliamentary History* 28(1): 137–149.

Smith, Jonathan Z. (1998) 'Religion, Religions, Religious' in *Critical Terms for Religious Studies*, M. Taylor, ed. Chicago: 269–294.

Smith, Morton (2014) *Jesus the Magician.* Charlottesville.

Smith, Stephen A. (2008) 'Introduction' in *The Religion of Fools? Superstition Past and Present, Past & Present Supplement 3*, Stephen A. Smith and Alan Knight, eds. Oxford: 7–55.

Smithies, Michael and Luigi Bressan (2001) *Siam and the Vatican in the Seventeenth Century.* Bangkok.

Sommerville, J. P. (1991) 'Absolutism and Royalty' in *The Cambridge History of Political Thought*, J. H. Burns and Mark Goldie, eds. Cambridge: 345-373.

Southall, Aidan (2004) *Alur Society: A Study in Processes and Types of Domination.* Münster.

Southwold, Martin (1979) 'Religious Belief', *Man* 14(4): 628–644.

(1983) *Buddhism in Life: The Anthropological Study of Religion and the Sinhalese Practice of Buddhism.* Manchester.

Souyri, Pierre F. (2001) *The World Turned Upside Down: Medieval Japanese Society.* New York.

Spencer, Herbert (1898) *The Principles of Sociology.* 3 Vols. New York.

Spiro, Melford E. (1982) *Buddhism and Society: A Great Tradition and Its Burmese Vicissitudes*, 2nd ed. Berkeley.

(1994) *Culture and Human Nature*, Benjamin Kilborne and L. L. Langness, eds. Chicago.

Srivinas, Smriti (2008) *In the Presence of Sai Baba: Body, City, and Memory in a Global Religious Movement*. Leiden.

Stark, Rodney (2001) 'Efforts to Christianize Europe, 400–2000', *Journal of Contemporary Religion* 16(1): 105–121.

Stern, Steve J. (1982) *Peru's Indian Peoples and the Challenge of Spanish Conquest: Huamanga to 1640*. Madison.

Stewart, Charles (2012) *Dreaming and Historical Consciousness in Island Greece*. Cambridge, MA.

Stirrat, R. L. (1992) *Power and Religiosity in a Post-Colonial Setting: Sinhala Catholics in Contemporary Sri Lanka*. Cambridge.

Stoneman, Richard (2010) *Alexander, A Life in Legend*. Yale.

Strathern, Alan (2007a) *Kingship and Conversion in Sixteenth-Century Sri Lanka: Portuguese Imperialism in a Buddhist land*. Cambridge.

(2007b) 'Transcendentalist Intransigence: Why Rulers Rejected Monotheism in Early Modern Southeast Asia and Beyond' in *Comparative Studies in Society and History* 49(2) 358–83.

(2009) 'The Vijaya Origin Myth of Sri Lanka and the Strangeness of Kingship', *Past & Present* 203: 3–28.

(2016) 'Religion and Empire' in *Encyclopedia of Empire*. N. Dalziel and J. M. MacKenzie, eds. 4 Vols. Chichester.

(2017a) 'Global Patterns of Ruler Conversion to Islam and the Logic of Empirical Religiosity' in Peacock (2017): 21–55.

(2017b) 'The Digestion of the Foreign in Sri Lankan History, c.500–1818' in Biedermann and Strathern (2017): 216–238.

(2018) 'Catholic Missions and Local Rulers in Sub-Saharan Africa' in *A Companion to Early Modern Catholic Global Missions*, Ronnie Po-chia Hsia, ed. Leiden: 151–178.

Forthcoming [CK] *Converting Kings: Kongo, Thailand, Japan and Hawaii Compared, 1450–1850*. Cambridge.

Strathern, Andrew (1970) 'The Female and Male Spirit Cults in Mount Hagen', *Man* 5(4): 571–585.

(1979) 'The Red Box Money-Cult in Mount Hagen 1968–71 (Part I)', *Oceania* 50(2): 88–102.

(1980) 'The Red Box Money-Cult in Mount Hagen 1968–71 (Part II)', *Oceania* 50(3): 161–175.

trans. (1993) *Ru, Biography of a Western Highlander*. Boroko.

Strathern, Andrew and Marilyn Strathern (1968) 'Marsupials and Magic: A Study of Spell Symbolism Among the Mbowamb' in *Dialectic in Practical Religion*, E. R. Leach, ed. Cambridge: 179–202.

Strathern, Marilyn (1968) '*Popokl*: The Question of Morality', *Mankind: Journal of the Anthropological Societies of Australia* 6: 553–562.

(1988) *The Gender of the Gift: Problems with Women and Problems with Society in Melanesia.* Berkeley, CA.

[MS] 'A clash of Ontologies? Time, Law and Science in Papua New Guinea' *Science in the Forest and Science in the Past*, Conference, Cambridge, June 2017.

Strong, John S. (2004) *Relics of the Buddha.* Oxford.

(2014) *The Legend of King Aśoka: A Study and Translation of the Aśokāvadāna.* Princeton.

Stroumsa, Guy G. (1986) 'Old Wine in New Bottles: On Patristic Soteriology and Rabbinic Judaism' in Eisenstadt (1986): 252–260.

(2009) *The End of Sacrifice: Religious Transformations in Late Antiquity.* Chicago.

(2010) *A New Science: The Discovery of Religion in the Age of Reason.* Cambridge, MA.

(2011) 'The History of Religions as a Subversive Discipline' in Krech and Steinicke (2011): 149–158.

Sullivan, Richard E. (1994) 'Khan Boris and the Conversion of Bulgaria: A Case Study of the Impact of Christianity on a Barbarian Society' in *Christian Missionary Activity in the Early Middle Ages*, by Richard E. Sullivan. Variorum Reprints. Aldershot: 55–139.

Swain, Tony and Garry W. Trompf (1995) *The Religions of Oceania.* London.

Tachard, Guy (1686) *Voyage de Siam des Pères Jésuites Envoyez par le Roy aux Indes & à la Chine: avex leurs Observations, Astronomiques, et leurs Remarques de Physique, de Géographie, d'Hydrographie, & d'Histoire.* Paris.

Tacitus (1931) *The Histories: Volume 3: Books IV-V*, Clifford H. Moore, trans. Cambridge, MA.

Tadmor, Hayim (1986) 'Monarchy and the Elite in Assyria and Babylonia: The Question of Royal Accountability' in Eisenstadt (1986a): 203–225.

Takagi, Shōsaku (2004) 'Hideyoshi and Ieyasu's View of Japan as a Land of the Gods and Its Antecedents: With Reference to the "Writ for the Expulsion of Missionaries" of 1614', *Acta Asiatica* 87: 59–84.

Tambiah, Stanley J. (1976) *World Conqueror and World Renouncer: A Study of Buddhism and Polity in Thailand against a Historical Background.* Cambridge.

(1984) *The Buddhist Saints of the Forest and the Cult of the Amulets.* Cambridge.

(1986) 'The Reflexive and Institutional Achievements of Early Buddhism' in Eisenstadt (1986a): 453–474.

(1990) *Magic, Science, Religion and the Scope of Rationality.* Cambridge.

Taussig, Michael (1987) *Shamanism, Colonialism and the Wild Man: A Study in Terror and Healing*. Chicago.

Taylor, Charles (2007) *A Secular Age*. Cambridge, MA.

(2012) 'What was the Axial Revolution?' in Bellah and Joas (2012): 30–46.

Taylor, Christopher C. (1999) *Sacrifice as Terror: The Rwandan Genocide of 1994*. Oxford.

Taylor, John Patrick (2016) 'Two Baskets Worn At Once: Christianity, Sorcery, and Sacred Power in Vanuatu' in *Christianity, Conflict, and Renewal in Australia and the Pacific*, Fiona Magowan and Carolyn Schwarz, eds. Leiden: 139–160.

Tcherkézoff, Serge (2008) *First Contacts in Polynesia. The Samoan Case (1722–1848): Western Misunderstanding about Sexuality and Divinity*. Canberra.

Teeuwen, Mark (2000) 'The Kami in Esoteric Buddhist Thought and Practice' in Breen and Teeuwen (2000): 95–116.

(2012) 'Comparative Perspectives on the Emergence of Jindo and Shinto' in *Japanese Religions*, 4 Vols. Lucia Dolce, ed. London.

ter Haar, Barend J. (1992) *The White Lotus Teachings in Chinese Religious History*. Leiden.

Thapar, Romila (1975) 'Ethics, Religion, and Social Protest in the First Millennium B.C. in Northern India', *Daedalus* 104(2): 119–132.

(2012) *Aśoka and the Decline of the Mauryas*, 3rd ed. Oxford.

Thomas, Keith (1971) *Religion and the Decline of Magic: Studies in Popular Beliefs in Sixteenth and Seventeenth Century England*. London.

Thomas, Nicholas (1991) *Entangled Objects: Exchange, Material Culture and Colonialism in the Pacific*. Cambridge, MA.

(1996) 'Marginal Powers: Shamanism and Hierarchy in Eastern Oceania' in Thomas and Humphrey (1996): 15–31.

(2010) *Islanders: The Pacific in the Age of Empire*. New Haven.

(2012a) 'Cosmologies and Collections, New Guinea 1840–1940' in Brunt and Thomas (2012): 130–157.

(2012b) 'European Incursions, 1765 – 1880' in Brunt and Thomas (2012): 270–297.

Thomas, Nicholas and Caroline Humphrey, eds. (1996) *Shamanism, History and the State*. Ann Abor.

Thomson, Rev. R. (n.d.) *History of Tahiti, 1767–1815* [incomplete MS], South Seas Journals, Box 3 1807–1816, CWM/LMS.

Thornley, Andrew and Tauga Vulaono (2002) *Exodus of the I Taukei: The Wesleyan Church in Fiji, 1848–74*. Suva.

Thornton, John K. (1991) 'Legitimacy and Political Power: Queen Njinga, 1624-63', *Journal of African History* 32: 25–40.

(1992) *Africa and Africans in the Making of the Atlantic World: 1400–1800.* New York.

(2001) 'Religious and Ceremonial Life in the Kongo and Mbundu Areas, 1500–1700' in *Central Africans and Cultural Transformation*, Linda M. Heywood, ed. Cambridge: 71–90.

Thurston, Lucy (1882) *Life and Times of Mrs. Lucy G. Thurston, Wife of Rev. Asa Thurston, Pioneer Missionary to the Sandwich Islands.* Ann Arbor.

Tilly, Charles (1990) *Coercion, Capital and European States, AD 990–1900.* Oxford.

Tomlinson, Matt (2009) 'Efficacy, Truth, and Silence: Language Ideologies in Fijian Christian Conversions', *Comparative Studies in Society and History* 51: 64–90.

Tomlinson, Matt and Matthew Engelke (2006) 'Meaning, Anthropology, Christianity' in *The Limits of Meaning: Case Studies in the Anthropology of Christianity*, Matt Tomlinson and Matthew Engelke, eds. New York: 1–38.

Trigger, Bruce (2003) *Understanding Early Civilizations: A Comparative Study.* Cambridge.

Trompf, Garry W. (2000) 'Millenarism: History, Sociology, and Cross-Cultural Analysis', *Journal of Religious History* 24: 103–124.

Tweed, Thomas A. (2006) *Crossings and Dwellings: A Theory of Religion.* Cambridge, MA.

Tyerman, Daniel and George Bennet (1831) *Journal of Voyages and Travels.* 2 Vols. London.

Tyler, Damian (2007) 'Reluctant Kings and Christian Conversion in Seventh-Century England', *History* 92(2): 144–161.

Tylor, Edward B. (1871) *Primitive Culture, Vol. I.* London.

Tymowski, Michal (2011) 'Early Imperial Formations in Africa and the Segmentation of Power' in *Tributary Empires in Global History*, Peter Fibiger Bang and C. A. Bayly, eds. London: 108–119.

(2015) 'African Perceptions of Europeans in the Early Period of Portuguese Expeditions to West Africa', *Itinerario* 39(2): 221–246.

Turchin, Peter (2011) 'Review Essay: Strange Parallels: Patterns in Eurasian Social Evolution', *Journal of World-Systems Research* 17(2): 538–552.

Uffenheimer, Benjamin (1986) 'Myth and Reality in Ancient Israel' in Eisenstadt (1986a): 135–168.

Umberger, Emily (2015) 'Tezcatlipoca and Huitzilopochtli: Political Dimensions of Aztec Deities' in *Tezcatlipoca: Trickster and Supreme Deity*, Elizabeth Baquedano, ed. Boulder: 83–112.

Valeri, Valerio (1985) *Kingship and Sacrifice: Ritual and Society in Ancient Hawaii*, Paula Wissing, trans. Chicago.

(1987) 'Response', *Pacific Studies* 10: 148-214.

Valignano, Alessandro (1944) *Historia del principio y progresso de la Compañía de Jesús en las Indias orientales (1542–64)*. Josef Wicki, ed. Rome.

Van Buitenen, Johannes A. B. (1962) *The Maitrayaniya Upanisad: A Critical Essay with Text, Translation and Commentary*. Mouton.

Van der Cruysse, Dirk (2002) *Siam and the West, 1500–1700*, Michael Smithies, trans. Chiang-Mai.

Van Engen, John (1986) 'The Christian Middle Ages as an Historiographical Problem', *American Historical Review* 91(3): 519–552.

Van Leeuwen, Richard (2017) *Narratives of Kingship in Eurasian Empires, 1300–1800*. Leiden.

Vansina, Jan (2004) *How Societies are Born: Governance in West Central Africa since 1600*. Charlottesville.

Vernant, Jean-Pierre (1991) *Mortals and Immortals: Collected Essays*. Princeton.

Versnel, Henk S. (2011) 'Playing (the) God: Did (the) Greeks Believe in the Divinity of their Rulers?' in *Coping with the Gods: Wayward Readings in Greek Theology*, Henk S. Vernsel. Leiden: 439–492.

Vilaça, Aparecida (1997) 'Christians without Faith: Some Aspects of the Conversion of the Wari', *Ethnos* 62: 95–115.

Viveiros de Castro, Eduardo (1998) 'Cosmological Deixis and Amerindian Perspectivism', *The Journal of the Royal Anthropological Institute* 4(3): 469–488.

(2011) *The Inconstancy of the Indian Soul: The Encounter of Catholics and Cannibals in 16th Century Brazil*. Chicago.

(2012) 'Immanence and Fear', *Hau: Journal of Ethnographic Theory* 2: 27–43.

Voegelin, Eric (2000–1) *Order and History*. 5 Vols. Columbia.

Wagner, Roy (1975) *The Invention of Culture*. Englewood Cliffs, NJ.

Walker, Anthony R. (2003) *Merit and the Millennium: Routine and Crisis in the Ritual Lives of the Lahu People*. New Delhi.

Wallace, Vesna A. (2015) 'Competing Religious Conversions and Re-Conversions in Contemporary Mongolia' in Papaconstantinou (2015): 49–63.

Walls, Andrew (1995) 'Christianity in the Non-Western World: A Study in the Serial Nature of Christian Expansion', *Studies in World Christianity* 1(1): 1–25.

Walsham, Alexandra (2008) 'Historiographical Reviews: The Reformation and "The Disenchantment of the World" Reassessed', *The Historical Journal* 51(2): 497–528.

(2010) 'Skeletons in the Cupboard: Relics after the English Reformation' in *Relics and Remains, Past & Present Supplement 5*, Alexandra Walsham, ed. Oxford: 121–143.

(2014) 'Migrations of the Holy: Explaining Religious Change in Medieval and Early Modern Europe', *Journal of Medieval and Early Modern Studies* 44: 241–280.

Walters, Jonathan S. (2000) 'Buddhist History: The Sri Lankan Pāli Vamsas and Their Community' in *Querying the Medieval: Texts and the History of Practices in South Asia*, Ronald Inden, Jonathon Walters, and Daud Ali, eds. New York: 99–164.

(2003) 'Communal Karma and Karmic Community in Theravada Buddhist History' in *Constituting Communities: Theravada Buddhism and the Religious Cultures of South and Southeast Asia*, John C. Holt, Jacob N. Kinnard, and Jonathan S. Walters, eds. New York: 9–40.

Waterhouse, Joseph (1866) *The King and the People of Fiji: Containing a Life of Thakombau; with Notices of the Fijians, Their Manners, Customs, and Superstitions, Previous to the Great Religious Reformation in 1854*. London.

Watson, James L. and Rubie S. Watson (2004) *Village Life in Hong Kong. Politics, Gender and Ritual in the New Territories*. Hong Kong.

Watts, Joseph, Oliver Sheehan, Quentin D. Atkinson, Joseph Bulbulia, and Russell D. Gray (2016) 'Letter: Ritual Human Sacrifice Promoted and Sustained the Evolution of Stratified Societies', *Nature* 532: 228–231.

Webb, M. C. (1965) 'The Abolition of the Taboo System in Hawaii', *Journal of the Polynesian Society* 74: 21–39.

Weber, Max (1948) *From Max Weber: Essays in Sociology*, Hans Heinrich Gerth and C. Wright Mills, eds. and trans. London.

(1978) *Economy and Society*, Guenther Roth and Claus Wittich, eds. 2 Vols. London.

Weir, Christine (1998) 'Fiji and the Fijians: Two Modes of Missionary Discourse', *The Journal of Religious History* 22(2): 152–167.

Weiss, Peter (2003) 'The Vision of Constantine', *Journal of Roman Archaeology* 16: 237–259.

Wenzel, Claudia (2011) 'The Image of the Buddha: Buddha Icons and Aniconic Traditions in India and China', *Transcultural Studies* 1: 263–305.

West, Thomas (1865) *Ten Years in South Central Polynesia*. London.

Wheeler, Charles (2007) 'Buddhism in the Re-Ordering of an Early Modern World: Chinese Missions to Cochinchina in the Seventeenth Century', *Journal of Global History* 2: 303–324.

White, Monica (2013) *Military Saints in Byzantium and Rus, 900–1200*. Cambridge.

Whitehouse, Harvey (2000) *Arguments and Icons: Diverging Modes of Religiosity*. Oxford.

Whitehouse, Harvey and James Laidlaw, eds. (2007) *Religion, Anthropology and Cognitive Science*. Durham, NC.

Whitmarsh, Tim (2016) *Battling the Gods: Atheism in the Ancient World*. London.

Wickham, Chris (2016) 'The Comparative Method and Early Medieval Religious Conversion' in Flechner (2016): 13–37.

Wiesner-Hanks, Merry (2016) 'Comparisons and Consequences in Global Perspective, 1500–1750', in Rublack 2016. doi: 10.1093/oxfordhb/9780199646920.013.37.

Wilde, Guillermo (2018) 'The Missions of Paraguay: Rise, Expansion and Fall' in *A Companion to Early Modern Catholic Global Missions*, Ronnie Po-chia Hsia, ed. Leiden: 73–101.

Willard, Aiyana K. (2017) 'Agency Detection is Unnecessary in the Explanation of Religious Belief', *Religion, Brain & Behavior*. https://doi.org/10.1080/2153599X.2017.1387593.

Willerslev, Rane (2013) 'God on Trial: Human Sacrifice, Trickery, and Faith', *Hau: Journal of Ethnographic Theory* 3(1): 140–154.

Williams, John (1837) *A Narrative of Missionary Enterprises in the South Sea Islands: With Remarks Upon the Natural History of the Islands, Origin, Languages, Traditions, and Usages of the Inhabitants*. New York.

Williams, Paul (2009) *Mahāyāna Buddhism: The Doctrinal Foundations*, 2nd ed. London.

Wilson, Bryan (1973) *Magic and the Millennium*. St. Albans.

Winter, Irene (2008) 'Touched by the Gods: Visual Evidence for the Divine Status of Rulers in the Ancient Near East' in Brisch (2008): 75–101.

Withington, Phil (2010) *Society in Early Modern England: The Vernacular Origins of Some Powerful Ideas*. Cambridge.

Wittrock, Björn (2004) 'Cultural Crystallizations and World History: The Age of Ecumenical Renaissances' in Arnason and Wittrock (2004): 41–73.

(2005) 'The Meaning of the Axial Age' in Arnason, Eisenstadt and Wittrock (2005): 51–85.

(2015) 'The Axial Age in World History' in *The Cambridge World History*, C. Benjamin, ed. Cambridge: 101–119.

Wolf, Arthur (1974) 'Gods, Ghosts and Ancestors,' in *Religion and Ritual in Chinese Society*, Arthur Wolf, ed. Stanford: 131–145.

Wood, Andy (2006) 'Fear, Hatred and the Hidden Injuries of Class in Early Modern England', *Journal of Social History* 39(3): 809–826.

Wood, A. Harold (1975) *Overseas Missions of the Australian Methodist Church*. 3 Vols. Melbourne.

Wood, Ian N. (1985) 'Gregory of Tours and Clovis', *Revus belge de philoslogie et d'histoire* 63(2): 249–272.

Woodhead, Christine (1987) '"The Present Terrour of the World"?* Contemporary Views of the Ottoman Empire, ca. 1600', *History* 72: 20–37.

Woolf, Greg (1998) *Becoming Roman: The Origins of Provincial Civilization in Gaul.* Cambridge.

 (2008) 'Divinity and Power in Ancient Rome' in Brisch (2008): 235–252.

Worsley, Peter (1957) *The Trumpet Shall Sound: A Study of "Cargo" Cults in Melanesia.* London.

Wyatt, David K. (2001) 'Relics, Oaths and Politics in Thirteenth-Century Siam', *Journal of Southeast Asian Studies* 32(1): 3–65.

Wynne, Alexander (2004) 'The Oral Transmission of the Early Buddhist Literature', *Journal of the International Association of Buddhist Studies* 27(1): 97–127.

 (2010) 'The Ātman and its Negation: A Conceptual and Chronological Analysis of Early Buddhist Thought', *Journal of the International Association of Buddhist Studies* 33(1): 1–76.

Xavier, Francis (1899–1912) *Monumenta Xaveriana: ex autographis vel ex antiquioribus exemplis collecta.* 2 Vols. Madrid.

Xygalatas, Dimitris (2012) *The Burning Saints: Cognition and Culture in the Fire-Walking Rituals of the Anastenaria.* Durham, NC.

Yai, Olabiyi Babalola 1993 'From Vodun to Mawu: Monotheism and History in the Fon Cultural Area', in Chrétien (1993): 241–265.

Yao, Yu-Shuang and Richard Gombrich (2017) 'Christianity as Model and Analogue in the Formation of the "Humanistic" Buddhism of Tài Xū and Hsīng Yún', *Buddhist Studies Review* 34(2): 205–237.

Yarrow, Simon (2014) 'Religion, Belief, and Society: Anthropological Approaches' in *The Oxford Handbook of Medieval Christianity*, John H. Arnold, ed. Oxford: 42–59.

Yorke, Barbara (2006) *The Conversion of Britain: Religion, Politics and Society in Britain, c. 600–800.* Harlow.

 (2016) 'From Pagan to Christian in Anglo-Saxon England' in Flechner and Ní Mhaonaigh (2016): 237–258.

Young, Richard F. and G.S.B. Senanayaka (1998) *The Carpenter-Heretic: A Collection of Buddhist Stories about Christianity from 18th Century Sri Lanka.* Colombo.

Zampol D'Ortia, Linda (2017) 'The Cape of the Devil: Salvation in the Japanese Jesuit Mission under Francisco Cabral (1570–1579)'. PhD diss., University of Otago.

Zarakol, Ayşe (2016) 'States and Ontological Security: A Historical Rethinking', *Cooperation and Conflict* 52(1): 48–68.

Zika, Charles (1988) 'Hosts, Processions, and Pilgrimages in Fifteenth Century Germany', *Past & Present* 118: 25–64.

Zuidema, Tom (1989) 'At the King's Table: Inca Concepts of Sacred Kingship in Cuzco', *History and Anthropology* 4: 249–274.

Županov, Ines G. (2008) 'Conversion, Illness and Possession: Catholic Missionary Healing in Early Modern South Asia' in *Divins remèdes: Médecine et religion en Inde*, Ines G. Zupanov and Caterina Guenzi, eds. Paris: 263–300.

Zysk, Kenneth G. (2003) 'Medicine' in *Encyclopedia of Buddhism*, Robert E. Buswell, Jr., ed. 2 Vols. New York: ii, 518–520.

Index

N.B. footnote material has been indexed sparingly.

9 781108 701952